The Last Guru

Robert Cohan's Life in

From Martha Graham to London Contemporary Dance Theatre

The Last Guru

Robert Cohan's Life in Dance

From Martha Graham to London Contemporary Dance Theatre

Paul R. W. Jackson

With commentary by Robert Cohan

Dedicated to the memories of
Dorothy Madden (1912–2009) and Walter Nicks (1925–2007)
Teachers, mentors, friends

DANCE BOOKS

First published in 2013 by Dance Books Ltd.,
Southwold House, Isington Road, Binsted, Hampshire GU34 4PH

ISBN: 978-1-85273-162-5

© 2013 Paul R W Jackson

Printed in Great Britain by Latimer Trend Ltd, Plymouth, Devon

Contents

List of photographs

Cover: Robert Cohan. Photo by Anthony Crickmay, courtesy of Victoria and Albert Museum, London.

(Between pages 56 and 57)
1. Billie Cohan, Cohan's mother. Courtesy of the Cohan family.
2. Walter and Billie Cohan. Courtesy of the Cohan family.
3. Baby Cohan on granny's lap. Courtesy of the Cohan family.
4. Baby Cohan. Courtesy of the Cohan family.
5. Cohan as Peter Pan. Courtesy of the Cohan family.
6. Cohan, Elliot and Dolly. Courtesy of the Cohan family.
7. Pte. Cohan in California.
8. Cohan in class.
9. Cohan and Martha Graham in *Deaths and Entrances*. Courtesy of the Lebrecht Collection.
10. Cohan and Pearl Lang in *Wilderness Stair*.
11. Cohan in *Shangri-La*.
12. Cohan teaching at Rochester, 1959. Courtesy of Dora Sanders.
13. Cohan teaching at Rochester, 1959. Courtesy of Dora Sanders.
14. Advert for performances by Cohan and Matt Turney.

(Between pages 152 and 153)
15. Cohan and Turney in the studio. Courtesy of Dora Sanders.
16. Cohan in *The Pass*.
17. Cohan in *Vestige*.
18. Cohan and Turney in *The Pass*.
19. Cohan and Turney in *Seaborne*. Courtesy of Dora Sanders.
20. Cohan and Noemi Lapzeson in *Eclipse*. Photo by Anthony Crickmay, courtesy of Victoria and Albert Museum, London.
21. Cohan and Robert Powell in *Hunter of Angels*. Photo by Anthony Crickmay, courtesy of Victoria and Albert Museum, London.
22. Cohan, Powell and Lapzeson rehearsing *Sky*. Photo by Anthony Crickmay, courtesy of Victoria and Albert Museum, London.
23. Robert North in *Cell*. Photo by Anthony Crickmay, courtesy of Victoria and Albert Museum, London.

(Between pages 216 and 217)
24. Cohan in pensive mood, 1970s.
25. Cohan teaching, 1970s.
26. Cohan and Ace. Photo by Anthony Crickmay, courtesy of Victoria and Albert Museum, London.

27. Robert Powell in *Stages*. Photo by Anthony Crickmay, courtesy of Victoria and Albert Museum, London.

28. Kate Harrison in *Class*. Photo by Anthony Crickmay, courtesy of Victoria and Albert Museum, London.

29. *Waterless Method of Swimming Instruction*. Photo by Anthony Crickmay, courtesy of Victoria and Albert Museum, London.

30. Siobhan Davies and Robert North in *No Man's Land*. Photo by Anthony Crickmay, courtesy of Victoria and Albert Museum, London.

31. Susan MacPherson in *Canciones del Alma*. Courtesy of Andrew Oxenham.

32. Robin Howard. Courtesy of Janet 'Mop' Eager.

33. Patrick Harding-Irmer in *Skylark*. Photo by Anthony Crickmay, courtesy of Victoria and Albert Museum, London.

34. *Slow Dance on a Burial Ground*. Photo by Anthony Crickmay, courtesy of Victoria and Albert Museum, London.

35. Celia Boorman as Hippolyta, Alan Innes as Theseus in *A Midsummer Night's Dream*, Scottish Ballet 1993. Courtesy of Bill Cooper

36. Rupert Jowett as Puck, Karl Burnett as Bottom, Galina Mezentseva as Titania in *A Midsummer Night's Dream*, Scottish Ballet 1993 Rupert Jowett as Puck, Karl Burnett as Bottom, Galina Mezentseva as Titania. Courtesy of Bill Cooper

37. Cohan and Janet 'Mop' Eager. Courtesy of University of Winchester.

Prelude

This book had its inception in 2004 at the run-up to Cohan's eightieth birthday in 2005. I was then chair of the Standing Conference of Dance in Higher Education, the umbrella organisation for UK university dance departments and I suggested that our 2005 conference should celebrate the legacy of Robert Cohan. The silence was deafening; no one was interested. In the end, I arranged a small panel consisting of myself, Christopher Bannerman, and Henrietta Bannerman, and we held an open discussion of Cohan's work and showed Darshan Singh Bhuller's then recently completed documentary on Cohan called *Another Place*.

It was a dispiriting experience. It was just over ten years since the closure of the company he founded, London Contemporary Dance Theatre (from now on LCDT), and two years since his most recent piece of choreography, *Aladdin*, for Scottish Ballet, and yet the British dance world seemed to have totally forgotten Robert Cohan, the man without whom, it is entirely correct to say, dance in these small islands would not be the same. As former LCDT dancer and now internationally successful commercial choreographer Anthony van Laast observes, 'It is incredible that what Bob had has so quickly been erased from the dance world and that is a huge loss to the world of dance.' I therefore decided to approach Cohan and ask if he had had any thoughts as to anyone writing his biography, he did not, and so began a fascinating journey.

The problem with Cohan is that his life has been spread around many countries – this is exacerbated by the fact that he is not a self-publicist and seldom talked of his achievements in one country to peers in another. Paul Taylor, Cohan's younger friend and former Graham dancer, is now described as 'the last living member of the pantheon that created America's indigenous art of modern dance.'[1] Well of course he is not, Cohan is as much a part of that pantheon as Taylor but he does not have a publicity machine perpetuating his legacy. Perhaps it is all down to promotion and here Cohan seems to have fallen between the cracks both geographically and historically and what little there is written about him is often not correct. In *Dance Studies: The Basics*, the most recent work to mention Cohan at all, Jo Butterworth writes, 'It was as if he saw his primary role as transmitting the Graham legacy to the UK rather than allowing himself the freedom to develop his own artistry.'[2] Nothing could be further from the truth. His primary purpose, the mission he was charged with by Robin Howard, was to develop a contemporary dance company and school in the UK. At the time, it was Graham's work which had completely bowled over the entire artistic establishment and Howard felt it was a suitable starting point for the venture. There was never any question that Cohan and Howard were going to transplant

Graham to England. It was merely the seed for both his work and the work his students developed. It proved to be a very fertile soil as the multiplicity of dance now seen in England demonstrates.

I have therefore tried in this book to bring together Cohan's own memories, memories of colleagues from around the world and reviews of Cohan's work as dancer, teacher, or choreographer over the last sixty years. It is not the intention of this book to sum up his life and draw conclusions – that will be for future generations who can do so with the benefit of the lens of time.

The title for this book, *The Last Guru*, appeared some way into the research and after many conversations with Cohan and his colleagues. Having a 'guru' may seem unfashionable these days but, certainly in the arts, dancers, musicians, and painters are always asked, 'Who did you study with?' Where you have come from seeming to be as important as where you are going. A guru in classical Indian culture (including the Hindu, Sikh, Jain, and Buddhist religions) is a revered teacher who passes their knowledge onto a shishya or disciple. The Sanskrit word literally means 'an uninterrupted row or series, order, succession, continuation, mediation, tradition'.[3] This knowledge – which may be political, philosophical, religious, or artistic – is transmitted over a period of many years through the developing relationship between the guru and the disciple. In this 4,000-year old tradition it is considered that this relationship, almost a contract, based on the integrity of the guru and the respect, commitment, devotion, and obedience of the student, is the best way for subtle or advanced knowledge to be conveyed. In the end, it is hoped that the student will eventually master the knowledge embodied by the guru. As distinguished Bharata Natyam dancer and guru V. P. Dhananjayan told Rama Natrajan in 2010:

> A real guru is a person who makes one think. Anyone cannot be called a 'guru' and it is unfortunate that when young teachers use this profound word liberally thus losing its sanctity and significance. A guru should be able to expel all of your ignorance and should be fully qualified to clear all of your doubts in your mind regarding what you are learning. Adhyapakas (teachers) can teach the basics, but it takes years of experience for a teacher to develop into a true guru.[4]

He went on to note that 'as a student it is important for you to choose the right guru'. For many of Cohan's students, he was the right person at the right time. Many stayed with him for long periods and took from him far more than just a physical training, as Christopher Bannerman and Ross McKim note in the book. Anthony van Laast puts 'Bob Cohan at the centre of my world; not only for what he taught you about dancing but for how he developed you as a human being.' Darshan Singh Bhuller is happy to acknowledge that 'Cohan has probably had the biggest impact on my life as anyone I have known'. Jonathan Lunn even uses the word guru, saying, 'Bob seemed to be able to see right inside your very being.

His work had a purity about it like a religious cult, he was something like a guru.'

So why the *last* guru? Simply because no one has emerged to take on the role. As Pandit Chitresh Das notes, even in India in the modern world the role of the guru is changing[5] and certainly in Britain, where the transmission of dance has become a far more egalitarian experience, few are prepared to accept the responsibility or indeed have the experience to take on the role. As Ross McKim notes in his study of LCDT, since the closure of that company 'a state of mind and an attitude towards dance making' has been lost. Cohan has a distinctly metaphysical side to his character, a deep interest in other states of being and, from his intense studies of the work of the philosopher, teacher, and mystic Gurdjieff, a belief that dance can change the self and in changing the self can change the world.

Cohan is not a documenter of his work, nor a collector of reviews or a diarist, and many people have helped make this book possible. His work dancing with Martha Graham is documented in reviews of her work, though it is odd that even with Graham, one of the giants of twentieth-century art, there is no substantial authoritative biography of her, twenty years after her death. For chronological details concerning the Graham Company in the late 1940s and 1950s, I am particularly indebted to Stuart Hodes for permission to quote from his autobiography, which was in manuscript while I was writing most of this book but is now available online as an e-book,[6] and which prompted Bob to remember stories and events from long ago. Dora Sanders and her husband Jim, who appeared late in the research could not have been more generous with their time and memories of the earliest days of Bob's choreographic career. They allowed me to have so many of the wonderful photographs that appear in this book. The British years are better documented in the papers of The Place now held at the Victoria and Albert Museum Theatre collection and in Mary Clarke and Clement Crisp's 1989 celebration of the first twenty-one years of London Contemporary Dance Theatre. This was supplemented by Janet 'Mop' Eager, one of the triumvirate who ran LCDT, and who allowed me access to many otherwise unavailable papers. She also read through and tweaked the manuscript on precise details of the LCDT years. For many years, Cohan worked in Israel with both the Batsheva and Bat-Dor companies, and from 1980–90 he was artistic adviser to the Batsheva Dance Company. All the material concerning Cohan's work there seems to have disappeared, and I am grateful to Mira Edels, formerly general manager for that company, for sharing her memories of those times. The Bat-Dor Dance Company closed in 2006 and none of its archive has been available.

Thanks are also due to Miriam Adams, Richard Alston, Yehudit Arnon, the late Clive Barnes, the late David Bedford, Chris Benstead, Paul Bloom, Primavera Boman, Karen Burgin, the late Geoffrey Burgon, Dolly Cohan, Elliot Cohan, Norberto Chiesa, Kate Coyne, Anthony Crickmay, Carl Davis, Susan Dinan-Young, the late Jane Dudley, Clare Duncan, David Earle, Janet Eilber, Sallie Estep

Bhuller, the late Nina Fonaroff, Anca Frankenhauser, Pat Fraser, Fred Gehrig, Elida Gera, Linda Gibbs, Rena Gluck, Barry Guy, Patrick Harding-Irmer, Jan Hartmann, David Henshaw, Mary Hinkson, Kazuko Hirabayashi, Linda Hodes, Stuart Hodes, Anne Jackson, the late Norman dello Joio, Daphna Jones-Jaglom, Danni Karavan, John Kehlior, Judyth Knight, Anthony van Laast, the late Pearl Lang, Noemi Lapzeson, Jayne Lee, Cathy Lewis, Bob Lockyer, Jonathan Lunn, Susan MacPherson, Marie McCluskey, David McInnes-Hughes, Ross McKim, Micheline McKnight, the late Dorothy Madden, the late Francis Mason, Andy Miller, Anna Mittelholzer, Barry Moreland, Namron, Robert North, the late May O'Donnell, Virginia Olney, Jann Parry, Valerie Preston-Dunlop, John B. Read, Moshe Romano, Clover Roope, Ned Rorem, the late Bertram Ross, Lizzie Saunderson, Rina Schenfeld, Darshan Singh Bhuller, Michael Small, Janet Smith, Gus Solomons Jr, Grant Strate, Philip Taylor, Kenneth Tharp, the late Dame Ninette de Valois, Yair Vardi, Carl Vine, Eli Wallach, the late John Wallowitch, Elizabeth Walton, Jane Ward, Anne Went, the late Joan White, Maggie White, the late Ethel Winter, Ben Wright.

Further thanks are due to the Lisa Ullmann Travelling Fund who provided financial assistance to travel to Israel and to the University of Winchester for research time and funds to complete the book. Ron Hillel translated Hebrew which was quite beyond me. Likewise, thanks to Barbara Loester for translations from German. Jane Pritchard and the staff at the Victoria and Albert Museum were of great assistance as were Jane Fowler and the staff at the Trinity-Laban liibrary. My editor Isabelle Dambricourt Carvalho did a remarkable job in questioning me about dates and facts and did much to rein in my eccentric punctuation. David Leonard of Dance Books was more than patient in waiting for the manuscript. To both of them I give much gratitude.

My partner Roger Peaple has lived through the long years of researching and writing this book and proofread many versions, to him thanks as always. He has as a result become a dedicated Cohan fan.

The book would not have appeared without Bob Cohan himself. He subjected himself to many hours of questioning in London, at his house in France, and to endless phone calls and emails. I am grateful to him for his patience, generosity, hospitality, and incredible cooking.

When I was writing the book, I had a conversation with the critic and writer Marcia B. Siegel and when I told her I was letting Cohan see the chapters as I wrote them, her look was more than incredulous. She went on to tell me that when she wrote her biography of Twyla Tharp she had said to Tharp, 'I will need your memories but you will not see the book until it is published', which is what happened. With this book, Cohan has seen the chapters as they were written – though not this prelude or the postlude, which contain my more personal observations – and suggested finessing of detail, though at no stage did he ask me to change anything. What we have done is adding a commentary by him at the end of each chapter in which he offers some personal observations in his own inimitable way.

Near the completion of this book, the film director Ken Russell died; after years of neglect the news was full of lavish tributes and the word genius was used. In the *Guardian*, Jonathan Jones wrote an article entitled 'The Mourning After: Why We Should Celebrate Artists While They Are Alive':

> Art is for the living. If someone has lived creatively and you are grateful, for goodness sake, write them a letter, or create a website about them; get an article about them published if you have the opportunity, or if you are an editor, commission tributes while she or he can read them. What is the point of making a fuss when they are gone? It is morbid and to me it seems inauthentic.

Art should not go gentle into that good night. The fire of it should illuminate the living, not sanctify the dead. Grand funerals are for soldiers, not for artists.... Instead of lamenting the lost, we should be celebrating their achievements, and saying thank you, while they are still among us.[7]

This book attempts to celebrate the achievements of Robert Cohan.

Chapter 1

God! Was he handsome! We all thought, 'Where did he come from?'

Elliot Cohan, 2007

1925–43

All of the few published accounts of Robert Paul Cohan's life give his date of birth as 27 March 1925 in Manhattan, but this is not quite true. 1925 and Manhattan, yes, but not 27 March. In the late 1950s, while living in Boston, he had his horoscope – a very detailed affair, now sadly lost – drawn up by a reputable and experienced astrologer. The astrologer called to tell him that he could not reconcile the personality that was appearing in the chart with what he knew of Cohan's life and work, and asked him to double-check the information. On speaking to his mother, Cohan was told that the astrologer was quite right, he had in fact been born late on the evening of 26 March at the Manhattan Hospital, but because of the lateness of the hour he was not registered until the next day. The astrologer was pleased, telling him, 'I knew you couldn't be an artist born on the twenty-seventh!'

Cohan shares his 'real' birthday with another trailblazing artist, the composer and conductor Pierre Boulez, and with him the characteristics of Aries the Ram: pioneering, adventurous, energetic, confident and courageous, all words which have at some time been used to describe both men. On the downside, Aries can also be self-obsessed, impatient and foolhardy, again, all words that have been applied to both men. But as the first sign of the zodiac, Aries are leaders and one of their key traits is to start new ventures and show the way forward. In this, Cohan – and Boulez – has proven himself a true child of the Ram.

Cohan's family, on both sides, had lived in the New York area for many years, having emigrated from Europe with thousands of other Jews escaping persecution under kings, queens, tsars and emperors. One great-grandfather was lost in the California Gold Rush, another great-great-grandfather lived in London where he ran a tailor's business in the poor working class East End, eventually moving to the wealthy West End after changing profession and becoming a purveyor of alcohol. After this, he made an even greater change to his life and moved to Stockholm where he met his wife Mary Anderson, with whom he moved to America in the 1850s. Her Scandinavian genes may have been responsible for Cohan's chiselled good looks which so surprised his family.

His father, Walter Cohan, was born in 1896, the son of Louis Slocombe Cohen and his wife Lena, the daughter of Mary Anderson. Louis was a professional gambler who, along with his brother, ran the casino in Central Park, the premises being an elegant affair in turn-of-the-century New York. During the day, patrons would drive up in their carriages to visit the casino, sit under the Wisteria Pergola at the western edge of the site and listen to the strains of music from the Wednesday and Saturday afternoon concerts on the Mall below. In the summer seasons, refreshments from the casino were served at tables placed under the archway leading to Bethesda Terrace. It was demolished in 1935 and is now the site of the Summer Stage theatre productions, however, long before its demolition Louis' fortunes had changed and he was working as a bookmaker on the Sheepshead Bay Racetrack near Coney Island, in the far reaches of Brooklyn.

Cohan's mother, Billie, was born in 1898, one of the eight children of Elias and Rose Osheyack. In complete contrast to the Cohens who were in no way religious, the Osheyacks were a devoutly Orthodox Jewish family, following in detail all of the commandments of their faith; Elias would eventually oversee the building of a synagogue in Brooklyn. Walter and Billie had met on the Lower East Side sometime before the First World War but any marriage plans were put on hold as Walter enlisted in the US Army as a cavalryman. During the course of the war, the cavalry were disbanded and he finished the conflict fighting in the infantry. Apart from the horrors of warfare, Walter Cohen also endured – along with many other Jews – severe anti-Semitic taunts, the more printable being 'kike' and 'Jew boy', so much so that on his return to America he changed his name from Cohen to what he felt was the more Irish spelling Cohan. There was never any doubt that Walter and Billie would eventually marry, since 'they were completely and totally in love with one another', but, prudently, they waited while they built up some semblance of financial stability. Billie worked for the US Postal Service alongside a brother who was a postmaster, while Walter established himself in a linotype print shop business based at 41 John Street in the Financial District in Manhattan. Aided by Billie's bookkeeping skills, he made a great success of it and the two were eventually married in 1921.

At the time of Cohan's birth, the family was living in Manhattan but all the extended family wanted to get out of the cramped conditions of the city which, after the First World War, had become even more crowded. The name Brooklyn conjures up images of the famous bridge, intensive building and the tenement world made famous in the novel and film *A Tree Grows in Brooklyn*. But in the 1920s the wider reaches of the borough were largely rural. From working at the racetrack, both his father and grandfather knew the area around Sheepshead Bay and suggested the family move there.

The area, named not after any geographical resemblance to the physiognomy of a sheep but after a particularly plentiful type of fish, was a small fishing port, home of the fifty or so ships of the Brooklyn Fishing Fleet in the far west of Long Island. The area is more famous for its beaches – Brighton Beach, Manhattan Beach – and for the world-famous funfair at Coney Island, a couple of stops down the line. The lure of extra space, fresh air, cooler summers, good transport links to Manhattan and cheaper rents – for $60 per month a family could take a whole, big house – proved irresistible and the extended clan moved to what they hoped would be a better life.

Depending on income, which did fluctuate – sometimes alarmingly – the families would often move to a smaller or larger dwelling but always stayed in the rectangle of 21st, 23rd, 24th, 25th and 26th Street, Sheepshead Bay (strangely they never lived on 22nd Street). It was a typically mixed Brooklyn neighbourhood consisting mainly of Irish, Jewish and Italian families, yet there were no problems. All the different racial and religious groups were perhaps living by the Brooklyn official motto 'Een Draght Mackt Maght', from the Old Dutch, which translates roughly as 'In Unity There is Strength.' Eli Wallach and his wife Anne Jackson (who like Cohan would both study with Martha Graham) recall that in Brooklyn at the time 'there were no problems, no troubles; everyone got along just fine'. Ultimately, there were seven Cohan/Osheyack families who all had two or three children, each living within a five-block radius of each other. They all got together at least once a week and Robert's parents saw the other adults nearly every night. The atmosphere was supportive but also claustrophobic, even more so from 1929 when his father's parents, Louis and Lena, moved in with them. The stifling normality would be something that Cohan constantly rebelled against.

The young Cohan relished the semi-rural life style. A cycle ride of a few blocks in one direction would find him in docks with fishing boats; while in another direction there were salt marshes, inlets and creeks filled with crabs and fish. Further afield, much of the surrounding area was countryside with farms guaranteeing locally grown fresh produce and was largely self-sufficient with local shops selling all the daily staples. The search for bigger items would necessitate a walk of ten blocks or so and a journey on the N or R line to downtown Brooklyn – indicated on the platforms as 'the city' – and the large department stores, of which the long-established Martin's was a favourite.

Because of the differing backgrounds of his parents, the family had a mixed attitude to the Jewish religion and there was therefore a balance between no religion and orthodoxy. All the children – himself, his sister Dorothy (known as Dolly, born in 1927) and brother Elliot (born in 1932) – were brought up in the Jewish faith. Candles were always lit on Friday night for the Shabbat and Cohan was taught, and can still recall, all the appropriate prayers. He went to Hebrew school until he was 13, but after his bar mitzvah he told his mother that he would not go to the synagogue at all. Being a believer herself, she found this stance very hard to understand but accepted it. For his father, it was not an issue at all and was one of the few things they had in common.

His mother felt that her marriage was more important than the strict adherence to her religious beliefs, so she made compromises. She still observed kosher cooking rules, keeping separate sinks and utensils for eggs, meat and fish, but she became used to, or immune to, cooking 'forbidden' foods such as pork, seafood, bacon, crab, ham, and shrimp because her husband loved them. Food was a major part of Cohan's upbringing, and once his grandmother Lena had moved into the house, there was a certain degree of competitiveness between the two women as to who could make the best dishes. Beef brisket, chicken casserole, goulash, a myriad of fish dishes (often caught by Cohan and his grandfather), knaidlach, and knish were staples while the high days and holy days would see the women try to outdo themselves. Much of this love of food has remained with Cohan and he is an extraordinary cook, as anyone who has dined with him will testify.

If the arrival of his grandmother livened things up in the kitchen, the arrival of his grandfather brightened up Cohan's outdoor life. Cohan's father left very early every day for Manhattan and therefore Cohan spent long periods of his youth in the company of Grandfather Louis who introduced him to the delights of fishing in the many creeks and inlets around the area which were alive with all manner of marine life. This was more than a hobby, for as money was often scarce during the years of the Depression, their piscatorial activities were an essential addition to the family diet. As well as fishing, Cohan was taught by Louis the convoluted and laborious method of harvesting the large crabs native to the area. For years, every morning before school, Cohan could be found on the seafront.

The times outdoors meant that Cohan could indulge in his passion for the natural world. By his early teens he was a member of the National Audubon Society, a respected ornithological association founded in 1905 and named after the great pioneer of American ornithologists. He became an avid bird watcher, devouring the society's field guides as they appeared. His rural location offered him plenty of scope to observe any number of bobolinks, grasshopper sparrows, northern flickers, American kestrels and a multitude of other native and migrating species, and he quickly filled his birdwatching cards. By the time he was 12, he had observed, recorded and noted over 140 different varieties of birds. By the time he was 14, he was certain that he was going to get a job that would have something to do with the natural world or biological sciences. This was not to be, but his love of the natural world never left him. Many years later, while teaching in New Zealand, Cohan would still be able to impress the composer Geoffrey Burgon by his ability to identify the most obscure of antipodean birds, plants and other wildlife.

Crabbing or fishing can be monotonous, and while waiting for the fish to bite, Cohan had plenty time to read and he became a voracious devourer of books; if his mother is to be believed, he began reading when he was three. Whenever it was, it happened during his early years, and he admits that he 'was always a dreamer', happily disappearing into the world of King Arthur, Robin Hood, and Robinson Crusoe. When he heard his peers talking about being engineers, he couldn't understand it and preferred to think of 'another world, a romantic world'.

His parents, although not great aficionados of literature, owned a ten-volume collection of poetry from around the world, an eclectic selection which included some Sufi poetry which, as a young teenager, made a tremendous impression on him. One, by the thirteenth-century Persian poet Rumi, could almost be seen as a map for Cohan's life:

> The Jesus of your spirit is inside you now.
> Ask that one for help, but don't ask for body-things…
> Don't ask Moses for provisions
> that you can get from Pharaoh.
> Don't worry so much about livelihood.
> Your livelihood will turn out as it should.
> Be constantly occupied instead
> with listening to God.[8]

His interest in other states of being and mysticism, the seeds of which were sown in childhood, would gather pace during his war service and inform his development as a human being and artist. In a physical sense, it would also save his life.

The highlights of Cohan's youth were the many visits he paid to Camp Raleigh, a summer camp owned by his Aunt Sophie and Uncle Emanuel and located in Livingstone Manor, in the beautiful Catskill Mountains area of upstate New York. Since the turn of the twentieth century, the area had been popular with Jewish families escaping the heat of the city and by the 1930s, there were – and still are – a great many Jewish resorts and summer camps in this rural oasis, just a few hours' drive from Brooklyn. So much so that the area is affectionately known as the 'Borscht Belt', after the beetroot soup popular all over *Mitteleuropa*.

The entire extended family went, for although it was very expensive, family members paid less. It was very well organised – his father acting as gardener and his mother easily filling the role of 'camp mother'. He, his brother and sister and the many cousins separated into the boys' and girls' camps, consisting of about 150 children each. They slept dormitory fashion in little bungalows and participated in all kinds of sports and activities, including tennis, baseball, volleyball, swimming, as well as music and nature classes with long hikes. Cohan's memories of the visits are of hugely enjoyable times. This bucolic paradise of forests, lakes, streams, and rivers was where he felt totally at home, and he filled his time indulging his love of nature with walks in the woods, fishing, searching for birds, insects, and animals. Less happily for his mother, he would often be unwilling to part with some of his new found 'friends', and a variety of snakes and insects would be smuggled back to the family home. As well as outdoor activities, Cohan had his first experience of stage success, performing a tap number to the song 'Swanee River'. Embarrassingly now, this was performed in the best – or worst – minstrel show fashion with a blacked-up face. Perhaps, not surprisingly, since Al Jolson was then one of America's most famous Jewish performers, well known for his black-face rendition of the song, Cohan was a huge success. The audience screamed and yelled for an encore and, although Cohan did not know what that meant, someone pushed him back onstage, rewound the gramophone and he did the whole number over again.

For family members, the visits were not confined to the summer and many times Cohan found himself there off season, making sure everything was in good repair. He loved the seclusion of the woods and once, when they were covered in snow, he found himself alone, surrounded by slowly darkening trees, as dusk approached. The silence was broken by the tiniest of sounds, a twig falling, the soft footfall of a distant animal, the sound of his own breathing. The concentrated memory of that transcendental experience would resurface years later in his work *Forest*.

On another occasion, Elliot remembers his father taking the two brothers and a cousin hunting in the woods for deer. Although his father had taught Cohan to shoot – and he was a good shot, even owning a small rifle – he never killed anything. On this occasion, Walter Cohan and the cousin went off in one direction, leaving the two brothers alone. After some time, they saw a magnificent stag and Cohan theatrically lifted his gun but then, to his younger brother's relief, slowly lowered it without firing. Both brothers were stunned by the beauty of the animal, regal in its natural environment; there was no question of them shooting it. The moment lasted only a few seconds, until all of a sudden the deer ran off and the two were left in silent contemplation. They kept their silence when they returned to their father. In spite of the age difference between the two brothers, there was a bond that wasn't instantly apparent, and they had much more in common with each other than they did with their father. Cohan became an important guiding light in his younger brother's life, encouraging in him an interest in the natural world and later in music and art. Elliot remembers his influence as 'marvellous… He has left me with so many intellectual and cultural things that I would not have had if he was not part of my life.'

As well as the natural world, Cohan was fascinated by art and this was something his parents, his mother in particular, were happy to indulge him in. Mother and son made regular visits to the Brooklyn Museum, the second largest museum in New York and one of the largest in the United States. Its huge collection of paintings and sculptures from every period of human history fascinated Cohan. At 13, he started taking the Saturday morning art classes there, and as the museum was on the edge of the world-famous Botanic Gardens, a great deal of time was taken up painting landscapes. This, however, proved to be a short-lived activity. When he was about 14, Cohan found himself attempting to paint a vase, but having seen many types of modern art in the museums, he decided to try something new. Instead of painting in a traditional still-life fashion, as a literal representation, which was something his father always encouraged, he took his palette knife and smeared a thick line of yellow paint onto the canvas and on top of his realistic painting of the blue vase. Leaving the painting for a few hours while he went on an errand, Cohan returned to find that someone had come into his room and made some changes to his work. The yellow paint had been scraped away leaving, once again, a traditional still life. At this point, his father walked in and demanded to know why he had made such a 'terrible mess' of a perfectly good painting. Cohan turned into blind rage, screaming at his father, destroying the canvas, and jumping on the paint box. He did not paint again for fifty years. His love of colour would, however, remain and would manifest itself in the lighting, costumes, and set designs he chose for his dances.

This episode was a low point in an already strained relationship. Cohan felt that his father had no idea of how to bring up children, which was probably true, as he mainly left it to his wife. If anything went wrong with the children, it was Cohan as the eldest who was punished. His father was never interested in anything Cohan did other than the occasional question on his fishing activities with his grandfather. Walter Cohan was slightly closer to his daughter Dolly, who feels that her parents 'had so much love for each other that they had no time for anyone else'. His brother Elliot acknowledges that his father was a hard and difficult man who simply could not understand his artistically minded son. He even goes so far as to suggest that his father was jealous, not only of his brother's gifts, but also because of his good looks.

The Cohans never went to see live theatre – for the family it was as though it did not exist. Cohan and Dolly did, however, try their hand at puppetry; using small hand puppets, they devised ongoing stories they presented in the garage, charging friends a penny to watch. Other activities involved the creation of dramas that evolved in an almost stream-of-consciousness fashion from afternoon to afternoon. Cohan would devise elaborate scenarios that were often set in the basement of the family home. Each room was a different part of some mythical wood, or magical environment and complex rituals had to be completed in order to progress from one room to the other. An interest in ritual is something that has stayed with Cohan all his life, and some type of formalised ritual appears in many of his dances. This mystical childhood world apart, it was to the cinema that Cohan and Dolly escaped – and to musicals in particular. Busby Berkeley and Ruby Keeler were enjoyed but Fred Astaire and Ginger Rogers were their favourites, their glamorous lifestyle portrayed in films such as *Flying Down to Rio* or *Top Hat* seeming to be a world away from life in Sheepshead Bay; little did Cohan know that he would later share the stage with Miss Rogers.

Cohan was taken to his first dance classes when he was about five years old, and although he did not know exactly what he was being taught, with hindsight he thinks it may have been something born out of the exoticisms of Ruth St Denis and Ted Shawn or some other form of 'modern dance'. The lessons took place in a very large wooden house, the kind now more associated with the Southern States than with Brooklyn, with a big porch all around it and a large living room that looked like a ballroom. Cohan remembers being taken by his mother to one of these houses where a large group of children were assembled. The lessons were led by two ladies, one in a long brown dress who taught the movements, and another who provided the music and who never moved from the piano. These occurred every Saturday and he loved them. It was unusual for boys to do dance and he has no idea as to why his mother took him – it was certainly not something his father would have encouraged. Sadly for Cohan, the lessons did not last very long, for on one occasion while he was in class his mother went to the toilet and saw something that shocked her so much that she took him out of the lesson and never took him back. No matter how often he asked her what it was she had seen, she would never tell. Classes of a different sort started when he was 8 or 9 and he was joined by his sister. This time they studied tap, gymnastics, and something called adagio, which with hindsight he realises was a form of ballet. His favourite discipline, however, was gymnastics, which stood him in good stead at school.

Cohan attended the local James Madison High School on the corner of Neck Road and 22nd/23rd Street. He was a likeable but middling student, working hard only at those things he enjoyed, such as geography, art, and English because he read a lot. He enjoyed some science, subjects such as biology, but the other classes held little interest for him and as he grew older, his strong independent streak became increasingly apparent.

Despite his naturally athletic physique, sport held no interest for him, though he spent some time on the fencing team and with the track team, excelling in running and jumping. Most of the time he got out of team sport by simply 'bunking off', cycling off on his own into the countryside. He discovered his vocation at the age of 14, when he joined the school cheerleading squad. This was not 'pompom' waving but very physically demanding, gymnastic routines for which a great deal of time was needed to work out the complex lifts, catches, drops, and backflips. These routines were not just for local consumption, as high-school football and basketball are an important part of the sport life of New York City. As such, the team performed to huge crowds in big arenas such as Madison Square Gardens and the Dodgers Stadium. For Cohan, performing was as important as the movements themselves.

His friends were very physical and they danced a lot – jive, rumba and jitterbug were all the rage and he and his sister loved going to parties. She would later tell him to his surprise that she got through high school on his coattails, meaning his popularity opened doors for her. Sex, he remembers, 'was always there, available without inhibition', and in his late teens Cohan realised he was attracted to both men and women, but sex for him was not that important a part of life, certainly there and available when needed but not a primary motivating need. His later colleague Stuart Hodes has more robust memories of adolescent sex:

Pre-teen males have their own folk lore. My bunch in Sheepshead Bay, Brooklyn, 11 to 13-year olds, talked about putting a 'boner' in a girl.

'They all want you to do it,' said Buddy.

'What if you take a piss in there?' asked Georgie.

'Probably kill her,' answered Buddy.

Buddy, 13, was our voice of authority because he'd actually 'done it' with Dorine, who was 14 and lived across the street. I could never look at Dorine without wondering what 'it' was like.[9]

But this was not Cohan's style or manner and his nature rebelled against the standard life, the routine that was mapped out and that said 'you would grow up, get married and have children, and that is it'. He 'didn't like the predictability of it, the claustrophobia of it'.

He was a very moody teenager, and Elliot, in spite of the affection between them, remembers him as often 'very in his head and very full of himself'. He did not know what he wanted to do with his life but he knew he was not finding it at home. He liked being on his own but this was difficult, especially with seven family members living in one house. He had no close relations with his cousins; no one, he felt, had similar interests or aspirations. He was always surrounded by people and yet he felt he was 'always the loner, always separate in a way'.

Like so many others, his teenage years, which should have been filled with so much hope and optimism, were blighted by the Second World War which began in Europe when he was 14. Being Jewish and of German extraction, the Cohan family had heard of some of the horrors that were being carried out by the Nazis and were both appalled and powerless. Once America entered the war after the bombing of Pearl Harbour in December 1941, when he was 16, all plans for a normal future changed. He and his friends knew that once they graduated, they would be called to serve their country; but here was no attempt made to evade enlisting. He was aware of a few conscientious objectors, but his family just thought they 'were plain stupid, because what could they be objecting to?' If Cohan had a plan, it was to try and control what part of the military he joined, and there were only two ways that this could be achieved. One was to enlist, in which case he would have been allowed to choose from the army, navy, or air force. Anyone who waited to be called up was simply told where to go. The other much more desirable option materialised in his final year of high school.

In early 1943, a notice appeared on the school bulletin board stating that army officers would be visiting the school to administer a special test to select those qualified to be in a special unit in the army. The teachers had been asked to nominate only the brightest of bright students to take part and, convinced of his own abilities, Cohan asked his teacher to put his name down. Her response, 'But Robert you shouldn't do it, you are not intelligent enough', was not what he was expecting. Controlling his anger – he nearly hit her – his Aries characteristics came into play, and he pushed and complained and was finally allowed to take the exam. It turned out to be an IQ test and Cohan's persistence was vindicated when he came out with an exceptionally high score and was accepted. Exactly what he was being accepted into he was not sure; but at least it was not the infantry, and it would get him out of Sheepshead Bay.

Commentary

Chapter 1

What Paul wrote about my childhood and early teens was spot on and made memories of that time flood back. It was an easy, happy and light-filled time. It was much more important to me to see and identify a sand plover in the marshes than to remember the declension of a French word in school. After all, the plover was on a journey of thousands of miles and just stopping in front of me for a few days. It is true, now that I live in France, I wish I had paid more attention to French than I did, but as a young man my imagination and the natural world I lived in were more important to me than anything else.

I was very good at geography but mainly because I had a book of maps at home in which I drew all the many trips I would make in the future. Not only would I visit every state in America, but I also had trips planned all over the world. I was sure I would make those journeys someday but little did I think I would make most of them, on tour, dancing.

Telling my mother that I would not go to the synagogue anymore was a very important moment in my young life. I had been through four years of Hebrew school, taught by very bad teachers, at the synagogue that my grandfather had helped to build. I could read Hebrew but I still did not know how to translate the prayers I was learning. I found that very frustrating. Like many young people, I think, I had my own personal relationship to God that I never talked about. Somehow I felt I needed to take that part of my inner life in my own hands and my bar mitzvah was the right time. I never thought my mother would agree but she was amazing. She said, 'You are a man now and even though I don't like that decision, I have to accept it, but you will go to the synagogue every Saturday at 10.30 a.m. (there was usually a break in the service at that time) and say 'Good Shabbat' to your grandmother.' I agreed, thinking I got off easy but I found out that being a man at 13 was not so easy.

Chapter 2

Hail, hail to the A.S.T.P.

(army chant, 1943)[10]

1944–6

Cohan found himself part of the largest college education programme in the history of the United States. The Army Specialized Training Program (ASTP) was a military training regime conceived by the US government soon after the attacks on Pearl Harbour. Held at a number of American universities, its aim was to meet wartime demands for junior officers and soldiers with technical skills. After much discussion in Congress, the ASTP was approved in September 1942 and implemented in December of that year.

The result of this was that during the academic year 1942–3 a national testing programme was conducted among the male students who were old enough to be conscripted. Enlisted men already on active duty were also tested, but could be accepted into the programme only at the rank of private. The military used a standard Stanford-Binet IQ test which consisted of thirty questions ranging from the ability to touch one's nose or ear when requested to do so, to the ability to draw designs from memory and to define abstract concepts. Mensa currently requires prospective members to achieve a score of 132, Cohan's was 150.

Cohan thus joined the over 200,000 men who were successful and were sent to 227 colleges across the United States to take accelerated courses in various branches of engineering, medicine, dentistry, personnel psychology, and thirty-four foreign languages. The huge influx of young ASTP'ers almost overnight changed many campuses into army reservations and included some names who would go on to be central to American culture, including diplomat Henry Kissinger, New York City Mayor Ed Koch, actor and writer Mel Brooks, and author Gore Vidal.

Cohan found himself with a group of highly intelligent and highly cultured men, not at all like the 'street gangs' he had been used to back in Brooklyn. It was here in the army that his life began to change; for the first time, he was with people who read because they enjoyed reading, not because they were told to, and who listened to classical music as a matter of course and not just when they were in music appreciation class. In short, they loved learning. For Cohan, this was a new attitude; the way in which they approached problem solving, whether in chemistry, maths, or physics, was a positive, fascinating experience, when for him it had been a chore at school. He had a lot to learn and they helped him, but the memory has stayed with him that 'often it was a struggle just to keep up'.

One of the most important areas these men opened to Cohan was not in maths or science but in philosophy, and specifically the work of the Armenian mystic and spiritual teacher George Gurdjieff (1866–1949) and of his pupil P. D. Ouspensky (1878–1947). Gurdjieff conceived a number of complex theories on the human experience and he developed teachings from many world religions, even calling his work 'esoteric Christianity' at one point. He believed that humanity had lost touch with the true meanings of ancient spiritual traditions. According to him, men could not perceive reality because they did not possess consciousness but rather lived in a state of what would be called by his followers 'waking sleep' – Gurdjieff wrote that 'man lives his life in sleep, and in sleep he dies'.[11] As a result of this condition, he taught that each person perceives the world from a completely subjective perspective. Of particular importance to these men fighting a war was Gurdjieff's assertion that 'evil' events such as wars could not take place if people were more awake. He taught that humans, in their typical state, function as unconscious automatons, but that one can 'wake up' and become a different sort, a better sort of human being altogether.

The idea was very appealing to men caught up in the relentless machine of war. Even more appealing was that in order to 'wake up', one did not have to renounce the world like in many traditional religions. Gurdjieff believed that most religions or spiritual movements tended to develop only one aspect of the human and not the whole being, namely, either the emotions, the physical body, or the mind. In addition to this, anyone wishing to undertake any of the traditional paths to spiritual knowledge, which Gurdjieff reduced to three (the path of the fakir, the path of the monk, and the path of the yogi), involved renouncing life in the world. Gurdjieff thus developed what became known through Ouspensky as the Fourth Way, although Gurdjieff himself never used the term, and which was intended to be achievable for modern people living modern lives in Europe and America. Instead of developing body, mind, or emotions separately, Gurdjieff's discipline worked on all three to promote an integrated and balanced inner development.

Gurdjieff's philosophy had something in common with other mystical or spiritual traditions: he taught that the path to 'awakening' would not be easy and required a great deal of effort – this he referred to as 'The Work' or 'Work on oneself'. According to him, 'Working on oneself is not so difficult as wishing to work, taking the decision.'[12] Gurdjieff's teachings addressed the question of humanity's place in the universe and the importance of developing latent potential. He taught that higher levels of consciousness, inner growth and development are real possibilities that nonetheless require conscious effort to achieve.

Gurdjieff's work taught people how to increase and focus their attention and energy in various ways and to minimise daydreaming and absent-mindedness. According to his teaching, this inner development is the beginning of a possible further process of change, the aim of which is to transform people into what

Gurdjieff believed they ought to be. These ideas became central to Cohan's whole outlook on life and art and when he discovered the work of Martha Graham at the end of the war, he saw a way to join all the areas of his life together into a transformational whole. The focus of his life and work has been an attempt to achieve a transformation in himself and to help others to discover their potential.

Had he known the level of intellectual debate the men entered into, Col. Herman Beukema, of West Point Military Academy and who ran the ASTP programme, would undoubtedly have been bemused, as he demanded that his men should be 'soldiers first, students second'. The ASTP'ers were under strict military discipline at all times; they wore regulation uniforms, were subject to Saturday morning inspections, marched to classes and meals, had lights out at 10.30 p.m. and generally behaved, and misbehaved, like all other soldiers. Or perhaps not, as Henry Kissinger was known to enjoy a good discussion on the merits of Stendhal's *The Red and the Black* rather than on Betty Grable's legs. The standard work week was fifty-nine hours of 'supervised activity', including a minimum of twenty-four hours of classroom and lab work, twenty-four hours of required study, five hours of military instruction, and six hours of physical instruction. Gore Vidal would write in his autobiography *Palimpsest*, 'We were a lean, sinewy, sweaty race, energised by sex and fear of death, the ultimate aphrodisiac.'[13]

Most of these men accepted their new assignments, whatever form they took, with unusually good humour, as one anonymous conscript wrote:

> Hail, hail to the A.S.T.P.
> Why did this ever happen to me?
> History, English, Chem. and Math.,
> Not even time to take a bath.
> They gave us assignments ten pages long,
> We did the problems. They were always wrong!
> But now throw your slide rule into the sea,
> And march on to the P.O.E.[14]

In the end, it did not matter too much because the course, which was at the College of Puget Sound in Washington State, lasted only three intense months and was then closed down.

At Christmas 1943, over 200,000 men were on campuses across the country. On 18 February 1944, the War Department unexpectedly announced that 110,000 ASTP'ers would be sent to active duty by 1 April. The reason for this was the catastrophic and seemingly unexpected losses that the military had suffered; all available bodies, no matter their IQ score, were now needed. But before he was shipped out, Cohan had his first exposure to ballet.

His newfound pals told him that Ballet Theatre were performing in Seattle and that he had to go and see them. Up until this time, his idea of a good dancer and good dancing had been Fred Astaire and Ginger Rogers, seen on the big screen with his sister. He had never seen any dance live on stage, and had never even been taken to a theatre. The Ballet Theatre had started in 1937 as the Mordkin Ballet, named after its founder, the Russian ballet dancer and former partner of Anna Pavlova, Mikhail Mordkin. He had been quickly replaced as director by a former student and financial backer Lucia Chase who, in 1940, renamed the company – it would only become the name by which is it now well known, American Ballet Theatre, in 1956. They had had huge success with modern ballets, including works by Antony Tudor, Agnes de Mille and Jerome Robbins and it was some of these works Cohan hoped to see.

Cohan travelled to the city with some friends but only he went to the theatre. Arriving early, he bought a ticket, wandered around for a while and went back to see the performance. Staring at the beautifully lit interior with its glamorous red stage curtain, and surrounded by smartly dressed people, Cohan was filled with anticipation and excitement. This was, however, short-lived because the usher came and told him he had to leave, as in his excitement he had bought a ticket for the matinee and it was now the evening show and it was sold out, and even his army uniform could not get him a seat. He had to wait until he was shipped out to Camp Roberts in Santa Maria, California, before he would see any ballet. Again, it was Ballet Theatre, this time at the Hollywood Bowl, and this time he got in. He was deeply moved by the dancing of Hugh Laing and Nora Kaye in Antony Tudor's 1942 version of *Romeo and Juliet*, and the ability of dance to carry this Shakespeare play which he had only recently discovered. Also imprinted onto his mind was the virtuoso dancing of André Eglevsky who 'seemed to touch the roof when he jumped'.

The majority of the displaced ASTP'ers joined the rest of the military still in training in the USA, but were scheduled for overseas assignment before the end of 1944. Cohan and his group were transferred to the 11th Army Infantry Division, which had been activated in Camp Polk, Louisiana. All thought of intellectual advancement went out the window as the division underwent combat training at Camp Polk and Camp Barkeley, Texas, desert manoeuvres at Camp Ibis, California, and combat readiness training at Camp Cooke, California.

The IQ of the division, Cohan remembers, was classified as too low to be sent overseas. To get around this, the army decided to boost the average IQ by adding into it the exceptionally bright men from the ASTP. If the former ASTP'ers had been expecting any special treatment in their new units, they were to be sadly disappointed. In spite of their intellectual prowess, very few were allowed to take officer training and practically none got non-combat ratings until they reached combat zones, where the carnage of war created unwanted openings for them to fill.

If anything, the inexperienced ASTP'ers were given a very tough time by the regular soldiers who considered them a bunch of overeducated college kids, or even worse, 'Jew boy college kids' who hoped their intellectual abilities would enable them to leap ahead in promotion; what they clearly needed was to be taught what life for 'real' men in the 'real' army was about. Cohan recalls this period as 'uncomfortable'. With five or six close friends, he made a deal to stick together and look after each other, always making sure that they all had enough money to be able to get out of the barracks at weekends and not return until Monday mornings. This was to escape the enlisted men who hated them and who 'by Saturday afternoons were mostly blind drunk and looking for trouble'.

One lengthier escape saw Cohan allowed home for a week during which he would have one of the magical experiences that were a regular part of his life. On this occasion, one of the family neighbours invited Cohan to join him and his daughter at the races. Cohan's grandfather and father had been brought up gambling on the racetrack but it held no interest for Cohan, and he had never been to one and knew nothing about betting. However, the neighbour insisted and he wanted to give Private Cohan a good time. The night before the visit, Cohan had a dream in which he called his Aunt Helen and asked her what horse was going to win at the races; her dream self obligingly told him to bet on Art of War. Cohan had only vague recollections of the dream when he woke up but when arrived at the racetrack and saw that a horse called Art of War was indeed running, the memory of the dream came back and he bet $2. The horse, which was an outsider, won and Cohan left with $60, much to the bemusement of his neighbour. This would not be the last time Cohan would experience what he terms 'foreknowledge', and often it would leave him better off financially and spiritually.

His brother also found him much changed. As most young people did then and do now, the teenage Elliot listened to the popular music of the day; not strange since no classical music was played in the Cohan household. But on his return from the army camp, Cohan, full of the excitement of his newfound knowledge, decided that his younger brother could do better and so borrowed a phonograph from an aunt, placed Elliot in a chair, and played Grieg's Piano Concerto to him, not once, but three times. This may have put some people off but not Elliot, who listened to the recording himself the next day and has continued an avid enjoyment of classical music to this day.

There was much uncertainty in the division, known as the Thunderbolts, as to where they would be going; one day it was the Pacific, the next it was Europe. It was finally decided they would be going to Europe, and on 12 August 1944 they were sent to Camp Kilmer, New Jersey, then on two troop trains. They were allowed into New York for a two-day leave. On 27 September 1944, an overcast, miserable, wet day, laden down with their packs, duffle bags, and weapons, Cohan and his division said goodbye to America. The coffee and doughnuts given to them by the Red Cross on the pier before they boarded the ship provided but little comfort. The division embarked from Staten Island, New York, aboard the troopships HMS Samaria and USS Hermitage to join the largest Atlantic convoy of the Second World War.

There was great unease on board the troopship as it crossed the Atlantic – every day brought the possibility of torpedo attacks from U-boats. Luckily there were no such assaults and the ship docked in Liverpool on 12 October. From the bustling seaport the troops were quickly dispatched by train to Longbridge Deverill in Wiltshire, then on 24 October they moved to Tilshead Barracks near Warminster.

While awaiting orders, Cohan and his friends were for once not exactly overworked. They made acquaintances with the local welcoming committee who put on art and music classes in the local church hall for the Americans. Most of the regular soldiers avoided this but the ASTP group were avid followers. On many weekends they were able to visit London. Nothing had prepared him for a city totally devastated by years of war. Since 13 June 1944 London had been subjected to a terrible assault by V-1s – *Vergeltungswaffen*, vengeance weapons – pilotless planes, launched from across the English Channel, which exploded on impact. Replaced in late August by the more deadly V-2s, these Doodlebugs had wreaked destruction on London. More than 1.25 million houses were eventually destroyed and parts of London looked like shanty towns. In her novel *The Girls of Slender Means*, Muriel Spark described the scene:

> The streets of the cities were lined with buildings in bad repair or in no repair at all, bomb-sites piled with stony rubble, houses like giant teeth in which decay had been drilled out, leaving only the cavity. Some bomb-ripped buildings looked like the ruins of ancient castles until, at closer view, the wallpapers of various quite normal rooms would be visible, room above room, exposed, as on a stage, with one wall missing; sometimes a lavatory chain would dangle over nothing from a fourth- or fifth-floor ceiling; most of all the staircases survived, like a new art-form, leading up and up to an unspecified destination that made unusual demands on the mind's eye.[15]

The bombs had destroyed thousands of dwellings, and London was filled to the brim with homeless Londoners, refugees and soldiers from every part of the globe and many, many Americans. An energy bordering on hysteria prevailed; drink and sex were available everywhere, but basics such as food were in short supply – the Americans' access to food made them doubly welcome. Often, Cohan and his friends would visit Watkins Bookshop, then and still now at 21 Cecil Court, to search out books on the occult and mysticism, and even on one occasion meeting the founder John M. Watkins himself. A leader on this interest in the esoteric was Walter Martin, who would lead Cohan in searching out other ways of thinking which would be so important to his later development. Entertainment was everywhere and performances – music, theatre, and cinema – were often sold out. As Dame Ninette de Valois would remember, 'There was nothing in the shops to buy so we were always sold out.' On one occasion, Cohan was victim of a conman, giving money to the man who ran off before handing over the tickets. Deciding to try his luck at the theatre, Cohan found that there was not even standing room. Tickets were usually available from a more reliable source, the United Services Organizations Club on Piccadilly, where most morning tickets were sold for theatre, ballet and concerts.

Under Ninette de Valois, the Vic-Wells Ballet did sterling work during the war, aiming to keep morale up by touring the country and presenting work to the troops and workers. Cohan would see them a few times in London and was particularly taken by performances of a new ballet, *Miracle in the Gorbals*, by the Australian Robert Helpmann with music by Arthur Bliss, which had only been premiered at the Prince's Theatre, on 26 October 1944. The dance, set in the slums of Glasgow, concerns a despairing young Scottish girl who commits suicide but is brought back to life by a Christ-like, mysterious stranger. In spite of this miracle, the inhabitants are terrified by the stranger's powers and he is murdered by a gang of thugs. Not exactly a cheering story but the theme of hope, resurrection and transformation was one that resonated with Cohan and his army pals and also with the public at large. The excellent cast included the choreographer Robert Helpmann, never a favourite of Cohan's, but who he felt in this work exuded a magical quality, alongside the radiant red-haired Moira Shearer. Other ballets included performances by Margot Fonteyn and Beryl Grey. One of Cohan's colleagues knew the editor of *Dance Magazine* in America and had been asked to write some articles about the works they saw; as a result, they were given some backstage passes and were able to watch the company take classes and to be introduced, briefly, to de Valois herself.

These almost carefree times in England were short-lived and on 17 December, the battalion left Wiltshire for Weymouth where five boats were ready to take them to Cherbourg. By 20 December, the men were in the resort town of Barneville, where they had orders 'to be ready at a moment's notice', as the news from the south was not good; in the Ardennes forest, the Nazis had attacked and burst through a fifty-mile line in a desperate attempt to force back the Allied Forces. Now known as the Battle of the Bulge, it was one of the bloodiest conflicts in the whole of the war, and Cohan was at its centre.

The Nazi surprise counter-attack through the Ardennes caused the abrupt change of orders they had been dreading, and on 22 December the battalion began one of the most gruelling forced marches in American military history. Travelling in freezing winter conditions, they struggled through the sleet and snow via Falaise, Dainville, Mantes and Paris, covering 500 miles in four days. Here Cohan saw the brutality of war, later telling Gordon Gow, 'We were moving so fast that there was no time to take prisoners. Well, usually we would go into a town and the Germans would be hiding in the houses. You would promise them anything to get them to come out and you would line them all up behind a building and then shoot them and go on.'[16] The horrors of these events would later be relived in his work *X* (1970). By 23 December, the division joined up with General Patton's US Third Army and was deployed defensively along a thirty-mile reach of the Meuse River, extending from Sedan to Givet. Shortly afterward, orders came to advance another eighty-five miles north-east into Belgium.

In spite of the Christmas season, Cohan and the men had little time to relax. Many were camped into dugouts painfully cut into the frozen mud by the sides of the destroyed roads and the men were made to work hard, with only a short break on Christmas Day for religious services. One bitterly cold night, Cohan and a friend decided to go into a nearby village to see if they could find some brandy. They began to walk before the moon came up but on their return it was high and bright in the sky, and looking around at the fields Cohan saw a scene from Dante. It was not clear in the almost surgical moonlight whether the dismembered arms and legs, disembowelled torsos or crushed heads frozen into the landscape were American, German or French. It was a scene he would never forget. Soon after midnight on Christmas Day the battalion moved onto Laon and Poix-Terron.

The Nazis had begun using saboteurs dressed as GIs, so extra tensions were added as all visitors or strangers were thoroughly checked. The checking caused Cohan some concern as the questions the men were told to ask strangers were often sport based, along the lines of, 'Who won the World Series in 1937?' or 'Who won the Rose Bowl in 1935?' Cohan's knowledge of such things was limited and he had to ask colleagues for assistance in both questions and answers. Looking back, he recalls that 'if they had been about movie stars I would have got them!'

The first battle occurred on 29 December, when the division engaged head-on with the fanatical Füher-Begleit-Brigade and the Panzer-Lehr-Division south of Remagne. Over the next few days a violent and bloody battle raged, as these enemy forces, together with the 3rd Panzer-Grenadier-Division and the 26th Volks-Grenadier-Division, fought to close the relief corridor into Bastogne from the south. The 11th armoured and supporting units fought them to a standstill. During this period, Cohan's division suffered heavy casualties from enemy action as well as from the bitter cold, and hundreds died. However, the enemy paid a heavier price, and the vital supply line into Bastogne remained open.

By 6 p.m. on 31 December, the battalion had taken the town of Rechrival, south of Morhet, and, as night had set in, the town was organised for defence. During the last night of December 1944 and the early morning of New Year's Day 1945, the village was the target of very intense enemy fire which caused numerous casualties; Cohan estimates that 80 per cent of his division were killed. He believes that most of them died because they got angry and simply threw themselves in a rage to avenge their fallen friends. He, however, was in one sense lucky as it was here that his war would end.

Cohan had a premonition that he would be wounded. His platoon was surrounding the exposed area of the village square, with another platoon opposite. His sergeant insisted that the two groups should be able to communicate and, as Cohan was acting as a scout, he was ordered to go. He said to his superior, 'If I go over there, I will be shot!' but he was told in no uncertain terms to obey orders. Cohan and another scout were made to go and, as they crossed the darkened square, they heard the shells coming.

Cohan saw a shell go off to his right before he heard it; his friend was killed instantly and he found himself being thrown a good distance onto his back. Lying on his back, frozen from the neck down, he became aware of two things: a man above him screaming, 'Oh my God! Oh my God!' and a huge jagged hole that he could just make out in the centre of his greatcoat. He was convinced he was going to die, because it looked as though the blast had blown away most of his chest. Fortunately that was not the case.

Knowing they were going into battle, the troops had been supplied with extra rations. Cohan had taken a package and pushed it down through his greatcoat and field jacket, where there was a large pocket. A sizeable shell fragment had indeed landed dead centre but what it had connected with was not Cohan's chest but a can of ham and eggs, from which it was deflected again off to one side. It then went through a leather wallet and, more poetically a copy of the *Rubáiyát of Omar Khayyám* purchased at Watkins Bookstore, which he had in his left-breast field jacket pocket. By the time the shell had hit him, it had expended most of its energy so it did not tear him apart as it should have done. It was, however, a very serious wound that would keep Cohan in hospital for six months, would ultimately require a skin graft taken from his left leg and would leave a scar the size of a man's hand. But he was luckier than most of the men he knew. Of the bright intelligent men he had started out with in Puget Sound, only two survived; one would indirectly lead him to Martha Graham and the other would share his life for nearly twenty years.

Back home, it was the young Elliot who answered the door to the stranger who came to tell the family in person that their son was seriously wounded. His mother became ill with worry, but there was nothing any of them could do but wait. The painful surgery and gruelling recuperation which for a long while took place outside of Birmingham in a hospital complex that would also house Robin Howard, had an enormous effect on his intellectual and spiritual development. The hospital had a marvellous library, in which he found hundreds of little library books especially printed for the use of the military. It contained 'all the classics, everything that a well-intentioned librarian would want a soldier to read', so Cohan built on the groundwork started the previous year and caught up on his education, devouring classic novels, plays, and poetry. He continued in this way when he was shipped back to America, in his own words he 'read like a sponge'. He was eventually moved back to New Jersey and ended his war as a librarian at a Boston transit camp.

The war in the Far East was still raging and Cohan, in spite of his serious injury, was expecting another overseas posting. Luckily for him, he discovered that he had one more Battle Star than he had thought. Battle Stars were awarded to soldiers for each campaign they fought in and each Battle Star was worth five points, once a certain number had been reached the soldier could be discharged. The forgotten five points got Cohan out of the army and, so he believes, saved his life. He was finally discharged in South Carolina and returned home. Along with 964,409 other Americans wounded in the war, he was awarded the Purple Heart and returned with it in hand to the Brooklyn home he had so wanted to escape from. Of his experiences, Cohan would later observe:

> Fighting in the war was an unreal experience, it is not obviously like anything else, it is not intellectually logical or emotionally logical. You are there and you must fight, if you do not you may be killed. You change completely. It is a matter of sheer survival and, if anything, it taught me what one can do, how much stress one can undergo and how easy, in the right situation, it is to kill. Not that to kill is ever right, but it is a definite question, you either kill or are killed.

Once back home, along with many war veterans, he had no idea what he wanted to do; throughout the final years of high school any plans had been put on hold as everyone expected to go into the war. Once back, these battle-scarred young people, mature beyond their years, suddenly had to pick up the pieces of a life they never thought they would have. To pass time, Cohan hung around with a group of ex-servicemen, most of whom he had little in common with apart from war service, and struggled to work out what he could do with the rest of his life. One of the group suggested that they all take the Civil Service Exam and see if they could get a job working for the government, in this case more specifically for the Veterans' Administration, the enormous organisation with a budget second only to that of defence, that looks after all American war veterans.

Cohan was called for interview and, after testing, received the good news that he had received a perfect score, something which was almost unheard of. He was duly offered a job, a very good, very well-paid job, with a starting salary of $60 per week, a huge sum in 1945 for someone who had never held down a paid job before. The only trouble with the job was that he never worked out what it was he was supposed to be doing and his routine resembled something out of a Kafka novel. Each morning, he would journey into Manhattan, enter a room full of large desks and sit at the one with his name on it. During the morning, various papers would arrive and he would dutifully file them. After a while, he would take his green blotter off his desk and put it into the top drawer and then take everything else off and put it into the other drawer. That achieved, he would get up and go for a walk around the streets of Manhattan, returning in the late afternoon to take out the blotter and sit down again. He did the job for about two months without knowing anything about it, or showing any interest in it. By the end, his grade was number seven although he was never too sure which part of the scale he had started on. Whatever it was, he realised this was not what he had planned for his life.

All this was to change when Arnold Horovitz, one of the two men still alive from the days at Puget Sound, called him to ask a favour. Horovitz had a friend called Diane Meredith, a dancer and singer from the West Coast who had appeared in a few movies including *Week-End at the Waldorf* and *Keep Your Powder Dry* in 1945, but, wanting more from her life she had come to New York to study with Martha Graham. Meredith had never been to New York before and Horovitz wanted to see if Cohan would be able to borrow his father's car and drive them around the sights. This he did; taking them on an extended tour covering the home turf of Coney Island and the distance of the Cloisters in the North Bronx as well as downtown Manhattan. Cohan felt comfortable in their company and as they drove they talked about the war, life, possibilities for the future. Then, something Cohan said prompted Meredith to tell him he had to study with Martha Graham, that she was exactly what he was looking for in his life. Apart from the ballet he had seen during the war, Cohan had never seen any art dancing, and although the name Martha Graham may have been mentioned in passing, he had never seen her dance. In any case, Cohan was still harbouring some idea that he would give up his job, go to university, and study biology.

Over the course of a week of touring, Meredith convinced him that he should at least have a look at the sort of dance she was talking about. A visit to Ruth St Denis, the mother of American modern dance and who Meredith knew, proved a turning point. St Denis' quasi-mystical approach to art, based as it was on magpie stealings from world philosophies, fascinated and intrigued Cohan. Her words seemed to open up other worlds and possibilities that were a million miles away from his mundane Kafkaesque life and he was hooked. Meredith was also friendly with Jane Dudley, an ex-Graham dancer who at the time was dancing with Sophie Maslow and William Bales as the Dudley-Maslow-Bales Trio. Since 1942, they had made something of a name for themselves with their politically motivated dances and as luck would have it they were performing in New York. After the show, Meredith took Cohan backstage to meet Dudley, even then a formidable statuesque character with a no-nonsense attitude and a complete contrast to St Denis. She was typically brusque with him, telling him she knew nothing about men dancing and that he should talk to Bales. Bill Bales was a much more approachable figure and he listened intently to Cohan, occasionally asking him questions about his life and hopes for the future. When Cohan stopped speaking, Bales told him that he really did agree with Meredith and that Cohan should seek out Martha Graham, saying, 'She would like you, I can see that.' This was particularly generous of Bales, who had studied not with Martha Graham but with her 'rival' Doris Humphrey, but saw something in Cohan that made him think Graham would be right for him. Cohan, however, did not go straight to the Graham Studio; intrigued by Bales, Maslow and Dudley, he went first to the New Dance Group studio where the trio taught and took class from all three of them. Excited by the experience and now able to agree with Bales that Graham's work would be best for him, he took himself off to the Graham Studio at 66 Fifth Avenue.

The first person he met there was Donald Duncan, who would eventually become editor of *Dance Magazine*, but who was then working as studio secretary/receptionist. Always with an eye for an attractive young man, Duncan was more than welcoming to the handsome war veteran. Students at the school were expected to take a minimum of three classes per week, but as Cohan still had his well-paid job, he could only make two. Duncan was happy to bend the rule a little, making an exception in this case, and allowed Cohan to take just two classes.

The Graham Studio at 66 Fifth Avenue was a good size, but the office and changing rooms were tiny. The stairs from the street led to a small room with a desk – the school and company were managed from there. There was a dividing wall behind the desk which acted as the women's changing room, consisting of a couple of benches and a clothes rack; it was also tiny. The men's changing room was if anything even smaller, providing just enough space for decency, and being only a curtained-off portion of a hallway. It was here that Cohan, nervous with anticipation, changed into his swimming trunks and T-shirt, the standard costume for men, and took his first class. This was with Marjorie Mazia, the wife of folk singer Woody Guthrie, and a beautiful dancer and teacher who had been with Graham since 1940. Mazia radiated freshness and warmth, with a voice that could reassure nursery children, and if as Stuart Hodes remembers, 'she did on occasion treat the beginners like babies, no one objected'. Five minutes into the class, Cohan had what he has described many times as a 'mystical experience'. He was overcome with a sense of excitement that nearly made him pass out as he realised that Meredith and Bales had been correct; he had found exactly what he had been looking for and that this was what he wanted to do for the rest of his life. The experience was almost religious, with feelings of oneness and identification, as well as an unbearable spiritual and physical excitement – he found himself trembling. All of this came from the material in the class, not from Graham herself for at that stage he had never even seen her. Was this, he thought, what Gurdjieff had talked about?

Cohan continued going to class and in the third one he saw someone whom he instinctively knew was Graham. On one wall of the 'office' section of the studio was a tiny bench and 'one day I saw this strangely beautiful woman sitting there, just waiting and very still. Everyone pretended, very quietly, that she wasn't there.

Of course, I guessed at once it was Martha, her presence was so powerful.'

She quickly took an interest in Cohan; talented, gifted, good-looking young men were in short supply and Graham needed men for her company. She pushed him along and although they never had a conversation, 'you didn't talk to Martha', she knew his name and urged him quickly through April and May, to move from the elementary class to the intermediate; then came the turning point. In June, there was to be an intensive course and he was expected to be in the advanced class for three hours every day. He had to make a choice, to stay in a well-paid job that he hated or to give that up and try to make something of dancing.

He chose the latter and this was the cause of a violent argument with his father. Up until this time, Cohan had been living at home and when he told his parents that he was giving up his job to dance they could not understand it. Dancing to them did not mean anything, at least not anything that could be considered a paying job for a man and he certainly could not explain mystical illumination to them. His father told him that if that was what he wanted to do then he would not support him and he would have to leave. Cohan slammed the door and left. It would be over two years before he spoke to them again.

Commentary

Chapter 2

These three years were certainly the most complex, difficult, and rewarding of my life.

The army was another world.

The purpose of the first eight weeks of basic training is to obliterate your sense of self-determination. All sense of personal will and privacy has to be wiped away. You sleep in a barracks of forty men with each bed two feet apart, you shower in one large room and there were seven or eight toilets in a row, the same with the sinks and of course you eat at a pre-assigned table. You are told what to do every minute of the day except for Saturday afternoon and Sunday. Of course this has its pre-designed purpose and that is to go into battle and shoot and kill another human being, or to put yourself in mortal danger without question.

The difficult part was the actual battleground itself.

Most of the time our cure for cancer is to cut it out. We are still not intelligent enough to deal with it or prevent it any other way. I think it is the same with our human and 'tribal' relations. We still are not intelligent enough as a world community to deal with our anger and desires for revenge and power other than to wage war and kill as many of the 'enemy' as possible, even if they are just like us, with lives to live and loved ones to mourn them. That is why most people who have been in battle don't talk about it. It is something strange, apart from our normal lives, an action that we do together, a permission to kill, under orders from others, which we try to leave alone the rest of our lives.

The rewarding part of my army experience was the men I met because of the ASTP which led, in its own time, to my working with Martha Graham.

When I look back on my first twenty years, it seems right to me now that I was heading for dance as a profession, although at the time I didn't know it. My early dance classes starting at five or six years old and then the Saturday tap and acrobatics. My obsession with the movie dance musicals by Busby Berkeley and then Astaire and Rogers, dancing the lindy hop all the time, the cheerleading in huge stadiums, my seeing dance during the army time, meeting Madame de Valois and Robert Helpmann which Paul described so well, and then through Diane seeing contemporary dance for the first time, meeting Ruth St Denis, Jane Dudley and then finally Graham – all comes to me now as a logical route to becoming a dancer.

One funny note to the racetrack premonition dream that Paul describes is that when my mother called my Aunt Helen to tell her the news, she became furious with me. She said, 'I cannot believe what you are telling me. You mean I was nice enough to come to him in his dream and tell him which horse to bet on and then when he wakes up he doesn't call me to tell me what I said! I am very angry with him.'

Chapter 3

What was your face before your mother and father were born?

(Zen Koan)

1947–51

After the war, Martha Graham was riding the crest of a wave of success. As one of her biographers, Don McDonagh, noted, 'When one thought of modern dance, one thought of Humphrey, Weidman, Holm and Tamiris, and, in a special category, Graham.'[17] She was, he felt, the most characteristic representative of the group of modern dance pioneers who had transformed the world of Western theatre dance in the early twentieth century. Her physical appearance was instantly recognisable through sets of carefully photographed images, including the semi-nudity of those by Imogen Cunningham and the vividly dramatic images taken by Barbara Morgan. Her style of dance, described by Agnes de Mille as 'an original way of communication… a code of technique which constitutes the most beautiful sustained movement by a living composer',[18] had – at least in America – entered the public consciousness sufficiently to be satirised in comedy routines on stage and in film. Worshipped by her dancers, her 'Graham-Crackers', they adapted their lives to suit her every need. In 1945, Graham was taken up by the impresario Sol Hurok, who was known for the quality of the artists he represented – which ranged from African American opera singer Marian Anderson through to dance artists such as Michel Fokine and Anna Pavlova. His offer to represent Graham was a major step forward not only for her but for modern dance as a whole.

Alongside Graham was her partner and principal male dancer Erick Hawkins. At least fifteen years Graham's junior, Hawkins had been a Greek scholar at Harvard and then danced and choreographed for Lincoln Kirstein and George Balanchine's early company Ballet Caravan. He was stunningly handsome, and when Graham first saw him she later admitted thinking, 'Where did you come from? I could just eat you up';[19] unfortunately, this is what happened. Hawkins, as well as being her lover – even though he was at least bisexual and slept with a number of men from the studio, including the composer Ned Rorem who worked there briefly as a pianist – was principal dancer, fundraiser, tour promoter, teacher, rehearsal director and general factotum. All of these things he did well, but everything he did was subject to Graham's will. In addition, the other dancers hated him for many reasons, not the least of which was that Graham would not hear a word of criticism against him, only she could do that, and she did. The relationship had almost floundered in mid 1945 when Hawkins moved out of their apartment, stopped teaching at the studio and underwent psychological counselling. By 1946 the two had reconciled some of their differences, though they never lived together again.

Added to this volatile mix was Louis Horst, the pianist, composer and Graham's mentor. Ten years older than Graham and with an estranged wife on the West Coast, Horst had also been Graham's lover for the fifteen years before Hawkins appeared. Where Hawkins was handsome, Horst was not; looking older than his years, portly, and with a dour expression, described by *The New Yorker* as 'white haired, corpulent, and calm...',[20] he was hardly the romantic ideal. But even if the sexual relations had long ceased, Graham still needed him to support her and he gave her this, acting as her music director and editing eye. He loved the dance and also the dancers. Over the years, he had many flirtatious dallies with the young ladies who took his respected composition course. At least one, May O'Donnell, remembered firmly removing his hand from her thigh during a private music lesson. But there was more than this, and his support for all modern dance was unfailing. This was recognised at the beginning of the June course when Horst received a fellowship from the Neighborhood Playhouse, together with a cheque for the sizeable sum of $3,500.[21]

The tensions between this triumvirate were immense and would spill over into the choreography, which became increasingly psychologically based, and the relationships within the company, which became strained. It was into this arena that Cohan was admitted in the autumn of 1946. But before that happened, he had more pressing concerns. After he moved out from his parents' home he needed somewhere to live, and so moved in with Walter Martin, one of the two soldiers still alive from the Puget Sound days. Martin had moved to New York to study art and as he knew no one in the city had managed, resourcefully, to track down Cohan. The two had not been particularly close in the army but Cohan was drawn to Martin who was 'very well read, very intelligent and seemed to have all of the knowledge about the world of art' that Cohan wanted. He was also deeply interested in the spiritual and mystical world that so excited Cohan. With him, Cohan had someone he could talk to about Gurdjieff, Ouspensky, and Krishnamurti, writers and mystics whose ideas promised so much more than the mundane life of post-war New York. Indeed with Martin, Cohan became very involved with the Gurdjieff circle in New York and so demanding did it become on his time that he ultimately had to make a choice between Gurdjieff and Graham. He chose Graham, although the teachings of Gurdjieff would continue to influence every area of his life and work.

Martin also introduced him to Zen Buddhism and it is from this aspect of Japanese culture that their relationship can be better understood. The senpai and kōhai relationship is a readily accepted part of Japanese society, where the senpai is a mentor to the kōhai, who can be seen as a pupil. Cohan and Martin's relationship was more physical and emotionally more complex than this, but both had something the other wanted – Cohan had beauty and a voraciously inquiring mind while Martin had knowledge and a greater spiritual maturity. Graham herself had been heavily influenced by Japanese culture, stating in her autobiography, 'I have always felt more Asian than American'; on a deeper level, she had studied Zen Buddhism with a Zen master named Ramiel, as she explained: 'Each day he left me a Koan to reason on, to brood on, to find my way. Through him I learned as much as anyone ever can about Zen. This knowledge served me in good stead, in terms of self-discipline and clarity of focus, and simple, pragmatic behaviour.'[22] From the outset, Graham's work promised Cohan answers to many of the questions he had been formulating during the trauma of active service and the long months of convalescence, and Martin provided a balance to this.

Cohan and Martin's relationship was not easily understood by Cohan's friends who could not comprehend why the beautiful Cohan was with a not so handsome and, in company at least, inarticulate man. Linda Hodes remembers him as 'Wally, Bob's boyfriend', whom she found 'a shadowy figure'. Graham always got their story wrong. In the war, Martin had been so traumatised – he saw his entire unit killed – that he refused to fight, operating instead as an ambulance driver and stretcher carrier. Cohan explained this to Graham who always mangled the story when she told it, choosing to say that Martin had saved Cohan's life during the war and that what was why Cohan was with him. She would continue telling the same wrong story into the 1960s. For all his gifts as poet, painter, and designer, out of his comfort zone Martin was quiet and withdrawn. Cohan also quickly found out that he was depressive, alcoholic, and had an unhealthy interest in drugs. But there was a bond between the two and despite all the problems, he would live with Cohan, on and off, for the next fifteen years, playing a major role in Cohan's personal life as well as creating the designs for Cohan's earliest attempts at choreography.

The apartment they shared on Avenue B was one of those terrible New York cold water affairs with no central heating – crushed orange crates and the hefty *New York Times*' Sunday edition burnt together in the open hearth provided the only warmth – or facilities. On the plus side, however, the rent was only $14 per month and between them they could just afford it. Neither Cohan nor Martin had jobs and so both had to rely on the GI Bill for money, plus the tiny amount Cohan received for having been wounded. The GI Bill enabled ex-servicemen to sign up for classes at approved schools; the classes would be paid for and monthly allowance was provided. Martin signed up for approved art classes, while for Cohan it was more problematic. Being on a scholarship with Graham meant that he did not pay for any classes, but neither was he paid, and unfortunately the Graham Studio was not approved under the terms of the bill to receive funding. To claim the $65 per month – a major come down from the $60 per week he had been earning with the Veterans' Administration – Cohan signed up at a ballet school run by Arthur Mahoney and Thalia Mara based in one of the studios in Carnegie Hall. He had been helped in his search for a school by Joanne Summers whom he had met while making inquiries about a suitable dance school. She was a show dancer from his area of Brooklyn 'and was very pretty and street-smart'. The two became very close for a while and she introduced him to the whole uptown dance world.

Cohan found that the whole scene at the Carnegie complex was 'crazy and wonderful' and a welcome antidote to the Graham Studio. Apart from the famous concert hall, the Carnegie building, located at 881 Seventh Avenue, contained two smaller concert halls and several large studios as well as apartments and offices. A number of artists had schools there, and many of the ballet stars from the Ballets Russes companies were either teaching or taking class. Cohan's classes were taught mainly by Arthur Mahoney or Tatiana Semionova, minor stars in the ballet firmament, though he also sometimes took class with the martinet Antony Tudor. The whole atmosphere, beautifully parodied in the musical *On the Town*, was fascinating and he regularly spent time just wandering from studio to studio to watch what was going on. For someone like him without any experience of the world of the theatre, it was an eye-opening and liberating opportunity as he had a lot of catching up to do.

Upstairs in the building were apartments and one day Joanne managed to get the keys to what had been Isadora Duncan's old residence. It was a high-ceilinged studio room, heavily curtained in dark maroon velvet with wood-panelled walls and an extraordinary, enormous bathroom completely tiled in Moorish ceramics. It was for Cohan a different world from anything he had been used to and 'it was a very strange time for me and utterly exciting'. Joanne could get cheap tickets for ballet performances and Cohan, always keen to be educated, happily went to see the surviving Ballets Russes, Ballet Theatre, and the Metropolitan Opera Ballet.

Looking back, he remembers:

I spent the mornings in the exciting decaying ballet world of expatriate Russians and assorted pretenders, just before Balanchine changed it all, and the afternoons in the sober stark world of Graham and the nights with Gurdjieff, Krishnamurti and Zen. I liked this whole world, it was undoubtedly filled with excitement and fun, but I knew that my world was really at the Graham Studio and after I started earning a little money teaching and performing with Graham, I left that world behind.

Cohan never told Graham about the ballet classes. A great mythology has arisen about Graham forbidding her dancers from taking other classes, particularly ballet, but she never stopped them doing other things. She was, however, very possessive of them, and as she demanded all their time and attention, she could never understand how they could possibly take class elsewhere. Any time away was time not devoted to her.

Any excitement Cohan may have felt as a result of his new artistic life was somewhat crushed when he and Martin realised they had roughly $130 per month to live on, which was less than half of what Cohan had been earning on his own, and even though it was possible to live cheaply in New York, by the middle of each month their meals consisted of only rice and beans. Cohan had to support himself in his new life on this spartan diet.

When Graham returned from her summer break at the Santa Fe home of her friend Cady Wells, she immediately began to prepare for a major tour that would travel up and down the East Coast. There was a great deal of work to do to prepare for the season. Since the last tour Merce Cunningham, the second male in her group, had left to pursue his own choreographic work with his lover John Cage, and his roles had been distributed between Mark Ryder and John Butler, with Cohan moving into the roles vacated by Ryder. Graham also, for the first time, allowed one of her dancers, Ethel Winter, to dance the solo *Salem Shore*, while Pearl Lang took over Graham's role in her classic trio *El Penitente*. Most of the other dances had new costumes made for them, including *Punch and the Judy*, one of Graham's comedic gems, and the strangely sexual work *Dark Meadow*.

The first Graham choreography Cohan learnt was the 'party step' from *Deaths and Entrances*, Graham's complex work based on the lives of the Brontë sisters. In the dance, the party scene establishes Emily Dickinson's narrow, male-dominated world and Cohan was taught the part by Ryder though it was Graham who rehearsed it. She demanded that he and other newcomer and fellow war veteran Stuart Gescheidt (he would soon change his name to Hodes) perform with a bearing more rigid, more arrogant than anything he had ever imagined. Before they donned costumes, Graham had described the tightly fitted clothing and stiff collars of the era, which the costumes would evoke, but made clear, as Hodes recalls, 'if your body does not bear its arrogance deep within, your costume will not give it to you!'

Another role Cohan learnt was as one of the four men, the partners of the five women collectively named 'They who dance together' in *Dark Meadow*. This piece had been premiered in January 1946 and had grown out of the 'marital' split between Graham and Hawkins. Both had gone into therapy; Graham under Jungian analyst Dr Frances Wickes. Graham had often been drawn to ancient mythic elements in her work and her time with Wickes seems to have strengthened her interest in this area. Jung's theory of a collective consciousness appealed to Graham and this new work seemed to take the difficulties of everyday life and expand them to mythic proportions. By the time the work was complete, Graham and Hawkins had reconciled their difficulties and the finished dance piece was life affirming rather than nihilistic.

The work includes in it a fetish dance, performed by the men alone. Each fetish was designed by Graham's long-term collaborator Isamu Noguchi as was the enigmatic set, which consisted of a phallic-looking object and something resembling a white face. Carrying the fetishes, the men had to burst out of the wing together with a double jump while violently shaking them. It was a deliberately clumsy, bull-like entrance and to some seemed the antithesis of dancing. They then stampeded across the stage, cutting the air with their fetishes, and on reaching the face above the platform, which Graham had just vacated, thrust them into fitted holes. Cohan's fetish was a lacquered wooden stick with three plumes of white horsehair; Hodes' was a crook-shaped clear plastic rod with a black ball on one end while Ryder's resembles a curved tomahawk. Cohan was protective of his plumed and lacquered prop, telling the other two, 'It's elegant, I like it better than either of yours.' Hodes' looked like a modern sculpture, and he said, 'Well. I like it better than yours.' Neither of them was appreciative of Ryder's stubby ornament, to which his response was, 'Well, I like it! And that's how a fetish should be. You're only supposed to like your own.'[23]

The dance is rich with meanings, and although none are clear, the phallic symbolism of the fetish dance was. In a programme note, Graham described the dance as 'a re-enactment of the Mysteries which attend the eternal adventure of seeking'. The possibilities for interpretations of the work excited Cohan tremendously. Not even Graham knew exactly what the piece was about, and as late as 1954, was writing to her psychologist Mrs Wickes, 'I am at last beginning to understand *Dark Meadow* a little and where it came from.'[24] Such was Cohan's induction into the mysteries of Graham's language of symbols. He was mystified and entranced, and although he did not see her then as a genius, he knew that he wanted to work with her, and for him that was enough.

While Cohan was being coached in existing roles, Graham was making a new work based on the myth of Oedipus and Jocasta to be called *Night Journey*. It would have a newly written score by William Schuman and would come to be regarded as one of her greatest works. Cohan was not involved in it but what struck him as fascinating and extraordinary was the preparatory reading list pinned to the noticeboard for the dancers:

Prolegomena to the Study of Greek Religion by Jane Harrison
Ancient Art and Ritual by Jane Harrison
The White Goddess by Robert Graves
Gods, Graves and Scholars by C.W. Ceram
The Hero with a Thousand Faces by Joseph Campbell
The King Must Die by Mary Renault

The education which had begun in the army continued apace with Graham, and Cohan revelled in it.

Now that he was officially a part of the company, he saw Graham dance, not on stage but in rehearsal. Beginning at 10 a.m., she would rehearse her solos, followed by her duets with Hawkins. But apart from peeking through the doors, none of the dancers were allowed to watch. They did, however, have plenty of time to watch her in their rehearsals, which began in the afternoon and would often run on until late evening. She was fanatical about detail and the company would frequently go over one small section for an hour and a half or two hours, as Graham was always looking for some special quality, some sense of excitement in the movement that was not always easy to find. There was no such thing as marking a movement or phrase, Graham expected the material to be presented full out every time. As she wrote in her famous speech 'I am a dancer': 'To practice means to perform, in the face of all obstacles, some act of vision, of faith, of desire. Practice is a means of inviting the perfection desired.' This she put into practice for she truly did want herself and her dancers to be 'athletes of God'.

Cohan recalls that in class and rehearsal, Graham would use using her poetic vocabulary like spells to create the 'magic' she required. On one occasion, she told them to 'wear your skin like a beautiful garment', on another to 'hold your bones with the muscles'. But often she would leave the poetry aside and simply address matters practically. While talking about centring the body, supporting the back and the centre, on the word 'centre' she 'would pull her body up as if she were glueing herself around an invisible core that by her action became visible, like a golden bar moving through her body, with a dynamic energy'. Cohan remembers that even in old age she had a remarkable ability to convince her audience that they could see more than what was on stage. It was this ability to project energy that Cohan noticed when he saw her dance the part of Medea in *Cave of the Heart*. As the cursed crown is placed on the princess' head, Graham would tremble her hand and Cohan was convinced he actually saw the magic energy, 'lightning bolts', that would kill the princess transfer from Graham.

As the rehearsals continued, Cohan began to relax around Graham, soon realising that she had no social life and had little small talk; all she knew and all she did was dancing and 'if you weren't in the studio she didn't love you'. As a junior member and on scholarship, he was expected to undertake other tasks such as cleaning the studio and running errands. On many occasions, Cohan was sent to the delicatessen across the street from 66 Fifth Avenue to get a cup of 'Ambrosia'. Costing 25¢, this magic potion consisted of a quart of orange juice, a raw egg and a scoop of vanilla ice cream. It was very thick, creamy, and high in protein and she and her dancers thought it was heaven.

Less often, but more than occasionally, she would give him $2 and he would have to go further up Fifth Avenue to between 13th and 14th Street where there was a liquor store. The $2 would buy a bottle of bourbon, which Graham always told him was for 'medicinal purposes', and he would believe her. Although he did think it was a lot of medicine, he never thought twice about why she needed it. Graham's drinking at this time was well under control, and the alcoholism that would plague her later years had not manifested itself. Cohan had grown up around 'Black Irish' in Brooklyn and was used to people who could consume vast quantities of alcohol without appearing the worse for wear. In her later years, when she became less able to physically conceal her drinking, she tried to make its consumption not too obvious, the vodka being always served in a mug with a brown substance in it and a spoon to make it look like tea.

Early on in his training, Cohan's career almost came to a swift end. Soon after he had joined the company, he was coming out of a class Graham had taught when someone in the office asked him how it had gone. He replied, 'Oh, it was the weirdest class I've ever had.' The youth of the 1940s were no different to the present day and regularly changed the conventional meaning of words and to Cohan 'weird', much like the current use of 'bad' meant good – strange but good. Suddenly Graham, with her hair hanging down, half brushed, looking like a banshee, burst from behind the curtain that was the women's tiny dressing room; she was furious, thinking he was criticising her class. She was radiating such anger that Cohan pushed himself flat against the wall to try and get away from her, 'Weird, was it?', she shouted. 'Get out! Don't ever let me see your face here again', and with that she threw him out of the studio. Cohan was shocked; he found the implied physical violence so overwhelming that he didn't sleep for twenty-four hours. He was of course allowed back once someone had explained to Graham what he had meant by 'weird'. But this was not by any means the last time he would see Graham in a fury.

On another occasion, without asking her permission, Hawkins had invited a small audience of backers to watch a rehearsal of *Every Soul is a Circus*, when it was really not ready to be seen. The dancers knew something was going to happen and could feel the tension build as time went by. Halfway through, Mark Ryder was supposed to present Graham with a flower, but was about two inches too far away so she missed it and the fury was unleashed; she screamed at him and he screamed back at her. She then flew across the floor, pulled open the door and slammed it shut so hard that it bounced back and flew off its hinges. The audience were quietly shown out through the side door. There would be many, many more of these occasions over the years, but eventually he realised that all of the drama was a part of Graham's performance, and that to be part of it was actually thrilling. In any case, it provided material to talk about later.

The dancers were expected to develop swiftly, and four months after he started Cohan found himself teaching his first class. All of the senior dancers had teaching engagements but as the company was intensely involved in rehearsals for the tour, scheduling could be a problem. Graham herself taught the company class as well as at least four classes a week at the Neighborhood Playhouse, where she was particularly well paid by its director, Mrs Morgenthal. Apart from the financial necessity of the work, she needed to teach, since it was in the classes that she could try out movements.

To free up Graham's studio, the company often rehearsed in Hawkins' studio on 17th Street. One day, after trying for some time, Ethel Winter managed to tell

Graham that she had to leave to teach; understandably, Graham was unwilling to allow this senior figure out of the rehearsals but Cohan was more than shocked when he heard Graham say, 'Ethel, you can't leave, I need you; Bob can do it.' Ignoring his protestations – Winter would remember, 'Bob's face was a picture, but what could you do, we had all been there' – Graham told him there was only one way to teach a class and that was in the classroom, teaching. He has no recollection of what he taught, that disappeared into a fugue of nerves, but the technique at this time was still 'brutal and hard'.

The tour they had all been working so hard to prepare for would be the second organised by Sol Hurok. Lasting from 11 to 22 February 1947, it would open at Hofstra College and then move on to Hempstead, Long Island, then to Pittsburgh, Philadelphia, Baltimore, Washington, Norfolk, Durham, and Lynchburg. The tour would finish back in Manhattan with Graham's week-long season at the Ziegfeld Theatre. The fifteen dancers were: Martha Graham, Erick Hawkins, May O'Donnell (billed as guest artist), Dorothea Douglas, Angela Kennedy, Yuriko, Nancy Lang, Pearl Lang, Helen McGehee, Natanya Neumann, Ethel Winter, Mark Ryder, Graham Black, Robert Cohan and Stuart Gescheidt (Hodes). It was, for the company, quite a glamorous affair as they travelled from city to city by train and not the bus which the older members had been used to.

Cohan's first dance partner was May O'Donnell, a long-time associate of Graham and an artist Graham respected so much that she was always billed as guest artist. A strong and dynamic dancer, she always gave her utmost to the performance and in rehearsals. This caused problems for Cohan's war wound; the large square of skin that had been taken from his left thigh and patched onto his chest had since the operations healed well but had unfortunately fused to his ribs, and it limited his torso movements. However, on the plus side, Cohan received a disability check from the army every month. While dancing, the enthusiastic O'Donnell had been lifting Cohan's hand so high that he could feel the pain in the scar. Cohan refused to raise the matter with O'Donnell, even when after one performance she raised his arm so high he felt something tear. After the tour, he visited the Veterans' Administration doctor who examined him and found that the muscle over his rib cage was now completely free, the dancing having acted as an extreme form of physiotherapy. He was pronounced 100 per cent fit, which sadly meant that the monthly payments stopped arriving.

In Philadelphia, Cohan's picture appeared in a newspaper for the first time. Stuart Gescheidt's sister Malvine lived in Washington, where she was married to Gordon Cole, a reporter on the *Washington Post*. Cole informed his editor that four war veterans would be dancing with Graham, and a reporter and photographer turned up at the rehearsal. The following day, there was a two-page spread in the paper under the heading 'Veterans Turn From Battlefields to Modern Dance'. Under the photograph of Mark Ryder, Stuart Gescheidt, Graham Black, and Robert Cohan was a profile of the men, with Cohan described as:

… [t]he baby of the group, who is just a big as the rest but only 21… Eloquent, despite his youth, Cohan tells us 'there is nothing to compare' with dancing, that it's the 'creative art I found most appealing'. Overseas with the 11th Army, Cohan holds a Purple Heart and two battle stars. When he was younger he planned to be a biology teacher. 'But let's not talk about that now,' he implores.[25]

The new performers did suffer from stage fright and, although Cohan tended to keep his feelings to himself, at the Syria Mosque in Pittsburgh even Hodes, a far more voluble character, confided to Cohan that he 'felt worse than when he was on bombing missions'.

Hawkins was still resented by the dancers, not least because 'he had a marvellous knack of saying the wrong things, at the wrong time, in the wrong way'. As soon as the curtain would come down, he would begin giving corrections, even when the dancers needed to get ready for the next dance. Summoning them to his dressing room, he would hold forth while putting on his make-up, covering himself only with an ill-fitting towel. As any criticism of him led to an outburst from Graham, the young dancers let their frustrations out in other ways. Just one such occasion happened during the tour, when the dancers gathered in Marjorie Mazia's room and made a big doll out of pillows. They gave it a red-lipstick penis, named it Erick and stuck pins into it. It was not a truly malevolent act and the dancers were relieved when they saw Hawkins arrive safely for breakfast.

The tour ended back in New York with a week of performances at the Ziegfeld Theatre. Getting the theatre had been something of a coup for Graham, as normally no Broadway venues were willing to take single-week bookings, as they could be losing out on a musical theatre booking that would run for months. Graham had to find one that was between productions; it was no mean feat in the limited theatrical space of Manhattan. The Ziegfeld was perfect; located at the intersection of Sixth Avenue and 54th Street in Manhattan, it was in the centre of the theatre district and had space before the musical *Brigadoon* was to be premiered on 13 March. However, its owner, the impresario Billy Rose, was not interested. Only after Graham had called on her friends, Broadway 'royalty' Katharine Cornell and her husband Guthrie McClintic, who in turn talked to Rose, was the booking taken. The Ziegfeld season included *Cave of the Heart* which, as *Serpent Heart*, had been premiered the previous season alongside another recent work, *Errand into the Maze*. Bookers in the 1940s were no different to those Cohan would encounter in 1970s England: if they had their way, they would only take popular, crowd-pleasing works. Graham, however, would insist to put all her dances forward, and the more challenging works would always appear.

The first role Graham choreographed on Cohan was in *Wilderness Stair*, later called *Diversion of Angels*. In the spring of 1947, Graham and Hawkins took a holiday in the South West and had been camping in the Sierra Madre. When she came back, she talked to the dancers about seeing the sun rise from the top of a mesa and wanting to make a dance about that. Cohan remembers that, 'She was feeling wonderful and life was great and she was going to make this romantic piece and she didn't mind she wasn't in it.'

She approached the composer Norman dello Joio, who was very surprised to hear from her as he had seen her work, which interested him, but he generally hated the music she used. He particularly disliked William Schuman's music for the recent *Night Journey*, which he found overly dissonant and unsuited for a dance piece. She visited him in his one-room apartment and talked at length about the work. He understood little of what she was saying until she mentioned that she wanted the music to 'sound like soft flesh around a hard core'. This he understood, as he saw it as a definition of musical texture, the sexual connotations being lost on him. He was excited by the commission, since for a young composer it would offer high-profile performances. He duly wrote a wonderfully lyrical and romantic work which he called *Serenade*; at the time, Graham had not given the work a title.

Graham's initial enthusiasm for the dance did not translate into a clear vision and she made a huge amount of material and threw it away or changed it. The first version began with Cohan coming from upstage left and Yuriko from downstage left; moving in the sequence 'tilt and step, step contract, step, step tilt'. This phrase would become a major structural motif in the final work but that opening disappeared. Another version began with three couples, and yet another with all the men and one woman. She had made almost two complete dances but it was not working for her and she gave up in the winter of 1947. She started again in the spring of 1948 to premiere the work at the American Dance Festival in the summer. Unusually for Graham, there is no mention of *Wilderness Stair* in her notebooks. This is no surprise to Cohan who remembers that she seemed to 'snatch the movements out of the moment'. He saw that when she created, she saw herself as the vehicle for her work but she did not know how it happened. When she was choreographing, she was in an almost trance-like state and the movement would just flow and flow, particularly for the women who had to run to keep up with her. He also learnt a valuable lesson in choreography from Graham. In a pattern that would be repeated, he saw that Graham would be willing to jettison an almost complete dance it if she did not think it matched her vision. She told him:

> The steps are not the important things, it is the steps that you select from all those steps in the world and how you select the possibilities, and give them to the dancers to do that makes it special and puts it in sequence. Do not get stuck on your steps, they are not special, not precious; if they do not work, get rid of them.

When they returned to the work at Connecticut College, Graham kept the central duet for 'Romantic Love' but changed almost everything else. Another choreographic tool Cohan learnt from Graham was to watch the dancers warming up. *Diversions* is well known now for a set of deep pitches and a contraction that the Woman in Red executes on the diagonal; this came from Graham watching Pearl Lang warming up. Lang would often to go to the barre at the back of the studio and stretch; pitching herself forward with one leg elevated on the barre until her loose hair touched the floor. After watching this impressive act for a while Graham said, 'Why don't you do that across the floor?' She did and one of the most famous entrances in dance was created. The technique of watching his dancers would be invaluable for Cohan in his later life as choreographer.

Working on *Wilderness Stair*, Cohan found he was able to add to the vocabulary and one of his favourite tricks of turning cartwheels would be incorporated into the work and ever after become a regular feature of Graham's choreography, especially for the men. Cartwheels had appeared before in Graham's work when Merce Cunningham had used them to humorous effect in *Every Soul is a Circus*, but with Cohan they became an artistically satisfying addition to the Graham vocabulary. Another standard addition to the Graham vocabulary would be the Bison jumps, so named because on first seeing the men execute them Horst commented that they looked just like those majestic creatures.

Work on the dance proved difficult, with the final section not finished until just before the premiere on 13 August 1948, but before that there had been a terrible scene with Horst. He had been having problems with the Juilliard Orchestra, a student group who were playing for the performances, and he continually interrupted their playing, disrupting rehearsals, until finally Graham said to him, 'Louis, this has got to stop.' Horst, appalled at being told off in front of students, put down his baton and walked out. He did conduct the premiere but after that wrote her a letter of resignation, even sending a copy to his union. After nearly thirty years, Graham was without her mentor.

Isamu Noguchi had been commissioned to design a set for the work but, like the movement, this went through a number of versions. The first was an enormous backcloth of beige Monk's Cloth, a large weave of soft cotton which Noguchi brought to Connecticut. He then hung the backcloth straight and had stagehands push poles – Bertram Ross, who was a student at the American Dance Festival at the time, remembered them as looking like giant toilet plungers – through the material. What appeared were peaks which gave a bird's-eye view of the South West landscape; the audience looked down and Graham's idea was that the dance took place at right angles to the earth. After the first performances, it was decided it would be too difficult to tour, so he designed three big plastic rocks illuminated on the inside which started on the floor and then floated up. These again were not satisfactory and would eventually be used in Balanchine's *Orpheus*, and the piece ended up on a bare stage. Again Cohan learnt a valuable lesson; no matter how much the sets cost, if they do not work, get rid of them.

The women's costumes became a groundbreaking classic. Around leotards of rayon jersey, Graham wrapped fabric from behind the waist scooping down to the thighs in front and fastened between the legs. From behind, the arrangement looks like a skirt, and from the front, trousers. The miracle of them was that the legs were free to move in any direction while giving the effect of a full skirt. The men, in contrast, wore earth-coloured tights with bare chests. Graham insisted that any naked flesh should be covered up with somewhat heavy body make-up. The men sweated so much in their highly athletic roles that every time they did the dance, the make-up would come off over the women's costumes which needed to be washed after every performance. This annoyed Graham who said, 'There's a limit to how much you need to sweat, and you are sweating more than necessary.'[26] When they objected to this she told them that 'there is something in a man that drives him to leave his mark on a woman!'

In its first performances, the work was not overly popular. Writing in the *New York Herald Tribune*, Walter Terry said, 'In its present state *Wilderness Stair* is not altogether successful…'[27] Frances Herridge in the *New York Star* thought it 'a far cry from a significant addition to her repertoire'. She felt this was partly to do with the poet Ben Belitt who 'unfortunately… has added a last-minute title and some pretentious notes that only serve to confuse'.[28]

> It is the place of the Rock and the Ladder, the raven, the blessing, the tempter, the rose. It is the wish of the single-hearted, the undivided; play after the spirit's labor, games, flights, fancies, configurations of the lover's intention; the believed Possibility, at once strenuous and tender; humors of innocence, garlands, evangels, Joy on the Wilderness Stair; diversion of angels.[29]

Belitt's verse, from which the title was taken, is not so confusing, covering as it does play, love, flights, and fancies. It is more Graham's selection of 'Wilderness Stair' as the title that confused the early audiences. Although Cohan does remember the Connecticut College version as being wilder than the final one, there was nothing of a wilderness about it. Graham continued working on the dance for five years, eventually settling on the more appropriate title *Diversion of Angels*, but also adding in the programme notes the final two verses of Thomas Traherne's poem 'Eden':

> Those things which first his Eden did adorn,
> My infancy
> Did crown. Simplicity
> Was my protection when I first was born.
> Mine eyes those treasures first did see
> Which God first made. The first effects of love
> My first enjoyments upon earth did prove;

And were so great, and so divine, so pure;
So fair and sweet,
So true; when I did meet
Them here at first, they did my soul allure,
And drew away my infant feet
Quite from the works of men; that I might see
The glorious wonders of the Deity.[30]

In this form, the dance would come to rival *Appalachian Spring* as Graham's signature work, its technical demands and lyricism heralding a new era in Graham's choreography. Indeed, the technical challenges bothered even the formidable Pearl Lang who Cohan partnered. The dance is noted for some very intricate partnering and one particular drop, which is now no longer in the work, worried Lang a great deal. She would bother Cohan to rehearse right up to the curtain, until one time he told her, 'Look Pearl, I have one more lift in me. Do you want to do it now or in front of the audience?' She opted for the audience.

After the festival, Graham and Hawkins headed off again for the South West where on 20 September they were married. This seems to have been a spur-of-the-moment decision they took in the middle of a fiesta in Santa Fe. It may have been prompted by Horst's departure or it may have been an attempt, on Hawkins' part, to put their relationship on a more 'normal' level. In any event, it did not work.

The company put on a brave face but no one was happy with Graham marrying Hawkins, and if it were possible, the marriage made him more unpopular than ever with the dancers. Graham would, however, do anything to keep him happy. She choreographed works for him and worse, had begun to allow his dances, including *Stephen Acrobat*, to appear on the programme alongside her own.

It was in this atmosphere that the company went on the first of three tours managed by Charles E. Green. The Hurok tour had lasted three weeks and they had travelled by train and performed only three or four shows a week in downtown theatres. Green booked eight shows a week in a different city every day, with matinees on Wednesdays and Saturdays. Green One began in Upper Montclair, New Jersey, then continued all over the East Coast for almost seven weeks. They then spent six months back in New York, then went on Green Two, a six-week tour followed by five weeks of rehearsal for a two-week season at the 46th Street Theatre and then another nine-week tour ending in April 1950. And they travelled by bus. Graham enjoyed this as she got to spend all of her time, both day and night, with her husband – even after their wedding he kept a separate apartment. Although she would sit in the front of the bus chatting and laughing with her new husband, she never missed anything that went on.

Even if the dancers actually got paid for the touring – receiving $75 per week, when a room at the cheapest hotel could cost as little as $1 – the bus tours were extremely tiring. The group would get up at 8 a.m., leave at 9 a.m., then usually travel for six hours in a bus which had no air conditioning and perform that night. The crew's lot was even worse as they would travel through the night, set up the theatre, and then wait for the dancers. After the show, they would have to try to 'find somewhere to eat where there were no hookers' and then get some well-earned sleep. Technically, the only day off was Sunday, though this often ended up being a travelling day, which on one occasion consisted of an eleven-hour journey from Atlanta to Baton Rouge. The tour could be made more agreeable or disagreeable, depending on their driver. For part of the tour in the Deep South, they had a driver called Bill who was on all counts an unpleasant character who refused to have anything to do with the dancers, preferring to align himself to Graham and Hawkins. According to the dancers, he always seemed to choose the worst rest stops with the filthiest of toilets – one restroom consisted of a shed reached by a walk through twenty yards of swamp.

The tours were also pioneering work. Most of the places they went to had seen little, if any, modern dance but the audiences were generally good. This review from the *Atlanta Journal* is typical of the many they received:

> There was so much the layman could not comprehend in this school of modern dance, just as in modern music and painting, sculpture, poetry and drama. The deepest imagination cannot unravel the mysteries. Yet, the onlooker can but hold esteem for the modernists' convictions and their artistry. The large audience gave mighty ovation for each dance, with seven or eight curtain calls.[31]

However, the tours were not without incident, and at Louisiana State University in Baton Rouge the audience talked throughout the performance so Graham did not allow the dancers to take their bows. In Montgomery, Alabama, where the group was presented by the Alcazar Patrol Shriners, the performance did not go exactly to plan, as a review in the *Montgomery Advertiser* of 26 February reported:

> Martha Graham's performance at Lanier auditorium last night, and that of her troop should end statements in this town that Miss Graham's dance style is grotesque and graceless... It was indeed humiliating to everyone present, however, to hear an Alcazar member announce that if the person who was shooting BBs [a pellet gun] at the dancers did not stop, the curtain would have to be dropped in order to save the dancers from injury.

Helen McGehee was indeed hit in the buttock but continued the performance nonetheless.

At this period in American history, segregation and racism were still rife in the Southern States, with restaurants, buses, and public seating reserved for whites or blacks. When Horst used to tour to these areas, making his own stand for integration, he always made a point of ignoring the signs and sitting in the 'blacks only' seats at stations and on buses. For Cohan, the appalling situation was brought home when in Chattanooga at a Saturday matinee, he saw out of the theatre's back window a well-dressed black family picking their way through rubbish to get to the back door to be allowed in to see the performance. The following year when two black dancers, Matt Turney and Mary Hinkson, joined the company, Graham would refuse to accept engagements in the South.

On tour, Cohan had another one of his mystical experiences. This was with Marie Louise Locheim, a very tall beautiful dancer and a very sensitive woman, who would be with Graham only for a short while. In one of the states where gambling was legal, and where every bus stop and hotel had one-armed bandits, Locheim would always know which one would win. She would never play herself, but if anyone was short of money she would say, 'That one', and on every occasion there would be a jackpot. She never failed; the dancers felt it was like magic and they all talked about it. The trick never worked if she played herself and she would only help people out if she knew they were out of cash.

Cohan and Hodes had become good friends and Hodes would later write: 'Robert Cohan is from Brooklyn, but there is no trace in his voice. I never heard him raise his voice, not in anger for any reason. Slender, sinewy, with dark curly hair, a sculpted poet's face, and a droll sense of humour, he inspires a crush in every female around the studio.'[32] Early on during his time in the company, Hodes was told by Mark Ryder, a decidedly earthy individual, that women 'were to be adored, not fucked'. However, Hodes tried to persuade a beautiful female dancer to spend the night with him but was rebuffed when she said, 'But I'm in love with Robert Cohan.' Hodes told her it would do no good but, saying she couldn't help it, he left.

He did not hold this episode against his friend when, in Chicago, Cohan asked Hodes a favour. His ex-'girlfriend' from the Carnegie Hall ballet class days, Joanne Summers, was dancing in Chicago. When the company arrived there, Cohan asked Hodes to go to the theatre with him, saying him that he was going to talk to her boyfriend and tell him that if she was not treated in an appropriate manner, then 'certain people' would not be happy. He asked Hodes to wear his belted tweed topcoat collar turned up and a dark green fedora with the brim pulled down. Cohan and the boyfriend huddled at the stage door of the theatre while Hodes stood some feet way, looking menacing. Afterwards Hodes asked, 'How did it go?' Cohan replied, 'He was nervous. You look like an Al Capone torpedo.' Hodes said, 'Wasn't that the idea?' Cohan did not answer. Hodes asked, 'So what kind of guy is he?' Cohan replied, 'Very decent, he will be good for Joanne.'

While Cohan became very friendly with Hodes, his closest friend would become Bertram Ross, who joined the company during the second Green tour to replace Mark Ryder who was leaving to marry and work on his own projects.

Ross came from a well-to-do Jewish family in the best part of Brooklyn. Where Cohan was quiet and serious, Ross was sharp, waspish, outgoing, and flamboyant. Cohan would advise, 'Don't touch your students, they will think they are in love with you', while Ross was more direct, saying to one girl in his class, 'Honey, if that's all you've got to give, I'm glad I'm not your lover!' They would stay by each other through thick and thin and they were indispensable for Graham in her later years, both eventually being billed as co-artistic directors. There was little competition between them since Graham, ever observant of their different personalities, tended to offer them different roles. Ross would be Oedipus to Cohan's Tiresias, Agamemnon to Cohan's Aegisthus.

It was while the company were in Los Angeles on 10 March 1949 that Cohan really began to understand how famous and important Martha Graham was when none other than Gene Kelly came backstage and took her out to dinner. She understandably received a very warm welcome in Santa Barbara, her home town, where the mayor declared 11 March Martha Graham Day. In a shell shop in the town, Cohan found a giant scallop shell and amused Hodes by holding the scooped out section at his solar plexus saying, 'If only I could do a contraction like this.'

By 23 March, and back in New York, the company had played in forty-three cities and travelled 8,000 miles. It had been exhausting but invigorating and it had enabled them to perform more times than they had in the previous two years. By the end of the tours, relationships had become a little frayed; Graham was not pleased with what she saw as slovenly dress and told the dancers that for the next tour it would be written into their contracts that, for touring, the men would wear shirt, tie, and jacket and the women dresses.

But it had been a wonderful opportunity for Cohan, who began to garner good notices while on tour. Hubert Roussell in the *Houston Post*, while commenting on his 'splendid physique and control', noted that 'Robert Cohan danced extremely well in everything he tried, especially so as the acrobat in the circus piece'.[33] Claudia Cassidy in the *Chicago Daily Tribune* found that 'Robert Cohan is instinctively and reassuringly an individual. He has the makings of a distinguished dancer.'[34]

To gain experience as a performer, Cohan did not restrict himself to dancing with Graham, though it was with her approval that he joined Hodes to dance for Jean Erdman in her work *Sea Deep: A Dreamy Drama*. Erdman, like May O'Donnell, was one of Graham's favourites and she was happy to encourage her work. In this piece, Cohan and Hodes played two shipwrecked sailors who sink to the bottom of the ocean and meet a mischievous mermaid there. The dance took three weeks of pleasant rehearsals but when she then invited her husband, mythology guru Joseph Campbell, to watch a run-through, he criticised the work so much that she threw the whole dance out and at the next rehearsal remade it completely. Cohan also joined Yuriko for an evening of her work held at the 92nd

Street Y Center on 23 October. There he danced with her in two duets, *Incident* and *Servant of the Pillar*, and they were joined by Sara Aman in a trio entitled *Suite*. Although it was an interesting experience, Cohan never joined in any of Yuriko's ventures again, feeling choreography was the least of her considerable talents.

During the tours Cohan grew tremendously as a performer and Graham began to trust him more and more and on their completion she gave him the role of the Fool in her dance based on Shakespeare's play *King Lear* and entitled *Eye of Anguish*. In 1944, Graham had thought of a dance based on *King Lear* but seen from Cordelia's perspective. She had commissioned a score from Carlos Chávez, which he had failed to deliver, and she created instead *Herodiade*. When Chávez's score did eventually arrive, she used it for *Dark Meadow*. Now, Graham intended to return to Lear but this time making a vehicle for Hawkins. Pearl Lang played Cordelia; Helen McGehee, Goneril; Yuriko, Regan; Ryder, Edmund the Bastard; Hodes Edgar and Mad Tom; and Cohan, the Fool.

Now a senior company member whom she trusted, Cohan found it exciting to work on the role of the Fool. Over the years, Graham had developed the ability to create movement that went straight to the emotional heart of a character, movement that furthered the psychological analysis of that character. She was able to choreograph for anyone but with men, she frequently wanted them to develop material themselves; with Cohan she would probe, push, and lean. Sometimes she would play the music and say, 'She is over here and he is over there and you don't know which way to turn, and you go to her first. Why don't you maybe run to her, or maybe run and crawl? What about run-crawl-run-crawl-run?' Cohan would make up the material, she would then add more directions saying, 'She turns and slashes her hand at your face and you fall backwards… Now when you are really back, stagger a little more.' Once this was achieved, she could add rhythmic patterns to the material and it would move from fairly naturalistic movement to that which was dance.

At other times, she would stand and show the movement. But as she trusted dancers more, she would simply play the music, describe the character and situation, and then leave the room saying, 'Now see what you can find.' She would return an hour later to see what material had been created, perhaps ten seconds or so, or if a substantial section had been made, she would take it and shape it herself, fitting it into her conception of the work. Dancers were sensitive to her needs, however, and would seldom present her with a fait accompli; they presented material to her, for her and never material that said, 'This is who I am, and this is what I did.'

She occasionally would say to the dancers, 'Now this time I'm not going to have credit for the choreography. It is going to say in the programme that you did this and you did that, and I directed it.' This never happened. But Cohan was happy with that situation no matter how much he had contributed, because the dances were not just her idea, they were her vision, and the memory has stayed with him that 'the vision was terribly personal to her and yet she was able to translate it to her dancers both emotionally and verbally so that they could participate in it as active actors. Then when it all came together and all the people she had inspired were on stage with her in front of an audience, then the audience would also see her vision.'

To begin with, the dance went well: the score by Vincent Persichetti was dynamic and exciting; the set, which included a tree trunk throne, was impressive; and the use of tubes of fabric reminded the dancers of *Lamentation*. And then it all went wrong, Graham began throwing out material the dancers loved and the work got stuck. Mark Ryder's view was that Graham was creating a role of a madman for someone who was already mad; what was seen was Hawkins' own madness, not Lear's.

The completed work was seen as a failure by critics; Margaret Lloyd writing in the *Christian Science Monitor* opined, 'Apparently a starring role for Mr Hawkins (now Miss Graham's husband), the result is a travesty. Mr Hawkins in a frightful wig and appalling costume does not even tear passion to tatters, he dissipates it.'[35] Horst would name it *Angst and Eyewash*.[36]

The season was notable for Cohan in that it marked his acceptance as a Graham dancer and he received very favourable notices from all the major critics. He had recently been 'promoted' to the role of the Poetic Beloved in *Deaths and Entrances*, and John Martin wrote in the *New York Times*:

> Second honors, and very high ones, belong to Robert Cohan, who was seen for the first time as the Poetic Beloved. The role has previously been a nebulous one, almost totally unrealized, but Mr Cohan's grasp of it and projection of it give new meaning to the entire work. He dances admirably and acts with a winning simplicity, and the character in his hands brings the only colour of normal light and sanity to a scene of morbidity and decay.[37]

This contrasted with Martin's review of Hawkins as the Dark Beloved who 'remained wooden and uncooperative, as an actor'.[38]

Meanwhile, Walter Terry from the *New York Herald Tribune* found that 'Mr Cohan, until recently a junior member of the Graham company has developed into the most valuable male dancer in Miss Graham's group and there is every reason to believe that his technical exactness, his incisiveness of movement and his sensitivity to gradations in dynamics will carry him far in the dance world.'[39]

The final review of the season in the *New York Times* of Sunday, 5 February 1950 summed up the two weeks:

> Robert Cohan, long a member of the company, blossomed forth as a full-fledged artist. Especially in *Deaths and Entrances* did he prove his gifts as a dancer with dramatic balance, but he distinguished himself also in everything else he did. His emergence was one of the major highlights of the season, indeed.

The season had been made possible partly with funding from Bethsabée de Rothschild; a daughter of the wealthy banking house, she had escaped the invasion of France and on arriving in New York, began to take classes at the Graham Studio. In spite of her background, she was a quiet, unassuming woman who did not like to draw attention to herself. Hawkins had first approached her for funding in 1943 when he needed $500 to orchestrate the score for *Deaths and Entrances*,[40] and since then she had provided small amounts as needed. She had also become more and more involved in the wider dance world, giving money to support a number of modern dance projects. After the season, he asked her if she would be willing to guarantee a tour of Europe to introduce Graham, and indirectly himself, to an international audience. She agreed with a pledge of $10,000 and Charles Green, who had managed the three bus tours, took off to Europe to secure dates.

The company was all very excited about the tour to Europe since for most of them, apart from the ex-servicemen, it would be the first time any of them had left the USA. Graham herself was nervous about it, as she said in a letter to Katharine Cornell:

> I think you know how much I want to go to Europe. I think I may meet with as great antagonism as I have met with here but it will be a challenge and I feel it is perhaps a responsibility. I hope it is not an indulgence or just to justify a vanity. I have thought deeply over it. I know how hard it will be and I know it will have griefs just as there are here.[41]

She had every right to be nervous, for in a rehearsal of *Night Journey* before they set off, Hawkins dropped Graham and she landed on her left knee, badly damaging it. This was not an unusual occurrence as Hawkins was not a very good partner, being more interested in what he looked like than supporting and over the years he had dropped pretty much all the women in the company. The injury got worse and worse but Graham would not hear of cancelling the tour. All the men in the company – Cohan, Hodes, and Ross – resolved to tell Graham that they would not go on the tour if she was incapacitated. In the event, they all backed down and it was only Cohan who told Graham this, but she simply could not or would not understand what he was saying; the tour, with the men, went ahead. Graham and Hawkins travelled to Paris in a Lockheed Constellation while the rest of the company travelled via Youth Argosy, a charter airline catering mainly for students. The lengthy journey involved stopovers in both Newfoundland and Shannon and it was an exhausted, dishevelled – though excited – company that eventually arrived at L'Hôtel West End.

The excitement was, however, short-lived as there were problems from the moment rehearsals began. For some reason, Hawkins began to argue with the conductor Ted Dale, a Hollywood arranger who had been called in to replace Horst. It was not that the music for the programme at the Théâtre des Champs

Elysées, which consisted of *Errand into the Maze*, *Eye of Anguish*, *Cave of the Heart*, and *Every Soul is a Circus*, caused problems for the musicians. As Bertram Ross remembered, 'It was not that the tempi were too slow or too fast, it was ... something intangible and Martha got involved and soon all three were screaming at each other. Eventually Martha said, "Come!! We'll start again", adding in a dramatic aside, "What does he know about art. That vaudevillian!" '

The tensions continued through the day and as the evening performance approached, everyone was a bundle of nerves.

During *Every Soul is a Circus*, Cohan heard a sound like a twig snapping and saw Graham wince in pain. She continued through to the end but after the curtain calls limped offstage to her dressing room. A mood of gloom settled on the company and after the performance they all left for their hotel rooms, fearing the worst.

The next day, Cohan and some company members visited Graham at her hotel. Propped up in bed, she told them that she had been examined by five doctors who had warned her that if she danced that night she would never dance again. When de Rothschild said that her dances would live forever, Graham retorted, 'If I can't dance, I don't care if my dances are never danced again!' That night, the performance went ahead without Graham, who stayed in her hotel room. In spite of their best efforts, the Parisian audience wanted to see Graham; it was not a success and the rest of the performances were cancelled.

Their next scheduled performances were to be in London a month later and so a somewhat despondent company headed there. In Britain at the time, the professional dance world consisted of classical ballet and very little else. Life in post-war Britain was bleak; the cities had not recovered from the bombings of the war, rationing of food and clothes was still in place and money was scarce. There had been early attempts in the century at building a British alternative to ballet, but the works of Madge Atkinson, Ruby Ginner and Margaret Morris were never successfully developed and had achieved only a modest following and even then, with the exception of Morris in Scotland, not on the concert stage. The German Kurt Jooss and his Ballet Jooss, who were exponents of an expressive Laban-based modern dance form, resided in Britain just before and during the war – when they were interned – but returned to Germany at its conclusion. In the intervening years, it was the work of Rudolf Laban and in particular his Modern Educational Dance that gave the English some experience of movement other than ballet. Modern Educational Dance was a creative expressive form that was taught to Physical Education teachers and then delivered by them to schoolchildren. As Betty Redfern would explain:

> Modern Educational Dance... does not require conformity to any one style nor depend on the acquisition of a specialised technique. It is not confined within the limits of a particular body-carriage, a set of steps and gestures, or

conventional floor patterns and group formations, but draws on the manifold varieties of all these which are possible to the human being and opens up a vast range of movement experience and mood.[42]

This work enabled people of all abilities to create movement material, but it was almost totally lacking in developing the high level of technique that a professional dancer needs.

But it was work based on these principles that was seen in the dances of Hettie Loman, a choreographer working with her 'British Dance Theatre' in a German Expressionist idiom. This group, which grew out of Laban's Art of Movement Studio in Manchester, was not enthusiastically received by the post-war British audience. As both Stuart Hopps and Valerie Preston-Dunlop, who danced for Loman, would recall, the work was indeed creative in dealing with socially responsive issues but was lacking in a solid technical base, and 'anything German was not going to be well received in post war Britain'. The public had very little idea as to what would be presented by Martha Graham and her dancers.

Publicity was already in full swing and the *Evening Standard* of 15 July printed a picture of Cohan and Pearl Lang in a lift from *Diversion of Angels*, under the heading 'Two of Martha Graham's dancers, Robert Cohan and Pearl Lang, performing one of the revolutionary dances, during a rehearsal of their "ballet" which opens in London next week.' But after a brief visit to the Piccadilly Theatre where they were due to perform, it was apparent Graham would not be able to dance. Hawkins called a press conference on 17 July and the season was cancelled.

Later that night, Cohan and Bertram Ross, who were sharing a room in a hotel in St James, were awoken at 2 a.m. by a noise at the window. On investigating, they found Hawkins in a terrible state, wanting to talk to Cohan who quickly dressed and went down to meet him. Graham was furious at the cancellation of the season and she and Hawkins had had a terrible argument, and he needed to talk to someone. The two walked along the Thames for over three hours, during which time Hawkins poured his heart out to Cohan about his needs and ambitions. He did love his wife but he did not see how he could stay with her, always being her shadow – he was always seen as Mr Martha Graham, which he found demeaning and emasculating. Also, he wanted to strike out on his own and make his own type of work; not the work he was making with Graham but something different – he hated her psychological approach. Knowing the company's antipathy to Hawkins' work and the detrimental effect he felt Hawkins' presence had on Graham, Cohan advised him to leave and seek a new life. Later, when Graham found out about the talk she would round angrily on Cohan saying, 'I don't know what you said to Erick that night but I will never forget it!'

The tour lost de Rothschild $75,000; but she loved Graham and with the enormous resources she had from her family, she was prepared to write it off and would continue to support Graham for many years to come. Initially, the company was told to leave London immediately, but after a revolt led by Stuart Hodes, they were given their money in traveller's cheques and told to make their own way home. After all, Graham didn't care; she felt her career was over. Cohan, Hodes, Ross, and Virginia Krollick stayed in England for a while. Hiring bicycles and led by Cohan, they went on a tour of the South West, taking in his old army haunts around Salisbury Plain and venturing down as far as St Michael's Mount and Penzance in Cornwall. Graham also went to the South West but for her it was Santa Fe and the home of Cady Wells. She needed time and space to recuperate, not only from the break in her marriage but from the terrible injury which now threatened her career.

Chapter 3

Commentary

It was a special gift to have had the experience Paul describes during the beginning of my first Graham class. To put it simply, it made my future sure.

It kept me directed for years and I never doubted where I was working or what I was doing. It also made the hard work on myself possible during that first year in the Company. I remember my body being so sore in the morning that I could not stand up straight to shave. I would lean on the sink with my left elbow, rest my left cheek in my left hand, and shave the right side of my face. Then reverse everything and shave the other side with my right hand.

In a superficial way, dance was easy for me. I was strong, well coordinated, and able to imitate what I was shown quickly. To make it real for myself was something else and required a special effort. This was what Martha Graham was so good at as a teacher. She was able to tell you what parts of your body to use in a specific way and give you inspiring images, but more than that, her very presence in front of you made you use yourself to your fullest. In her classes, there was never a moment when your attention wandered. It was fantastic training.

The first tour I went on was just like a fairy tale. I was used to seeing Pullman sleeping cars on trains from the movies I was brought up with in the 1930s. There were always scenes of a musical show on tour and that was exactly what I was doing. The touring life suited me and that was a good thing because that was what I would do for the next forty years or so.

In spite of my visits to Carnegie Hall, my main focus was learning to dance on stage and finding my way into the Graham repertory. I was lucky, as at that time there were many performances and opportunities every night to be on stage with Martha Graham herself. That in itself was a very special gift. There are many articles you can read about Graham's incredible power as a performer. I can personally assure you that to be on stage with her was a revelation. Her skills of dance and projection were so strong that the stage had an uncanny sense of power and place. You either learnt to lift yourself up into that place or you were wiped away by it. Martha always used to say, 'When you leave the stage you take it with you.' She did, and if you were unfortunate to be left on stage when she left, you had to be able to take it back.

Paul telling about my talk with Erick Hawkins that dark sad night in London brings it all back with an upsetting memory. I don't know why he chose to talk to me, but he did. I don't think I ever told what happened to anyone before except maybe to Bert Ross. Erick had a very bad relationship with the entire company when I joined. Maybe it was inherited from the time when Martha brought him into her all-women company in 1939. I know that the women resented him then, not so much for his coming into the company but because Martha was so obviously in love with him, and that changed their close rapport with her.

Erick contributed to this dislike by usually acting badly in rehearsals. He would frequently stop the rehearsal and try to explain the way things should be done in a very naive and pretentious-seeming way. He would also give us interpretations about what Martha meant or said, sometimes right in front of her, and we usually thought that he had it all wrong. She would excuse all this because she loved him but we knew it irritated her and she would later lose her temper and take her frustration out on one of us. He also changed what Martha was teaching to suit his body, but what was inexcusable to us was that he would show his version instead of the real exercise while teaching in her studio. That, of course, confused the students.

When I say us, I think I speak for most of the company because when we were together, the favourite topic of conversation was Erick and what he did and said today. This went on for all the years I was in the company until he left. That night walking along the Embankment in London, I had to be very careful and not let all this history influence what I said. Erick talked nonstop about what he wanted to do as an artist and how he could not choreograph while under the powerful influence of Martha. He did choreograph several works while in the company and Martha put them on the stage alongside her works. They unfailingly got bad reviews and I think were not good, but what he was talking about that night was that very problem. He said that he had very different ideas about what a dance should be and do and that, while under Martha's influence, he could not create that way.

We walked for hours, in the middle of the night along the Thames.

He did most of the talking and it was obvious, to me, that he was talking himself into a position which he felt justified his leaving the company. What I advised him to do is what I would say to anyone else who felt so passionately about his or her artistic life – do it. You must follow your dream. If you don't follow your dream, whose life are you living? I did not advise him to leave Martha but I knew he had to if he wanted to do what he was saying. That left me feeling sick at heart about what would happen in the future to Martha, her life, and her company.

Chapter 4

*Martha's work was so completely satisfying to me at this time, I did not
need to do anything else, not my own, not anyone's.*

(Robert Cohan, 2008)

1952–6

While Graham was recovering from her injuries, the studio was kept open mainly
by Helen McGehee, Bertram Ross, and Cohan; most of the other dancers, out of
financial necessity, scattered to find other forms of employment. These were
dangerous times, for without Graham's presence, students drifted away and there
was a real possibility that the whole enterprise would collapse. Things got so bad
that, unknown to Graham, Hawkins was persuaded to return to teach. He was
a 'name' and an experienced teacher and charismatic draw for students, even if
what he was teaching was his own idiosyncratic version of Graham Technique.
After years of dancing with her and teaching her technique, he would for example
say odd things like, 'Now, I know this movement is very hard for men to do but
I have changed it to this as it is much easier on the hips and you should be able
to get it to look sort of right.' The other teachers, although they had their own
particular take on the technique stayed as close to Graham's wishes as possible.

All the regular core of teachers at the school had been, or were, dancers in the
company and before Graham's injury had taken regular classes with her. In their
own teaching, they would try to repeat her classes; what Graham did was what
they taught. Cohan and his colleagues 'conscientiously tried to formalise what
she did, so we would discuss timings, repetitions, etc. and we would set it and she
would say yes or no'. Graham often thought that what they did went beyond the
call of duty and one day, on hearing Cohan and Hodes trying to break down an
exercise, said to them, 'You're going to count it to death!' But no one went their
own way, 'we taught Martha's class as we took them, although of course we may
have emphasised things we liked doing, turns, jumps or whatever'. But Cohan
was happy to teach 'what Martha taught because it was exciting'; and in the
1950s the technique was still developing at a pace; dancers who came back to the
studio, after even a few months of absence, found a whole new development of an
exercise or a wholly new sequence of movements. John Butler commented that 'if
you leave for a few months you may as well go back to the beginners' class!' Some
of the older generation of Graham dancers who visited always left with the latest
material, even if they did not always approve of what they saw as a softening of
her work. The percussive brutality that had characterised so many of the works
up until 1948 had given way to a dynamic lyricism that had come to the fore in

Diversion of Angels, this, together with the continued exploration of the spiral, had influenced all aspects of the technique.

Cohan developed into an exceptional and charismatic teacher, and his lack of salary from rehearsing with Graham was made up by teaching. At the Graham Studio, teachers received $8 per class but when Juilliard Dance Department opened in 1951, teachers were paid $18 per class. Cohan became a very popular teacher there and Elida Gera remembers him as 'the most beautiful man you have ever seen, all the students were in awe of him. It took a long, long time before we could follow his instructions because all we could do was stare. He looked you straight in the eye, which was very nice. We were totally frozen sometimes.'

But more than his looks, he was an extraordinary teacher,

> … because although he was an Adonis he had none of the show-off or ego, he was very honest, very centred and had the ability to inspire you without forcing anything on you that wasn't you. His personality was so strong [but] he spoke very softly, never shouted. He was an honest teacher, you understood that the necessity to teach was important for him and that you understood was important for him.

This necessity to teach fitted in very well with Cohan's interest in Gurdjieff's teachings and the passing on of the knowledge of self-discovery.

Graham's insurance doctors had wanted her to have an operation on her knee but she held off and while at Cady Wells' home the doctor prescribed weight-lifting exercises. When she returned to New York, she demonstrated to her dancers what she had been doing. With her feet dangling from a chair she would lift her left knee a few inches, straighten it over eight counts hold it for eight counts, and then lower it over a slow count of eight. She had begun in Santa Fe using a three-pound weight, by the end of the summer had moved onto five pounds and by the end of the year was lifting thirty pounds – a tenpin bowling ball weighs on average fifteen pounds!

Once back, she began reshaping the company and Cohan initially found himself given some of Hawkins' roles, though he admits to not being a very good imitation Hawkins, and his parts usually went to Bertram Ross. He did, however, take over the role of Jason *in Cave of the Heart* and Graham totally re-choreographed the part for him. There is no film of Cohan in the role but Martha Swope's 1960s photographs of this dance show Cohan as a vigorous sexually charged character, heartlessly parading his nubile love interest before the sorceress Medea, the mother of his children. It was, however, always a problematic role, and after one performance a reviewer wrote of the central duet between Jason and the Princess, 'Wisely Miss Graham's choreography for this duet ends just this side of ludicrousness. Had it continued a bit longer, the gymnastic gyrations would have begun to look too much like "Muscle Beach" set to music.'[43][sic]

1 Billie Cohan, Cohan's mother.

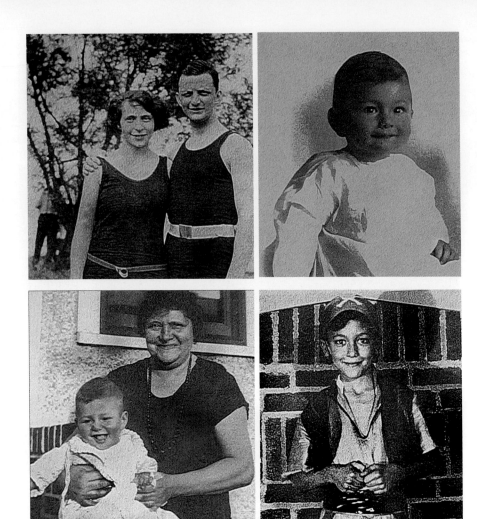

2 Walter and Billie Cohan, Cohan's parents.
3 Baby Cohan.
4 Baby Cohan on granny's lap.
5 Cohan as Peter Pan.

6 Cohan with his brother Elliot and sister Dolly.
7 Pte. Cohan in California, c. 1944.
8 Cohan in class, early 1950s.

9 Cohan and Martha Graham in *Deaths and Entrances.*

10 Cohan and Pearl Lang in *Wilderness Stair*, late 1940s.

11 Cohan in *Shangri-La*.

12 Cohan teaching at Rochester, 1959.
13 Cohan teaching at Rochester, 1959.

14 Advert for performances by Cohan and Matt Turney, late 1950s.

In other works, he partnered Graham more often and found her extraordinary. Lifting her, he found, was like lifting sprung steel and marble, an unusual combination. In the course of his career, Cohan partnered many women but none were like Graham. Pearl Lang, with whom he worked on many occasions – he likened the experience to wrestling – was strong but felt heavy, as did a later dancer Noemi Lapzeson. Graham, however, felt light, even though she weighed about 110 pounds; she had the ability to move, or at least manipulate, her centre while she was being lifted. She did of course lead, but Cohan found this a challenge and they both enjoyed it. In a sense it was like a contest between the two of them, and although he would never have described dancing with anyone else in this way, that was how he found her. It was a contest with the strongest winning: 'If she leaned on you then you had to lean back, this was true of her daily life as well as stage performance, if she pushed you had to push back, if you could not cope with it then you could not be in her company.'

In the 1950s when Graham returned, although devastated with the loss of Hawkins, she entered the most creative years of her life; she was no longer the rebel in woollen tights of the 1930s and 1940s, but settled into creating her mature complex masterworks with the finest dancers she ever had working with her. Graham had not made any group work since *Eye of Anguish*, having concentrated during 1951 on her solo *The Triumph of St Joan*. Cohan was therefore pleased when she announced that she would be starting a new work for the group alone. The dance would be based on the writings of St Francis of Assisi, who 'sang canticles in praise of the sun and fire and his friends the birds', although the title *Canticle for Innocent Comedians* would, as had *Diversion of Angels*, come from lines by Ben Belitt.

The dance was commissioned by the newly opened Juilliard Dance Department and much of the rehearsals took place at their premises near Columbia University. Stored on the stage area were designs by Frederick Kiesler which consisted of wooden flats, steps, cubes, curves, and a hinged door frame, all of which could be arranged in endless permutations for the student opera productions. Ever inventive, Graham leapt on this serendipitous encounter and started working with them at the first rehearsal; one reviewer later described them as the dancer's 'inanimate partner'.[44]

Of the 'animate partners', Cohan and McGehee were to be Stars and in a separate duet he was Wind with Matt Turney; Ross and Yuriko were Brother Sun and Sister Moon; McGehee was Water; Hinkson, Earth; Lang, Death; and Hodes, Fire. A Star cluster was danced by Linda Margolies, Patricia Birch, Miriam Cole, and Dorothy Krooks. The dance critic Clive Barnes felt it was

> … as easy to understand as *Genesis*. A group of people gather together to praise the Sun, the Earth, Wind, Water, Fire, the Moon, the Stars and Death. Death is birth and man continues in his praise. Each element is praised with

an expressive dance, and the work is linked together by the dancing of the
'Participants' which separate the episodes of praise by the Celebrants.[45]

Although all the cast knew the dance was centred around the duet for Ross and
Yuriko, for Cohan it was a joyous and happy experience as he was partnered with
two of his favourite women, Helen McGehee and Matt Turney. In remembering
working with him on the dance, McGehee in a tribute written for his eightieth
birthday gave an insight into his special qualities as a partner:

> You were just an incredible dance partner. There is no substitute for the
> instinctive. Your dancing instinct was so apparent that I never had the slightest
> hesitation when we were experimenting with movement, especially lifts. There
> was total trust that your nervous system and mine would collaborate and
> something exciting would happen. And so I never hesitated to fling myself
> at you, fully confident of being caught and changed into something else,
> unforeseen and unpredictable. That is the treasure, the experimenting and the
> discovery, finally providing so much rich material to be structured and shaped
> towards the vision.[46]

As McGehee notes, the dancers in Graham's work felt they were changed, and
this 'change' or transformation, a voyage of self-discovery, was what made the
whole experience so satisfying, and for many, certainly Cohan, made it seem like
a mystical journey, that could perhaps lead to awakening. With his other partner
Matt Turney, Cohan had a special bond. He admired her as a dancer and as a
very special and rare type of personality. When she died in 2009, he wrote to this
author that 'she exuded a kind of mystery when she moved and her presence,
when still on stage, was even more mysterious'. He made much of her 'mysterious
presence' when she joined him as the first member of the Robert Cohan Dance
Company in 1958.

Clive Barnes felt that Graham coined 'phrases hot-fresh from the mint,
seldom repeating herself, she babbles magic words like an idiot child or poet'.[47]
Had he been in rehearsals he may have written 'prophet', for as Mary Hinkson
remembers in the studio, 'Martha would sit on one of the benches, seeming to
meditate; when her eyes rolled into the back of her head leaving only the whites,
she would rise and in a trance-like state begin to choreograph.' Like Stravinsky,
who said he was the vessel through which the *Rite of Spring* passed, Graham
was a vessel through which her dances appeared and on one occasion, in the
Philippines Cohan heard her say, 'I am a witness to my work.' Looking back he
can see that 'she had this way of talking which everyone knows, she talked in
mystical and poetic terms, riddles, poems, pronouncements, not the language of
the everyday world. But that was Martha, that was how she was.' This connection
to other states of consciousness was one of the reasons Cohan wanted to work
with her, and he told at a Martha Graham Study Day in London in 1999 that 'it

was as though she existed on a different plane, as an archetypal figure of greater depth than those around her'. He was fascinated by her and her work, finding that 'she seemed to have all the connections most of us have lost'. Connections or not, she was still human and not a deity, and Pearl Lang's comment on being given some new material – 'Yes, I think I can work with that' – helped to keep things grounded.

The score was by Thomas Ribbink, a young Texan musician and sometime dancer who had studied in Paris with Darius Milhaud. Although it was effective, it caused problems for the dancers as his music began at the first duet for 'Sun and Moon' but Graham wanted a prologue. At one rehearsal, she had the dancers push all the stage props to the centre and then stand among them, then push them offstage, leaving the curved flat used for the Sun and Moon duet. Ribbink, in a fit of artistic temperament, refused to compose any music for this, feeling that his score was perfect just as it was. When Paul Goodman, a Juilliard professor, suggested that they could add soft timpani strokes for the opening, Ribbink was furious and threatened to remove his score. At the time, Ribbink was dating Bertram Ross, and after Ross had argued with him that he should write the extra music, Ribbink went home and took all of Ross' clothes to the cleaner's, leaving Ross with the receipts and a huge bill. When the work was shown in London, David Hunt – not knowing anything of its troubled history – wrote in *Dance and Dancers*, 'Long silent sections in the dance of the moon in which the undulating rhythm of the choreography gave the illusion of being part of the musical design showed how closely composer and choreographer had worked together.'[48]

A revised version of *Canticle*, with an orchestration of the score for small orchestra and baritone, was presented at the Alvin Theatre in April 1953 when de Rothschild sponsored a gala for eight dance companies: Martha Graham, Doris Humphrey, José Limón, May O'Donnell, Nina Fonaroff, Pearl Lang, Helen McGehee, and Merce Cunningham. Sadly however, after that gala, the sunniest of Graham's works disappeared from the repertoire, the only record being some studio shots taken by Carl van Vechten, one of which shows Cohan positively twinkling in his Star costume. An attempted reconstruction by Yuriko for the Martha Graham Ensemble in 1987 was like the ghost image of the tail of a comet.

The membership of Graham's company settled down in the early 1950s and a number of dancers stayed with it for ten years or, in some cases, many more. Not everyone got on with each other, but in their various groupings they felt comfortable. Cohan was always something of an enigma, and to some extent he cultivated an air of mystery. He had, indeed still does have, an eccentric, off-the-wall sense of humour that could amuse, perplex, or simply annoy depending on personal taste, as the following story from Stuart Hodes shows:

> We had a break from rehearsal of about an hour and a half as Martha was doing something else, so instead of going to our usual drugstore across the

street, someone said, 'There's a real nice diner just up Fifth Avenue', so Bob, myself, Bert, and Natanya [Neuman] went and sat in a booth. Bob, myself, and Bertram were watching the cashier; she was sitting up really high and she was young and healthy looking, but she was obese, and we were just astonished that she looked the way she did, and we all said, 'How could she let herself get like that?'

Bert: 'Maybe she was born like that?'
Natanya: 'She looks healthy enough.'
Bob: 'She's beautiful!'
Bert (infuriated): 'Oh of course Bob, you would have to say that!'
Bob (calmly): 'If people were raised for food, they would all look like that.'
That's the sort of way Bob's mind worked!

More than any of the other dancers in her group, Cohan was in tune with Graham's sense of the mystical and in addition to the reading needed for researching her dances, would often be seen carrying, as Hodes recalls, a philosophical or occult treatise from Ouspensky or Krishnamurti. But his sense of humour could elicit a playful response from Graham, and although she never really socialised with her dancers, she did occasionally take a break from rehearsals with them. On one occasion, Hodes remembers:

Bob decided to have a saffron coloured necktie, so he bought a pure white silk one and spent a lot of money on some pure saffron, from which he made a rich infusion and dyed the tie. Martha saw it and said, 'What a pretty yellow tie.' 'It's not yellow', replied Bob, offended, 'It's saffron. I dyed it with real saffron.' Martha put on her glasses, peered closely, took off her glasses stared at Cohan and barked, 'It's yeller!'

In 1952, Bethsabée de Rothschild, in another show of uncalled-for generosity, offered to buy Graham a new building to house her studio. Before agreeing to the move, Graham took her dancers to view the three-storey building at 316 E. 63rd Street. At first glance, it seemed unpromising as it faced Second Avenue and was largely derelict and full of junk; but walking around it, Graham and the dancers were taken by its quaint charm, partly provided by the small garden, and could see the possibilities for three studios. They decided to accept the offer. The large room on the ground floor was covered in a heavy but chipped varnish on top of a good maple floor. Cohan and Hodes volunteered to strip it, and hiring a large sander they began work at dawn one morning, finishing at 4 p.m. when Graham arrived, alarmed to see them smothered in dust and chippings. The following day, they put down a sealant and once dry, Studio One – the company studio – was ready for work. The other two smaller studios were soon renovated and crammed with students. Studio One did have a problem: there was a large pillar right in the middle, and Graham felt her choreography was always drawn to it like a magnet. After a year of dealing with this unwelcome intruder, de Rothschild, while the company were on tour, had the pillar removed and a cross beam put in its place. With a few Noguchi benches and Nakashima chairs, the studio was able to double as a small theatre accommodating about fifty people. With its petite garden creating a haven of green amongst the high rises of the Upper East Side, it would remain the Graham School until the late 1990s when it was sold and razed to the ground. The school and company were offered a minuscule space in its replacement's sunless basement; above them is a forty-room apartment hotel.

Without de Rothschild's support, it is unlikely that Graham would have had the success she did and many times the Rothschild fortune saved her from financial disaster. She was at a loss as to how she could ever repay her and told Cohan on one occasion, 'The only thing I can offer Bethsabée is success in the eyes of her friends. Money isn't success to them, they have had it for generations; but spending it well is difficult. If I have a successful season, Bethsabée is congratulated by her friends.'

It was to the new studios that Helen Keller made a visit. She had known Graham since the early 1940s and, although deaf and blind, was fascinated by the idea of dance. For the visit Graham arranged a special technique class followed by a rehearsal of *Canticle for Innocent Comedians*. To begin with, Cohan and the dancers found it a strange experience as they danced for Keller seated in front of them,

> … but then Martha put her in the centre of a circle and we all danced round her, occasionally touching her hands and then all touching her, one after the other. Then Helen [McGehee] stood on my thighs – the lift at the end of our duet in *Canticle* – and she came to us and touched us both very lightly, trying to make sense of the positioning of bodies that she couldn't see or hear. She must have worked it out because she suddenly threw both arms in the air in surprise and let out a wonderful happy sigh.

The sound of her sigh has stayed with Cohan throughout his life.

Cohan found dancing with Graham so engrossing and interesting that he had no thought of choreographing himself, even though he had taken both of Louis Horst's composition classes – Pre-Classic Forms and Modern Forms – twice, beginning in spring 1947 and continuing until 1949. When Cohan started working with Graham, Horst was still teaching composition in her studio three days a week in the afternoons. Each course was about ten weeks long, with projects set in class but with students expected to choreograph in their own time. In this Cohan was lucky because he had access to the studio, which many of the other students did not. At the time he took the courses, no one from the company was participating though many did, or had, at different times.

Being a musician, Horst based his courses on musical forms and compositional ideas. He had no dance material of his own nor did he ever demonstrate any, thus the students had to be self-sufficient in developing their own movements according to his exacting and precise demands. For Cohan, the courses were 'remarkable' and Horst, he found, was a brilliant teacher; under his watchful eye – often more watchful when he looked as though he was asleep – it was not possible to fake anything. If he thought a dancer was improvising, he would make that person repeat the material instantly and woe betide anyone who could not reproduce the material, because even if Horst could not dance the material, he would almost invariably remember exactly what he had seen. The worst case scenario was when a student had improvised something and Horst would, with a twinkle in his eye, say, 'Great, we will put it in the Saturday performance.' In one study, Cohan did actually improvise and did it again, and so well, that Horst couldn't tell. He was amazed that he managed to do it, but was also disgusted at himself for having done so. He knew that he was there to learn and that the only person he had cheated was himself. The courses were extremely intense and required very hard work and application; they were not – as is so often the case nowadays – about self-expression but about learning a craft. Over many years, Horst had taught many dancers, who had been very successful and he knew what he was doing. Of course, his greatest success had been Graham herself. She frequently talked about how he had told her she should walk 'like a lioness' and that he had taken her to the zoo and made her watch the lions pace in their cages while he sat and read the newspaper. She always said that she was angry that he got to read while she had to work.

Horst's great 'rival' in teaching choreography was, as she was for Graham, Doris Humphrey; although Cohan never took class with Humphrey, he watched her teach on many occasions. He thought her a good teacher but, in contrast to Horst, easier on the students, less demanding of the specific task at hand. When Horst critiqued his students, he would say, 'You didn't do this, didn't do this, but you did do that, you need to rework that section because it wasn't right.' He made the student stick to what he had asked them to do and they had to sublimate their expression to the technique. He told Cohan on one occasion that he covered 'a host of choreographic faults by moving so well'. This was worthwhile criticism for Cohan because he did move well and the beauty of his performance could easily make up for poorly constructed work.

Horst was very strict about form and the forms he used were often simple and clear – rondo, binary or ternary. This meant that he could be very demanding in what he required and this helped the dancer to compose. This was enormously important to Cohan and would later affect the way he taught composition. He made Cohan understand that it is the form of the dance, whether it is classical, contemporary, or movement against vibration or whatever, that contains the dance. Cohan believes that,

When a choreographer choreographs a movement sequence, if it all existed in space at one moment, out of time, then it should be a beautiful sculpture. Beautiful not meaning pretty, but beautiful in that it should have its inherent beauty, no matter how simplistic; angular or raucous, the movement should have its own integrity and that is how a choreographer builds a dance, out of its own integrity.

This is what Cohan tried to pass on when years later he was a much sought-after choreography teacher.

Cohan found Horst's method particularly useful in the long run as, by the end of both courses, the student knew the ten or twelve forms and was able to listen to music and identify a form without being abstract or just guessing:

You might say, 'I want a procession at this stage', or 'I might want a rondo'. It could be an abstract rondo but you would still have a coming and going back. What you do intuitively is that you recognise that is what it is and that helps you to find the steps to finish it. To recognise what form you are suddenly doing is what is important.

At a Cohan study day held at The Place for his eightieth birthday, Cohan was questioned by a student as to why he paid so much attention to form. Cohan's reply was simple: 'Can you tell me anything in your daily life which does not have form?' Anthony van Laast has found this approach invaluable in the highly pressured world of commercial dance in which he has been so successful. Here, speed and preparation are essential attributes and the clarity of form and structure he learnt from Horst via Cohan has aided in the choreography of shows as diverse as *Song and Dance*, *Mamma Mia* and *Sister Act*.

Cohan's first choreography was called *Perchance to Dream* and was based on lines from Shakespeare's *Hamlet* in which the prince contemplates suicide:

To die, to sleep;
To sleep, perchance to dream – ay, there's the rub:
For in that sleep of death what dreams may come,
When we have shuffled off this mortal coil,
Must give us pause – there's the respect
That makes calamity of so long life.[49]

It came about almost by accident, and he certainly had not sought out the opportunity. At the 1952 American Dance Festival held at Connecticut College, Graham had declined to teach the first week of the course and had given this to Cohan. It was usually expected that teachers would show some of their work at the end of the week and so Cohan's first choreography was born.

He was understandably nervous about doing something on his own and so Graham had agreed to help him, as even though she was not teaching, she was still in the area. She told him to get into the studio and begin work and that she would come in and help him shape the movement. Cohan was, by his own admission, 'feeling in a very romantic and expressive mood at the time' and chose to choreograph to Debussy's lush *Première Rhapsodie* for clarinet and orchestra. He had a fairly clear idea as to what the work would look like on stage and to this end he bought, in a Boston antique shop, a (fake) medieval dagger, the blade of which he had sprayed a gaudy silver for effect. At Graham's suggestion, he used the ornate ceremonial chair that Oliver Smith had made the previous year for Graham's not very successful solo dance *The Gospel of Eve*. Alongside this he had constructed a coffin-like structure, the top of which was covered in cork, so that when he threw the dagger at it, it would stick and stand up straight.

Cohan began work and in a few short hours had begun to amass a useful amount of movement; but there was no sign of Graham. He tried calling her and when he eventually got through, she said not to worry as she was held up but that he should continue working and that she would be along soon. This continued for three days, during which Cohan created more and more movement but got more and more frustrated each day when his mentor would not arrive. When, on day four, Graham did eventually appear, the dance was almost complete. She made some suggestions for changes, moved certain movements around and altered dynamics and speeds; but basically the choreography was by Cohan. As she knew, he was more than capable of making a dance – all he needed was a push. The first performance took place in the Palmer Auditorium on Sunday, 27 July 1952, with Louis Horst introducing the mixed programme which, as well as Cohan, included work by Muriel Mannings and Irving Burton.

Being a trained Graham dancer, he constructed the dance using the classic Graham Technique and also incorporating her methods of staging with the props being integral, not extraneous, to the dance. Coming out of his favourite step, the cartwheel, Cohan threw the dagger at the top of the 'coffin' a number of times. In rehearsal, this had always happened perfectly with the blade standing upright in the lid at every throw. Not so in performance, when each time he flung it, it either bounced off or fell down. After the performance Louis Horst's comment to him was, 'You threw that dagger once too often my boy.' This was not picked up by Thomas Hughes Ingle who reviewed the concert in the *New London Evening Day* on Tuesday, 29 July under the banner 'Young Professionals Seen at School of the Dance':

> To music by Debussy, Robert Cohan has set an enigmatic soliloquy, avowedly based on Hamlet's 'To be or not to be' transmuted into the air of the nineteenth-century romanticism. Despite a certain diffusion of plastic content, this piece appeared to be the most mature and absorbing work of the evening, both for the dancer's elegance of line and for his sensitive development of it. Mr Horst announced this as the dancer's first original creation, and it is a work of great

promise with something of the suave balance and mordant poetry of a story by Henry James.

Although this was a very favourable review and Cohan was happy with the work, he did not feel the need at this time to continue choreographing. Unlike some dancers in Graham's company he did not need to prove himself as anything other than a dancer. Where Helen McGehee, Ethel Winter, Pearl Lang all felt the need to make dances to prove themselves against Graham, Cohan found 'Martha's work was so completely satisfying to me at this time, I did not need to do anything else, not my own, not anyone's'.

This may not have been a bad move since around this time Cohan, for reasons of conscience, became a vegetarian and involved with health food. In the 1950s, there was only one shop in Manhattan – on Lexington Avenue –where one could buy vitamins and organic food. There Cohan discovered macrobiotic food and juice diets. The concept of a macrobiotic diet was something new in the early 1950s and Cohan embraced the idea wholeheartedly. He went on cleansing juice diets every month, processing the raw food himself on huge primitive juicing machines on which he invested quite some money. This regime lasted for about a year, during which time he had another choreographic idea, a protest piece about the inhumanity of meat eating. He decided that he would rent the theatre at the Young Men's Hebrew Association, acquire a live cow and slaughter it on stage during the performance of a dance. The meat would then be handed to the audience who, so he hoped, would be so disgusted by the spectacle that they would never eat meat again. There were of course many problems to be solved, not the least of which was how to get the cow into the theatre! The problems proved insurmountable and what could have been one of the precursors of 1960's German Live Art was shelved. The vegetarianism only lasted a year as Cohan found that he was too weak to do the Graham Technique without meat in his diet. He did think that, had the piece worked, he would have become famous overnight.

Later in the 1950s, the juicers became useful for other things. Cohan never showed any interest in excessive alcohol, which had become an increasing part of Walter Martin's life, but he had a great interest in mind-altering drugs, and admits, 'Yes, I experimented with everything'. Influenced by Aldous Huxley's book *The Doors of Perception* about the taking of mescaline, Cohan decided he 'had to try it as it sounded extraordinary', but where was one to find the peyote cactus, from which mescaline is derived, in New York City? Here his love of all things botanical came into play and looking in the back pages of a gardening magazine, he discovered adverts for the cactus that produces mescaline. He sent off the $2 required and very soon a two-foot-square box arrived, full of decomposing cacti.

The problem with Lophophora williamsii, the small mushroom-like peyote cactus, was how to extract the mescaline, as it did not come with instructions; this was when his juicing machines became useful again. It is well documented that the taste of the plant is vile and that it is violently emetic – if it is taken straight, the moment it hits the stomach it comes back again plus everything else in there. After a number of unsuccessful experiments Cohan found that the best way was to use the juicing machines, to make a smoothie mix of sweet raspberry syrup with the peyote, a 'Smoothie Williamsii'. The drug has a long history in the religious and ritualistic ceremonies of certain Native American tribes where it is used to induce a deeply introspective metaphysical state. Cohan found the drug dark, primitive, and mysterious and that the world it opens is inhabited by the Peyote Lady, who he saw as 'a faceless woman, who, if a person, looked like a mushroom or if a mushroom looked like a person – that is what she would look like'. He found her 'very dark and very feminine'; he could see a little of her eyes but not much of her face; but he knew he was in the presence of magic and something mystical. Many years later, when Cohan was living in London, he was walking in Mayfair in a street full of art galleries when he saw a painting of the Peyote Lady. He went in and it was full of paintings of her. When Cohan told the assistant he knew the figure in the paintings, the assistant was shocked and asked him how he knew her; he said, 'I've met her.' He was informed they were from an American artist who had indeed mentioned how he 'knew' the Peyote Lady, the acquaintance of whom the gallery assistant had not made. Cohan told him they were very nice paintings and were very exact.

Mystical experiences were not limited entirely to drugs and with his great interest in alternative teachings on life, Cohan found himself one day in the presence of Merwan Sheriar Irani, known to his followers as Meher Baba. Baba was an Indian mystic who had since the 1920s developed a worldwide following and who had in 1953 declared himself an Avatar or earthly manifestation of the Supreme Being. Meher Baba had become very popular in New York dance circles, largely through the ballet teacher Margaret Craske, who was a devotee; indeed it was Baba who had instructed her to leave his ashram in India and go to America. Over the years, she would introduce many to his teachings, including Viola Farber, one of her favourite pupils who would be an adherent, wearing a locket with his picture in it until the end of her life. Not so Cohan who in 1956 attended one of his meetings at the Hotel Delmonico at 502 Park Avenue in Manhattan. The Baba had not spoken since 1925, preferring to communicate via an alphabet board and intricate hand gestures which were interpreted by close disciples. Vocal or not, during the meditation session Cohan was convinced that he felt something – certainly not sounds, but something he could not quite identify – trying to enter his mind. He left and never went back finding the experience 'just too disturbing'.

After her split from Hawkins, Graham had become more and more reliant on the masculine energies of her three main men, Cohan, Stuart Hodes, and

Bertram Ross. In her autobiography, she wrote, ' after Erick there was no one,'[50] which for Graham was a struggle, as she had always been a highly sexualised woman having affairs with a number of her collaborators, even during her time with Hawkins, including Arch Lauterer, Hunter Johnston and Saint-John Perse. No sexual act took place with her dancers, although Hodes remembers one interviewer for an oral history project offering to turn the tape recorder off if he would 'admit to fucking her'.

Although the dancers were colleagues and friends, they were also in a sense rivals and when they felt they were not getting the right roles, they would fight for them. Unlike in a ballet company, there were no named positions of seniority as such but Graham observed some sense of order, which in the case of the men placed Cohan ahead of Stuart Hodes and Bertram Ross. However, Graham enjoyed the play of human relationships and she loved nothing better than drawing people under her hypnotic power and then arranging them to suit her own needs. In her only work from 1952, entitled *Voyage*, she took as her subject matter her relationship with these three men. Graham did not make this theme explicit to any of them, and none of them had any idea where the dance was going. Each had a character: Cohan was a creative creature, Ross a beloved, and Hodes a demon. Hodes saw them as the Hindu trinity, Cohan as Brahma the creator, Ross as Vishnu the preserver and himself as Shiva the destroyer; but Graham did not explain this herself.

The setting for the work, as the programme note told the audience, was 'the terrace of a mansion at the edge of a desert, with a man and woman facing each other. Within an out-of-sight mansion, a party is in progress from which the two have momentarily escaped. Before them stretches a desert, barren of people yet rich in mystery.'

The set was again by Noguchi and it had arrived at 316 E. 63rd Street in two parts. In the centre of the stage was a high arch, a doorway of the house perhaps, the other was unmistakeably a ship. The trio asked Graham why Noguchi would design a ship when she had asked him for a desert. Graham's response was that that was the way of the Oriental mind, Noguchi seeing the sea as a kind of desert. Hodes did not accept this and said, 'But one represents death, the other life.' To which Graham responded, 'To the Japanese, life and death are the same!'

The work progressed slowly and Graham tried out hundreds of movements, discarding most of them. After a long rehearsal in which only one tiny phrase was kept, Graham in positive frame of mind said, 'Well at least we found one little treasure today.' Another time Graham's inspiration dried up – 'I have the inspiration of a gnat' was a favourite phrase – and she didn't know where to go next and began to get very frustrated. Before the situation could boil over into disaster, she told the three to go out while she cleared her head. They went and had coffee and then walked around for a while, window shopping; on 63rd Street and Madison Avenue, they found a very exclusive Chinese shop in the window of which they saw displayed some beautiful carved mahogany flowers. Each chose one they thought appropriate and presented them to Graham when they returned. She immediately rushed out of the studio and came back with a big switch of fake hair attached to her head into which she had inserted the three flowers. Leaning against the set, she told each of them to take a flower, which they did; the hair collapsed and the dance continued.

It was only years later when her notebooks were published that the three were able to see what she had been aiming for:

> One sees her as a Goddess to be placated and paralleled in all things. Bob
> One sees her as one to do battle with. Stuart
> One sees her as part of his own being. Bert
> Each man changes into a costume denoting his aspect of mankind
> Bob – the youth
> Stuart – Don Juan
> Pirate
> Matador (if so can he use a cape?)
> perhaps he also has
> dagger--&it is a duel
> Bert – Orpheus?[51]

She had indeed been trying to make a dance from their actual relationships, though their actual emotional involvement was much more complex than the characters she had noted. Cohan may not have seen her as goddess to be placated, but he would never intentionally upset her or rile her. After he left the company, Cohan did write to her explaining why and she told Hodes, 'Bob is very put out with me.' She did on the other hand regularly have fiery, violent arguments with Hodes, who as much as he loved her would not put up with any of her tantrums. Ross probably did see her as part of his own being. He had a selfless devotion to her and after Hawkins left – although there would never have been any question of a sexual relationship between the two – was her right-hand man, until he was unceremoniously dismissed in a telephone call in 1973.

When the dance was finally completed, Graham costumed it in a contemporary style, but had great difficulty in deciding what she herself should wear, eventually choosing a beautiful evening gown she had bought some years before from Hattie Carnegie. The men were costumed in formal evening wear purchased from a shop on lower Fifth Avenue. Cohan's tuxedo was dark green, Ross' midnight blue and Hodes' maroon. At the climax of the dance, each of them removed his dinner jacket to dance bare chested in a savage dance, only to put them back on like a civilised veneer at the end. A similar idea would appear twenty years later in Paul Taylor's *Cloven Kingdom*.

The work was premiered on 23 April 1952 at Juilliard and was not a success, the reviews being either hostile or puzzled. Arthur Todd got to the heart of the matter when he wrote that although it 'was performed magnificently' it failed 'because the identities and characteristics of each of the men had not yet been clearly defined and thus their relationship to the central character was obscure'.[52] Graham was interested enough in it to return to the work and in 1955 renamed it *Theatre of Voyage* and showed it again. It fared little better with John Martin writing in the *New York Times*:

> What she has given us looks like a series of fragmentary improvisations held together only by a mood of neurotic frustration. Occasional phrases by herself and the three men who work with her – Mr Cohan, Mr Hodes and Mr Ross – have interesting movements in them but there is little 'theatre' about it and if it is a 'voyage' it is a singularly becalmed one.[53]

After these few performances the work was dropped while the set would be reused to great success in *Circe* of 1963.

Graham's second international tour came about as a result of the Cold War. Russia had begun to consolidate its position on the world stage by initiating a series of cultural exchanges, sending ballet, music and theatre around the world. Not to be outdone the Americans began sending some of their cultural icons abroad. Since 'the modern dance' was an indigenous art form and Graham was seen as its leading artist, and she had a number of supporters in the State Department, it was only natural that she should be among the first to be sent. The pull of working for Graham was extraordinary: at the time the tour was announced, Stuart Hodes had been offered $1,200 per week to dance in the Dave Garroway Show on television but he turned it down to earn $200 to dance with Graham on tour. For Hodes it was an act of faith and dedication since he had recently married fellow Graham dancer Linda Margolies and the two could certainly have used the larger salary to start a life together. But the dedication was not unexpected. On the weekend of their wedding Graham had promised them the time off, but called on Saturday night to ask them to come for rehearsal on the Sunday; they of course agreed.

In February 1954 the company, which included Graham, fourteen dancers, and their new Music Director Eugene Lester, set sail on the Queen Elizabeth. In addition to England, the tour would continue on to Holland, Sweden, Denmark, Belgium, France, Switzerland, Italy, and Austria. This was an enormous undertaking, and Graham and the dancers, who had been on the 1951 tour, were nervous and fearing another disaster. The week-long voyage across the Atlantic affected the group in different ways. Graham turned green as soon as the ship left harbour and stayed either in her cabin or on a deck chair bilious for most of the voyage, panicking that no one would like her or the work. The dancers, however, made the most of the time on board; touring the ship, staying up late and generally having a good time. When they finally disembarked in

England the dancers found that their equilibrium was gone and they could not stop swaying. Graham on the other hand was suddenly perfectly well and forced them straight into a rehearsal as soon as they arrived, for Linda Hodes it was 'a horrible experience'.

On arrival in London, the boat train was met by Peggy Harper, a dancer born in South Africa who had met Cohan and his assigned room-mate David Woods while she was studying at the American Dance Festival in 1952. Harper had more than a passing crush on Cohan and when he told her he was not very happy with the hotel room they had been given, she told him of a friend of hers who owned the Gore Hotel in Queensgate; she was sure he could give them a good rate. Via Harper, the owner Robin Howard did offer them a good rate, but Cohan turned it down, saying he would feel too much in his debt and it was too far from the theatre. He persuaded Woods to move with him to a smaller hotel close by the Saville Theatre where they were performing, and closer to Soho, where certain substances could be purchased.[54]

Very soon after their arrival, Cohan did manage to purchase some marijuana – he had a reputation for being able to find a supply of drugs within one hour of arriving in a new town – which he and Woods shared with two other company members back at their hotel. This was Woods' first attempt at smoking the drug and in his autobiography he noted somewhat wistfully that 'the effect that the marijuana had on each of them was immediate and complete. I on the other hand, in my novice state, had no idea what sensation to look for. As my friends moved into those strange worlds, I began to feel I was far behind.'[55]

The 'solace' of the marijuana was sought out frequently as the first week of performances went very badly. The theatre was virtually empty – on some performances there were only about twenty people in the audience. Cohan remembers that every night the cast would peek out from the curtain and count the number of spectators, hoping that it would fall below the number which legally let them cancel the show – unfortunately it was usually just one or two above. The reception was mixed, with audiences being generally lukewarm, while the press took violently opposing points of view. Long-established ballet critic Cyril Beaumont, writing in *The Times* was appalled by the 'complete negation of normal conception... Miss Graham's intense expression, gaunt features and body, suggest a being mentally wrecked.' And 'her abstractions and philosophies leave one exhausted rather than entertained'.[56] Less informed critics were even more affronted such as the anonymous critic in *Empire News* who thought: 'If lack of grace and grotesque contortions are the essence of modern dance, America's Martha Graham and Company succeed admirably.'[57] In this Graham should not have been too upset since the British had long had a reputation as dance philistines as the poet Heine had observed almost a hundred years previously:

As I hear, Taglioni met with no applause last year in London; that is truly her greatest claim to fame. Had she given pleasure there, I would begin to doubt the poesy of her feet. The sons of Albion are themselves the most awful of all dancers, and Strauß assures me there is not a single one among them who could keep time.[58]

As well as feeling the stress from performing in empty houses, the dancers were worried about an unfinished work. For the tour, Graham had promised a new piece, *Ardent Song* to music by Alan Hovhaness; she had begun it in New York but at nearly fifty minutes long, it was nowhere near complete by the time they had arrived in London. The score, typical of the composer, making use as it did of non-European scales, sensuous and lush melodies, was meditative yet exuberant and with a driving beat that Graham found herself too often being pushed along by. There was little time to rehearse and added to this the British musicians had never seen or heard anything like a Hovhaness score and behaved badly when they saw it.

Each night after the performances were over, the company would go back on stage and rehearse for an hour or so. Graham kept putting the premiere off until well into the second week when she decided to cancel. Her manager Gert Macy stood up to her, calling her 'unprofessional' – which infuriated Graham – and demanded that she showed her how much of the work existed. There were nearly fifteen minutes of choreography missing and so the dancers had to improvise. In this Cohan took the lead, arranging material for four couples who danced around the solo figure of Yuriko. He would start off a phrase which would be picked up by the next couple in canon and so on; in this way the holes were filled, and there was no empty space on stage. After the run-though Graham, who was not in the work herself, came backstage and said, 'I don't know what you just did but you are going to do it again tomorrow night!' then walked off in her best imperial fashion.

This they continued to do until the end of the run, and on each night what they did became more fixed. It was not an ideal way to present a new company in a new city but it was not unheard of and at least it was exciting. By the end of the tour most of the dance was set, though a fast trio for Mary Hinkson, Linda Hodes, and Patricia Birch was in fact never completed, and Hodes was heard to shout, 'When is she going to set this fucking dance?'

It looked as though the whole visit was going to be a disaster until a magically poetic review by Richard Buckle appeared in *The Observer* on the Sunday:

I have long thought myself the most diehard abonné of classical ballet in town. 'Modern' dancers have always embarrassed and bored me. Now, I conjure every idle habit-formed fellow in need of a third eye to see new beauty that he should visit the Saville Theatre and watch Martha Graham. She is one of the great creators of our time.[59]

And everything changed. The second week more and more people came, though not the thousands who would later claim to have been at these performances. Even *Ardent Song* was well received, with one critic finding, 'The new ballet *Ardent Song* which Miss Martha Graham produced for the first time on any stage at the Saville Theatre last night, is the most successful she has shown us during her present season.'[60] At the end of the run, Mary Clarke could write in *Dance Magazine*, 'Martha Graham's London season ended March 20th in a blaze of glory.'[61]

One person who was there was the hotelier and businessman Robin Howard. Howard came from a very well connected family, he was the son of Sir Arthur Howard MP and grandson of Prime Minister Stanley Baldwin; his great-grandfather had been Canadian railway magnate Lord Strathcona and on his mother's side he was related to Rudyard Kipling. Money, power, and influence were in his blood. Educated at Eton and Cambridge, he had followed a traditional career pathway for one of his class, which saw him as a lieutenant in the Scots Guards during the Second World War. He tragically lost both his legs when, during a shell attack, he had thrown his large frame over his batman to protect him. Howard's interest in ballet grew after the war when the Sadler's Wells Ballet was installed at the Royal Opera House and for a few exciting post-war years many foreign companies performed there. Amongst these were Roland Petit and his company, [American] Ballet Theatre, Ballet du Marquis de Cuevas, and the New York City Ballet. Ballet, however, never really satisfied him and it was Peggy Harper who alerted him to Graham's work; she also persuaded Cohan to go and talk to him.

This first meeting did not go smoothly, and not because Cohan had turned down his offer of accommodation. Cohan was shown to Howard's suite at the Gore Hotel in Kensington which, as the owner, Howard had been able to deck out for his own needs. This meant that around the edges of the walls was a sort of raised cushioned walkway, banquettes really, on which Howard could manoeuvre himself without benefit of his metal legs. He opened the door to Cohan without his legs attached – this was a common ploy Howard used as a way of challenging newcomers and assessing their character. Howard was in a pugnacious mood and led straight into the modern dance, questioning why it was needed when we had ballet. How, he demanded to know, could something that had been around for twenty-five years possibly be as satisfying as an art form that had taken 200 years to develop? It must be noted here that he echoed the sentiments of Dame Ninette de Valois who told this author on one occasion near the end of her long life, 'Well why do we need it [contemporary dance] we [ballet dancers] can do it all anyway.' Howard seemed to take no notice of Cohan's explanation of the technique, the choreography, the philosophy, or its frank success in the USA. This greatly antagonised Cohan, which was undoubtedly Howard's aim, and he left saying, 'There's no point in me wasting any more time with you, and I don't care if you come or not!' With Howard as with Graham, if he pushed you had to push back, which Cohan had certainly done, and the next night Howard came to the performance, and the next night, and the next night.

Enthralled by Graham and her work, Howard would later write:

> Though I did not realise it at the time, my life was undoubtedly changed on that night… because not only did I change my immediate arrangements for the following nights so I saw every performance but one… but I also got to know Martha Graham and various members of her company. Ultimately much the most important to me was Robert Cohan, whom I admired immensely as a person and as an artist at that time. Many years later when I was doing something that I never expected to do then – starting my own dance organisation' – Bob Cohan was my only choice for artistic director.[62]

Howard held a party for Graham and her company at the Gore; in the Elizabethan-style banquet room Graham was seated, of course, in the Queen's chair. He became an ardent supporter of Graham and her work, and from the inauspicious initial meeting with Cohan were sown the seeds that would ultimately change the face of dance in Britain. Overall, the season, in terms of critical and audience reception, had not been the unqualified success that they had all hoped, but enough people had been sufficiently impressed to realise that there was more to dance than simply ballet and that Britain needed to enrich its cultural life beyond European boundaries.

The rest of the tour went generally better than in England. In Holland, the performances – some of which were visited by the royal family – were sold out and so Graham put on the first of what would later be called lecture-demonstrations. In these Graham would not dance but as interlocutor introduced her work, the dancers showing some of the class exercises and then some of the choreography. This was a new idea and one that became important in the world of dance and which Cohan brought with him to England. It developed into educational residencies and become the backbone of the work of his company, introducing the world of contemporary dance to new audiences and demystifying the most ephemeral of the arts. Back home, the US State Department were overjoyed with the reports they received about the tour and immediately began to prepare another. This time it was to Asia, and would be a mammoth undertaking lasting from October 1955 to March 1956.

A year to arrange such an enormous venture was not long but with the aid of the State Department and Charles Green, the tour began to take shape. Back in the studio Graham continued to work; too distracted for any wholly new works, she returned to some old ones. The unsuccessful quartet *Voyage* was revised and was equally unsuccessful, her thirty-minute solo *The Triumph of St Joan*, based on the life of Joan of Arc, was recast as a group dance. With spectacular designs by Noguchi and a glorious score by Norman dello Joio, it would, as *Seraphic*

Dialogue, become one of her most successful works, although the only male role –that of St Michael – went to Ross and not Cohan. To everyone's relief, she finally set *Ardent Song*, which, even after numerous performances, still had sections of improvisation in it. She made some radical changes to the work, adding into it a new role for the youthful Donald McKayle who joined the company for the tour. But finished by whom was the question, as at a rehearsal Graham watched Ethel Winter and McKayle perform a duet they had been working on and as she walked out of the room she said, 'It needs more… sa-da, sa-da',[63] and left. The bemused couple completed the duet themselves but endeavoured to add 'sa-da, sa-da' throughout.

Everyone was excited about the forthcoming tour; the world seemed a larger place in the 1950s, travel was difficult and now the dancers were going to be sent to places they had only read about in books or seen on newsreels. Cohan was doubly happy to be leaving New York again as his relationship with Martin had got more and more difficult. Martin's depression and dependency on alcohol and drugs made life very difficult; on one occasion, Cohan had returned home to find him burning his paintings in the fireplace. To keep his sanity, Cohan spent as much time as he could at the Graham Studio and so the opportunity to be away for longer periods was more than welcomed. Even then it was not in Cohan's nature to desert someone in need, and in one form or another he continued to look after Martin for another ten years. Looking back, he remembers it as 'like sharing doom for a long time'.

The Asian tour began, after the six men, ten women, and nine technicians and musicians had endured many inoculations and a thirty-six-hour plane journey, in Tokyo. Sending Graham on tour before any of the American ballet companies proved to be an unusual but sensible decision. It gave the Asian countries an opportunity to see a dance form entirely American in origin, which offered no comparison to European ballet – the first performances in Tokyo followed on from Alexandra Danilova's ballet company.

Graham and her dancers had become used to performing before large audiences and in June 1955 had performed at Boston's Public Garden Theatre in front of 15,000 people as part of the Boston Arts Festival. This event prompted Margaret Lloyd to write in the *Christian Science Monitor* that we should 'never underestimate the power of a public to recognize what is good, what is great in art'.[64] That the Asian public should recognise this power was something that the US State Department could only have hoped and prayed for. The extraordinary reception that greeted Graham and her dancers throughout the tour far exceeded this.

From the start in Tokyo, the reviews were ecstatic as Irene Pines wrote in *The Mainichi* of Thursday, 3 November 1955:

Here was dancing in the fullest sense of the word; every movement full of life and significance and performed beautifully by Miss Graham and her company of artists. Without meaning to disparage some of the very fine dancers and choreographers among the Japanese school of 'moderns,' they must all surely look at themselves anew in the light of these performances and ask whether they have used 'modern dance' as a license for unabashed, undisciplined self-expression, or as a shield for lack of technique, or as an excuse to make a pantomime spectacle.

A State Department report noted that, 'large numbers of people stood in the aisles at every performance and the final curtain brought a thunderous ovation of applause, cheers, exploding firecrackers, confetti, serpentines and flowers. Miss Graham's presence was a revelation here. Her works disclosed a theatre of drama the Japanese thought the Americans could not create.'[65]

Such reviews and reports continued for the whole of the tour; even if the size of theatre changed from large to tiny stages, the warmth of welcome did not. In Rangoon, there was no theatre and the company performed for an audience of 6,000 in the temple courtyard of the golden Shwedagon Pagoda. In every country, royalty, presidents, premiers, diplomats, and celebrities turned out for the company. In Tokyo, the Crown Prince and the Emperor's brother were there, while in Burma the opening night began with a speech by Prime Minister U Nu, and in India President Nehru was in attendance. Photo opportunities abounded and Cohan was often called upon to escort Graham. A picture of Cohan and Graham perched on a statue with Madame Sukarno, Indonesia's first lady, appeared in a number of magazines and papers.

Part of the success of the tour could be attributed to the lecture-demonstrations that Graham presented before each engagement. Both the critics and the public responded enthusiastically to these demystifications of the work. The very first one, in Tokyo, had, however, got off to a bad start, when in rehearsal, Graham got into an argument with Paul Taylor over the position of his hands, 'Paul watch your hands', she said. His response, 'What do you want me to watch about them?', infuriated Graham who was nervous about the performance anyway and as a result shouted that only the older dancers would be in the lecture-demonstration, everyone else was to leave. This in turn infuriated Ellen van der Hoeven who hung around and waited for Graham, asking, 'When will I become a senior member of the company?' 'When you become a dancer' was Graham's serious response. Van der Hoeven began arguing with her and Graham slapped her across the face, to which she responded, 'You should be glad you're an old woman or I'd slap you right back!'[66] A later attempted suicide by a depressed young company member further added to the stress.

Dancers from Japanese dance schools flocked to the performances and attended classes; most had only ever taken ballet classes but some took to Graham's style instantly. Two, Kazuko Hirabayashi and Takako Asakawa, were offered scholarships at the Graham Studio, where they would become key players in Graham's work, Asakawa as a star dancer and Hirabayashi as one of the leading teachers of Graham Technique and no mean choreographer.

Initially, the tour was exciting. In Tokyo, Cohan and McKayle set off together to explore a burlesque show in the Yoshiwara, the city's red light district, then had an amazing meal in an exclusive Tepanyaki restaurant. Performances of Noh and Kabuki were challenging but enthralling. But as the tour progressed and the company saw dance after dance, monument after monument and had one official dinner after the next, they became jaded. When they arrived in India, all the company did was play bridge; most did not leave the hotel, suffering from sensory overload, exhaustion, and Delhi belly.

On New Year's Eve in Calcutta, Cohan and Matt Turney got completely drunk on a gift of some aqua vitae which resulted in them arriving late to a glamorous party, held on the rooftop of, as Cohan remembers, 'an exquisite building with panoramic views over the city'. By the time they got there everyone was seated and watching a Kathak dancer in full flight and Cohan was 'horrified to see Martha summon me over to sit with her. I don't know how I did it but I swayed through these beautifully dressed Indian women and managed to sit by her without falling down. I thought the evening would never end'. The night did end, with Turney and Cohan still drunk, lost in a market, being pointed and laughed at by the stallholders. He has no recollection as to how they got there nor how they found their way back to their hotel. Looking back, Cohan is appalled by this, realising that 'it was a terrible sensation to be so satiated'.

Other sensations were achieved through the use of drugs and Cohan remembers that it was the authorities in each country which inadvertently pointed would-be imbibers in the right direction in their search for illegal substances. At all airports in the various countries there would be a large illustrated board or poster detailing banned substances spelt out in many languages. So even if the visitor did not know the name for a drug before arriving, they did by the time they had cleared customs. In Dhaka, Cohan and David Woods once again found a supply of marijuana. Unfortunately, one day, just as they had settled into an intense and marvellous high, the phone rang. It was LeRoy Leatherman asking them if they wanted to join Graham and himself in a chauffeur-driven Christmas shopping trip. They briefly considered asking Graham and Leatherman to join them instead but wisely thought better of it. Sitting in the car giggling inanely, the two infuriated their hosts who at the earliest opportunity left them alone in the middle of a market and drove off. They had almost been discovered and realised they would have to be more careful in future; the only drug Graham tolerated was alcohol.

In Burma, the plan was to try something a little harder than marijuana and once settled into their hotel in Rangoon Cohan and Woods headed off in a rickshaw to find supplies. They became worried as they were driven by the wizened old driver to what looked like a very disreputable part of the city. There they found a dealer who sold them, quite cheaply, a considerable amount of hashish and what they hoped was opium. Back at the hotel, word spread among the company that they had been successful and most of the new members and some of the older ones joined them in one of the bedrooms.

The room had in it a stairway that led up to an unlit area just below the cupola of the hotel, but above that was a glass room that gave incredible views around the city. There, illuminated by the light of a full moon, nearly the whole company spent an enjoyable evening getting high on what turned out to be very good hashish. The irony of taking drugs on a State Department-sponsored tour was not lost on Cohan. If the hashish was good, the group could never get high with the opium which requires a specific technique, unknown to them, to get it to unleash its wonders and wisely Cohan disposed of it.[67]

The official tour was to finish in Tehran before de Rothschild, who had accompanied them as a sort of wardrobe mistress, took them at her own expense to Israel; but the company almost never made it. Owing to bad weather, the group had had to wait in the tiny airport at Abadan for a flight. After a couple of false starts, they eventually gained clearance and boarded the small two-engine plane. Abadan and Tehran are separated by a high mountain range and the plane was not able to go over them but needed to go through a steep-sided canyon. Seated behind Ross in a window seat, Cohan had spectacular views of the mountain as the pilot made a 360-degree turn. In order to get through, the plane needed to be on a tail wind which the pilot seemed unable to find. Then suddenly, the weather changed and they were caught in a storm. The plane was thrown about like a toy, and the cabin was soon full of dangerously mobile bags, cameras, coats, and souvenirs. The intrepid stewardess was almost concussed while she moved around the cabin attempting to restore order and the dancers sat screaming in their seats. Graham, however, sat calmly at the back of the plane. She would later tell the story that she calmed herself by mentally dancing through *Errand into the Maze*, facing up, as does the character in the dance, to her fear. The pilot did make it back to Abadan where the passengers, very definitely shaken, disembarked. The stewardess apologised to Graham who replied, 'My dear, I may spend the rest of my life in Abadan, but I will never fly in that plane again.'

The following morning, a larger but unpressurised plane arrived. It was so large that there were plenty of empty seats and Graham grandly told the airport staff to allow some of the other waiting passengers onto her aircraft. This caused problems for at 20,000 feet the oxygen masks appeared, but there were not enough to go around with the extra passengers and Helen McGehee's husband, the artist Umana, who had a heart condition, turned blue and looked as though he was about to die. The lack of oxygen caused symptoms similar to inebriation and the US Embassy and Iranian officials at Tehran airport looked surprised at the condition of the passengers as they descended the steps of the plane.

At the end of the tour, Graham went to Rome, Athens, and Paris to lecture while the company returned to America. Cohan's souvenirs included some drugs he had in his bag. Linda Hodes knew this and started teasing him saying, 'Oh I can't wait to see you getting arrested!' When they arrived in New York, she hung behind him in the customs queue, watching. Cohan's customs officer was an old Irish woman who, on seeing the name Cohan on the passport and his dark good looks, beamed at him and said, 'And where have you been darlin'?' He replied and she said, 'Let's open the bag.' Hodes was beside herself by this time, waiting to see what would happen. But, on the very top of the bag the first thing the official saw was a large book entitled *The Spiritual Life of our Lord Jesus Christ*, and with a twinkle in her eye, she closed the case saying, 'Oh, I think that's fine me darlin'. You go on through.'

The group had been away for a long time and were exhausted after the tour; the changing time zones, food, climate, had all taken their toll. As Graham was not due back in America for some time – after her lectures she went to Berlin to dance her solo *Judith*, with the Berlin Philharmonic – Cohan took the opportunity to get away from the claustrophobic atmosphere of the company, and, to broaden his horizons, by appearing in a musical. It was fairly common for dancers from the modern dance world to appear in Broadway shows – Stuart Hodes regularly left Graham in order to earn more money, Yuriko had created the role of Eliza in the Broadway and film versions of *The King and I*, and it was more unusual that Cohan had not tried it until this time.

The musical he chose for his Broadway debut was *Shangri-La* based on James Hilton's novel *Lost Horizon*, with music by Harry Warren, book and lyrics by James Hilton, Jerome Lawrence, and Robert E. Lee. The choreography was by Donald Saddler, whom Cohan had met when Saddler was dating the critic Walter Terry, and who cast Cohan as the Perrault Dancer. Hilton's famous story about plane-wrecked Europeans who discover an Asian Utopia where life is serene, desires are moderate and people live long and mellow, was an odd choice for a Broadway musical. As *Time Magazine* noted, 'A Broadway musical is one of the very few places where a controlled frenzy and a tasteful immoderacy seem in order.'[68] This was almost the exact opposite of the needs of this musical. In spite of beautiful sets by Peter Larkin, costumes by Irene Sharaff and a great comic turn by Alice Ghostley, it was not a success. In an out-of-town preview in New Haven it was 'given a warm reception by a capacity audience generous enough to overlook the weaker aspects of the play because the production was beautiful overall.'[69] But not in New York, where it lasted only twenty-one performances when it opened at the Winter Garden Theatre on 13 June. Cohan had, however, been noticed as 'ballet dancer [sic] Robert Cohan who executed some fine interpretive ballet.'[70] And after the show closed Saddler offered him a part in another musical.

This was in Dallas, Texas, in a production of the musical *Can-Can*, starring the Incomparable Hildegarde, a famous cabaret star who described herself as a 'luscious, hazel-eyed Milwaukee blonde who sings the way Garbo looks'. In it he danced the part of the serpent in the dance section about the Garden of Eden. This was fortunate indeed as on returning to New York he began working with Graham on a new work based on the story of Adam and Eve.

Back in New York, Cohan joined Pearl Lang and Toni Cook in Lang's television dance series *Look up and Live*. Based partly on a young girl's discovery of the sanctity of marriage, it was broadcast on Channel 2 on 1 October, at a time when television networks still showed non-commercial dance. His next work would also involve cameras, but would have a larger audience than Channel 2. For someone who had always avoided documenting her work, it came as a surprise to the company when Graham announced that she had agreed to a film being made of herself and her dancers. Before the Asian tour, Nathan Kroll, a violinist turned producer and director, had approached Graham with the idea – of course she had refused. Like many of her generation, she felt that dance could not be caught successfully on film. In addition, she was in her early sixties and although on stage this was not so apparent, she worried that in front of the scrutiny of a film camera, the wrinkles would be visible to all. Furthermore, she knew nothing about film production and felt that she would not be in control. But Kroll persisted and she had given in.

Entitled *A Dancer's World*, it would be produced by Nathan Kroll, although Graham's friend the director John Houseman had a major input into its direction. The format they agreed on was a type of lecture-demonstration, in which a short demonstration of the technique would be followed by extracts of her dances. In the film, Graham is seen dressing for the role of Jocasta in *Night Journey* and talking into the mirror, outlining her thoughts on dance. Then the camera moves into the studio and her dancers move into the space, and begin what is a short technique demonstration, to the piano accompaniment of Cameron McCosh. They then move into pairs and present three duets from *Diversion of Angels*, and then a fourth couple dance the sarabande from *Dark Meadow*.

With the miracle of editing it all appears seamless, however, it was a more difficult a process. Graham was happy with the staging of the dancers – the section she does not appear in – and became fascinated by the technicalities of shots and angles. But when it came to film her, she became panicked, locked herself in her room and refused to come out. After much discussion, it was agreed she would not dance, but would be filmed as noted, preparing her regal self for a performance.

These problems passed Cohan by, and he found working on the film a 'wonderful experience', remembering that 'I was in good shape and I enjoyed every minute of it.' The project offered him the opportunity to be involved firsthand in the production of a film. His inquiring mind meant that he was interested in all aspects of the filming, from the lighting requirements to the

camera angles and shooting technicalities. There were some problems with the
costumes as the men hated 'those stupid polo shirts we wore! We wanted to wear
our usual class tank tops but Martha's administrator went to Bloomingdale's and
came back with those ordinary polos and convinced her they were right. We even
had a fight about buttoning the top button which we felt was choking us, which
we lost!'

Those slight problems apart, this is one of the only documents of Cohan
dancing in his prime, and although he does not demonstrate anything like
the extensions that would be expected of male dancers only a few years later,
what is seen is his gossamer light jumps and landings, razor-sharp timing and
a mercurial presence that radiates from his every movement. In spite of its
extremely dated staging – Graham is aided in her dressing room by a black maid
– and Graham's portentous dialogue, the film went on to have great success
in introducing the world to Graham's work. In the UK, where it was shown in
teacher training colleges, it helped open the eyes of Laban-based students to the
possibilities of American modern dance, making Cohan's work in Britain in the
1960s easier.

In addition to the film, Cohan was in rehearsals for a new quartet of Graham's
entitled *Embattled Garden*. Set in the Garden of Eden, Cohan was the Stranger
– in reality the serpent – Ross was Adam, Yuriko was Eve and Turney was Lilith
(Adam's first wife). Cohan thinks he may have given Graham the idea for the
work as he had talked about his experiences in the Garden of Eden ballet of the
musical *Can-Can*. If that was the case, then Graham had moved with the idea
very quickly, commissioning a flamenco-inspired score from Carlos Surinach
and a large set from Noguchi. The set which is now used, consisting of wooden
platforms with flexible poles in them in imitation of trees, is only a fraction of
the one he made. What had been delivered initially to the studio was a large
wooden platform that covered so much of the area that there was nowhere to
dance. Unfazed, Graham got one of her stagehands to cut the set into pieces
and rearranged those to suit her needs. With these trusted dancers Graham was
happy – after she had given detailed explanations of character and relationship
– to let them develop material themselves that she would then move and shape.
However, her comment to the very proper Yuriko that she 'should be like Gina
Lollobrigida'[71] was met with some bemusement. Graham found the dance
difficult to work on; at the time she was drinking heavily, and she kept putting
it aside. It was not complete by the time Cohan left the company and he did not
appear in the first performance.

As well as working on the new dance, Cohan had persuaded Graham to let
him try to reconstruct her classic trio *El Penitente* which had not been performed
for a number of years. He had performed the Christ figure in the work but did not
know the other parts, so with Ethel Winter he set about restoring the movement.
Graham refused to help, saying that she could not remember any of the dance

and that it was a stupid waste of everyone's time to try and bring it back. She was always loathed to restage works in which she had performed (which was most of them) but which she was not able to do anymore. When *Appalachian Spring* was staged for the first time with Pearl Lang in the role of the Bride, Graham said to her, 'You must know this is the worst day of my life.'

It did prove problematic to retrieve the movement and the dancers even got Hawkins to come to the studio to tap into his memories of the work. After a great deal of effort, the piece was finished and they tried to show it to Graham, who wanted nothing to do with the project. She arrived repeating that it was 'a waste of time as I can't remember any of it'. Cohan, getting annoyed, said, 'Martha, just sit down. You don't have to remember any of it, it is all done', 'No', she said, 'I can't remember anything', and walked out of the room leaving the flabbergasted performers to stare after her exit.

Tensions were therefore already running high in the company; they had been rehearsing and rehearsing, had given no performances since Asia, and everyone was frustrated. Then one day Yuriko came running into the studio, saying that she had heard LeRoy Leatherman, the company manager, on the phone saying that as Stuart Hodes was going to fulfil a Broadway contract and as he was so central to company's current repertoire but would not be available for the coming season, then it would be cancelled. This may have been a ruse since nothing in Hodes' schedule indicated he was planning on being away, but everyone was outraged that this could be even considered without consulting them, as in their opinion Hodes' roles could easily be taken by others. They demanded a meeting with Graham.

Graham hated any form of public confrontation and reluctantly agreed to see them, but at her apartment and on her terms. Lined up were all the company, facing Graham and company managers LeRoy Leatherman and Craig Barton. The company had little faith in Leatherman and Barton who they felt had no skills in financial or personnel management and only had the job because Graham was in love with Leatherman, and he possibly with her, but who in any event had a relationship with the tall good-looking Texan Barton.

In the meeting no one started to speak so Cohan led off, then Graham attacked him straight away because she felt he was attacking the administration. The administration meanwhile were sitting in the room and not saying anything. Graham insisted on knowing who had said what but Cohan said, 'I can't do that to you because the person is in this room. You trust that person. We all work on that trust, and if that person can't tell you that they did it, I can't continue working in this organisation.'

Graham stated that she and no one else made all of the decisions, both financial and artistic. Cohan challenged this, repeating what Yuriko had said, although on this Yuriko now backed down, saying she may have made a mistake. The company pianist Cameron McCosh spoke up, agreeing with Cohan, but Bertram Ross, his boyfriend, and always the dominant character in their relationship, shushed him and he refused to get involved. The arguments, now only between Cohan and Graham, became more personal and heated and the pair were screaming insults at each other. Cohan amazed himself by deliberately riling her, demeaningly calling her 'Honey' and 'Darling'. They even had to stop for refreshments and then continued in the same acrimonious vein. Eventually Cohan said, 'Honey, you can't talk to me like that. I'm leaving you and your company.' The shocked silence that followed was broken by consoling comments from all around; even Cohan was shocked to hear himself utter the fateful words as he had never entered the discussion expecting that outcome. Things calmed down and on leaving Graham went to hug Cohan, saying, 'Don't you know I'm a tiger and I have claws I can use', at which point she dragged her nails down his back, breaking the skin. Cohan's response was, 'Lady, so do I', and he clawed her flesh in return.

Chapter 4

Commentary

You might be excused, after reading this chapter, in thinking that this biography was of the Martha Graham Company and not me. But Martha and the company were my life. I remember going to the studio in the morning to take class or teach class, and/or rehearse and get back to where I was living around ten or eleven at night. Seven days a week. Graham thought Sunday or any holiday was the best time to rehearse, as there were no distractions like classes.

The studio was like a hothouse as Graham was not only choreographing but also still changing and increasing the range of her technique class, as Paul noted. Her choreography was changing and the movement skills needed were becoming more complex. She was also challenged by having a large, committed, and skilled group of dancers, women and now men also, who were taking her advanced class every day.

I just should note here something very simple that is not usually said. Critics and audiences knew Martha Graham as a great artist with a magnetic presence on stage. Well, in the studio we had that same magnetic presence just a few feet away from us every day; she and the creative energy that flowed into the studio from her mesmerized most of us and me for sure. It was as if we were at a convergence of ley lines. She was a constant performer and class was no different than the stage. We were there to learn and she responded by constantly inventing new exercises that advanced the quality and scale of the training.

The process itself was a learning experience. She would see something on a body that was not working well. She would then devise a small movement to correct the problem. Over the next few classes that small movement would perhaps be extended by repetition, and a counter movement have timing added, and a structure would gradually develop. It would then become an exercise in itself. As was said, we teachers would help by trying to keep all the classes tuned to what Martha was teaching at the time. Several of us would demonstrate for her and that meant that we knew what she wanted at each of the class levels. This coordination was needed as more and more young people were coming to dance as a means of expression and there was a kind of competition going on as to what studio you would choose to study.

The modern dance world was still very small in New York in the 1950s. There were Doris Humphrey and Charles Weidman developing their technique, also derived from Denishawn, and Hanya Holm, who came from Mary Wigman and several teachers of different techniques at the New Dance Group. There were not so many choices as to where to study then. I don't think that Martha thought of them as competitors but all the studios needed students to survive and we, the company members who were teaching, knew how much we needed them.

As Paul wrote, we did not get paid for working with Martha during the extensive choreographic and rehearsal periods but only for the actual performance weeks and maybe the rehearsals just before, and even then, we only got the Equity Union minimum. Martha choreographed or we rehearsed for several months before a performing season.

It is hard to imagine now how we survived financially. It was a matter of teaching, if you could, and getting enough weeks in the year to qualify for unemployment insurance the following year. We were actually unemployed and registered as dancers. That meant that the unemployment bureau had to find us work as dancers. Of course, there was no way they could do that and we could usually get the full twenty-six weeks of unemployment money we were entitled to each year.

By the way, this was true of all dancers in New York in those years and you would often meet other dancers standing in line. The only excuse for missing a rehearsal that Martha accepted without question was the day you had to go to the Unemployment Bureau to sign for your unemployment cheque. She knew that the New York State Unemployment Bureau was unknowingly giving her 'grants' to make new work.

I need to say something about all the references to my taking of drugs. I started after reading about drugs being used in several religions and by shamans in the effort to reach some kind of enlightenment, or at any rate a deeper understanding or meaning to life. Drugs that now go by the nice name 'entheogens' (literally meaning 'god within us'). The theory being that our normal everyday cluttered mind is incapable of opening the doors of perception, as Aldous Huxley called them, and that through the use of these mind-enhancing drugs, gates could be unlocked that would otherwise remain closed. I am not qualified to talk more about this other than to say, I think I found them useful for a time but I stopped all that many years ago. It sounds like the Graham Company were taking drugs all the time. That's not true, it certainly was very few of them and on only one or two occasions, mostly organised by me and usually on a dare!

My leaving Martha after the violent argument we had was more than I could take. How strange that was, because I can't remember before that meeting that I ever wanted to leave. As I remember, those ten years with her were the happiest and most fulfilling of my life. I had that rare feeling of being in the right place at the right time, doing exactly what I wanted to do.

Chapter 5

Our Man in Havana

(and Boston, and Rochester, and Buffalo, and New Haven, and…)

1957–62

Cohan returned to his loft in a state of shock. The meeting had not gone as anyone envisioned, certainly not Cohan; he had not entered Graham's home with any scripted speeches and what he had heard himself say had surprised everyone, especially himself. But he knew that what he had said, shocking as it was to hear, he had meant and it needed to be said. After a few days, he received a phone call inviting him to have dinner with Graham and some company members. He agreed to go, but when he heard from Ethel Winter that it was simply a set-up to get him to return to the fold, he stayed at home. There he wrote Graham a long letter, now sadly lost, putting into writing – and in more temperate language – what he had said at her apartment, and finished by saying that it was best that he left the company. A certain mythology, mostly untrue, arose in the company as to exactly what he had said to her, but Glen Tetley's assertion to Robert Tracy that Cohan just walked out and left a note on the piano is not true.[72] Graham never responded to the letter, but in any event, he had stopped answering the phone and cut off all contact with Graham and her company; he even managed to avoid Bertram Ross who lived in the same building.

In his own words, he 'went into a deep, deep, deep, depression, almost a midlife crisis', but he was only 32. All of his working life had been with Graham and he had never thought of working with anyone else. The sudden and unexpected nature of his departure completely debilitated him. He had no idea of what to do with himself, as he had not planned to leave and had therefore not planned a future path. For over a month he hid himself away, sleeping, eating a little, and escaping into his occasional 'dream world'. Realising this was not a healthy attitude and to occupy himself, he purchased a small kiln and began to make copper enamel jewellery, ashtrays, and ornaments that he gave away. His only income was from some savings and a small amount of unemployment insurance, so when a friend, who was creating shop window designs, asked him to help he leapt at the chance. This small bit of work motivated him and he began to venture out and to answer the phone; as a result, more dance work came in. June Taylor, a well-known teacher and choreographer for television and Broadway, asked him to teach some classes in her school. Out of this developed some television work and he appeared on a number of occasions with the June Taylor Dancers on the *Jackie Gleason Show*, featuring in some of her Busby Berkeley-inspired kaleidoscopic numbers.

An important contact was made with the city of Boston when a local arts group asked him to teach some masterclasses. Although the music scene in Boston was well established, with its famous symphony orchestra and nearby Tanglewood Music Festival, there were fewer opportunities for dance. There was no resident company – the Boston Ballet would not be formed until 1963 – but with a large number of young people attending the many universities in the area, there was a ready market for modern dance. Cohan regularly made the 400 mile round trip between New York and Boston and sowed the seeds for what became a very fruitful relationship with the city. This tiring routine went on for a few months when, out of the blue, Jack Cole called him, said he had heard he had left Graham and asked if he would like to join a company he was putting together that was to perform at the opening of the new Havana Riviera Hotel in Cuba. Cohan who had always admired Cole happily said yes, glad to get out of the exhausting travelling and to get away for a longer period from Walter Martin, whose habits and problems had not improved.

Jack Cole, born John Ewing Richter in New Jersey in 1911, has been credited with inventing what we know today as jazz dance. Like Martha Graham, he had trained under Ruth St Denis and Ted Shawn at the Denishawn School and danced in their company; later he performed with Doris Humphrey and Charles Weidman and was a member of Ted Shawn's all-male group. He soon left the world of modern dance for the far more lucrative world of commercial dance, performing in nightclubs and casinos, and eventually on Broadway and in Hollywood where he created choreography for many classic films and shows including *Kismet*, *Gentlemen Prefer Blondes*, *There's No Business Like Show Business*, *Gilda* and *Moon over Miami*. He was highly disciplined, sought absolute perfection from himself and his dancers, and was known as a tyrannical taskmaster. This did not faze Cohan who knew that working for Graham had prepared him for anything.

But, before he could escape, he was called back secretly to the Graham Studio to teach his role in *Embattled Garden* to Glen Tetley. Tetley had been called in to replace Cohan in some roles, notably in *Diversion of Angels* and the part of The Stranger in *Embattled Garden*. The dance which Cohan had worked so hard on was not complete and Graham was struggling with it. Teaching Tetley the part without the person it was made on was proving challenging and so Bertram Ross took it on himself to renew contact with Cohan and to ask him to return and help. This he did on a quiet night when no one else was in the building; the rehearsal took the entire evening and Tetley took over the role, even though Cohan was surprised at how difficult he found some of the movements which had been developed on Cohan's body. Graham did eventually finish the work but it would not premiere until 3 April 1958. Cohan would eventually return and claim back the role as his, but that day was some years off.

Cohan found Cole's work fascinating. His movement was not overtly similar to Graham's but because both came out of Denishawn, it was possible to see the common origins; Cohan had experienced some of the Denishawn material when he had taken class with Ted Shawn at Jacob's Pillow in the early 1950s. He remembered that 'you could see where some of her material came from, especially on the floor, particularly in fourth position'. The theatricality for which Denishawn was famous was still evident as 'Ted showed up [at 9 a.m.] in full make-up and wearing a beautifully embroidered silk kimono, stood at the piano and said, 'Let's begin', shimmied his shoulders and [the kimono] fell to the floor and he was revealed in all his glory in a tiny white leotard.'

Cohan loved Cole's energy; he knew he was strong performer but he found that he was also an excellent teacher, because he knew what he wanted and he would give clear instructions both physically and verbally. Where Graham's work engages large muscle groups to create powerful impulses as in her contractions, Cole would aim to articulate separate muscle groups: shoulders, hips, torso, ribcage, and arms and to these he added movements and hand gestures from Bharata Natyam, the Indian classical style which he had studied in depth. He also blended in a variety of styles of dance – lindy hop, rumba, samba, and Haitian vodoun dance.

Cohan had wanted to study Indian dance with La Meri, but Graham had dissuaded him from the idea, so doing Cole's movement was very exciting to him and he found that part of Cole's work very easy to do. The other movements required more practise; Cole's lindy jazz was incredibly fast and although Cohan as a teenager had lindyed whenever he could, it was never at the speed Cole required. Cohan was good at big, broad movement on a large scale, not fast moving steps, and he had to work very hard on the small intricate material and only just barely got it together. The classes were immensely enjoyable, though after not performing for nearly a year, proved very taxing and Cohan had to get back into shape very quickly as the show was to open on 10 December 1957.

In spite of the excitement of the work, Cohan found Cole lived up to his reputation as a very difficult man: 'He was a perfectionist and he could be very mean in getting what he wanted from his dancers.' Cole's approach was to make them feel small and worthless and he frequently made the women and some of the men cry, much like Antony Tudor and Jerome Robbins did. Cohan feels it was some type of a power game and that these fundamentally aggressive people needed to push the dancers to give them an adrenaline rush so that they could get through their rehearsals. Cole's aggressive temperament was also fuelled by his addiction to amphetamines, which he took to keep him awake during the long hours he worked. He did work harder than anyone else; in this show he put himself into almost every dance. Cole tried some of these tactics on Cohan, who found that 'after Martha it was like amateur night and he couldn't get anywhere with me'. Attempting to belittle and make fun of Cohan over a step he had difficulty getting, Cole said, 'Can't you dance in shoes?' to which Cohan replied,

'No! Can I take them off?' He would remove them and dance barefoot while Cole shrugged his shoulders and gave up.

Some of the dances were complex and involved careful manipulation of often elaborate costumes. In one dance, Cole was in a central position while a woman in a very elaborate gown moved around him yet always ensuring that her back was facing him. At the climax of the dance, she turned around and the audience saw what Cole had been viewing all the time, which were her naked buttocks. The beautiful gown was held together at the back only by tiny chains. The dance was Cole's homage to Cuba, because he thought all Cubans liked large rumps.

Cohan was part of an exceptional company which consisted of four women, including Gwen Verdon, Cole's assistant, fresh from a Tony Award as Eve in the musical *Can-Can*, and two years before becoming Bob Fosse's wife. And four men, one of whom was Ron Field who went on to become a choreographer and whose major success was the opening of the 1986 Los Angeles Olympics. Cohan's main companion during his six months' contract was Canadian jazz singer Anita Ellis, who often provided the singing voice for Rita Hayworth if she were called upon to sing in films. All were support acts for the show's star Ginger Rogers. At this stage in her career, Rogers never danced and was there as a singer, even though the drunken Mafiosi who were often in the audience, attended by ladies of the night, would shout out, 'Stop singing Ginger and dance. Give us some steps!' She always refused. Mafia Boss and hotel owner Meyer Lansky was heard to complain, 'Rogers can wiggle her ass, but she can't sing a goddam note!'[73] Cohan found his childhood hero still attractive and very charming, although the two never became friends.

The hotel, which cost $8 million to build, was controlled by Meyer Lansky and no expense had been spared. In a country where most of the population lived in poverty, the hotel staff had vacuums with which they sucked up excess sand that escaped from the beach and when the vacuums broke, they bought new ones. The dancers were housed in comfortable apartments near the hotel but as it was the end of the Batista regime, Fidel Castro and his revolutionaries were in the mountains and there was security everywhere – Cohan was frequently stopped and searched. As well as living in comfort, they were very well paid, and the casino was lavish; huge amounts of money was won and lost in it each day. This was something of a problem for Cohan, who after his wartime experience at the races had discovered something of a fondness for gambling.

There were three shows a night, at 10 p.m., 1 a.m., and 3 a.m. and either between or after them, Cohan would find himself in the casino. He would go and gamble and by the end of the six months he had lost about $400, not a huge amount but enough to be noticeably missing from his savings. Carlos, one of the conga players, told Cohan that he could always win at the casino. He said that if he played, he would lose but that if he didn't, he could always predict the winning numbers. One night, Cohan found Carlos standing by the roulette machines and he said, 'Number 34 will come up', and it did, and he looked at another machine and said, '16 will come up', and it did. Cohan tried to predict the winning number but failed; Carlos would predict seven out of ten numbers. Cohan was intrigued by the mystery and tried each night to tune himself into predicting the winners. After some effort, he suddenly knew what the number would be and put a dollar down on number 36, which won. The croupier, who knew Cohan as regular loser, looked at him and said, 'Good, Bob, good!' For the 'system' to work, Cohan found he had to stand between the three machines while all three were in use, and by carefully observing which two machines did what, he would know what the third one would do. Over the next five nights, Cohan made back over $500.

In spite of the dangers, Cohan was relaxed about dancing in Cuba, he did not view the work as serious but he enjoyed every minute of it. Some of the dances were tricky and he had to work extremely hard at them to get better and better and to keep up with the other dancers, many of whom had worked with Cole before. He found Cole to be an extraordinary performer, who could light up the stage and exude a similar dynamic energy to that which he had experienced with Graham. Like Graham, Cole on stage was absolutely of the moment and his dancers had to be there with him, and Cohan was used to this. The few numbers Cole did not dance in were difficult because the energy he had created had to be carried on with the dancers alone.

To break up the monotony of three shows per night, Cohan taught some classes at the Cuban Ballet. A dancer who knew him from Graham brought him in for some work but he found the style too balletic and too different from his aesthetic, and it was not something he actively pursued. The rest of his time he spent indulging his fascination with Cuba. There was some scuba-diving, but mainly he was struck by the richness of the culture. Travelling about Havana and beyond, he saw 'real' rumba, which was completely unlike the commercial rumba seen in the West. What he found were groups of about 'five or six old men drunk or high on drugs, making music on drums, bottles filled with water, no recognisable instruments except for an occasional old violin or a flute'. The music, betraying its African roots, would die out under Castro who banned it, but while Cohan was there he revelled in it. Dancing was on every street corner and people always danced either singly or together as couples or groups. In spite of the poverty, the Cubans did not look or act poor; they were very friendly and welcoming. The problem Cohan found 'was with the political situation which meant there were police everywhere and there was a lot of corruption and prostitution'.

Cohan could have extended his contract, and the excitement of winning more money was enticing, but he listened to the drummer, Carlos, who warned him that he would start losing his winnings if he stayed, and after his contract was up, Cohan packed and returned home. Those who stayed were almost caught up in the revolution of 1 January 1959 but luckily caught the last plane out of Cuba.

He got back to a cold, damp New York with no work; he also got back to find Walter Martin's drinking problems had, improbably, got worse, and he did not want to stay. He picked up some teaching again from June Taylor and the dance club in Boston were happy to have him back, the classes quickly moving from monthly sessions to weekly. Building on his recent Cuban experience, Cohan added to his modern repertoire and began to offer jazz classes as well.

Hearing that he was working in New England, Dora Sanders, who was setting up an extramural dance programme at the University of Rochester, asked him if, in the autumn, he would come to teach at the university. Sanders was a gifted musician, dancer, and photographer who started as a protégée of Hanya Holm and was then, like many before and after her, pulled into the world of Martha Graham. As well as playing for classes at the school, she took as many classes as she could fit in, and Cohan's were her favourite. She asked him if he would be willing to come and teach a packed schedule of classes and he agreed. He wrote to her on 14 October 1958:

> Dear Dora, This is the confirmation you want – I am really looking forward to this – it is always exciting to start in a new place – especially when there is so much enthusiasm – I know it will be a completely rewarding semester for all of us.

It was, as it turned out, a very rewarding experience, not least because over the two years he would work there, he got to know Dora Sanders and her husband Jim very well, as he stayed at their house when he was teaching in Rochester. He became part of the family, which included the Sanders' young son Robin who became very fond of Cohan, not least because on every visit he would bring him some new toy or interesting gadget. Jim, who was a rising young star in the world of theology – he would go on to become one of the most distinguished biblical scholars of his generation, being one of the translators of the Dead Sea Scrolls – was very tolerant of his wife's relationship with Cohan, which he understood from the start was not going to lead her into trouble. Not so others at the university, which like many such insular institutions, had a network of gossips. On one occasion, after a late class, Cohan and Dora had gone to a late-night diner for a meal when they were spotted by one of the secretaries, who eyed them knowingly. Dora was worried, knowing the woman to be a gossip monger, and she did not want her husband, who was then untenured, to be put in an awkward position so she raised her concern with him. The next day, he went into the office, saw the secretary and said, 'Hi, I hear you bumped into my wife last night. What were you doing out so late?' No rumours were started. Jim Sanders would later observe, 'For me Bob was the most perfect example of a secular Jew; he knew that he could never be perfect but that there was no harm in trying to attain perfection.'

The relationship was a fruitful one and the open classes held on Thursday evenings attracted over fifty students, as the *Rochester Democrat and Chronicle* reported under the banner:

'A Way of Freedom Through Movement'

Every Thursday evening some fifty women in the city don a costume for two hours that has nothing to do with the latest fashion.

Most of them are married and have children. Some are businesswomen who work 9-5 type jobs and still others are high school and college graduate students. None of that really matters because while they are together they have one strong common interest – a love of the dance.[74]

Sanders was a tireless and enthusiastic promoter and many articles appeared in the local press about Cohan and his classes. Numbers soared after one writer described him as 'a dark-haired young man, who had about him a kind of Byronic aura'.[75]

Cohan's teaching career in New England went from strength to strength and he became the major teacher of modern dance in the region. He soon found himself with over twenty-two classes a week criss-crossing the region between Rochester, Buffalo, Boston, New Haven, and Rhode Island. It was a punishing schedule and Cohan flew or drove; he invested in a very fast NG3 Roadster and he could make the 200 miles from New York to Boston in three hours. On more than one occasion, he fell asleep at the wheel, nearly coming off the road and crashing. He was eventually joined on his journeys by two companions; the first was a pug dog named Charlie and then a more unorthodox pet iguana called Mr Iguana. The snuffling of Charlie and the scratchings of Mr Iguana helped to break up the monotony of engine noise and provided interesting discussion points when he arrived at his destinations.

Eventually the travel became too much and so did Walter Martin, and he made the decision to open a studio in Boston and concentrate his work there, although he maintained a tiny apartment in New York. This made sense as he had substantial classes at Harvard's Loeb Drama Centre, Radcliffe College, and the New England Conservatory. The studio was opposite the conservatory in the Gainsborough Studios, at 295 Huntington Avenue. Actually, there were two studios that constituted the Robert Cohan School of the Dance; they were loft rooms that Cohan kitted out with linoleum floors and mirrors and he would rent one out and use the other.

The school proved very popular and offered classes in modern, from beginners to advanced, modern jazz at intermediate level, modern dance for young people, and rhythmic movement – a special class for non-dancers designed to 'develop balance, coordination, and perfect the body [sic]'. The classes were competitively priced in sixteen-week courses; one class per week at $40, two classes at $64, and three at $90; young people paid $30. Most of his students were gifted amateurs but there were occasional exceptions, and Cohan found himself teaching the young Gus Solomons Jr, then an architecture student at the Massachusetts Institute of Technology, and Elizabeth Walton. Both would go onto exceptional careers in modern dance, Solomons working with Graham and Cunningham and then into a long-lasting career as an independent artist while Walton would become one of Paul Taylor's leading dancers.

For many of his pupils, Cohan was their only teacher, and he swiftly realised that he needed 'to be the right teacher for everybody'. His students, for the most part, were not going to be professionals but they were serious and committed and he had to give them challenging enough material to develop as well-rounded dancers. He therefore opened up the strict form of the Graham Technique – which was always his basic working model – to incorporate other techniques; more balletic work for the calves and feet, arm isolations from Indian dance, and isolations from jazz. As a result of these changes and additions, the Graham Technique became less percussive and a more lyrical, flowing movement quality evolved.

The core for Cohan in this evolution was the use of breath. Graham Technique is fundamentally based on the act of breathing, a pillar in most schools of yoga. Pearl Lang remembered that 'many exercises [in Graham], particularly on the floor, bore relation to tantric thought which underlies hatha yoga'. Cohan investigated this further and became fascinated by the concept of Body Breathing. This involved finding a way of developing the understanding that as you breathe with your lungs, you displace the lymph in your body. Visualisation techniques such as imagining breathing in the arms or the legs assisted in this process. The aim was to develop a strong sense of the ebb and flow of the fluid in the body, which in turn has an impact on the performance of movement.

Even with amateurs, Cohan's class exercises had more than a physical purpose, and he would write later in his book, *The Dance Workshop*, 'dance exercises the whole being.' Cohan sees this as taking place in part through a quasi-religious confrontation with the self as in Jungian analysis. He observes: 'As you try to improve your body's movements, you will collide head-on with your emotions – which may have been in control of your body until now.' These were large themes for amateurs to engage with, but Cohan had been trained by an artist and knew no other way; it was always serious.

In these years of freedom, Cohan worked on and developed a more focussed sensory experience of the body. Gus Solomons Jr found Cohan's teaching inspirational and counts himself lucky that to have studied with Cohan before he went to the Graham Studio. He believes that at the time, Cohan was rediscovering Graham for himself and that he needed to jettison the emotional base for so much of the movement to rediscover the physical truth of the technique. This 'cooler' form of Graham which Cohan began to explore in Boston is what he would ultimately bring to England, where it found a welcoming audience. He would sum up his approach to teaching in an interview with Isabel Ferguson which appeared in the *Christian Science Monitor*. She noted that, though he had danced with Graham, he had now 'developed his own mode of movement' and that,

> Freshness, dynamism, immediacy are qualities much sought-after in modern dance. As Mr Cohan explains, the aim is always to break the form, to have no set style. The dancer must respond to each new mood, create afresh each movement.

> Mr Cohan finds teaching beginners a renewing process: 'The more I teach the more concerned I am with basic things – a walk, the lifting of the arm. The teacher tries to do two things: give the student a physical description so that he knows how the body makes an action; and also charge that action with meaning, so that the full implications are seen. For example the plié, a basic down-up movement, can mean no, yes, black, white, etc.'

> But doesn't teaching become irksome sometimes? 'No', he replied, 'not if you look for something new in it each time. If I can't do a plié or a walk fresh for myself each time, I might as well stop teaching. There are no finite limitations to the body', he continues, 'Is there and end to the number of sports records being broken? Someone will always run an 1/8th of a second faster than the last man. In teaching I always look for fresh understanding of each movement. A new understanding of an old understanding.

> People who know how to dance come into your class and dance the first day. You can't force anyone to learn. You can only produce the atmosphere conducive to learning. Make it easy for the student. Give everything you know. Sometimes it is difficult to teach a good student everything, because you think, 'He will be better than I', Mr Cohan admits frankly, 'but you have to see that you are not going to lose anything. You are free if you teach the very things which you think maybe executed better by someone else. It is because you teach them that you become better yourself. It requires love and sympathy.'

Out of all this teaching, Cohan developed work as a choreographer. Sometime in 1958, he had made a solo for himself for a now forgotten performance in Boston. The work, entitled *Streams* was inspired by a haiku-like poem by Walter Martin which appeared in some early programme notes:

> Streams
> Of a half remembered attitude
> Ease a now
> With
> Poses of perfection

Set to piano music by Alan Hovhaness, it was a short solo which, from its open Buddha-like pose, moved to convey the spirit of calm or turbulent waters which one reviewer perplexingly felt 'combine[d] plasticity of movement with angularity of pose';[76] he was keen to perform it again and to add to it. This happened at the University of Rochester on 14 March 1959, when at Dora Sanders' insistence, he danced the solo in a curious mixed bag of a performance which included the ball scene from Menotti's opera *Amelia Goes to the Ball*.

It was a success and Cohan was asked if he would like to present some more work at the university as part of their 1959 Festival of Contemporary Arts, which would be held in the autumn. The festival was a three-day event that included music, poetry, and drama – a production of Dylan Thomas' *Under Milk Wood* – and it was just the opportunity Cohan had been hoping for and he happily agreed. Realising he would need more than solos, he asked Matt Turney from the Graham Company to join him in the evenings and the Robert Cohan Dance Company was born. Over the next three years, he would work with Turney, creating a number of solos and duos which they performed whenever and wherever they could. Cohan and Turney were perfectly matched as dancers – both had a mystical, other-worldly air about them and Turney was completely in tune with Cohan in his approach to dance. She had found that 'Martha's stage was ritual, completely, literally ritual for me… the first and purest vehicle of meaning',[77] and in Cohan she found a perfect partner to carry on this tradition.

Cohan had known Alan Hovhaness and admired his music before Graham had used it for *Ardent Song*, having been introduced to him by Eugene Lester. Cohan liked his simplicity both as a man and in his musical materials, which drew on Middle Eastern elements, much like the music used in Gurdjieff's dance exercises. Hovhaness was not precious about his work and he was happy to suggest music to dancers and then allow them to perform it free of charge. He was also somewhat eccentric and Cohan remembers one time sitting with him and a few friends with the composer improvising at the piano for over two hours. His wife told Cohan that 'sometimes he plays until his fingers bleed; when the keys get dirty he stops'. Hovhaness' music was written for all sorts of unusual combinations of instruments and he offered one of his works for marimba and percussion ensemble for Cohan's new dance entitled *Praises*.

The work opened with two indistinct figures standing silhouetted in the shadows of deep blue lighting, Hovhaness' bell like sounds gently ringing in the distance. Once the scene was set, the dancers began to move; 'silently the figures swung, turned, leapt, bended, swayed, sometimes in unison, sometimes alone'. The effect for one reviewer was 'as though the air were a solid mass to be pushed and moulded by their liquid forms'.[78] The movements Cohan devised for himself implied fluid shapes which contrasted with those for Turney which were more bird-like with rhythmically intricate flutterings and sculpted, beautiful use of hands and arms. For a work entitled *Praises*, it was a somewhat slow-moving dance emotionally; but was a perfect concert opener, and later would often be used as such, allowing both dancers and audience to warm to one another. It was more of an *alborada*, an awakening of the dawn, and a blossoming to life, than a work of praise.

Turney's beautifully expressive hands had spurred Cohan to begin a solo for her set to some cool jazz. In India, he had purchased a beautiful jacket with numerous tiny embroidered buttons; the dance was to consist of Turney simply yet exquisitely putting on the jacket and buttoning it up, all the interest being in the sensuous articulation of her fingers. It sadly never made it to the stage.

Ever interested in things esoteric, Cohan had been reading Schoff and Carus' 1912 text *Tammuz, Pan and Christ: Notes on a Typical Case of Myth Transference and Development*, in which the authors chart the development of the myth that on the night Christ was born the great god Pan died. This complex and involved theme was the subject of *Vestige*, to piano music by Eugene Lester. Cohan's performance as Pan was praised as exciting and dramatic, but the work was seen by critics as too literary a concept to be the subject for a successful dance. A further criticism was that the large cloak that Cohan manipulated à la Graham obscured too much of the material and was used in too melodramatic a way.

Streams joined *Praises* and *Vestige* as the three dance works in the concert on 8 November 1959 in Kilbourn Hall, a space not really suited to dance performance. The dances were sandwiched between a lecture on Modern Church Architecture and a recital of Kodály's *Missa Brevis*. They were such a success that they were invited to perform again on 4 December in a performance shared with the university percussion ensemble. The request had been happily received, but what was not so well received by Cohan was Sanders' request that he talk to the audience before each piece. Surprisingly, looking at where his career would take him, Cohan has always had a horror of speaking in public, it was one of the reasons he danced, but Sanders was persuasive. He duly went out before the dances, explained to the audience the style of the piece, the ideas, the music, and the costumes, before stepping back into role for the dance. In spite of this horror, he remembers it as one of the best performances he ever did.

They performed again on 2 April 1960 when they joined the Modern Dance Club in a programme that included folk dances as well as modern work. One of these was Dora Sanders' own dance *Pandora's Box* in which a packing crate was wheeled on stage and out of which continually appeared an unbelievably large crowd of dancers. Among this fun Cohan and Turney presented two new dances, *Seaborne* and *The Pass*. These same works would be presented at the more prestigious setting of the Ted Shawn Theatre at Jacob's Pillow in Lee, Massachusetts, on 2 August, where they garnered some good reviews, particularly from Walter Terry, chief dance critic for the *New York Herald Tribune*.

Seaborne, to music by James Anderson, a young composer who played for classes at Cohan's studio was an abstract work that Walter Terry found 'notable chiefly for the beautiful dancing of the two young artists'. Choreographically, he thought it 'somewhat formless' though it did contain a central adagio exhibiting 'some lovely passages of freshly conceived and well-ordered movement'. *The Pass* was, however, in a different category with Terry feeling that,

> … Mr Cohan has found form as well as purpose and come up with a highly exciting work in which he probes the evil nature of the Greek Sphinx, transforming allure into a snare of destruction and hot physical passion into frightening evil. It's an absorbing work of theatre, with marvellous score by Eugene Lester, and both Mr Cohan and Miss Turney dance it with technical bravura and telling dramatic power.[79]

The Pass would go on to become their most popular duet, appearing in almost all of their performances. The dance concerned the Theban Sphinx (Turney) and her attendant (Cohan) and was set fifteen minutes before the arrival of the first victim. The sets and costumes were by Walter Martin, who when sober proved himself a gifted designer and would design most of Cohan's early work. Even so his Catwoman-like designs for Cohan in this dance, complete with jewelled mask and morning gloves, do seem a little elaborate, more suited to Las Vegas than the world of modern dance.

The music by Eugene Lester, a score for flute and percussion, was in the Hovhaness tradition of using Middle Eastern scales and intervals to create an atmosphere of gentle exoticism. Lester and Cohan were good friends who had known each other before Lester had begun working as Graham's music director. He was 'retiring and reticent with a big lanky English body', and 'did not look as though he would be very creative', but he was. Like Louis Horst he was happy to invest a lot of time with his dancers, watching rehearsals, making notes, and then playing extracts of his music so that they could select what was most appropriate for the dance. Cohan found working with him ideal, more like two friends collaborating than a formal composer-choreographer relationship, and Lester would go on to become the music director of Cohan's small group.

Most of Cohan's works from this early period have almost completely disappeared, existing only as photographs and reviews. Three works – *Streams*, *Hunter of Angels*, and *Eclipse*, were later staged in London, and the latter two have become dance classics. *The Pass* was thought to have been lost, but this author found a recording of it in the archive of Israeli dancer Rena Schenfeld, made for rehearsal purposes when Cohan staged it on the Batsheva Company in 1964. It provides a fascinating insight into Cohan's movement material at this time. He says of this period, 'I had studied with Louis Horst so I knew the rules and I had danced with Martha, watching her make it up in front of me, so I knew her rules. I knew how she worked and it was all self-evident.' Taking this into account, it is not surprising that the work is heavily indebted to Graham's narrative style nor that it was not staged in London, where its narrative-driven formula would certainly have looked dated, even less than ten years after it was made. In London, Cohan developed the style of stylised abstraction he would demonstrate in *Hunter of Angels* and *Eclipse*. In *The Pass*, characters are broadly drawn in 'an exotic series of manoeuvres which at times seems more reminiscent of the Hindu world and art of the thuggee than ancient Greece'.[80]

It is almost melodramatic, a point brought home by the final offstage scream which occurs as the assistant closes the curtain and which was noted as over the top even by a number of writers at the time. Nonetheless, Cohan knows how to create and develop character and to tell an erotically charged story, and throughout the dance Turney was perfect as a mythologically seductive yet cruel creature, who perfectly complemented Cohan's catlike eagerness. Terry ended his review by telling his readers:

> The two duets which I saw them dance augur well for the future of this new modern dance duo, for they not only make an exceptionally handsome team but it is also apparent that Mr Cohan already possesses the instinct and much of the skill to create effective and challenging pieces for the two.[81]

More positive feedback had come from José Limón, who visited Cohan backstage to tell him how much he had enjoyed the dances, but advised him to always show his work to Louis Horst before the public. Cohan was struck by the comment and, as soon as he could, telephoned Horst to arrange an appointment. When he arrived at Horst's apartment, the first thing Horst said to him was how much he had enjoyed the pieces and that if he had been a choreographer, that was the way he would make dances. Cohan was tempted to say thank you and leave, but stayed and the two had a useful discussion about minor details in the works and what Cohan would do next. What he planned would be a major undertaking but first he had to get through a busy summer.

The summer of 1960 was taken up with teaching classes in modern and jazz at the Ellis Memorial Gym in Boston and working on an unusual project. This was a musical called *The New Boy*, presented by the Pilgrim Fellowship of the First Church, Congregational, in Cambridge. The book was by Pastor Jay Buell, lyrics by Warren Blackstock, jazz music by Yusuf Emed, a recent graduate from the New England Conservatory. The story concerned Denny Simpson, the 'new boy' at a high school who, in his efforts to do 'something big', gets into trouble. But eventually, through the interest of a local pastor and his daughter Ginny, Denny starts to grow up. The cast was a mix of regular church-going youth and students from Harvard and much was made, at a time of racial tension, of the integration of 'Negroes' and whites. *Youth Magazine* commented, 'One can only be grateful that Robert Cohan, a stranger to the group, was willing to work months with a gang of kids, most of whom had no dance experience.'[82] Cohan remembers it as being a time-consuming but a worthwhile experience. The few images remaining from the performances show his staging to have been influenced by his experience with Jack Cole and Jerome Robbins.

The performances at Rochester and at Jacob's Pillow had made Cohan realise how much he missed performing. Flush with the success of his choreographies, he decided to add to the repertoire of the duo and actively seek out more engagements. Even with their reputations this was not so easy, as outside the university circuit the possibilities for young choreographers to show work was limited. But with Sanders' help he received a commission from the University School of Liberal and Applied Studies for two new dances. These would be added to his existing works to form an all-Cohan evening which would be performed at Rochester on 8 and 9 October, followed by a further performance at John Hancock Hall in Boston on 15 October. These shows to guaranteed audiences – if no one else came then his students would – were preparation for a performance at the Hunter Playhouse in New York which he had booked for 29 October. A New York performance was a major step and he had no guarantee as to how his works, successful in the northern regions, would be in the critical gaze of a sophisticated New York audience.

Cohan had to work intensively with Turney to prepare for the October performance. There was a great deal to do! Turney had commitments with Graham and he had extensive teaching engagements, including a new course in movement for actors at the Loeb Drama Centre beginning in the autumn. The performances would include *Streams, Praises, The Pass, Seaborne,* and *Vestige,* and the two commissions, *Veiled Woman* – a solo for Turney – and *The Quest,* a duet. All three works would be in the classical narrative style, exploring intriguing quasi-mystical subjects.

Cohan loved working with Turney and the movement for the new works flowed easily. He usually demonstrated the material he wanted her to do; being a good mimic, he could move in the way he knew she would and be like her. But there were no hard and fast rules which some choreographers apply. One approach he never took, however, was to improvise in the search for a movement, rather he 'improvised what I thought it should be and then in that sense of improvising I made the movement. If it wasn't right I threw it away and I did it again but I was always working on movement with a sense of continuity.'

Cohan's inspiration for *Veiled Woman* came from a small primitive statue of a woman that had been found somewhere in the Middle East; for Cohan, 'it was very mysterious as the face seemed to be covered'. When the opportunity came to make a new solo for Turney, the statue seemed a perfect starting point and he made a dance that was very personal to her as 'as she was a very complicated woman, covered with a beautiful, quiet and composed physical elegance'. The dance, set to an aggressive, complex piano score by Leonard Taffs, was 'a revealing of the complications under a calm elegant exterior' and for Cohan it 'worked very well because Matt performed the personal process of unveiling so well'. The theme of unveiling or revealing is one that Cohan would return to many times in his career. For critics, the dance was seen as 'rather obscure in meaning', but Turney's performance was 'ravishing' with 'her slim graceful form, torn and agitated like a bird escaping from a net'.[83]

Cohan is philosophical about critics and the problems they have in writing about dance, noting that 'people sometimes look for meaning in a literal sense where a dance can give you the meaning in an experiential sense that you cannot put into words. That makes it very difficult for critics who want to write the meaning in words.' Over the years this 'problem' – for the critics, not Cohan – would surface frequently in relation to his work.

The second new work, *The Quest, an allegory of the soul*, with music for small ensemble by Lester, was based on the story of *Sleeping Beauty*, and both dancers where suitably attired, Cohan's costume in particular resembling that of a romantic ballet prince. The idea was to undermine the classic tale by asking the question: 'What would happen if the princess was not overjoyed at being awoken by a kiss?' As with *Vestige*, the quality of the dancing was praised: 'Mr Cohan as the Knight and Miss Turney as the Lady performed with great beauty and purity of style.'[84] But the literary nature of the work was not made apparent in the movement which P. W. Manchester in *Dance News* felt 'suffered from an all pervading vagueness'.[85] She went on to complain that 'it never became clear as to why the Lady lying seemingly dead, on her tomb, should have got up and been so extremely active while the Knight went through all kinds of torments without resolving anything'.[86] These quibbles apart and the comment that a number of reviewers made that the work was too long, most felt that there was much to admire in terms of movement and staging pattern. The dance had an elaborate set design by Walter Martin – one writer commenting that 'it was all moonlight and marble',[87] however the marble was not real but skilfully painted wood. It was in this artifice that it became clear that certain dramaturgical aspects of the dance had not been thought through, as P. W. Manchester scolded Cohan saying 'although it is perfectly permissible to paint a piece of wood to resemble marble, it is not permissible to hurl a dagger so that the point buries itself in the slab. Wood, yes; marble, yes; but make up your mind which you want it to be.'[88]

The concert was a great success in both Rochester and Boston where it was presented to a hall 'filled with an audience composed mainly of young people in their early twenties who were deeply absorbed and most enthusiastic'.[89] Isabel Ferguson, writing for the *Christian Science Monitor*, summed up the whole evening positively: 'Mr Cohan's choreography is imaginative and convincing flavoured with spices of ethnic and oriental dancing, yet well blended as a whole. There are passages breath-taking in their poignancy.' Another part of her article shows how closely related Cohan's teaching of technique was to his choreography as the review could just as easily relate to his classes: 'Mr Cohan works for the whole body, making the audience just as aware of his back muscles and spinal vertebrae as of his curling fingers and upturned toes.'[90]

In spite of the success of the performances, Cohan was still nervous about New York. It was for him a major event, he had not presented any work in the city before but the fame of both he and Turney as dancers meant that they would play to a capacity house, which as it turned out included most of the modern dance world, including Graham, Ruth St Denis, and Horst. He needed not have worried for as Walter Terry wrote, 'because they are such an unusually handsome pair, it is a pleasure just to look at them and because they are superbly trained, it is an unalloyed joy simply to watch them move. But pictorial delights are not enough in dance and it is fortunate that as choreographer Mr Cohan has something to deliver.'[91]

Terry, who generously gave a sizeable and well-thought review to the concert, went on to write:

> This is not to say that Mr Cohan is yet a master choreographer. In certain respects he is still a novice, still a searcher for a style of his own but both imagination and adventure are present in his creative efforts. As a Graham product, it is understandable that there are Grahamisms in his work. Some he has assimilated and used for his own purposes; others seem like interpolations from the Graham past. But this, at present was no great fault, for in time, these will disappear.[92]

He then pinpointed an aspect of Cohan's work that over the years many more critics would highlight:

> Before I turn to the considerable virtues of the program, I would like to touch upon one other flaw. No matter what the theme, there is a cool remoteness about Mr Cohan's work. If passion is present, it is as if it were remembered and not of the instant. Perhaps this is due to a form which Mr Cohan uses and this is in the shape of rituals. A ritual is a formalized memory. Rituals are wonderfully suitable to dance but I would wish that Mr Cohan would balance ritual with dances suggestive of dramatic immediacy. He comes close to it but not enough.[93]

Many of Gurdjieff's teachings emphasise ritual approaches to life and in his early dance works his aim was 'to plunge participants into intense and formative experiences';[94] Graham, particularly in her early dances, also often adopted a ritualistic approach, and was certainly intending her audience to have intense experiences. Louis Horst's approach to the teaching of choreography was in a sense ritualistic, depending as it did on the completion of a number of set forms which changed only a little over the years. It is not surprising therefore that Cohan should adopt a ritualistic approach in his dances. The problem with rituals, which by definition largely use actions for their symbolic value, is that they can, as Terry suggested in his review, seem remote, passionless, and alienating for those uninitiated to their mysteries. Over the many years of his

career as a choreographer, critics would often comment on the remoteness of
Cohan's dancers, their performance style, super cool and iconic, separated by
more than the fourth wall. Had the concept of a fifth wall – the barrier between
critic and practitioner – been prevalent during Cohan's active years, a whole
barrage of mystified reviews could perhaps have been avoided.

On the whole however, Terry's comments were positive and for him:

> … the high points of this recital far outnumbered the faults. First of all, Mr
> Cohan is not afraid of the theatre. He used elaborate, but pertinent lighting
> effects, his costumes (with one glaring exception) were stunning, the décor
> was striking indeed and, as a choreographer, he had no fear of dealing with
> romance, heroics, melodramatics, pathos and those emotions which make
> the theatre exciting. In this, he differs from certain of his contemporaries who
> tend to purge dancing of feeling.[95]

The doyen of New York dance critics, John Martin, was more forthright in his
criticism:

> Choreographically, Mr Cohan found it tough going at times to create a long
> programme for only two dancers. The two dramatic works that constituted
> the body of the performance, however, have strong ideas behind them, and
> they contain a number of striking inventions and stirring phrases. It may be,
> indeed, that there are too many of both; the choreographer has not yet learned
> to quit when he has made a point.
>
> Certainly he moves marvellously as a dancer, and with a deep expressiveness.
> That he still employs the essential style and a great deal of the specific vocabulary
> of Martha Graham is not surprising since he spent eleven years practising and
> teaching them. It is nevertheless a handicap for him, for hers is a personal
> style resulting in a personal vocabulary. The method of its production is what
> is basic and impersonal, and if only the dancers who come out of her school
> could track down the method and produce by the same process their own
> vocabulary, how great a step they would take forward.[96]

It is curious that Martin talks of finding a new vocabulary, a new syntax yes,
but looking for a new vocabulary would be like asking a ballet dancer not to
use ballet steps. Over the years, Cohan would not develop a new vocabulary
but his syntax would be recognisable as wholly his own. Other reviewers were
generally complimentary, though none were as perspicacious as Terry, and the
risky venture was deemed a success.

The success of the performances did not lead to any great change in Cohan's
working life, if anything he was working harder. In addition to his school he was
still touring all over New England, teaching – a new post delivering movement
for actors had begun at the Loeb Drama Centre in Boston. He was also asked

onto panels and to give talks on dance. April 1961 saw him joining Dora Sanders at Rutgers University in New Jersey as part of a symposium on dance in colleges, an area on which he had fast become an expert. And in a pattern that would continue when he moved to England he found his time taken up with panels on choreography, technique, the role of dance in education, and in this one at Rutgers University in New Jersey, 'What dance means to me'.

Bolstered somewhat by his choreographic successes he decided to renew his contact with Martha Graham. It had been over three years since the split and there had been no communication between the two. She had had notable success with her two works from this period (her evening-length masterpiece *Clytemnestra* and *Embattled Garden*) and it still grated on him that he had missed being part of the premiere of the work made on his body, so he called and asked for a meeting. She was very polite and so was he and she was charmed by the white orchid in a pot he brought as a gift. Never one to skirt an issue however, she asked him, 'Bob, just what is it that you want?' His response, 'Nothing. I just wanted to see you' broke the tension between the two and Graham immediately became giggly, flirty, and charming. She chided him for leaving her and they both admitted they had missed one another. He had truly gone to see her without any idea of looking for work but within a couple of weeks, he received a phone call asking him to take over the Saturday morning children's classes at the studio.

More choreographic work appeared when he created the movement for a staging of Purcell's opera *Dido and Aeneas*, shown on 18 May 1961 at the New England Conservatory's Jordan Hall. Shown as part of a mixed bill, including two ballets by Esther Brooks, to music by Rossini, it 'proved the masterwork of the bountiful evening'.[97] The dancers included Cohan's star pupils Elizabeth Walton and Gus Solomons Jr, and Kevin Kelly in the *Boston Globe* thought the dancing 'remarkable' and 'brilliant', though he attributed the choreography to Solomons, which was not the case.[98]

At the same time as working on *Dido* in Boston during the week, at the weekends he was busy at Jean Erdman's studio on 17th Street and Fifth Avenue in New York working with Turney on a new duet to be premiered at the American Dance Festival to be held at Connecticut College in the summer. This work called *Eclipse*, became one of his great successes, and continued to have a life into the twenty-first century, being frequently staged for a variety of performers.

This 'interplanetary duel', as one review called the dance, developed out of Cohan's reading of various mythologies and one particular Native American myth of what happens when the woman of the moon eclipses the male of the sun; this fascinated him and he felt would be eminently suitable for dance. He was most interested in the relationship possibilities, the form of the eclipse being that moon and sun are joined together but also wipe each other out – in one sense a relationship that goes wrong, something with which Cohan was very familiar.

For Cohan, 'the interesting thing about the dance was the direction the movement took. It doesn't have the usual flow of lyric choreography I like to do, it is very minimalistic and static. It was partly due to the way I made it to Eugene's music.' Lester was fully conversant with all of the latest trends in music, and when Cohan said to him that he wanted the score to sound 'out of space', he was happy to oblige. The electronic score to the 1956 film *Forbidden Planet*, a space-age take on Shakespeare's *The Tempest*, by Louis and Bebe Barron, was well known at the time and Lester's score clearly owes something to that classic work. For Cohan's score, Lester had the idea that he wanted all the notes to sound backwards, but with the minimal equipment he had this proved impractical. But what he could do was to cut individual notes from his sound tapes – approximately a quarter inch of tape – and splice them together in such a way that the effect was almost what he wanted. This was incredibly time-consuming and problematic in Erdman's noisy studio; in the end, Cohan bought huge sheets of soundproofing which he and Lester stuck together to cover the windows. Lester worked all night, when there was not so much traffic, and timed his recordings so that he would miss the roar of the Fifth Avenue bus as it pulled up outside. Each morning, he would have completed five feet of spliced tape and he would play it while Cohan would choreograph. This fragmentary approach – five feet of tape is only a few moments of sound – accounts for the fragmented nature of the movement material, so unlike anything Cohan had done before or did afterwards. But Cohan found the whole process 'very exciting', and despite the fragmentary nature of its construction, it was for him one of those dances which 'appeared' and he 'witnessed' its birth. Cohan likes 'dances that come when you don't have to go back and redo a section, and what you do is right… and that the movement stays and you go on until the end and your mind is whirring all the time. You are remembering it all and putting it into context but you do not have to do it over again.'

Eclipse was such a work. He even dreamt one of the key images of the piece. At the beginning of the dance, the two figures enter from opposite sides and take the 'eclipse position', show their relationship and then exit. Cohan worried about the actual 'eclipse position' but then one night he dreamt it 'knees bent back to back arms outstretched'; he was so excited he could barely wait for the next rehearsal. As he knew it would, the position worked instantly on both of their bodies, and so clear was this image that it became the poster for the next season.

Even though Cohan always revises works when staged on different bodies, the dance movement in this piece has never changed, 'its simple angularity is fairly easy to recreate', and the material allows for the dancers to relate in different ways. The costumes were, however, changed a number of times over the years. At the first performances, Cohan and Turney wore tights and leotards; she in pale mauve as the moon and he in red/orange as the sun. The tights and leotards were covered in Indian embroidery of moons and suns appliquéd onto the costumes. This pre-hippy stuff was new at the time and no one had seen it, but it very quickly became dated and Cohan adapted the costumes, finally settling on designs by Peter Farmer.

Although it became one of his signature pieces, at the time it was often criticised for being too long or overly repetitive, with one writer even suggesting it should be cut down by half.[99] But it has stood the test of time and at celebrations for his eightieth birthday in 2005, Judith Mackrell wrote: '... in its attempts to channel hot emotion through cool, geometric form it feels very 50s, very experimental. As the two dancers prowl around each other, their rhythmic spatters of dance and bold gestures flare with danger. The emotion is coiled tight in the movement, waiting to spring – a trademark of Cohan's work.'[100]

The artistic success did not – as ever – mean financial success and in the *New York Herald Tribune* of 18 June 1961, Walter Terry gave some space to Cohan's plight, outlining a situation which was as familiar then as it is now:

'Subsidy Urgent as Costs Climb'

'As your accountant, I strongly advise you to stop giving dance recitals.' This discouraging comment was delivered to Robert Cohan, a superb dancer and a gifted choreographer. The accountant, of course had a point... Mr Cohan and his beautiful partner Matt Turney had given four recitals and Mr Cohan had lost $6,000 on the venture. Attendance had been excellent, but income from the box office did not meet expenses. It rarely if ever does with dance events these days.

In order to give these recitals, Mr Cohan worked hard at teaching. Each week, his circuit carried him from New York City to Boston to Rochester and back again. He averaged nineteen classes a week and frequently taught five classes, each one hour and a half long during a single day. While pursuing this schedule of instructing others, he also had to keep in training himself, rehearse his repertory, and create new works. That he was carted off to hospital for two days was understandable. Diagnosis? Exhaustion. His accountant to the contrary, Mr Cohan is planning a similar teaching-performing schedule for next season.

One venue missing from the schedule was the University of Rochester which Cohan had left in May. His time there had been enormously successful not only for himself but for the development of dance in the city, but after three years he decided it was time to leave. Without the support of Dora Sanders' and the University of Rochester, it is unlikely Cohan's career as a choreographer would have taken off as rapidly as it did. An article in the *Rochester Herald* noted with pride that his Hunter College success had been nourished by the university, 'the result of the combined faith of many Rochesterians who believe in the importance of young artists having a chance to make their statement.'[101]

Cohan gained more choreographic opportunities in the coming years, which saw an expansion of his group from a duet to an ensemble sometimes numbering eight. His 'muse' Matt Turney would not be among them. Her husband, who was of a jealous and overbearing nature, and who had never really approved of her dancing with Cohan, encouraged her to leave and so Cohan turned to a pool of dancers working with Graham to replace her. Over the next few years, the company included, at different times, Bertram Ross, Mary Hinkson, Linda Hodes, Robert Powell, Juliet Fisher, Carol Drisin, and Noemi Lapzeson.

It was back 'in the fold' at the Graham Studio that another of Cohan's most successful and lasting works was made. Cohan knew he wanted another man to dance with and he turned to his close friend Bertram Ross who agreed. Over the years the two had grown into the leading male Graham dancers, but the two could not have been more different. Cohan in his teaching and performing was enigmatic, cool and mercurial, whereas Ross was his opposite, fiery, dramatic, and flamboyant; their differences provided a perfect coupling for a duet.

Searching for a theme for the new work *Hunter of Angels*, Cohan remembered a phrase from the mystical *Emerald Tablet* of Hermes Trismegistus: 'That which is above is like that which is below and that which is below is like that which is above, to achieve the wonders of the one thing.'[102] In a stream-of-consciousness fashion he linked this to the Bible, conflating stories surrounding Jacob and Esau – the brothers' fight in Rebekah's womb to see who will be born first and thus inherit everything; Jacob's wrestling with the angel; and the dream of the ladder to heaven with angels climbing it. The dance therefore concerns transformation, from earth to heaven, from man to angel, from the hairy, brutish hunter Esau, to the smooth-skinned thinker Jacob. In the final image of the dance Esau is seen hanged and Jacob is transformed into an angel-like figure. This is achieved in *Hunter* with great economy of means and the choreography developed out of a serendipitous discovery. One day Cohan went into the large studio at the Graham School and found a very tall ladder lying on the floor. Someone had been changing the light bulbs, and for some reason had gone off and left it open on the floor forming a wide V shape. Cohan looked at it 'and thought that was a godsend! It looked like the wings of an angel.' His mind began racing and he immediately called Ross and asked him to hurry to the studio, which fortunately had no classes at the time.

Cohan found working with Ross very easy; the two were good friends, Ross – who was a choreographer in his own right – was very creative and 'it was just magic to make it up together'. With Ross, Cohan did not need to demonstrate everything, he could show a phrase or movement and Ross would be able to develop and extend it – they were trained in the same technique and shared a common vocabulary and outlook. Of course, if Ross' vision strayed from Cohan's, he was able to bring it back, gently. They began playing with the ladder, seeing what images they could create with the apparatus, and they were lucky for right at the beginning of the process he found the 'key'. At the time, Cohan had a theory

> ... that at one point when you choreograph, either you work and make the
> dancers improvise, or more like me, you find a movement that is suddenly
> like a key, and that movement is the key to the dance. And once you have that
> key the rest is not so hard because you can then see the style of the material
> and you can expand both forward and backward and you can rearrange the
> material, add that movement at the end and the beginning, and it can become
> a theme and variations. But it becomes a key, or source, and you can play with
> it, but once you recognise that, you can use the material and in these years it
> was an important compositional tool.

The 'key' here was the first image they settled on and which would be the final
image of the dance, thus giving a firm anchor to work towards. It is a striking
image in which Esau is seen hanging upside down from the centre of the ladder
while Jacob sits atop in the form of an angel. From this, the pair experimented with
what Cohan described in a 1982 study tape of the work as 'ritualistic movement...
filled with consciousness'.[103] In the tape, Cohan is at pains to explain he searched
for 'interesting' movement – there is little literal gesture in the piece, a point worth
noting as it was choreographed at the same time as the Judson Church group
were experimenting with everyday movement as choreography. Cohan and Ross
rather searched for intriguing shapes and conjunctions of their bodies in relation
to the ladders, which in the work are manipulated into Rebekah's womb, the
angel's stairway to heaven and the manifest separation of heaven and earth. They
never simply climbed the rungs, instead they sculpted their movements to it in
an almost gymnastic way, or more appropriately like 'acrobats of God', their legs
extended in arabesques, their knees threaded through the rungs enabling their
backs to arch and bend, freeing the arms to become wing-like.

All this material was arranged to Bruno Maderna's 1957 *Serenata No. 2* for
eleven instruments, a score Cohan had in his record collection; when he played
it, he could see almost the complete dance. Like *Eclipse*, it 'was one of those
dances that was made before and all I had to do was do it' – the pair completed
in two or three rehearsals.

It was well received at its first performance with the *Boston Herald* finding it

> ... exciting and impressive. With Bertram Ross as a darkly redoubtable, crafty
> Jacob in red tights and Mr Cohan as a majestic shining impartial angel in blue.
> On a lofty double ladder the dancers moved with acrobatic ease in striking
> patterns of combat; sometimes one was in the ascendant, sometimes another.
> The music by Bruno Maderna blended so perfectly with the action that one
> was almost un-conscious of it.[104]

It had its first performance at the Loeb Drama Centre at Harvard on 25 May 1962
where it joined two other new works in a programme performed by Cohan and

Ross with Linda Hodes and Mary Hinkson. The other new works were in marked contrast to the austerity of *Hunter of Angels*. Both had music by Eugene Lester, one was a solo for Cohan and the other a quartet finale for a programme that also included *The Pass* and *Eclipse*.

Chamber of the Liar was 'a none too serious take on the snake in the Garden of Eden', a theme which had continued to interest Cohan since *Can-Can* and aroused the curiosity of the *Christian Science Monitor*'s reviewer who felt that,

> … *Chamber of the Liar* a solo danced by the choreographer, was an intriguing composition, suggesting probably different significances to each spectator. Mr Cohan was discovered in a huge glittering sunburst cage, which may have been the nacelle of a balloon. He continually tried to climb higher in the rigging, but always slipped back. His costume of fleshings was feathered with bright multi colored motifs like trout flies hooked into the skin – perhaps a symbol of fretting entanglement in his own webs. In a final straining to climb once more the whole cage collapsed.[105]

Even this piece did not end his interest in the myth and he would return to the theme in the following year.

Luna Park: An Excursion could not have been more different from the rest of the programme as it was a humorous work drawing on Cohan's childhood visits to Coney Island and concerned two couples having fun at an amusement park. It proved a crowd-pleasing finale with the *Boston Herald* finding it 'was an irresistible spoof, both comic and lyrical, with many tiny dance gestures like trills of laughter'.[106]

The whole Loeb programme, which was repeated on 26 May, garnered mainly good reviews, with the *Christian Science Monitor* lavishly praising Cohan: 'Mr Cohan is one of the most creative and engaging personalities in modern dance. He has virile but not extravagantly muscled technique with the smooth strength of a python, and a dazzling variety of movement refreshingly devoid of clichés.'[107] The *Boston Herald*, while noting that 'the dances, except for *Luna Park*, concerned unrelieved nervous and mental suffering', was magnanimous to acknowledge that 'the dancing was done with extraordinary skill', and that 'a large audience, most of whom were women, gave every sign of pleasure'.[108]

Cohan continued to give pleasure with his enlarged group, travelling the limited circuit of performance spaces and continuing to teach an inordinate number of classes, which now included children's classes at the Graham School. It was, as Terry's article had pointed out, very difficult financially and Cohan couldn't decide what to do when one day, as he was sitting at the desk in his studio in Boston in the morning, the phone rang. Cohan found himself speaking to LeRoy Leatherman, who was as usual very cordial and polite but quickly got to the point, telling him that Graham had been wondering if he would be interested in coming back to join the company. Cohan instantly knew there was more to it than that and said he would have to think about it, but was there anything else? Eventually Leatherman confided that yes, there was a problem, the company had a season in a few weeks and Paul Taylor had suddenly resigned, and Graham wondered if Cohan would learn his roles. Cohan thought very quickly about the problems he was having in running an unsubsidised company:

> I was earning round about $50 a class for teaching twenty-five classes a week and I was flying a lot; though I made over a $1,000 a week, $600 was for flights – that was fine. The problem was the money I had to spend on the company: studio space, costumes, lights, travelling, buying a station wagon to carry the sets; it was hard work and I suddenly thought, well I am 36, I am in good physical shape, I should dance.

These thoughts did not take long and Cohan said yes, he would be interested; however, he was not prepared for Leatherman's request that he come to rehearsal that night. He explained he was in Boston, not New York, and that he had a number of classes to teach and, no, it was not practical. But Leatherman was persuasive and Cohan agreed to make phone calls and find people to cover the afternoon and evening teaching. This he did, and in the late afternoon he boarded a plane and went straight from La Guardia to the Graham Studio.

On entering the tiny changing room, he found himself alone with Paul Taylor and asked him what was going on. Taylor, who at this stage had had some success as a choreographer, explained that he was unhappy with his billing on posters and publicity material and that he wanted more money. Cohan asked him outright if he was planning on leaving and he said he was; with that the two walked into the studio where Taylor was to teach him his part in the new work *Phaedra*. As they went in, they found not an empty room but something resembling a Roman amphitheatre, for assembled on the seating were the entire company with Graham in the centre. Let the games begin! Like some latter day Livia, she had carefully arranged the event to punish Taylor for wanting to leave her and Cohan for actually doing it. It quickly became apparent that it would not be an easy night as every time Taylor demonstrated a move Graham would jump up and say, 'No he doesn't do that, he does this', and whether it was right or not, she would alter the choreography. She would elbow Taylor aside, and pulling Cohan by his hair, would push him to his knees or onto his back saying, 'You go here, then there, not what he wants!' As it went on, Cohan and Taylor found it more and more hysterical, and they did their best to restrain from laughing. A lot of the younger company members were embarrassed by the whole spectacle as Graham was truly angry and they feared that it might spill off onto them. But at that point in his life, Cohan knew her very well and he was not at all frightened by her anger; he and Taylor quite enjoyed themselves as it was such a bizarre, surrealist scene. The 'rehearsal' went on for nearly three hours and by 11 p.m. Cohan knew the piece, and Taylor found that what he thought he knew was not the piece!

Cohan made his farewells and stayed overnight in New York. Not a word had been mentioned about coming back to the company – 'There was no talk of a contract; nothing!' Back in his apartment, he replayed the events in his mind and something made him realise that Taylor was not serious about leaving Graham. He had a busy schedule the next day and had already inconvenienced people, and was not going to do so again, so in the morning he got up very early, caught the first plane to Boston – and waited.

But his hunch had been correct, Taylor danced the season and Cohan never heard anything again – no mention had been made of reimbursing him the plane fare. With hindsight, he believes that Taylor had probably thought of leaving and that as he was being threatening to Graham, her response was to call his bluff by sending for Cohan. As it happened, Taylor's demands were met and he did get more money and his name on the poster, but at the end of that season he left Graham to set up his own group which would go on to become one of the most successful modern dance companies in the world. He and Cohan would continue a very cordial relationship, and a number of Taylor's works would become popular additions to the repertory of Cohan's British company. The events at the studio had triggered something in Cohan and in Graham, and by general agreement it was accepted that Cohan would come back to the company at the next season.

It was with some relief, tinged with sadness, that he closed down his school; although it was very successful, and had played a key role in transforming the dance scene in Boston, it took a great deal of time and energy to run and both of these would be needed elsewhere. So he packed up his small living area, took down the posters, advertisements, and schedules and tried to sell the large and expensive mirrors, but to no avail. Unwilling to just ditch them, Cohan had them transported to his parents' garage where they languished until the mid 1990s when his mother sold the house and moved from Sheepshead Bay to Florida. Then, still unable to find anyone who wanted them, they were smashed up in the front yard by the removal men and the shards thrown in the trash.

With the closure of his school, the Boston connection was not totally severed as he kept his classes at the New England Conservatory which were sponsored by the Special Student Department. He taught three technique classes on Monday and Tuesday: elementary, intermediate, and advanced, and an additional composition class. In these, he was assisted by Virginia Olney who had replaced Mary Ita Hoffman and it was she who taught on Wednesday an additional elementary class. The rest of the week, he was in New York with Graham, where news of his return were warmly welcomed by the dance press – Arthur Todd, writing in *Dance Magazine*, celebrated 'the return of Robert Cohan, a truly superlative dancer, with an unmatched romantic quality, who is now at the peak of his performing powers'.[109]

Chapter 5

Commentary

As it is easy to see, these years were chaotic. It was as if, at first, I gave up the idea of dance as a serious art form. Not that 'show business' can't be serious. Gene Kelly proved that in his amazing dance to *Singin' in the Rain*.

In a funny way, I sometimes think it all goes back to my six-year-old first appearance on stage tapping to 'Swanee River' and then subsequent appearances in several musicals for children. Then I must not forget my fascination, also at a very young age, with the Busby Berkeley and Fred Astaire movies. I know that these early interests keep surfacing all through my life.

After all I have never lost my early interest in seeing and naming trees, birds, and all sorts of snakes and lizards that I used to keep in my bedroom.

So I have to expect that deep inside me lives this nostalgia for show dance. I especially enjoyed being a backup dancer to my childhood crush Ginger Rogers and on top being able to lie next to her and chat a little at the swimming pool.

How strange life can be at times.

At any rate that's what happened to me. I also found myself thirty-one years old, without a job and I had to find a new way of working. In the end it all worked out because I learnt to really teach. In the Graham Studio and at Juilliard, one was part of a teaching team. If you didn't cover something, most likely another teacher did. But being the only teacher meant that if a student was doing something you thought was wrong, you could not blame it on another teacher, it was your fault and your problem.

I worked out for myself these three simple rules, which I have put in print before:

Teach only what you know.

(If you try to teach something you do not know or understand, you can be teaching wrong material. That is simply unfair to the students. We also all know how hard it is to unlearn badly taught basic movements.)

Teach everything you know.

(I have seen teachers keep back as they teach, or not explain details that would help the students to learn faster.

I also discovered that if you teach everything you know you, in some strange process, learn more than you knew before. There is a simple analogy. If your cup is full, nothing more can be put in it. If a student thinks they know everything, you cannot teach them anything.

The same applies to the teacher.)

Teach with love.

(This is simple even though it sounds strange. You must clearly project involvement and care to your students. You must honestly care about their learning and what you are teaching.

In a dance class, the students are very vulnerable. That very vulnerability also makes them very sensitive and aware. It makes them sensitive to criticism but also aware of the teacher's attitude and even honesty.

In teaching dance, you are teaching a personal art form.

If it becomes just a way of earning money or makes you feel good to have authority or power, you should not be teaching dance, as I understand it.)

My entering into choreography had a very simple motive. I wanted to dance on stage again. Choreographing for yourself was the time-honored way for modern dancers to work, at that time. I asked Matt Turney to work with me because we were such good friends, and although we had very different temperaments, we trusted and understood each other. The fact that she had an unusual kind of beauty, physically and in her dancing, helped make that choice easy. I knew that even if the choreography was not brilliant, people could relax and just enjoy seeing the two of us dancing together on stage. That's what happened, sometimes.

I slid into choreographing very easily because I did it when I wanted to, on my own time and in my own time. That way of working was natural to me because I saw Martha working that way for years. Of course, that way of working is lost now for most choreographers. Dancers seldom work for any pay, and if you get an Arts Council grant you will have pressure put on you to perform, perhaps before the work is finished. At that time, we finished the work first and then, if we thought it was ready, we tried to get the dates to show it.

That's called research and development now.

Chapter 6

The Lady of the house of sleep

'A good artist uses their entire life as the basis for their art; everything in
your life becomes part of the driving force that makes the art work.'

(Robert Cohan, 2008)

1963–9

By the autumn of 1962, Cohan was back in the Graham fold just in time for
an extended tour covering central Europe, Scandinavia and the Middle East;
he found the company much changed. Of the older women remained Helen
McGehee, Ethel Winter, Mary Hinkson, and Linda Hodes, to which were added
some newcomers such as Juliet Fisher, Phyllis Gutelius, Carol Fried, and Takako
Asakawa. Of the men, David Woods was rehearsal director and Bertram Ross
remained as Graham's right-hand man and confidant. The rest were an excellent
group of young bucks including Richard Gain, Richard Kutch (known as the Two
Dicks), Robert Powell, Dudley Williams, Peter Randazzo, and Clive Thompson.
Cohan found that the dancers naturally divided themselves into two groups,
old and young, with the youngsters thinking they were the bee's knees, which
in a sense they were. They were all much more technically skilled than the older
dancers, and this thrilled the younger members of the audience, but in terms of
stagecraft they 'were very lightweight'. In the big dramatic roles, which were still
an essential part of Graham's work, they tended to flounder and so she was more
than happy to welcome Cohan back; she needed Cohan and Ross around her and
on stage with her.

At the age of, at least, 68, Graham's abilities were still considerable, but the
previous year she had experienced great difficulty in completing her new work,
Acrobats of God. Her drinking got out of hand – Robert Dunn, her pianist,
thought she was drinking more than a bottle of liquor a day. Her liver had
swelled, she developed diverticulitis, and she began fainting in rehearsals and it
was only with the help of Dunn, and more particularly Bertram Ross, that the
work was completed. The piece turned out to be one of her comic successes, but
its creation set the pattern for the next few years. Cohan remembers that in her
old age, in the studio, when she was confident and relaxed Graham could turn in
'spectacular, hair-raising performances', as good as any he had ever seen her do
in her prime.

But in front of the audience on the stage, where she looked old next to her
dancers, she became frightened, unable to trust her abilities and she began to fail.

Occasionally in public she could excel and Bertram Ross recalled taking her to a party on Fire Island, popular as a gay summer getaway and only a few hours from New York. The assembled queens begged her to dance for them, she refused, but smelling blood they continued baiting her until eventually she began to dance. When she had finished, they were silent, stunned by what she had just done; then the applause began. The magic was still there but too often hidden.

The tour began in Israel with a performance on 24 October at the Habima Theatre in Tel Aviv; in a gesture of goodwill to her benefactress de Rothschild, Graham decided to premiere a new work in her honour. The dance, *Legend of Judith*, would set the pattern for many of her later works in which she created a semi-danced, dramatic role for herself, in this case as the aged Judith looking back on her life, while a younger dancer, in this work Linda Hodes, would play the younger version of the character. Bertram Ross was cast as the evil Holofernes, while Cohan was included as one of three angels. In a further homage to de Rothschild and to Israel, the music was commissioned from the Jewish composer Mordecai Seter, who had been a pupil of Dukas and Boulanger in Paris and which Graham had begun working with in New York. The set, which Graham had only seen in miniature, was by the talented young Israeli artist Dani Karavan; the dance was to be completed in situ, in Israel.

In the set, Karavan had placed in the centre of the stage what looked like an enormous rock that had an overhang that jutted erotically forward, and underneath was a multipurpose shape that could be used as a bench, bed, or table. Graham loved it and as soon as she saw it began climbing all over it with almost childlike glee; she found it so inspiring that she completed the dance soon after her arrival. She felt confident in her use of the structure but during the first performance, at a point when she was perched precariously on the top of the rock, it began to shake and looked as though it was going to fall over, but somehow she got down. The back section had metal supports coming out of it which had not been screwed down into the floor and seeing this, Cohan asked the stage manager for a hammer and some nails which he hid in the folds of his voluminous cape. He indicated to the other two angels that they should follow him out onto the stage which they did with a series of step arabesques. They circled to the back of the set where they adopted a suitably dramatic pose, and then on every drumbeat of the score, Cohan hammered the nails in and it saved the night. Graham, who loved this sort of theatrical drama, would tell the story for years after.

Before they had left New York, Cohan had been thrown in the deep end of company life and also came to the rescue of the costumes. One unfortunate evening, he found himself in the studio with Graham and her long-term wardrobe mistress Ursula Reed. Ursula Reed fitted very well with Graham as she was very temperamental and moody; she and Graham regularly fought like two old sisters, having arguments that frequently saw them not on speaking terms. That evening, they were working on the large and elaborate cape for Judith and Graham asked Cohan if he would help; he agreed and marked out the costume with the two women. He left them alone for a short while and when he returned, Graham was there but Ursula Reed had moved to the other room. He asked Graham where they were working on the cape and Graham curtly said, 'Ask her!' He went to Ursula Reed and asked what was going on and she said, 'I'm not talking to her!' Cohan tried to save the situation, saying, 'Come on, we have to get this done!' She replied, 'You do it.' Graham said, 'She's impossible, I want nothing to do with her!' So Cohan was left with the cape spread out around him and with neither women talking. It took hours, but by 4 a.m. they had both returned to the studio to help but they would still not acknowledge each other's presence, and stayed on opposite sides of Cohan.

The company were in Israel for two weeks and, as well as the major cities, toured to the outlying villages and kibbutzim. For Graham, Israel was a major success and as a result of it many Israeli dancers appeared at the Graham Studio on scholarships paid for by de Rothschild. Israel was also a success for Cohan and he was able to lay the building blocks for what would be a substantial career in that country.

A seasoned tourer, Cohan found that touring itself had changed. When in the past most of the company had stayed together, this time some of the members brought lovers or partners. Sometimes the dancers dated each other – Richard Kutch and Richard Gain were a long-term couple, and Cohan himself had begun a relationship with Robert Powell. Powell – ten years Cohan's junior – was one of the leading dancers of his generation. A strikingly beautiful man originally from Hawaii with a lean boyish physique, he was much in demand on the New York dance scene. The two found they had much in common although Powell, like Martin before him, was haunted by demons which would eventually overcome him. The younger members tended to stay together while the older ones were often corralled by Graham to assist her in official functions. They would all reassemble at the theatre for the warm-up before the show; this was never an official class but everyone was expected to be there to do what they needed to prepare for the performance. Graham's was a huge plié with her hands clasped above her head, meditating. It was on tour that Cohan realised how wide the gap was between the young members and the older ones. In conversation, the question was asked, 'Is it true Martha used to dance really well?' Cohan realised that none of the young people had seen her dance at her peak and that the decay in the transmission of her aesthetic had already begun.

After Israel, the tour continued to Ankara, Athens, Belgrade, and Zagreb. In Ankara, Cohan was taken by Graham, de Rothschild, and her assistant François Shapira into the empty ballroom of the hotel, a grand setting for a grand proposal. De Rothschild told him that she wanted to set up a dance company in Israel, and that she and Graham had discussed the matter at length and wanted to offer him the job as first artistic director. Cohan looked at Graham when he heard this but she avoided his eyes. His credentials ticked all of the boxes; he was Jewish, a seasoned performer, a very experienced teacher, an accomplished choreographer and company director. Cohan was of course flattered and interested – the opportunity to not only direct but to create what would be a fully funded company had to be given serious consideration.

The company may have been fully funded from de Rothschild's fabulous wealth, but if Cohan moved to Israel she would, she told him, only be able to pay him state-controlled wages which would amount to about $50 per week. Of course living expenses in Israel were well below those of New York, but the sum was still less than ten per cent of Cohan's weekly earnings. Even her offer to buy him an apartment on Rothschild Boulevard, the most desirable part of Tel Aviv, did not in his eyes make up for what he would lose in New York especially since she refused to consider paying the rent for his apartment there, something she could well have afforded to do, and he sadly declined her offer. There was no acrimony involved; Graham, having just recovered Cohan, was relieved not to lose him but had suggested he was the most suitable, and after all de Rothschild had done for her, she wanted to give her the best. For her part, de Rothschild was not an aggressive personality and accepted his decision, promising to involve him in the Israeli troupe's work.

Graham and her company were fascinated by the cities they performed in as many were in communist countries generally closed to Americans. The reception they received in all these places was for them incredible; they found that there was no animosity against the USA and they were a staggering success, far more so than in their homeland. Most of the countries they visited had only been used to seeing Russian ballet – which was very old-fashioned in terms of narrative and stage production – and the audiences were astounded by Graham's theatrical style. It was not just the dancing they were fascinated by but the whole Grahamesque way of using sets, costumes, props, and lighting.

In Belgrade, the dancers found life horrific and they were glad to leave; everything seemed to be in shades of grey and black, all only partially illuminated by flickering fluorescent lights. The shops were devoid of anything but the most basic stock and food seemed to consist mainly of sausage, potato, and cabbage, and 'to find an egg was a revelation'. It was tragically sad at night, when people seemed to shuffle around the streets in which there very few cars. One day, the company were all taken on a special bus tour to see a new football stadium and everyone noticed there were no cars on the roads. Cohan asked the guides why, to which the answer was, 'Oh, we are being very logical here; we are building the roads first.'

Cohan had almost not made the journey to Yugoslavia, as while in Athens, the company was treated to an after-show party where Cohan ate something that disagreed with him. He was used to an upset stomach from visits to strange and interesting restaurants on tour, and initially tried to ignore it, but as the hours moved on he realised this time it was more serious and bore all the symptoms of severe food poisoning. He called the tour manager, who had to get in touch with the American Embassy as they could find no doctors that would treat him. The embassy sent over 'a very sweet old man who had only one hypodermic needle which he had to sharpen before he used it', painfully filling Cohan with an unidentified and curiously coloured medication. Whatever it was, the medicine had little effect and Cohan found that he was fainting constantly and when he was not prone in bed, he spent his time in the bathroom; it was clear to all he was in no fit state to perform. The only work Cohan was dancing in that night was *Night Journey* in the role of Tiresias, the blind seer, while opposite him Graham was playing one of her favourite parts, Jocasta. She would not hear of the performance being cancelled and ordered David Woods to go to Cohan and learn the role. By this time, Cohan was confined to bed and attached to a drip, so the rehearsal consisted of Woods standing in front of him asking for directions and when Cohan passed out, Woods would shake him to wake him up. In this fashion, they got through the whole dance which Woods duly performed that night. When he returned the next day, Cohan asked how it had gone and Woods told him it was fine but Cohan had neglected to tell him how to get onto the large Noguchi-designed bed which was a major part of the set; the vertically challenged Wood found the bed came up to his chin and its navigation nearly brought the dance to a standstill.

The following night was more problematic, as Cohan was dancing the major role of Aegisthus in *Clytemnestra* and he had to do it. For this leg of the tour, Graham had been assigned a hugely impressive Yugoslav driver who was over 6' 5' tall. She explained the problem to the driver, telling him that she was going to put Cohan onto a camp bed by the stage, and every time he needed to enter the driver was to pick up Cohan, who was dressed in his small jockstrap of a costume, and move him to the stage, then catch him when he came offstage and return him to the makeshift bed. In spite of his weakness, Cohan recalls 'being in heaven'.

Although the tour had begun in the heat of the Middle East, it ended in the far north in Helsinki, where the sub-zero temperatures caught the company unawares. They had only been allowed limited luggage, and foolishly none of them had thought to carry large winter boots – they found to their dismay that their little leather shoes froze on the icy Finnish streets.

It was on this tour that Cohan at last was able to perform in *Phaedra*, the dance he had 'learnt' with Paul Taylor the previous year. The work, which was about a woman who fell in love with her stepson, saw Ross cast as the son Hippolytus and Cohan as Theseus, the husband and father coming back from wars to find out she had lied about the son whom she accuses of attempting to have sex with her. The dance was erotic and Graham had choreographed twenty minutes of

lust and sexual obsession. What made the movement shocking was the set by
Noguchi which was not very subtle, the 'home' of the goddess Venus being a
thinly disguised vagina. There was also a shōji-type screen which had moving
panels – Hippolytus is behind it and his body is shown in sections, rather like a
striptease show. This was too much for two Americans, Peter Frelinghuysen and
Edna Kelley, members of the House of Representatives who saw the work in the
final stages of the tour in Cologne and found it obscene. Once back in America,
they tried to have Graham removed from the list of approved artists.

The tour finished in Germany and the British press sent a number of critics
to review the work. All the reviews were positive and there began a campaign to
bring Graham to the United Kingdom. Graham was keen to come back to the
UK, and Cohan and David Woods gave Robin Howard's name to Craig Barton,
the company manager, as a possible source of funding. Howard was appalled
when he heard Graham was not to come to Britain, and with his wide knowledge
of the political world – since 1954 he had been involved with the United Nations
refugee organisations – called Francis Scarlett Mason, the Cultural Affairs Officer
at the American Embassy in London, and told him he was interested in helping.

It was a good move on Howard's part to contact Mason, who was a great
supporter of Graham. His interest in dance had begun in the 1950s when he was
a passionate supporter of Balanchine, and later wrote a very successful book on
that choreographer. His first exposure to Graham had been *Eye of Anguish*, which
he hated, but later he saw *Canticle for Innocent Comedians* which stunned him
and he invited Graham onto his arts programme on radio station WNYC. He
interviewed her for forty-five minutes and found her 'one of the most fascinating
women in America'. The two liked each other's company and he became a regular
visitor to her apartment, where they took 'tea' – the 'tea' consisting of large
tumblers of neat bourbon whisky. He was therefore very sympathetic to helping
Graham in any way he could.

Mason brought Clive Barnes along to the lunch with Howard, and he
explained to them both that although the US administration was spending a
lot of money sending American cultural institutions abroad, in response to the
Soviets exporting theirs, the UK was not in the Soviet sphere and the Americans
were not trying to influence the UK in that way. Clive Barnes then proposed the
idea that if the Americans could send Graham on another tour then perhaps,
if money could be found, she could stop off in the UK. Howard asked how
much such a stopover would cost and Mason told him in the region of £20,000.
Although shocked by this – for the time – gigantic sum, Howard told Mason that
it was possible.

Thereafter events moved swiftly, Mason spoke to Washington to arrange a
short tour for the following year and Howard set about finding a British venue.
He spoke first to his old friend from his Cambridge days, the Queen's cousin
Lord Harewood, then Director of the Edinburgh Festival, who agreed to invite

Graham to perform. He also asked him if he would be willing to split the cost of any financial shortcomings. Howard said he was able to cover the first £10,000, but that the second £10,000 would be difficult for him. In a remarkable gesture, of the sort no longer seen in the arts, Harewood agreed to this. It was more remarkable in that he had no particular love of the dance, his main passion being opera. He was risking more than just money as dance, apart from the big classics such as *Swan Lake* and *Sleeping Beauty*, had never been popular at the festival. But Harewood was keen and supportive and it was all beautifully arranged.

Back in America, life continued as before, the company rehearsed a great deal, while Graham busied herself with a new work for Britain. *Circe*, with music by Hovhaness, was based on the Ulysses myth and in it she cast Mary Hinkson as the sorceress, Bertram Ross as Ulysses, and the young men in the company as his crew. Using Noguchi's set from the discarded *Theatre for a Voyage*, it would be an enormous success. It also bore the dedication, 'This work was created in homage to Robin Howard', in acknowledgement of all he had already done for her.

Cohan was not involved with the new work, which was fortunate as he had projects of his own to complete. On 6 April, he performed his solo *Streams* in a gala supporting the Dance Circle of Boston with an interesting programme that showed the variety that now constituted the American modern dance. In addition to Cohan, the programme included works by Doris Humphrey, James Truitte, Erick Hawkins, Joseph Gilford, and Jack Moore, as well as Cohan's former student Gus Solomons Jr who, after completing his degree in architecture, moved into the dance world with great success. Talley Beatty should have been in the performance but, true to his temperamental nature, did not appear. In distinguished company, Cohan gained positive reviews for his performance; Elinor Hughes, writing in the *Boston Herald*, felt that 'there was a truly distinguished solo work by Robert Cohan in his own *Streams* set to music by Alan Hovhaness, and with each appearance here the quality of this dancer's technique, personality and choreographic ideas take on added quality [sic]'.[110] While Margaret von Szeliski, who had clearly studied with Cohan and fallen under his spell, wrote in *The Harvard Crimson*,

> Cohan once told a dance class at the Loeb that his most treasured compliment came from his young niece who ran up to him after a performance and told him, 'Uncle Bob, I understood every word you said.' One loses complete comprehension after childhood, but the beauty of Cohan's dance is still powerful and awesome; at the same time it is delightful. I have never seen a dancer change levels (move, for example from an upright to a sitting position) with such grace; guessing how he will rise to his feet again becomes an interesting game. And he never disappoints his audience by doing so unimaginatively.[111]

The good reviews for this brief appearance helped ensure a sold-out John Hancock Hall a few weeks later when on 28 April, Cohan's company appeared in an all-Cohan programme. The group had grown and now included Cohan, a newly returned Matt Turney, Robert Powell, Carol Drisin, and Juliet Fisher. The Sunday night performance presented by Ruth Greene consisted of *Eclipse*, *Luna Park*, and *Hunter of Angels*, together with two new works, *Ceremony for Serpents*, and *Ornaments and Ashes*. The *Boston Herald* of Monday, 29 April 1963, in a review that would presage his British years, wrote: 'There is strict economy of means and materials in Mr Cohan's choreographies… props were used sparingly, and the music was relatively restrained – all exposing the arts of the participants in merciless transparency'. The critics found the works 'visually exciting but… not always easy to understand at first view', as they dealt 'with the inner world of characters'.[112]

Ceremony of Serpents had been inspired yet again by the myth of the Garden of Eden and was an extension of his solo *Chamber of the Liar*. Cohan's take on the story saw three serpents instead of one: Cohan was the emerald green liar, Carol Drisin and Juliet Fisher were cast as smaller white snakes, their tights embroidered with ophidian motifs. Matt Turney was Eve, dressed in a purple leotard with a flowing yellow cape. The slight story saw Cohan suspended in a beautiful stylised gold cage, or perhaps a trap, designed – as was all the décor – by Walter Martin. Eve enters, unaware of the serpent's presence, and dances a solo; he sends the two white serpents to intrigue her; once close to the cage, he comes out and dances a duet with her, luring her into the cage as the curtain closes. As always, the dancing was praised:

> Mr Cohan adapted the serpentine forms with subtlety and originality to an extraordinary variety of leaps and progressions, as well as to complex group arabesques. His own dance style featured smooth but powerful curves and the girls echoed them in gentler fashion. Mr Cohan and Miss Turney are ideal partners. The word for her is silky. She can drape herself into any shape and then hold it with marmoreal stillness.[113]

While praising the dancing, some reviewers found *Ceremony* slightly obscure, but generally found *Ornaments and Ashes*, the other new work, more accessible. Its 'highly ornamental dances sometimes light hearted, and at others seductive, were performed by Matt Turney and Robert Cohan in shades of red and Carol Drisin and Robert Powell in violet blues'.[114] Cohan again used music by Alan Hovhaness and, as one reviewer noted, allowed the music to infuse the dance with 'an oriental aura that delighted the audience'.[115]

Hunter of Angels, which he danced with Powell, and *Eclipse*, danced by Powell and Drisin – were well received. However, Isabel Ferguson for the *Christian Science Monitor* voiced a reservation about *Eclipse*: 'though it had some good moments … [it] would be better cut – possibly in half'.[116] *Luna Park*, which completed the programme, had the audience in 'gales of laughter'. In spite of the success of the concert – Isabel Ferguson described him as 'one of the most interesting and inventive choreographers of modern dance' – this was the last appearance of the Robert Cohan Dance Company. Events in Britain and a serious injury changed the course of Cohan's life.

All the Graham dancers who remembered the 1954 visit to the UK were nervous about this tour. The memories of virtually empty houses had not been swept away by recalling the success at the end. There was something of a military feel as the company left the American soil; they were going to do battle and win no matter what. Bertram Ross' partner, the pianist and cabaret singer John Wallowitch, even wrote him a goodbye song entitled 'My Love Went to London.'

> My Love went to London
> And left me behind
> I'm going to London
> And I'll find him

(With genders changed, him to her, it would become a hit for Tony Bennett.) They would indeed get to London but first they had to get to Edinburgh.

Since their last visit, British society had been slowly but surely changing, as critic Michael Billington later noted:

> In the early Sixties, the chasm widened. If the previous decade was marked by generational division and conflict, the Sixties saw the young not merely rattling and shaking the culture but increasingly taking charge. Youth which had been knocking at the door in the previous decade finally attained the commanding heights in theatre, film, television, pop and fashion.'[117]

To the list he could have added dance as the 1954 visit had, towards the end at least, shown the public and in particular the young the possibilities of American modern dance. When, in the late 1950s, José Limón had visited with his company, he was very well received. When the company did appear again in Britain, the audiences would be full of young people.

Of major importance in the dissemination of modern dance was Ruth Foster, a school inspector for PE who, in the early 1960s, began to question the situation at major educational conferences. While attending a PE conference in Washington DC in 1961, Foster, together with Marie Crabbe, principal of I. M. Marsh College in Liverpool, saw the work of and were introduced to Dorothy Madden, who had founded and directed the dance programme at the University of Maryland. The performance was a revelation as it was art dancing from an educational, not conservatory, setting. Madden had extensive experience, having studied with the great figures in modern dance, including Hanya Holm, Doris Humphrey, Graham, and most significantly Louis Horst. What so excited Crabbe and Foster was Madden's ability to combine technique with creative work and it was this ability that convinced them to invite her to teach for a term at I. M. Marsh.

After the initial trip, Madden made regular visits to various colleges of education throughout the UK, most significantly at Dartington Hall in Devon, and set the groundwork for an interested group of young people who wanted to see modern dance. There was therefore, from the mid 1960s onwards, an almost military pincer attack of American modern dance on Britain; Howard in London was developing his school and company while Dorothy Madden, in her choreography courses, was disseminating an American-based approach to choreography. The word was spreading rapidly.

In addition, in 1963, the same year as Graham's visit, Teresa Early had formed an organisation called Ballet-makers Ltd (the company would receive funding from Howard) whose aim was to make and show work independently of the established ballet companies. To begin with, the work was ballet based as many of the dancers, although trained in ballet, had seen their hopes of a ballet career scuppered by not having what was seen as the perfect bodies for major companies. But as contemporary dance began to appear, it was embraced by the group who 'believed that dance was one thing... and that good [dance] of any kind was good'.[118] So a good foundation, from dancers in training and trained dancers who wanted something different to ballet, was very definitely in place at the time of the company's visit.

Robin Howard and Francis Mason met Graham in Glasgow, drove her to Edinburgh and helped her settle in. The two, Howard especially, were a little worried about the response of the genteel Morningside ladies and the Lord Provost of Edinburgh, Sir Duncan Mackay Weatherstone, who was a little more than formal. However, they need not have worried because he liked Graham, as did the Morningside ladies, and in the end it was successful, but not unconditionally so.

For the performances, which ran from 26 to 31 August, Graham brought an ambitious range of works consisting of *Seraphic Dialogue*, *Secular Games*, *Phaedra*, *Diversion of Angels*, *Legend of Judith*, *Acrobats of God*, *Embattled Garden*, *Night Journey* and, if that were not enough the full-length and taxing *Clytemnestra*. The reviews varied from the mystified as in the *Glasgow Herald* of 27 August: 'The tradition, the method of the dance, is the most difficult to understand at first seeing. It is both more and less original than the works of Jerome Robbins. It still lives, as Robbins does not, within the framework of ballet, and yet the barefooted dancers move with a freedom of gesture that is utterly original to us in Scotland.'[119] ...To the mystifying: 'The dancers moulded to a style that is strongly unemotional but with all the power concentrated on making the human form respond to music... Though strictly in its own class, it is action more nearly related to yoga than ballet...'[120] Most viewers would not find Graham's work 'unemotional', and quite exactly what form of yoga the writer had seen is a mystery.

But the majority were positive: 'Surely nothing quite like the Martha Graham

Dance Company has ever been seen in Edinburgh before. In technique, dance creation and performance they are utterly unique.'[121] Cohan himself was singled out by Richard Buckle, who wrote in the *Sunday Times*,

> The scene when Graham flirts with Robert Cohan as Aegisthus is wonderful. Graham wiggles, looks coy, trails her mauve veil. She shudders when he puts the idea of murdering Agamemnon into her head; then rehearses the crime as a dance. Cohan acts realistically; he is extraordinary, he is sick. He relaxes on the throne, fiddling unconsciously with her veil, twisting it, watching, smiling, basking.[122]

The not uncritical success of Edinburgh could not have prepared the group for the enormous and unqualified success of the performances at the Prince Of Wales Theatre in London. Barnes, Buckle, Williams et al., did a good job prepping their public and the two-week season was sold out every night. The company was even asked to extend it but could not owing to other commitments. The entire arts world came – painters, sculptors, dancers, choreographers, actors, anyone who was anyone wanted to see what had been missed ten years earlier. They were not disappointed. The new work, *Circe*, was saved for London, and Mary Hinkson scored a personal triumph in the role. Graham had originally intended the part of the sorceress for herself but wisely realised it was beyond her. Even then, she identified so strongly with the part that when in a rehearsal Hinkson got stuck on the set, Graham shouted out, 'Get me down! Get me down.'

Everyone wanted to meet the company and the resourceful Marie Rambert managed to get backstage while the men were all just standing in their jockstraps and she patted Cohan playfully on the rump saying, 'All you beautiful naked men.' It was Rambert who, more than anyone, pushed Howard to do more, saying to him, 'Mr Howard, I don't know who you are or why you have done this, but don't stop now!' Her enthusiasm and encouragement carried Howard forward. In truth, he had no idea what to do. He had wanted to present Graham in London and this he had done, but without Rambert's encouragement he may have stopped. But he did not; what he did was to ask Graham to provide training for dancers at her studio, with all their expenses paid for by him. Graham agreed but warned him, saying, 'If you really want to do it I will help you, but I do advise you not to, because very soon you will find you have no money, no one will like you, and you'll wish you hadn't done it.'[123] These would prove to be prophetic words indeed.

Nothing could dampen Howard's enthusiasm and by Christmas 1963 Eileen Cropley, the first British dancer, was in New York. She was soon followed by Anna Price, Christian Holder, Timothy Hext, and Ross Parks. Three other dancers – Irene Dilkes, Anna Mittelholzer, and Clover Roope – who had made their own way to the Graham Studio, Roope on a Harkness Fellowship, were helped financially. These three would soon be the backbone of the new developments in

London, though for Mittelholzer a talented young dancer of Trinidadian descent, the outcome would not be entirely satisfactory.

The whole visit had not been a comfortable one for Cohan. Before leaving America, Graham, in one of her wilful moods, decided she wanted to run the entire repertory over one Sunday. For some, it did not matter as they were not in many pieces, but for Ross and Cohan, who were in everything, it was a nightmare. By late afternoon, when they were well into *Clytemnestra*, Cohan executed a back fall and felt a twinge in his Achilles tendon; a perhaps telling place to feel injury in a work based on the Trojan War. The problem persisted, and all through Edinburgh and London, Cohan was receiving treatment in the form of cortisone and novocaine injections for the problem. It was so bad that he had to adapt some of the more strenuous aspects of the dancing to accommodate the pain. When the British season ended, the company travelled onto Portugal, a visit that was for Cohan mercifully short.

The pain continued back home, but with the aid of Dr Cobert, a medical practitioner renowned in the artistic community of New York for giving his patients whatever it took to get them through a performance, Cohan completed the two-week season at the Lunt-Fontanne Theatre. The performances, in terms of audience members, were a tremendous success, as much as the season in London had been. The Lunt-Fontanne was, for New York, a large theatre seating 1,478 people but even it proved to be too small to hold all who wished to see Graham and her company. Every night the theatre was full of the maximum amount of standees and in the second week, hundreds were turned away at the box office. Reviews were generally favourable but in the *New York Times* of 28 October, Allen Hughes became the first to question the quality of Graham's performance: 'It is regrettable that Miss Graham's performances were not equally compelling throughout the two weeks. It is a fact, however, that they did vary considerably, although those of her company did not.' After the success of London where Graham herself had been praised to the roof, these comments came as a shock, but similar ones would appear all too regularly over the next few years and contribute to Graham's psychological and physical decline.

Two weeks after the season ended, Cohan was teaching a class at the University of Connecticut, when he demonstrated a simple skip across the floor and heard a sound like a pistol going off and realised he had snapped his Achilles tendon. This is one of the most serious injuries that can befall a dancer, and many do not resume their careers afterwards. Cohan thankfully was not one of these. The University of Connecticut has a well-established American football team named the Huskies, and as such there was easy access to a medical team well versed in torn and damaged ligaments. Rather than going back to New York, which had been Cohan's first choice, he was persuaded to stay and be seen by the athletic team doctors, and it was they who confirmed the nature of his injury and performed surgery the next day. After the operation, Cohan spent six weeks

in a plaster cast and then underwent months of therapy, which put him out
of performing action for the first half of 1964. This caused some problems for
him as he was scheduled to choreograph for the New England Conservatory a
production of Menotti's Christmas opera, *Amahl and the Night Visitors*, which
was to be broadcast – as *Dido and Aeneas* had been – on the television station
WGBH. Although stuck in a chair he was, with the help of his assistant Virginia
Olney, who did special research into the tarantella, able to complete the project.
This was the first time he had not been able to demonstrate any movements
and he found the experience so useful that whenever he taught a choreography
course, he always gave the students a task of creating a dance while seated. The
opera was broadcast successfully with a cast of dancers led by Olney herself,
Henry Atlas, and Flora Cushman, the latter of whom became a central teacher in
the early days of the London venture.

The injury did not affect the Graham Company too much since Graham had
no new works planned for the year. She turned down the offer to make a new
piece for the 1964/1965 New York World's Fair as she had agreed to go to Israel to
help de Rothschild with her new Batsheva Dance Company. The year, however,
had begun badly with the death of Louis Horst. After her divorce from Hawkins,
the two had become close again and his death was devastating to her. He had
appointed her one of his executors, and one of her first actions was to go through
his papers and destroy all their personal correspondence. She had followed a
similar pattern when her mother had died, but attempting to seal off the past was
not so easy this time.

The Connecticut College Dance Festival wanted to honour Horst and asked
Graham to reconstruct three of her works for which he had composed the music:
Primitive Mysteries, *Frontier*, and *El Penitente*. Graham, as ever, showed no
interest in reconstructing works, and left that task to the company. Cohan helped
with *El Penitente*, and Ethel Winter struggled with the poor film record of the
solo *Frontier*. *Primitive Mysteries* was recreated by many of the original 1930s
cast, but after seeing a couple of rehearsals Cohan purposely stayed away unable
to bear the constant bickering and fighting of the aged dancers all of whom were
convinced that their memories were the correct ones. In spite of Graham's lack
of interest in the reconstructions they were a great success, especially *Primitive
Mysteries*. As well as the Graham works, the evening gala included Humphrey's
Lament for Ignacio Sánchez Mejias; this had been created on José Limón and he
and Graham entered from opposite sides of the stage to receive the applause. The
two acknowledged each other, then unannounced he raised his hand to silence
the audience, and choking back emotion said, 'Because of this woman we have
seen one of the greatest masterpieces ever made.' She may not have wanted her
works to be revived but she was more than gratified when they were and were
well received.

In the summer, Cohan was sufficiently recovered from his injury to travel to

Israel where he had been invited to teach modern dance as part of a summer programme, which was paid for by the America-Israel Fund and the Jerusalem Academy of Music. His classes proved very popular, filled with students from all corners of the country. Members of the newly formed Batsheva Dance Company also participated in some of the classes. This was good preparation for them since in the evenings they worked with him on three dances that he was preparing for the company's first performances. These were a new work for the whole company: *Celebrants*, danced to Carlos Surinach's *Concertino for Piano, Strings and Cymbal* and two existing works from his company's repertoire; the duet *The Pass* and the humorous quartet *Luna Park*.

Cohan had been friendly with Surinach since before his work for Graham on *Embattled Garden* and *Acrobats of God* and the composer was happy for him to use his twenty-minute concertino. It is a dynamic, vivacious work, full of exciting rhythms, solos, and ensembles and Cohan created a corresponding piece of choreography. Cohan was the consummate professional and realised that this new company needed developing, and the work was very formally divided into sections for men, women, together with duets and solos, each section giving everyone the opportunity to shine, while at the same time pushing them physically and artistically. The dancers remember it as being hugely satisfying for them to do, particularly in the women's sections which had some very intricate Indian-based arms with very strange turns of the legs. It was, however, a challenge to make.

The company were an unruly bunch, typically Israeli, with each one seeing themselves as a soloist and unwilling to give ground to anyone else. Some, such as Rena Gluck, who had given up her own company to help de Rothschild in the venture, and Rina Schenfeld, were extraordinary performers and Graham would entrust her roles in *Herodiade* and *Errand into the Maze* to them. The men were more undisciplined and rehearsals often went like this:

Cohan: I want you to step right, turn and drop to the floor.
Ehud Ben-David: Yes, but I could turn left.
Cohan: You could, but I want you to turn right.
Ehud Ben-David: Yes, but if I turn left it would look better and then I could . . jump.
Cohan: No! Just turn as I have shown you, please.
Ehud Ben-David: Well…

It took all of Cohan's considerable tact and diplomatic skills, which he would soon need in London, to complete the work. Cohan laughs a lot – his infectious masculine giggle, able to diffuse many a difficult situation, is remembered fondly by all who have heard it. In this he is following Gurdjieff's teaching: 'Laughter relieves us of superfluous energy, which, if it remained unused, might become negative, that is, poison. Laughter is the antidote.'[124] There would be a lot of laughter in the coming years.

He did complete the work but then needed to return to America before the premiere. In the meantime Graham arrived and decided that some sections did not work and she changed them. In particular, she altered the finale and added a section with three women and a solo for a girl which gave the dance a focus that had been missing. The dancers were worried that Cohan would be angry when he returned for the premiere, but he agreed that Graham's changes were for the better and was happy to let them stand. This was not so for Donald McKayle who had created a work entitled *Daughters of the Garden*, to music by Ernest Bloch. Graham tampered with that work as well though McKayle let her know in no uncertain terms that her changes were not welcome.

Cohan worked closely with Rina Schenfeld on the duet *The Pass*, even turning up at her apartment at 1 a.m. to give her make-up tips, and the two filmed the work, albeit in practise clothes. This black and white film is the only record of Cohan performing in one of his own works and shows his immaculate use of timing and the sinister relationship between the Sphinx and her assistant. Rather like in the 1960s classic film *The Servant*, one is never sure who is master and who is servant until the very end.

The whole venture was a remarkable success and marked the beginning of Cohan's career as an international choreographer. He had proved himself not only as a popular teacher with the Israeli dancers but also as a popular choreographer and he would return to Israel many times throughout his career. His decision not to take on the job of artistic director at $50 per week had been a good one as de Rothschild paid him handsomely for each of his visits.

In England, Howard had moved on with his plans for bringing modern dance to Britain and on 25 November 1964, a paper entitled 'Formation of Trust for Modern Dance' was sent out to interested parties. This Robin Howard Trust was to stimulate British interest in foreign dance developments and particularly in American modern dance. It would do this by:

A) Bringing American companies here or cooperating with those who were doing so.

B) Bringing American teachers here, two top members of the Graham Company have promised to come over for a minimum of two months between April and June 1965. Ballet Rambert, the Rambert School, Western Theatre Ballet, London Dance Theatre and the Arts Educational Trust have already asked to use these teachers and other organisations will be approached. Classes for individual dancers are guaranteed.

C) Martha Graham has promised to give free tuition for up to ten students per year in each school for the next few years. And a basic selection committee has already been formed, Dame Marie Rambert, Miss Christyne Lawson (the only former member of the Graham Company permanently resident in this country), Mr Francis Mason, Assistant Cultural Attaché at the United States Embassy and Mr Robin Howard. Other British dancers and teachers have promised to help with the auditions.[125]

An initial £20,000 had been placed in the Trust by Howard with the aim that, through fundraising, this would rise to £50,000 within six months. It was hoped that this would be enough to set up a small studio space and later aid in the development of a performing company if one proved necessary. It was also envisioned that exchanges with countries other than the USA would develop. The money was also used to support other organisations with funding going to Ballet Rambert, Ballet-makers Ltd, and Norman McDowell's London Dance Theatre.

The setting up of the Trust coincided with Paul Taylor's first season in London, which like Graham's had been guaranteed by Howard's money. Taylor in return had offered full cooperation to anyone wanting to mount his works in the future (the bottles of vintage champagne placed by Janet Eager in each of his dancer's hotel rooms helped sweeten him). Merce Cunningham and Alvin Ailey likewise had London seasons sponsored by Howard and also agreed to help with the venture. It is worth noting here that Howard had not chosen the Graham style blindly, he was well aware of the variety of dance styles available and he had made his choice as he told *Dance and Dancers*, for valid reasons:

> Our object here is not to try and transplant American modern dance to this country; it is to try and develop a native style appropriate to the bodies and outlook of British people, to our climate and the rest of our culture. We have chosen to base it upon the Graham approach and technique because we feel that this is far more developed than any alternative – it is out and away the best.[126]

Janet Eager, who aided Howard in all his work, had been known since her boarding school days as Mop, owing to her big bush of unruly hair which resembled a floor mop. From a comfortably off family she had, by her own admission, drifted through various jobs suitable for a middle-class girl of the time, including a few stints as an au pair, one being with the family of the Greek President. She had been introduced to Howard through mutual friends and had initially worked with him on a celebration of Shakespeare's four-hundredth anniversary. She was enthralled by his baby blue eyes from the start and by his decision, straight away to call her 'Moppity'. In spite of her poor spelling and typing, Howard could see her special qualities and he offered her a job. She would eventually become one of the triumvirate who would run London Contemporary Dance Theatre, her slightly vague and diffident demeanour masking a steely determination and a sharp business brain.

The Trust Deed was signed on 2 April 1965 and stated in torturous legalese that Robin Howard, 'being desirous of establishing a charitable trust to foster, promote, and increase the interest of the public in the knowledge, understanding, and practice of the art of the ballet and to promote and assist presentations of the ballet and the training of ballet dancers and choreographers', had set aside certain sums and that 'the ballet shall mean ballet and modern ballet in all its forms and expressions'.[127] The word 'ballet' was used instead of 'contemporary dance' as Howard had been advised by his lawyers that 'dance' may have been seen as non-cultural and therefore non-charitable, whereas 'ballet' was acceptable. It would be three years before the deed was changed and the word 'ballet' replaced by the word 'contemporary dance'.

Cohan made a full recovery from his injury and 1965 proved to be a very busy year for him. Graham was preparing two new works for the New York autumn season, *The Witch of Endor* and *Part Real – Part Dream*. Both had roles for Cohan, in fact he pressed Graham into making them as athletic as possible, realising that at the age of 38, time was catching up with him.

James Anderson, who had worked with Cohan as an accompanist at his school in Boston, had created a musical version of Herman Hesse's play about the life of the young Buddha entitled *Siddhartha* which was presented on 4, 5, and 6 March at the Loeb Theatre in Boston. He asked Cohan not only to choreograph it but to dance in it, design it, and direct it. It was a large-scale production with a big cast of actors and dancers and an orchestra that blended Western instruments with Indian ones. With his fascination in things spiritual, the play held great interest for Cohan and he invested a lot of time researching material for the elaborate production. As with the music, he was able to indulge his knowledge and love for Indian classical dance, blending this with his contemporary work. Perhaps borrowing from Graham's choreography, Cohan split the character of Siddhartha into three separate roles played by a dancer, a singer, and an actor; another three played his love interest. Cohan played the dancing Siddhartha role and Matt Turney the dancing love interest. The other dancers came from the Boston Dance Circle and included Gus Solomons Jr.

The piece, which combined symbolism, mysticism, and contemplation, had mixed reviews. The lighting, which used back projections, was praised while Margo Miller writing for the *Boston Herald* felt that 'as a stage work it was rather short on the dramatic tending to rely on descriptions and meditations', but that 'Robert Cohan's liquid dances were most welcome'.[128] Alta Maloney, writing for the *Boston Traveller*, was more than sarcastic when she wrote, 'Mr Cohan and Miss Turney attempt to achieve nirvana or oblivion to external reality and almost accomplish it. Mr Anderson's music too works to paralyze portions of the brain. Some tones come perilously close to inducing nose bleed, others drone like a distant saw mill.'[129]

Cohan's final visit to Boston would be in May to teach two classes sponsored by the Christian Fellowship at the Community House. The *Connecticut Daily*

Campus of Tuesday, 24 May gave him a glowing press which is worth printing here to highlight how much his work had been appreciated in the Boston area:

> Robert Cohan is a phenomenon rarely found in the arts. He has achieved equal status as both performer and teacher. In the years he has been a part of the dancer's world Cohan has made four national tours and performed five seasons as a lead dancer in the Martha Graham Dance Company. He has toured internationally with the company on six occasions. In addition he has appeared in numerous stage, screen, and television productions. In his role as choreographer, Cohan has presented his works both here and abroad. He has five full concerts to his credit the last of which, an adaptation of Herman Hesse's SIDDARTHA [sic] was recently presented at Harvard's Loeb Drama Centre, in Cambridge, Mass.
>
> The other side of the ledger reveals an equally impressive list of activities as a teacher. Cohan has been a senior instructor at the Martha Graham School for a number of years. He has served as instructor at the Juilliard School of music, Connecticut College School of Dance, the June Taylor's School, the University of Rochester, Sarah Lawrence College, Harvard, New York University and is presently director of the dance department at the New England Conservatory of Music in Boston.
>
> Robert Cohan is a dedicated artist and teacher. His excellence as a demonstrator in class is surpassed only by his power of communicating to students the all-important feeling behind a movement. He is a truly inspired artist and teacher.

After the Boston engagement, Cohan finally severed his connections with Boston to devote himself fully to Graham and his developing international career. He handed over all of his teaching responsibilities to Cunningham dancer Albert Reid and went straight to Israel where he had again been invited to teach and to make another work for the Batsheva Company. This was *Tent of Vision*, to a new score by the young Israeli composer Noam Sheriff, with designs by Dani Karavan.

The programme printed part of the fifth of Rilke's *Duino Elegies*:

> But tell me, who *are* they, these acrobats, even a little
> more fleeting than we ourselves,—so urgently, ever since childhood,
> wrung by an (oh, for the sake of whom?)
> never-contented will? That keeps on wringing them,
> bending them, slinging them, swinging them,
> throwing them and catching them back; as though from an oily
> smoother air, they come down on the threadbare
> carpet, thinned by their everlasting
> upspringing,[130] [sic]

Cohan took the poem's wonderfully physical language as a starting point for a dance that looked at the backstage lives of a troupe of circus performers. Linda Hodes, listed on the programme as The Enchantress, was more a mistress of ceremonies, guiding the players as they cavorted on Karavan's elaborate, tactile, and interactive set.

Graham's willingness to allow the Batsheva Company to perform her works caused some friction in her own group. There was some jealousy that young dancers in the Batsheva Company were being given parts that Graham had taken years to bestow on them. On one occasion, the dancers were asked to film *Dark Meadow* as a rehearsal document for the Israeli company. Cohan and Ross were so angry that they deliberately made mistakes in the dance – Ross would point instead of jumping and they would walk from spot to spot. The Batsheva Company learnt and performed it with the mistakes and somehow that version ended up back with the Graham Company who, Cohan insists, still performs it to this day with errors in the dance/music phrasing.

The international developments continued in England with workshops held between May and July by Mary Hinkson, Ethel Winter, and Bertram Ross, all teaching across London. Classes cost 7s. 6d. each and students were expected to participate in three classes a week for a minimum of one month. The dancers were also to give classes to ballet companies and schools and the auditions for the scholarships to the Graham School were held in June and July. This scheme was to prove unworkable, however, as the excellent students who were sent to America more often than not stayed there, joining modern companies, rather than returning to no work in Britain.

Adverts were placed in *Dance and Dancers* and the *Dancing Times* looking for students to participate in a long-term training programme. In the event, over two hundred applied and the plans had to be changed to offer more courses of shorter duration. With no building to its name, the Trust had to find space where the classes could take place. This was not easy and on many nights Mop Eager travelled in a van around London, laying a dance floor and taking it up after class, ready for the next day. Mondays and Thursdays at the Arts Educational Trust in Hyde Park Corner, Tuesdays and Fridays were at the Mercury Theatre, Notting Hill (the birthplace) of Ballet Rambert. Wednesday afternoons were at the Africa Centre in Covent Garden. On Saturday mornings, the venue was the Victor Silvester Ballroom in the Odeon Cinema, Chelsea. This schedule of three or more classes a day around London was too much for Mary Hinkson who was the main teacher for the first two months. She had been persuaded to go by Graham after Robert Powell had refused, however, she missed her husband and daughter, hated where she was staying, and found the schedule of introducing the technique and teaching to what were largely beginners, too dispiriting.

Things improved when Ross and Winter arrived from New York and the trio teamed up with Eileen Cropley and Christyne Lawson to prepare for some performances. Here they joined with the Royal Ballet's education group Ballet for All and present a lecture-demonstration on Graham together with excerpts from Graham's repertoire. The performances took place at the Theatre Royal Stratford East in the first week of July and were an enormous success. Plans began to develop a performance group to tour the UK and also to establish a permanent, not peripatetic, school to teach contemporary dance. After the Graham dancers had departed, Eileen Cropley, who would eventually become a leading dancer with Paul Taylor, fulfilled her part of the bargain with Howard and in September became the regular teacher of the British students in Howard's peripatetic school.

The classes were 'reviewed' by Pat Hutchinson and Teresa Early for the *Dancing Times*. Hutchinson noted that the demands of the Graham classes 'come as something of a shock to some students who associate modern dance with limited technique and unlimited freedom of expression'. Early noted that some students 'were often so fascinated by watching both teacher and demonstrator (Hinkson and Cropley) that they would forget that in one moment they would be doing the movement for themselves!' She went on to admit to a general mystification as to what a contraction and release actually was, but that 'all the students I spoke to were most enthusiastic about the classes and eager for more'. She concluded her report writing,

> It is too early to tell what the future for a modern dancer could be in this country. What has been proved to us is that this kind of contemporary dance is founded on a technique as rigorous and demanding as that of classical ballet and this surely must be the starting point from which our own explorations will be made.[131]

It was not clear to anyone how it would develop but there was now a strong movement of support for Howard's work. His hunch that contemporary dance could take hold in Britain was now supported by unshakeable evidence; all he had to do was to keep it financed.

Back in America, for Cohan the year culminated in a three-week season at the 54th Street Theater in New York. This would be one of the Graham Company's longest and most successful seasons, with the opening night audience comprising 'celebrated dancers, composers, choreographers, painters, educators, and patrons and patronesses of the arts',[132] But the season would also emphasise the huge gap between Graham and the new generation of dancers and theatregoers. Cohan gained good reviews for his performance as the Husbandman in *Appalachian Spring*, Walter Terry finding he danced the role with 'virility and marvellous intensity',[133] while Clive Barnes thought that as Jason in *Cave of the Heart*, 'Robert Cohan looked self-indulgently handsome, pouncing through the choreography with acquisitive mastery [and] proved himself Jason to the death.'[134]

Of the new works *Part Real – Part Dream* caused puzzlement as Clive Barnes' review for the *New York Times* shows: 'what looks like a giant-size Roman shield, all grim with encrustations, revolves to reveal Robert Cohan, who apparently lives in it, and who loses little time, understandably, in trying to persuade Miss Hinkson that even on the inside of a giant-size shield two can live as cheaply as one.'[135] The other new work *The Witch of Endor* in which Cohan played David to Ross' Saul and which he feels was the best role Graham made for him, was not received well, with Clive Barnes writing that 'the final impression is that of a number of very well contrived theatrical and dramatic effects separated by choreography that never fully jumps to life'.[136] Walter Terry was more charitable towards the work and Graham's performance in it, writing that 'Miss Graham has not had time to discover the fullest range of dramatic colours inherent in the title role, nor has she yet completely integrated her own acting patterns with the dance designs she has devised.'[137] During a performance of *Part Real – Part Dream*, Cohan managed to get the big toe of his right foot caught in Mary Hinkson's cloak, and as she moved away his toe badly twisted and he severely damaged the joint. He got through performances with Dr Cobert's magic potions, but the problem caused severe pain for many years and was only alleviated by surgery in 1979.

The season was a success though, not least because of the revivals of *Primitive Mysteries* and *Frontier*, which enabled the younger audience members to see what would later come to be called 'Radical Graham' – movement stripped down to the bare essentials without all the trappings of costumes and theatrical effects that had by 1965 become such a part of Graham's dance world. But within the success came some criticism of Graham herself, with Clive Barnes writing:

> The mordant wit and charm of Miss Graham in *Acrobats of God* make this currently one of the finest performances in the present day dance theatre. One wishes one could say as much of her appearance last night in the title role of her own excellently conceived tragedy *Phaedra*. This was ill advised. We all owe Miss Graham so much that if it is her pleasure to appear in such arduous roles then perhaps we as an audience should show gratitude. Yet this is hardly fair to either her great reputation as a dancer or to her reputations one of the world's major choreographers. This is not easy to say but it should, however, softly and gently, be said.[138]

This was a devastating criticism from a leading critic and one who had always been a staunch supporter of Graham. It cut Graham to the bone and hastened her decline as both performer and choreographer.

1966 was a year of consolidations and changes, for Cohan, for Graham, and for dance in Britain. In Britain, plans were already in place for Ballet Rambert to reinvent itself under the direction of Norman Morrice and they would give their first performance in this guise on 28 November. Their work moved from small-scale productions of the classics and intriguing contemporary ballet to ballet-based contemporary dance. In this they were greatly influenced by the choreography and teaching of Glen Tetley who had built up an international career based on a style that merged ballet technique with Graham and whose work was perfectly suited to a company which would often begin class with a ballet barre before moving to a Graham floor work.

Early 1966, Robin Howard had arrived at Graham's studio to help her by working – free of charge – as administrative director of the company and the school. He also arrived with more formalised ideas for dance in Britain. The success of the open classes meant he had moved ahead with plans for a permanent school and some sort of performance group and he wanted someone senior from the Graham Company to run it. He did not at the time have any fixed idea that Cohan would be 'the one' and a number of dancers were mentioned as possibilities, Yuriko being one. However, when Howard asked Graham who she would suggest, she had no hesitation in naming Cohan as her first choice. He had been dancing for twenty years, he was a very experienced teacher, he had run his own company and school, and he was developing rapidly as a choreographer. In addition to these artistic pluses, he was a consummate diplomat; he had exactly the same virtues that had interested de Rothschild a few years earlier. She broke the news to Cohan over a dinner at her apartment which Howard also attended. His first reaction was to ask what she wanted, but she answered in only the vaguest of terms so he did not pursue the topic. A day later when they were alone, he asked her again and she only replied, 'I think we owe it to Robin', but when he again pushed her for what she wanted, she seemed to indicate he should accept. This may seem puzzling, but Graham was herself torn by her need to have Cohan close by to support her, and what she felt was a moral obligation to assist Howard in return for all the support he had given her. Howard later told Richard Alston that Graham had regretted her decision, as Cohan was far too valuable an asset to 'give away'. Cohan was intrigued by Howard's suggestion but not overly so; he was a born and bred New Yorker and he had a life in that city. Besides, he was not sure, having been a pioneer of modern dance already, whether or not he wanted to do it again in another country. In any event he could not commit yet as Graham had a busy year ahead.

In the autumn of 1966 the company went on their first coast-to-coast tour of the USA since 1950. Aided by a grant of $141,000 from the National Council on the Arts, Sol Hurok organised an eight-week tour that began on 2 October in Hartford, Connecticut, and finished in Ithaca, New York on 2 December, taking in, on the way, twenty-nine other cities from the Midwest to the West Coast. At the end of the tour, Cohan and Ross were named as co-artistic directors of the company but exactly what this meant in practice was open to debate. Graham of course had the final say over all details, but the three worked together discussing casting and repertory. It was, however, a small acknowledgment on Graham's part that at her advanced age she could not continue doing everything as before.

In addition, she was working on a new dance to be premiered in February

1967. Returning to Greek myth, she had chosen nothing less than the fall of Troy, in a complex work that would see Graham herself as the matriarch Hecuba. The piece, to be called *Cortege of Eagles,* would have music by Eugene Lester and it would be her final collaboration with Isamu Noguchi who designed the majestic sets. The rehearsals were not without some difficulties but the story of the ageing queen Hecuba seeing all she treasured being destroyed around her struck a chord with Graham, the House of Atreus being a metaphor for the Graham Studio; she was able, mostly, to stay focussed and inspired. The opening ten minutes, in which Graham sums up the story and introduces all the characters, stunned the dancers. Cohan still recalls it as an astonishing piece, although he feels that some of the power was lost once, as was usual in Graham's work from this period, the costumes and set got in the way of the movement.

For the work, Noguchi made two enormous shields, one each for Achilles and Hector; seven feet tall, three feet wide, and two feet long, they were simply too big. Cohan and Ross were supposed to fight with them but they were so huge that the two 6-foot dancers looked like toys when they picked them up. Graham was about to discard them when someone pointed out that the shields would perhaps look good as portals for an entrance. Intrigued, she told Ethel Winter to use the two handholds as steps and climb on them, imagining them to be the walls of Troy. With some assistance, she made it and the image worked, and Graham had the stage manager remake them in heavier material so they could be durable. This development was unknown to Noguchi, who did not see them until he was in the audience at the dress rehearsal. Seeing the dancers climbing on what he thought were his creations he said, 'But Martha, they are shields, they should fight with them', and then he ran onto the stage and tried to grab them. Finding he could not lift them, he got very angry and shouted at Graham, demanding to know what she had done. Graham shouted back, 'Isamu! They are not shields they are the gates of Troy', and he said, 'No, no Martha, they are shields!', to which she retorted, 'Get off my stage; they are the gates of Troy.' Graham of course had committed one of the worse insults towards a Japanese, which was to make him look foolish. The two artists had worked together so long, however, that they quickly resolved the argument. The finished work was probably Graham's finest from this late period. It was filmed in 1969 and shows her as the consummate dance/actress. She dances little but controls the stage by her presence, sitting majestically on a stool surveying the carnage. In a perfect piece of casting, Cohan was Hector, noble and heroic, to the flamboyantly dramatic Achilles as portrayed by Ross.

After the February season that included the premiere of *Cortege of Eagles,* the company left for England to perform a three-week season at the Saville Theatre. Again they received a warm welcome and although many of the reviewers concentrated on writing about the young dynamic dancers in the company, such as Robert Powell, Bill Louther, and Noemi Lapzeson, Cohan was recognised as a consummate, seasoned performer whose 'Husbandman in *Appalachian Spring* sums up the whole story of the West in the way he touches a wall of his new home or gazes over a fence', and whose 'Jason in *Cave of the Heart* has both love and fear in him'.[139] Richard Alston, who had previously been addicted to the work of Frederick Ashton, went initially to see the company because of Graham's collaboration with visual artists. He attended most of the performances and was struck by 'this sense of a company on stage who did not like each other, but [who] were amazingly mature strong performers, very rooted [and] much grounded.'

Cohan stayed behind after the season was over, as Howard had eventually found a permanent home for his school which was based at 5-7 Berners Place in London's West End. The premises, an old clothing showroom above a furrier's shop, was sixty feet by thirty feet, had a small unisex changing area, no showers, no toilet, minimal heating and a leaking roof. The wartime British spirit of 'making do' was still prevalent but as Marie McCluskey, one of the early students, remembers: 'Walking up those creaking stairs was like walking into an Aladdin's cave.' It was into this 'Aladdin's cave' that Cohan appeared in the spring of 1967, looking to the young student Richard Alston 'extraordinarily glamorous, very American, like a film star'.

On his arrival, Howard had told Cohan that he wanted to put on a performance as soon as possible, and that everyone who was involved in the classes should take part. This was too much for Cohan, for although he had taught every level of ability, he came from a professional performing background and Howard's idea smacked of amateurism. In addition, Cohan quickly realised that with the technical levels of many of the students, there was no possibility of success in the short period of time available. He told Howard that if the performance could be postponed until the autumn, then he would stay and work with the dancers. Howard agreed and booked the Adeline Genée Theatre in East Grinstead for a programme of new works to be premiered in October. Cohan told Howard, 'The dancers are not ready and they are not going to be ready. What they are going to be able to do is to perform the works that we are going to rehearse all summer. I don't guarantee that they can dance anything else, but I guarantee that they will dance those works.' Howard agreed and Cohan stayed to drill the students into shape.

This was no easy task as Howard's endeavours had had an almost Pied Piper effect on the dance world, and Cohan found himself working with a diverse group. Some came from careers as ballet dancers and were retraining in contemporary, some came from PE colleges, some from the commercial world, some were young beginners, and some came from Europe having heard about developments in Britain. Anthony van Laast remembers that Lindsay Kemp, who became one of Britain's greatest mime artists, would often appear in class along with his partially sighted boyfriend Jack, which always added a certain frisson to proceedings. These varying levels of ability caused a problem for Yuriko who had been asked to help with the teaching. After her first class, she said to the group, 'Now Bob knows I am honest and I have to speak as I find, and I have to say you have all been very badly trained.' This was hardly the pep talk they needed, and after that one class she disappeared, never to return. Cohan was more accommodating and told *Dance and Dancers* that,

> … I am trying to be very careful in not forcing on these students here in London what is sometimes defined as the American style… There is a tendency in teaching, to teach as you taught before. But you have to be able to change everything, to grow with everything, to let it all move in a slightly different direction. It is all very dangerous and very delicate, but it has to happen. When it happens you will have what you may call English contemporary dance.[140]

This was some way off and the October programme would include work by choreographers of mixed nationalities, including Trinidadian Anna Mittelholzer, Canadian David Earle, Patrick Steede, and of course works by Cohan himself. In these he would be joined by two of his closest friends from the Graham Company, Noemi Lapzeson and Robert Powell, who, although their relationship had ended was still very much part of Cohan's circle.

Out of the large group of students Cohan selected eight of the most technically able to dance in his works. His first work for the group was *Tzaikerk*, subtitled *Evensong*, to music of the same name by Alan Hovhaness. In it he used six of the women, and the work is ostensibly about the coming of evening. This is not apparent in the dance which is very formally structured, beginning with the six women dancing together then three, then two, then one, and then the work disappears. It is for the most part a very fast dance and Cohan certainly pushed the techniques of the women involved. There is in *Tzaikerk* a clear use of the Graham Technique, but straightaway one can see Cohan's love of stretched lines, fast falls, and recovery to and from the floor. No narrative is apparent but a feel of Middle Eastern or Indian dancing is given by certain arm and hand gestures – for example in the turns with arms in a wide V with flexed hands reminiscent of Sufi dancing – although a starting point for the dance had been the beautiful arms of the young group member Xenia Hribar. Also immediately apparent is Cohan's characteristic use of the music, in which he never 'mimics' the musical rhythms or textures but like Graham takes large sections as blocks to form his movement phrases on. This is Horstian choreography at its best, fully understanding of the music but not a slave to it. Anna Mittelholzer remembers the dance as very fast and very tricky to perform, the problems in it being exacerbated by the different standards of performance skills of the six women. This was not a group of seasoned performers who had bonded over years and the pairings and groupings caused some arguments. Mittelholzer was paired with a particularly temperamental dancer and she had to race to keep up with her. None of these difficulties were observed by the critics and Peter Williams noted that 'it was ingenious in that everybody had a chance of doing something; nor did it tax the young dancers beyond their limitations'.[141]

His other work, *Sky*, with music by Eugene Lester was based on Native American mythology about the Sky and the Earth coming together, and explained in a simple programme note: 'The first people lived beyond the stars because there was no earth beneath.' The cast of nine women and five men were variously the Storm People, and the Rainbow People, while the main focus of the dance was on Robert Powell and Noemi Lapzeson as Father Sky and Mother Earth. The chorus included Robert Dodson, who would change his name to North, and Norman Murray, who would change his name to Namron; along with former London Festival Ballet dancer Clare Duncan, they became long-serving members of his company.

Into the opening Storm scene, Lightning (Powell) appeared with forked flashes attached to his wrists and danced an energetic solo of power. This was followed by a gentle solo for Rain (Lapzeson) who was swept away by the female chorus pulling a gauze across the stage. The Sky women then entered, holding peacock feathers which they waved as though attempting to purify the way for the entry of Mother Earth. Here, after a quick change, Lapzeson returned dressed in a brown dress from which hung strips of material representing the roots of the earth. Her majestic solo was supported by three duos that created closely entwined patterns. Mother Earth was then joined by Father Sky in a sensual duet which ended with them running to the four corners of the earth and away. The storm over the chorus enters in shades reminiscent of a rainbow and heralds the arrival of the First Man and Woman who dance another duet; the material is picked up and developed and this most poetic of works for an inexperienced company ends.

Writing in *The Times*, John Percival found the work 'in form… reminiscent of Martha Graham's early nature myths. Without any direct narrative it proceeds from an evocation of storm to rainbow and at the same time from sky to earth, chaos to creation.' Of the dancing he found Powell's and Lapzeson's 'excellence is backed by some interesting group dances which valuably force the ensemble just past their real present capacity'.[142]

The first performances of the Contemporary Dance Group were at the Adeline Genée Theatre, East Grinstead, Surrey between 10 and 14 October in a programme entitled 'Dance, One, Two, Four'. The gala premiere, on 10 October, began with *Tzaikerk*, *Piece for Metronome*, and *Three Dancers* by Patrick Steede – this work had already been seen in choreographic workshops led by Dorothy Madden at Dartington College and was in a markedly different style to the others; it included Mop Eager as one of the three 'dancers'. After the interval came Anna Mittelholzer's *Family of Man*, a twenty-minute work, the first piece of dance to come from the London school's tradition. Inspired by a recent photography exhibition of the same name, it followed Howard's wishes by including all the levels of dancing ability. This was followed by Cohan's *Eclipse*, danced by Powell and Lapzeson and finally the premiere of *Sky*. Later in the week, Cohan and Powell danced in *Hunter of Angels*, and David Earle's work *Witness of Innocence*, based on the life of Lady Jane Grey and previously seen in Canada, were shown.

Just as the critics had supported Graham, so too did they support the new venture, with all of them writing in broadly positive terms about the performances. Alexander Bland in *The Observer* wrote, 'It is fair, then, to record that the Contemporary Dance Group has got away to an excellent start.'[143] Nicholas Dromgoole in the *Sunday Telegraph* was glowing in his praise for Robert Cohan, writing that 'on this showing Robert Cohan is a major choreographer and we are indeed fortunate to have him among us'.[144]

Not everyone was entirely happy and Richard Alston remembers that before Cohan had arrived 'there had been [around Howard] a whole range of eccentric misfits from the motley British dance scene' but that,

> … very quickly as Bob began to formulate what he wanted to do, all sorts of other people had to let go of their own little dreams. It became clear the company was going to be run by one person and that would be Bob and we would do this and not that. No, we would not do happenings in the street or hug trees. There were lots of little resentments, but we were part of the new young gang who were going to be part of Bob's work.

Happy, at first, to be part of this, Alston admits that he and Siobhan Davies were so smitten by the whole enterprise that they 'were like groupies'. Even at this early stage, Howard had decided that Alston was going to be a choreographer and, feeling it would be good for him to understand all aspects of dance production, had sent him to East Grinstead to work overnight with the technicians. This plan quickly changed when it was apparent Alston did not know one end of a wrench from the other and more suitable jobs were found for him. But he was in the theatre and was fascinated by the theatricality of it all. He and Davies were astonished watching 'Bob and Noemi warm up in their extraordinary Graham make-up; they would wear two pairs of false eye lashes, bejewelled with melted wax. It looked amazing and exotic on Noemi but on the men it was just weird.' Weird or not it was a huge success, for Cohan, for Howard, and for the dancers. They had shown that it was possible to produce quality contemporary dance in Britain, and everyone wanted more.

From such success and high praise in England, Cohan returned to a Graham company in a state of decay. Graham was still working on choreography and for the May 1968 season at the George Abbott Theater was preparing three works: *Plain of Prayer*, *A Time of Snow*, and *The Lady of the House of Sleep*. No one thought these works were up to the standard of her previous dances and in most she cast herself as an observer with little dance movement. In both of the latter works, Doris Hering felt that 'Miss Graham almost becomes an intruder' and that *The Lady of the House of Sleep* 'seemed like a parody of other Graham works'.[145]

It was remarkable that the works were even made as Graham found it difficult to drag herself from her apartment to come to the studio; she was depressed and drunk most of the time and Cohan almost always had to telephone her and coax her to the studio. The dancers, who had often been given leeway in devising their own parts, now began to create them entirely on their own. On the Monday morning, when they were due to start rehearsals on *A Time of Snow*, Graham did not appear and Cohan called her, asking where she was, to which Graham replied, 'Oh darling, I'll be there soon, just work on bits and pieces.' He had to tell her it was a new piece and there were no bits and pieces to which her response was, 'Oh God.'

In *A Time of Snow*, a heavy piece filled with violence, Graham was tortured by the realisation that she could not dance anymore and upset that she had to give the young part to Noemi Lapzeson. She found it difficult to cope, knowing that Cohan and Ross, who were thirty years younger than her, could still dance. There had been a time when there was a huge age difference between her and her company but no one noticed. In the film of *Appalachian Spring*, in which she played the Bride, she was in her mid sixties while Stuart Hodes as her husband was just thirty, but she did not look it. Now in her seventies, it was obvious and it hurt her. David Earle saw her sitting in her dressing room one night, staring into the mirror, and thought that she looked like the loneliest person he would ever see.

In the work, Graham cast Cohan as the evil Fulbert, Héloïse's uncle who orders the castration of Abélard, and Cohan relished it. He remembers it as one of the best parts she ever made on him and he impressed Doris Hering who thought 'Robert Cohan's Fulbert, with its hard gait and demoniacal facial expression was one of the most distinguished portrayals of the season. He was as cold as a shard of medieval stone.'[146] The work was Graham's last collaboration with Norman dello Joio, who wrote his *Songs of Abelard* for the dance; Graham was not entirely happy with the score and in one rehearsal barked, 'I asked him for a ballet not a goddammed opera!'

Despite all of this, the company got through the May season and a second one in the autumn garnered fairly positive reviews, particularly because Graham danced less. Even when she did the critics were a little kinder as when Allen Hughes wrote of her *Clytemnestra*, 'Miss Graham herself was especially effective as performer in this entire sequence. At the beginning of the work, she was quite unsteady in her opening solo dances and had difficulty with the passages in which she had to rise from a kneeling position. Once these moments had passed, however, things went well in every respect.'[147]

In addition, old masterworks including *Dark Meadow*, *Alcestis*, and *Errand into the Maze* were brought back into the repertoire and the younger dancers were given leading roles. In a long article in the *New York Times* of 26 November entitled 'Blueprint for the Future', Clive Barnes was unusually enthusiastic for the future of the company: 'it has become clear that the company's future is clear [sic] and determined. Miss Graham – one of the greatest of all American artists – has already prepared the blueprints.' These blueprints included major revivals, the purchase of the school premises, and a triumvirate of Cohan, Ross, and LeRoy Leatherman under Graham running the company, and in a new season works by Cohan and Ross as well as Graham's own. Barnes finished his article with, 'It has often been maintained that modern dance needs a show-case repertory company comparable to the classic ballet companies. It would be supremely fitting and for that matter, extraordinarily convenient if such a company simply grew out of Martha Graham and her dancers.'

The article was so optimistic for the future that it seemed too good to be true, and unfortunately it was. The positive gloss Graham and her lieutenants put on the picture for the press was not the reality of the studio. She wanted to dance, she could not; she wanted to choreograph, she could not; and if she could not do those things, she did not care what happened to her works. Cohan tried to 'read' her; he wanted to support her but did not know what she wanted. In the UK, the plans for a permanent school and theatre had moved ahead and premises had been found. At Christmas 1968, Cohan found himself alone with Noemi Lapzeson when he finally decided he would move to England; a major factor in this decision was when he had been mugged on the street and realised that perhaps New York was not the place to be after all. The two pooled the money in their wallets and he called British Airways to find out when the next flight to London was available.[148] It turned out to be the following morning so the two had a meal together, she then drove him to his apartment where he packed and wrote a note to Graham explaining his actions. As he recalls, 'I realised that when I was away from New York the Graham company got on quite well without me, while the London Contemporary Dance Group started to fall apart if I was away.' He would not return for some time, subletting his apartment to his brother and beginning a new life in England.

Chapter 6

Commentary

I came back to the Graham Company with a great sigh of relief with regard to the kind of teaching I was doing and all that it required, especially the complicated travelling I had to do every week. As Paul wrote, I did not allow myself to teach even one class for a year. I knew that I had been teaching too much but when I gave my classes up, the freedom I felt proved to me that it was the right decision. I had to stop teaching for a while.

I also wanted to dance again and although I was still in good physical shape, I was not in good 'dance' shape and I had to focus on myself to achieve that. I was also going to be on stage with these much younger dancers, some of whom were technically very good. It wasn't a competition in my mind. I knew that dramatically I was still powerful but I had to strengthen my body enough to be able to hold my own physical space on stage.

If I taught at the Graham school, I would again have to teach the Graham method. There was no actual requirement placed on the teachers to teach a certain way, but it was clear that dancers came to the Graham school to learn her technique and I thought it was wrong to stray too far from the basic canon.

Reading about this time when I left the Graham Company and came to London is not easy for me because of the enormous life change involved. I had become especially close to Martha those last few years. As is well known now, she was drinking heavily and more and more she could not control it. I knew from personal experience that there is not much one can to do to stop alcoholism. Whatever help you try to give inadvertently makes you an enabler. I tried to protect her. Whenever she didn't show up for a rehearsal, I would call her or go to her apartment, which was just down the street from the studio, and try to coax her to come. If it was too impossible, I had to make some excuse and take the rehearsal myself or get Bert to do it. This, as you can imagine was – emotionally – desperately wearing.

It is, I think, not an uncommon problem with certain kind of creative performing artists who so devote themselves to their art that when they end up unable to perform, they find themselves old, alone and without a family or partner to protect them. It is an intolerable situation and alcohol or drugs are the only way they can find to make each day possible. I am not being overdramatic, Maria Callas immediately comes to mind and I am sure there are many more. I also know it from my own experience, when after a particularly exciting performance, with many curtain calls, I would go home alone with maybe a Chinese takeaway for dinner.

That's not what most of the audience would think happens to those glamorous dancers they just applauded on the stage. Who would think that Martha Graham, the genius of dance, who was considered as one of the most acclaimed dance artists of her time, would be home alone drinking because she could not face coming to her own studio to work. That's the way it was and is.

I knew that if I stayed in New York, very possibly Bert and I would inherit the Graham Company but London was calling. I have said many times before, you don't get the opportunity to start a school and dance company in the way you think is best artistically very often. I had the offer once before with the Batsheva Company, which did not work out; so this time I had to take the opportunity.

Chapter 7

Such a mind, is indeed,

That of a Buddha!

(Shinkei, 1406–75)

1970–3

It is not entirely fair to say that the group fell apart when Cohan was not with them; although it would be true to say that it lacked firm direction. Howard had made his choice for director and that was Cohan; anyone else was there to follow as best they could Howard's wishes and was simply treading water. The two this fell upon were David Earle and Anna Mittelholzer who Howard had brought over from the Graham Studio with promises of work in England. The Canadian Earle had been ecstatic when he had received his American green card, but the joy was short-lived, as along with the opportunity to live and work in the USA, he found he was eligible for the Vietnam draft and received his call-up papers soon after the card. Howard saw the highly gifted Commonwealth citizen as an ideal person to work with on his projects in England and to Earle it seemed like a gift from heaven. But he sensed there would be problems with Howard, as when he suggested that his partner, the dancer and Graham Company member Peter Randazzo, could be offered work as well, Howard replied, 'Oh no! I want to keep the homosexuals down to a minimum.' Mop Eager points out that this was not down to any homophobia on Howard's part, rather he wanted a 'happy balanced company'. After his experience of working with another company where the majority of the men were gay and the women spent their spare time with either the technicians or the musicians, Howard resolved that the sexual make-up of the company would be conducive to good working and social relationships all round.

Anna Mittelholzer also encountered difficulties with Howard. In his efforts to get her to join the group he, in her eyes, offered more than he could deliver. It is unlikely that Howard would have offered the directorship of the company to such a young and fairly inexperienced artist, but he made it sound as though he had. In addition, she felt she suffered from some degree of racism when a dancer said to her, 'Oh come on Anna, someone like you is not going to direct the company.' This is not a view supported by Namron, another black dancer in the company who did not experience any form of racism. Indeed, it was the multiracial nature of Graham's company that had attracted him in the first place; prior to seeing the half dozen or more black dancers in Graham's troupe, the only black male dancer he had seen was one in the TV pop series *Cool for Cats* which ran from 1955 to 1961. Nevertheless, Britain in the late 1960s was a deeply racist country but LCDT would prove itself a pioneering company in promoting complete integration of all races.

Mittelholzer and Earle, in Cohan's absence, provided leadership as best they could, taking the group on tours that seemed more like expeditions to damp outposts of the United Kingdom. But when it was clear that Cohan would be moving permanently to Britain, they left. Earle went back to Canada and with Randazzo founded the Toronto Dance Theatre, becoming one of that country's most celebrated dance artists, while Mittelholzer moved to a career in Europe and then America. She could have had a place in the group as a dancer, but she did not see herself as a performer, preferring to choreograph and to teach. As an educator, she has had a highly successful career which continues to this day, although a trace of hurt at her treatment by Howard, not Cohan, for whom she has nothing but the greatest respect, has stayed with her.

On 16 January 1969, the Contemporary Ballet Trust released a press statement stating that it would be setting up a new arts centre in London. The centre would be housed in the disused Drill Hall of the Artists Rifles in Duke's Road, near Euston station. Above the door of the somewhat grubby building just behind St Pancras Church is the crest of an army regiment founded in 1859 which was to be a volunteer corps of the arts professions – painters, actors, musicians, and sculptors. If to modern ears this sounds like a recipe for a scene from Peter Nichols' play *Privates on Parade*, to the patriotic Victorians it sounded like a good idea. Among the early members were John Everett Millais, William Holman Hunt, William Morris, and G. F. Watts. The regiment was called many things over time but the name by which it is best remembered as is the Artists Rifles. Eventually, it became an extremely successful officer training corps and part of the Special Air Service (SAS) but did keep some curious special functions such as mounting the guard at the Royal Academy Summer Exhibition and providing a small guard of honours at the dinner of the Worshipful Company of Glovers. From 1889 to 1967, Duke's Road had been their headquarters and drill hall but until Howard took on the lease, it had stood empty.

It was to be an ambitious project with the 15,000 square feet housing an experimental studio/theatre suitable for a range of art forms, and seating 300; in addition there would be five large studios, three rehearsal rooms, and a canteen with additional plans for a 150-seat restaurant. England had seen nothing like it and there was much excitement.

The building would also house the London School of Contemporary Dance and the Trust's offices. In addition it would be the home of Peter Maxwell Davies and Harrison Birtwistle's music theatre group the Pierrot Players. There would also be a ballet studio for Madame Cleo Nordi, who had been a member of Pavlova's company. The expenses for the project, it was hoped, would be met by renting out the spaces to other groups. 'Other groups' included the New Cinema Club, which turned out to be an adult film club, and Siobhan Davies and Richard Alston remember with horror the nights when, working as student helpers, they had to clear the building of dubious men in shabby raincoats. The Trust's own dance group planned to present a number of performances each year in the theatre which would initially be open to members only.

Before settling on The Place, Howard and Mop had spent months looking for suitable premises, even at one time considering the empty Old Vic Theatre in Waterloo. When Cohan and Howard had discussed a permanent building, Cohan was adamant that as well as rehearsal rooms, it had to have a small theatre. What he wanted was something along the lines of the YMHA Theater in New York, which emerging artists could hire for a small fee that included technical support, and thus have a platform for showing their work. The venue, though small, was uptown and did attract critics, who often refused to travel to downtown performances. Cohan had been shown The Place in the summer of 1968 and was satisfied. A decisive moment came when, under Cohan's instructions, Howard marked out the size of the proposed stage by laying his walking stick on the floor, the generous depth of the stage being something Cohan was insistent on. The original idea had been to call the building The Artist's Place, building into the name a tribute to its original tenants, but very early on someone pointed out that the name would be truncated by press and public alike, and so The Place was born.

While a home for the Trust had been found, Cohan yet had to find one. Initially, he stayed at the Gore Hotel and then tried various flats around the capital before settling on a small mews house in Thurloe Place, South Kensington, which, with Howard's help, he would ultimately purchase. Although this was to be his London base for many years, he never seemed to truly inhabit it; months after he moved in, Robin Howard arrived to find the place still full of unpacked boxes. This so perturbed him that he even asked Mop Eager if she thought Cohan was actually planning to stay in the UK. To begin with though, Cohan had to think carefully if he could afford the rent. He had not entered into his contract with Howard to make large sums of money, but he did need to live and so Howard agreed to pay an adequate salary of £45 per week, in addition to which 'I had an account at The Place and for a while my general expenses were taken from the account and in the end it was all worked out'. Generally though, Cohan had little opportunity to spend money, as he spent most of his time working. He would 'arrive at The Place at 9.30 a.m. to teach at 10 a.m., and then I left twelve hours later. I taught, choreographed, then taught again.' There was little time for a social life, most often he would eat with Howard and Eager and discuss work. Occasionally at weekends he would join Peter Williams the editor of *Dance and Dancers*, and his group of largely gay intelligentsia, including choreographer Kenneth MacMillan; designer Nick Georgiadis; critics Clement Crisp and Andrew Porter and Porter's wife Sheila; journalist John Higgins; TV mandarin John Drummond and his partner director Bob Lockyer; and photographer Anthony Crickmay. The last three would become lifelong friends, with Crickmay his closest confidant and valued collaborator. This work pattern was, however, nothing new to Cohan, he had worked long hours with Graham and he was used to it. The difference now was that he was in a new country without family and very few friends. He had persuaded Howard to employ Noemi Lapzeson and Robert Powell, even going so far as to tell Howard to keep some money he was owed to enable them to come. They provided some sense of family for him but mostly he was alone. While he and Powell had ceased to be lovers, the younger man still exerted an influence over Cohan and Clare Duncan remembers that in rehearsals Powell always put his own particular 'spin' on the movement, and Cohan let him get away with it, but she and others noticed that 'you only had to see the way Bob [Cohan] looked at him to see he was still in love'.

As work moved ahead to convert The Place the dance group continued on an extensive tour of the British Isles. These were often to out-of-the-way places where sometimes there would only be two or three people in the audience, but the dancers were so keen to perform that those not dancing in a particular piece would sit in the audience to bolster numbers and give moral support. The tours always began with a demonstration of Graham Technique, which Cohan had choreographed and which he would introduce. More often than not, the accompanist was Judyth Knight, a former pupil of the distinguished concert pianist Peter Katin, who had worked extensively as a ballet pianist and who had been sent by Howard to New York to see how contemporary dance was accompanied. There she was mentored by Bertram Ross, who was himself a fine musician, and she brought these skills back to England where, as principal accompanist at The Place for over twenty years, she trained generations of dance musicians. Although she knew Cohan well, playing for him was not always plain sailing and she observes that,

> I don't think he liked music much, although he tolerated it well in the class; but I felt that he often found it inhibiting as it imposed certain rhythmic restrictions on his teaching of technical exercises. Many of the dance combinations he devised and for which it was required to improvise music were lengthy and contained changes of metre, and sometimes he would have liked them to include changes of tempo too, which was an element I firmly resisted...!

After the demonstration the group were able, even at this very early stage, to perform a range of works by Place choreographers. A typical eclectic second half programme included Steede's *Piece for Metronome* and *Three Dancers*, a love duet from Mittelholzer's *Family of Man*, an extract from Cohan's *Eclipse*, *Sky* and *Tzaikerk*, and the Hand Dance from Paul Taylor's *Piece Period*. The sheer variety of styles was a challenge for the young dancers to perform but this was what

Howard and Cohan wanted and always would be a feature of the company. But this is how they learnt to dance, by dancing.

Later additions to the repertoire included more complex dances such as Barry Moreland's *Summer Games*, Clover Roope's *Ô Saisons Ô Châteaux*, and Ruth Posner's *Four Poems*. All three used contemporary sounds, the Moreland being set to Samuel Barber, the Roope to Elisabeth Lutyens, while the Posner was danced to the poetry of Keats, Yeats and e. e. cummings. Moreland and Roope seemed set to become part of the backbone of the company as choreographers, but it soon became apparent that Moreland's real area of interest was ballet and he left, working extensively with London Festival Ballet, while Roope, for personal reasons, moved into other areas and developed into the leading British-born teacher of classic Graham Technique.

The summer saw the dancers make their first European visit when in July they performed in Vichy, Châteauvallon and Les Baux, in France. Cohan was still very much a performer at this stage and his experience, together with that of Powell and Lapzeson, was much admired by the younger dancers. Of the open air performance at Châteauvallon, Linda Gibbs remembers that 'Bob and Noemi danced *Eclipse*. Against the starry night sky it was absolutely magical. Bob seemed huge and overpowering as the Sun & Noemi small and vulnerable as the Moon.' The performances were well received although there was some confusion in the press who thought Robin Howard was the choreographer for the group.

Before The Place was officially opened, the building was shown off to great advantage in what could be described as a 'happening'. Entitled 'Explorations', it was devised by Howard and shown between 24 and 26 July and 29 and 31 July, and involved the whole building being taken over by art and artists – even corridors and broom cupboards. In programme one, *Green Maze* by Alan Beattie saw three dancers move slowly between some green plastic sheets. In the unfinished theatre, there were mobile sculptures by Andrew Logan buzzing around the floor while *Event with Air Structure and Costumes* by Peter Dockley saw an aerial performer slowly lowered from the ceiling in a spacesuit. The long hallway in the basement was taken over by *Corridor and Room for Robin Howard* by Peter Logan, with music by Brian Hodgson, which saw the space covered in paper. It had holes cut into it through which various people put their legs and other body parts. Richard Alston was one of these and he remembers that his body was in a room being used for a rehearsal by Geoff Moore's Moving Being group while his cramped leg was waving at the audience in the corridor. Art Bauman's first work, *Burlesque/Black & White*, included a striptease in reverse; while his second was a dialogue between a dancer (Bauman) and a film of himself in an office. Programme two started with *X-IT* by Leopoldo Maler; it was a large work for sixteen performers and included forklift trucks which lifted audience members into their seats. *Cronus 111* by Taller de Montevideo, a Latin American collective, saw the audience move around the white set while lights played on the performers clad in white leotards. *Moving Being Benediction* by Geoff Moore was his expected blend of movement, light, speech, and sound. It was an exciting and unexpected prelude.

The building finally and officially opened its doors, behind schedule, on 2 September 1969 in a more formal ceremony presided over by Lord Goodman, Chairman of the Arts Council. After the gala, performances continued in an ambitious three-week season from the group which presented a repertory of twelve dances by Cohan, Patricia Christopher, Barry Moreland, Clover Roope, together with Alvin Ailey's *Hermit Songs*, performed by guest artist William Louther, and Martha Graham's *El Penitente*, performed by Cohan, Louther and Lapzeson. Louther, a pupil of May O'Donnell and member of the Graham Company, would become one of the main players at The Place, as a charismatic performer, teacher, and occasional choreographer. His performances of *Hermit Songs* and later his own *Vesalii Icones* have become the stuff of legend.

El Penitente was always one of Cohan's favourite dances and in his career he had performed both the male roles. He had become somewhat identified with the title role, as Judith Cruickshank noted: '*El Penitente* for me means Robert Cohan who danced the role of the penitent with such passionate conviction, such total commitment, that he could make the audience feel the penitent's pain, his remorse, his joy.'[149] He had returned to America to ask Graham's permission to stage the work and also to get the props which included a cross and an apple, hand carved by Noguchi. Cohan fretted on the flight back to England as to how he was going to get these objects held in his brown leather hand luggage, valued in the tens of thousands of pounds, through customs. He need not have worried, however, as the customs official was only interested in how much alcohol or cigarettes he had with him and he was waved through.

The programme cover for the opening season was by Cohan's friend Norberto Chiesa, the estranged husband of Noemi Lapzeson. Chiesa had visited Cohan in London and had effectively 'made' the theatre at The Place. He designed and built the floor and built all the risers, bleachers, and steps. Disenchanted with New York, he eventually moved permanently to England and became Cohan's regular designer, as well as partner in various small-scale property developments the two would be involved in. Although Howard came from a family of politicians, he had not inherited his family's diplomatic genes and he opened the programme with bad news, noting that the group had performed to over 25,000 people, but went on to say that,

> ... the financial position of the Contemporary Ballet Trust is simple but sad. The building and the Artists' Place Society cannot continue without the Trust, but the Trust itself cannot continue without more money from somewhere. Our main donor [i.e. Howard] has contributed all he can and unless money is found by Christmas, the Trust must close down. It is hard to believe that

Britain cannot find at least as much money for its only contemporary dance organisation as it finds for eight or nine ballet organisations, each of which on average receives over five times as much as we do.

The bleak warning finished with a tribute to Cohan with Howard challenging 'anyone to name one person in the world who is a better choreographer-performer-teacher-inspirer-explainer-leader-helper-bag-carrier-floor-sweeper and friend'.[150]

Cohan's contribution to the opening programme was *Side Scene* set, interestingly for him, not to a twentieth-century score but to a selection of pre-classical music. It was in a way a companion piece to *Tent of Vision*, Cohan's work for Batsheva, and may have included material from that dance; in the Batsheva work, he had explored the inner world of circus acrobats and in this one, he wanted to show the backstage world of the performers. What the audience saw was the behind-the-curtain life of the performers before they went on stage. The dance was concerned with their relationships, and using a variety of circus props and materials, it was a somewhat sombre affair. What may have started the idea for the work was a gigantic ball, far bigger and more solid than the currently modish exercise balls that Cohan found in the building. Robert Powell demonstrated expertise in balancing and walking on it, but sadly he was not to be in the dance and all the cast – William Louther, Barry Moreland, Xenia Hribar, Dinah Goodes, and Linda Gibbs – fell off; Namron twisted his ankle so badly that his role had to be reworked and his involvement limited to some static strongman partnering, swinging Linda Gibbs and Clare Duncan from his extended arms. In spite of this, and ignoring Linda Gibbs' protestations that she was not going to work with it, Cohan and his designer Norberto Chiesa incorporated it into the dance and all that remains of the work is a striking photograph of Gibbs balanced on the ball in a precarious penché arabesque, holding the hands of William Louther.

Two days later, on 4 September, Cohan's second new work, *Shanta Quintet*, was premiered. This work was very much of its time and fitted in with the world of the hippies and the then current interest in all things Indian. The music was by the Anglo-Indian composer and violinist John Mayer and Cohan had heard the music, a blend of jazz and Indian ragas for sitar and string quartet, on record and found it very exciting. His long-standing fascination for Indian culture was given full rein in this technically demanding work for two men and three women and which he described to them as 'a perfumed love song' though some realised it probably had come from the Kama Sutra. The men wearing beautiful harem trousers and the women swathed in luxurious silks giving the impression of flowing saris, Cohan set about creating 'a beautiful dance smelling of incense', almost something Ruth St Denis would have been proud of. He had thought of intensifying the atmosphere by having incense blown through the heating system, but this was not followed through. In what became a long association with Cohan, Linda Gibbs remembers *Shanta Quintet* as being the only time he ever got angry with them, when they could not get some particular tricky combination he was asking for. He was, for his young dancers, a presence similar to Graham, and despite his laid-back ways and trendy clothes, he was still 'the Boss' and Gibbs recalls it took some time before she and the others felt comfortable talking to him.

Cohan's third and final contribution to the season, on 11 September, could not have been more different to the others. *Cell*, set to a musique concrète score by Ronald Lloyd, was a dark expressionist piece seeming to concern a group of people imprisoned in their own way of thinking. He had been introduced to Lloyd through Primavera Boman, the daughter of expressionist dancer Hilde Holger and one of the company dancers and who had worked with him on projects while a student at Saint Martins College of Art.

It is typical of Cohan's searching mind that he chose such a figure as Lloyd, who although he had been a professional oboe player, was hardly mainstream as a composer. Influenced by the American Harry Partch, he built his own instruments, was interested in microtonal tunings and created some of the earliest examples of British electronic music. From an aristocratic family, he was well travelled, fluent in many languages, and just the sort of person Cohan liked to work with.

The dance explored three ways of living – a personal one, an abstract one, and a sensual one, all of which end in disaster. The inspiration for the piece was his one-time lover Robert Powell. Powell was an immensely gifted dancer – Anna Mittelholzer remembers him as one of the five greatest dancers she ever saw, who should have had great success, but 'no matter what he did, which way he went, whatever choices he made, the ultimate result was a disaster', and dependency on alcohol and drugs ultimately ruined his body and his career. Cohan 'saw him as a beautiful dancer who couldn't make anything of it. He could have been a star in a company but he had to be told what to do and be kept under control, he drank so much. There were a lot of pills around at the time.' And 'he just never really stuck with anything and that was the story of *Cell*'.

Cohan was able to place the dancers into a stunning set of 'Mycenaean simplicity' by Norberto Chiesa. Cohan had described to Chiesa a white enclosed room and his friend worked through many designs until he came up with the final version of off-centred walls and floor that were easily assembled, easily transportable, and claustrophobically effective. Cohan gave Ronald Lloyd a definitive minutage and the composer assembled the collage of shrieks and everyday sounds which were every bit as disturbing as Chiesa's set.

With all the components in place, Cohan found the choreography easy and it was for him one of those works which seemed to appear fully formed. He knew where everyone was going to be on stage and he made no changes as the choreography progressed. As noted, the work moves through three movements, or stages, all contained in a white walled space whose only entrances and exits are on each side upstage. Into this come six characters, three men and three women – Cohan told them to imagine they were going to a party, with some people they liked and some people they wanted to avoid; they fall and balance but always return to the walls which, ambiguously, may be their support or their prison. In the first section, they are dressed in everyday clothes, and although their interactions are fleeting they are disturbingly aggressive. They leave one by one. In part two, they appear in tights of primary colours, their outer clothes stripped away, perhaps suggesting the more obvious nature of their relationships. Out of the group one man (Powell) emerges as the central character but once again they all leave one by one. In part three, they enter stripped down to the barest minimum for decency, their clothing offers no protection and emotionally they are fully exposed, and they panic. Richard Buckle described the section as 'falling, embracing, sliding, hiding in corners, photographing Powell, a scarlet starfish on the floor'.[151] They again leave one by one and this time the man is left to panic alone. In a dramatic solo, the man throws himself at the walls and each time he does, a section lights up, exposing a hanging figure.

Here Cohan got stuck; he knew it had to finish in catastrophe and he had this image of strobe lights and bricks flying through the air, but he could not see exactly what Powell should do. Then in a lighting rehearsal on the set, Cohan suddenly looked up and saw 'Powell was sitting there on the floor with all these bricks around him and he took them and piled them up and I said, "That's it."' What 'it' was confused the critics, was the man building a sanctuary or a prison?

The question was part of the power of the piece – Pinteresque, it raised more questions than it answered and the critics were unanimous that Cohan had created a masterpiece. James Kennedy found it 'strong, disturbing choreographic stuff', while Alexander Bland thought it 'outstanding… one of those works in which conception, collaboration and execution come together in what seems inevitable conjunction'.[152] Nicholas Dromgoole enthused that 'no dance enthusiast should miss it'.[153]

The lighting for *Cell* was by a young lighting designer called John B. Read who would go on to light twenty-three of Cohan's dances, in fact the vast majority of his British work and some of his overseas commissions as well. Read had studied at the Rose Bruford College in Sidcup, Kent, and had moved into lighting dance for Ballet Rambert, where he worked particularly closely with Glen Tetley. He developed a close relationship with the Royal Opera and the Royal Ballet, as well as working internationally in contemporary dance, ballet, opera and in the commercial world. In *Cell*, he and Cohan set up the relationship that sustained them over the next twenty years, one of mutual trust. Cohan never told Read how to light and Read never asked Cohan what he wanted. Like a jazz musician, Read improvises with his lighting board; he may view a rehearsal, may see some swatches of costume material, but fundamentally approaches the actual lighting in the theatre as a creative task integral to the success of what he sees before him. The sculpting of the stage and the bodies in light and shadow is what he does in the theatre, not from a set of notes or plans. With Cohan, he found someone who 'was open to any ideas, totally unselfish and totally generous', who allowed him free rein to explore his creativity and craft. Of course, in the early LCDT days, owing to financial considerations, the lighting possibilities were limited, but he used this to his advantage, creating for them a lean, clean look which would become something of a trademark. In *Cell*, his restricted lighting fitted in with the simplicity of the set and costumes, creating from the simplest of means a look that was at once brilliantly surgical yet claustrophobic.

Cell became one of Cohan's most enduring works – it was restaged throughout the company's existence and, even when the central part was danced by characters as different as Tom Jobe and Patrick Harding-Irmer, the strength of the vision came through. When the piece was performed in Poland, the audience stood and applauded for twenty minutes because they saw it as representing their life under communism – at the end everyone was in tears. At an early performance in Southampton a policeman came on stage to tell the audience to leave the theatre as there had been a bomb threat, thinking he was part of the dance, the audience stayed put. After a London performance a friend of Cohan's brought backstage a man who had suffered the bastinado at the hands of the Greek Generals. He wanted to thank Cohan for understanding what torture was like. In Chile, Madame Allende told Cohan it was the first time she was able to cry since her father had been murdered.

This was exactly what Cohan wanted his work to do; he felt it was his job as director and choreographer to create work that gave people a cathartic experience. He felt very strongly at the time that dance should have meaning for an audience and therefore, once he got hold of a theme with a strong social message, he tried to use it as profoundly as he could and deliver a meaningful theatrical experience. This and later works in the early 1970s followed in this vein, tapping into popular counterculture at the time which frequently questioned the status quo and the relationship of the public, and often youth, to authority.

The critical reception to the first season was mainly positive with Richard Buckle noting the 'amazing labours which are producing such shining results',[154] though John Percival in *The Times* sounded a word of caution, observing that 'some of the present works are clearly ephemeral'.[155] At the end of the season, Howard was feeling in a positive mood and produced a document that would highlight, in as optimistic a way as possible, developments over the next ten years. However, all of this came crashing down when at the signing of the lease on the building, an event Howard had encouraged to be public with a strong presence of the press, David Reynolds from the Arts Council handed him a letter and said that it should be read at once. It was a rejection of Howard's request for increased funding.

15 Cohan and Turney in the studio.

16 Cohan in *The Pass*.

17 Cohan in *Vestige.*

18 Cohan and Turney in *The Pass*.

19 Cohan and Turney in *Seaborne*.

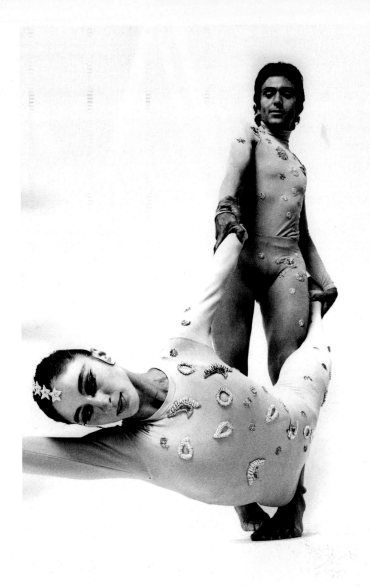

20 Cohan and Noemi Lapzeson in *Eclipse*, 1967.

21 Cohan and Robert Powell in *Hunter of Angels*, 1967.

22 Cohan, Powell and Lapzeson rehearsing *Sky*, 1967.
23 Robert North in *Cell*, 1969.

In spite of this, and showing enormous courage, Howard signed the lease. Even then, he had to tell the dancers that after December there would be no more money and that they would have to cease operations. Then, Howard received two strange yet welcome phone calls. One was from Alexander Dunbar, the director of the Gulbenkian Foundation in Britain, who said that if he could keep the company going until April, then Dunbar would provide funding in the region £30,000 over three years. The second call was from John Cruft, Head of Music at the Arts Council, reversing the decision of the Reynolds letter and agreeing to an increase in money from 1 April 1970. There was no explanation given for this extraordinary change of heart, though perhaps there was a feeling of guilt within the Council, prompted by the generosity of the Gulbenkian Foundation. This would not be the last of the Trust's dealings with an unhelpful Arts Council, but does serve to demonstrate the quixotic way in which public money was spent at the time. So at the end of 1969, the group was technically closed down but born again in 1970 as London Contemporary Dance Theatre, Howard finding more of his own money to cover the bills until the new funding came into effect.

The Trust's work continued along with renewed energy and before the London season in May and June they presented a series of choreographic workshops showcasing the work of company and school members. On 29 April, this included Flora Cushman's *Raga Shankara*, William Louther's *Divertissement in the Playground of the Zodiac*, and Richard Alston's *Something to Do*. Cohan's generosity of spirit and the excitement in the early days of the company paid dividends in the amount of new work that was produced, certainly some was of variable quality and did not last long, but from nothing came a rich seam of invention that lasted decades and spawn in Britain a whole new way of moving. Richard Alston, in an interview in *Dance and Dancers* of June 1978, remembered some of the excitement he felt as a student at this time: 'I made my first piece after studying for nine months. In those days the workshops were entirely un-delineated; you would find yourself working with somebody like Noemi Lapzeson although I was only a first year; anyone could choose anyone to work with since they were feverishly looking for choreographers.'

The second London season lasted from 27 May to 14 June and was so successful that an extra seven days were added to the original run. Even at this early stage, it is worth remembering that it was never the 'Robert Cohan Dance Company' and this season included works by eleven choreographers as varied as the experienced Cohan, Ailey, and Taylor, through to newcomers like Alston and Barry Moreland.

After the season ended, the company continued on its pattern of touring the UK and Europe and first they went to Oxford where they gave the premiere of Cohan's latest work, *X*. Set to music by Mauricio Kagel, *X*, like *Cell* before it, dealt with fears and tensions and anxieties in group of young people who seemed to counteract the stress by smoking marijuana. It had been inspired by the My Lai massacre, although the catalyst to start the work had been the music, a typically challenging piece by Argentinian composer Mauricio Kagel called *ACUSTICA, Musik für experimentelle Klangerzeuger, Lautsprecher und zwei bis fünf Spieler*, which Cohan found very exciting.

The My Lai massacre, in which a unit of American troops sexually abused, tortured, mutilated, and killed a group of about 500 civilians, took place on 16 March 1968 in Vietnam and two years later was still a much discussed topic. The story that Cohan recalled at the time was that the American soldiers were high on hashish and this he wanted to include in the piece. The music in a sense dictated the shape of the dance as it built up to a tremendous explosive climax. Cohan wanted to open up the whole stage, strip it bare and have the dancers sitting at the back as though they were smoking hash and then, zombie-like, they would get into a line and walk forward and back. The idea was that the work would be an illusory drug-induced dream that would end in catastrophe, and it continued logically until they were all in a straight line and then they were shot. Chiesa created for the work an extraordinary inflatable set which added to the spaced-out atmosphere of the piece. A great deal of smoke was blown onto the stage so, like the nudity in the then current musical *Hair*, it was difficult to see exactly what the dancers were up to, some guessed it was drug-taking, some did not. At the first performance some knowledgeable critics were certain they recognised a certain smell, but it was incense, not marijuana, which Cohan had blown into the theatre, following through the idea he had not used in *Shanta Quintet*. The dancers then slowly walked forward, some occasionally kneeling, others going back again; to them this was like moving in and out of a hallucination. They then ran about and performed short personal solos. Events became more chaotic, or hallucinatory, as they rolled, slapped their thighs, and walked. Some order was discernible in the chaos, perhaps a reflection of *X*, 'the incalculable influence or factor' (this quote from the Oxford Dictionary was the only programme note). The chaos became more organised and regimented, and the dancers more zombie-like. Near the end, each of the men picked up a girl who would fall as soon as she was lifted, then one woman (Xenia Hribar) was chosen by the men to be lifted high, as for a sacrifice, but she too flopped. The dance ended with the cast walking forward to the audience. Peter Williams found it an odd dance in which 'nothing happens and everything happens',[156] and yet thought it more successful than *Cell*, feeling it dealt with relationships in more complex ways. The photographs of the work, which are now its only record, show a dance which more resembles the works of Merce Cunningham than Cohan. When the company performed it at La Fenice in Venice, the audience hissed it as they thought it was evil. Cohan was intrigued by the ideas in the work but was not happy with the end product, and a few years later wanted to return to it and extend it, but Kagel had altered the music and was not happy for it to go ahead. This was fortuitous as it enabled Cohan to take it into a totally different direction when it would resurface as *Mass*, one of his most intriguing works. Cohan's only other work in 1970 was a resetting of his early solo *Streams* on Noemi Lapzeson.

Cohan had been distracted for part of 1970, when at one of Peter Williams' dinners, he had met Rudolf Nureyev, who was then dancing in Rudi van Dantzig's *The Ropes of Time* with the Royal Ballet. The two found each other fascinating and an affair of some months ensued. Cohan found Nureyev to be an 'extraordinary thinker' with 'an amazing imagination', and his personality on stage was only a fraction of what he displayed offstage. He showed a great interest in Cohan's company and wanted to dance with them, but Cohan had to turn down the request, telling him it was not a company of guest artists and that he felt his presence would 'disrupt the balance'. Nureyev understood fully and never pushed the matter, but it was a brave decision on Cohan's part, as any company that billed Nureyev, as even a guest artist, would be guaranteed large audiences and vast amounts of publicity. Graham herself, as well as Paul Taylor and many others, would take advantage of Nureyev's presence to swell audiences and coffers, but not Cohan, it was not his style.

After a two-week break the company went on tour to Yugoslavia, Czechoslovakia and Italy where, apart from the aforementioned *X* in La Fenice, the performances were well received. The hazards of international travel were brought home to the company when they discovered that, on one of the flights, another passenger was found to have cholera. As a result, and possibly more for political than medical ends, they were forced to stay quarantined in a chalet in the mountains of Czechoslovakia while tests were carried out.

The critical success abroad contrasted, on their return, with the reception at the Windsor Festival, where a disappointingly small audience was less than enthusiastic. This was a salient warning to the company that what was popular in London would not necessarily travel outside. The Windsor event was further marred by an incident at a reception held at the castle, when one of the technical crew, who had drank far too much, was found relieving herself on the green.

Even London could not be guaranteed to welcome all of the work and this was the case with Pauline de Groot's work *Rainmakers*. De Groot, a Dutch choreographer influenced by Erick Hawkins, was a friend of Lapzeson and Cohan had visited Amsterdam to see her work, which he found interesting. He thought it so different from his that it would be good for the company to work in her style. The piece was not popular with many of the dancers, as it seemed to be about cabbages, though a number of them were happy to partake of some of the Dutch cakes she brought with her. Her visit set up the pattern for most of Cohan's tenure as director of the company, when he would bring in a wide range of choreographers because he wanted the company to experience them as people. This, for him, was the key point and he admits: 'It was not so much that the work was good, but the way those people worked, which would enrich the dancers and the company.' They learnt to be dancers through performing.

He did get it right with his next visitor, Talley Beatty, who came to work on his ballet *The Road of the Phoebe Snow*. Beatty was a great name in African American dance; having performed with Katherine Dunham in the 1940s, he then went on to have a distinguished career on Broadway and in the cabaret. This work, set to the music of Duke Ellington and Billy Strayhorn, had been created for the Ailey Company in 1959. One of the main roles had been made on William Louther, and it was he who set it on the company. When Beatty arrived, he worked with the dancers on performance style and nuance and they loved it, even though he was a strict disciplinarian, in the mould of Cole and Robbins. At one rehearsal, Namron found himself 'raping' Linda Gibbs repeatedly, until Beatty saw exactly what he wanted, and Namron retired to the corner with severe muscle strain. Barry Moreland, who had entered LCDT after some years in commercial theatre, was, however, in his element. The audiences loved it as well and at the premiere, they applauded so long that Beatty and Cohan, who were at the back of The Place's theatre, had time to go all the way around the auditorium to the stage and still arrive to thunderous applause. The success of the work was a reward for a difficult time for Cohan, as he had to look after Beatty, who was more than temperamental and would many times announce for no reason: 'I'm leaving! You can't do the piece!' and storm out. On one memorable occasion, Cohan took him to his hotel and watched him while he packed, then drove him to the airport, where Beatty refused to leave the car, and the two returned together.

At this time, Cohan was far more than a choreographer, as Howard had noted in his preface to the opening of The Place. Yet, Cohan downplays his creative role: 'I wasn't choreographing for myself, I was choreographing for the company. I was making work for the dancers that they would enjoy doing and that the audience would enjoy. It wasn't about pieces I wanted to do. If anything, I wasn't a choreographer, I was teacher, teaching by choreography and, OK, that was fair enough for me.' This is typical of Cohan's self-deprecating style. None of the critics or audiences would have thought that he was anything less than a master craftsman creating new and interesting work for a new and interesting company. That he was teaching by enabling the dancers to dance seems to be a laudable endeavour. Helping others to reach a higher level of attainment is central to Gurdjieff's teachings and Cohan certainly put the idea into practice with his company.

His new work, in the same programme as Beatty's, was *Consolations of the Rising Moon*, a development of some material from *Shanta Quintet* which was, by his own admission, 'a weird piece'. Set to a selection of early Spanish guitar music arranged and performed by guitarist John Williams, it was a 'Spanish/ Moorish ritual about the rising moon and nothing else, nothing else, that is, except interpreting the music'. The music and Williams were integral to the piece; he was on stage, dressed in white, seated inside a white circle – the rising moon of the title. Near him were two oriental-looking benches around which the dancers, dressed in sexy oriental costumes – the men in jockstraps with skirts and tassels of red and the women in blue and black – moved.

The dance had been designed by Peter Farmer, who would become a frequent collaborator of Cohan and the company, and who, in the early years, did much to give it a visual identity, even if on occasions Cohan found his work a little too balletic. Another key element in the visual identity of the company was the lighting. Often, the name Charter would appear in programmes, sometimes with a biography:

Charter

Started lighting for dance early in the 1960s in the United States of America and since moving to London has been involved in helping to establish the lighting pattern for the LCDT and has gone on to design lighting for several of their productions including *Reflections, Step at a Time, Then You Can Only Sing* and *Forest*.

The biography was fictitious as Charter was Cohan's alias, much like Paul Taylor's pseudonymous costume designer Tacet. Cohan, who had spent many hours watching the great Jean Rosenthal light Graham's work, brought this style of theatrical lighting to the UK. In the ballet which Britain was used to, the lighting more often than not lit the soloists and little else. In Graham's and Cohan's theatre, the lights were used to highlight the space and bring it to life.

Initially, Cohan's decision to light his own dances was purely financial; he could not afford to pay anyone else to do it. But he also realised early on in his career that the dances he made in the daylight in a studio were, when transferred onto a theatre's black stage, at the mercy of the lighting designer. For the lighting to be successful, choreographer and lighting designer need to have a close relationship. Cohan worked well with John B. Read on many occasions but he knew how he wanted his dances to look on stage, and so trained himself to be able to design his own lighting plots.

Another figure who shaped the image of the company, even to those who never saw them, was photographer Anthony Crickmay. Cohan had first met Crickmay when he had taken photographs of the Graham Company – his well-known portrait of Graham in a position of angst taken at 5 a.m. during the Edinburgh Festival visit is one of the finest of the artist. They became good friends, and from the earliest days, Crickmay photographed the school and the company. Described by writer Ann Nugent as 'the greatest living photographer of Western theatre dance',[157] whose photographs 'crystallise the aims of the interpreter and the creator', he had no formal training in photography as such, having been a protégé of the London-based Austrian photographer Lotte Meitner-Graf, who encouraged him in his work. Then through various serendipitous encounters, he found himself taking photographs of opera at Covent Garden and then of the ballet – he broke the monopoly of photographer Houston Rogers, who had a prerogative on ballet for years.

His exquisitely composed photographs – Crickpix – with lighting orchestrated to perfectly highlight the form and shape of the bodies, and yet give volume to the space they occupy, fitted well with Cohan's approach to lighting. The images, like Cohan's choreography, which on first viewing can sometimes seem cold and rarefied, the perfect technique distancing viewer from performer, reveal on closer inspection a 'humanity, vulnerability and pride' which holds the viewer's attention, allowing them to focus on the 'fragility of the individual'.[158] His approach here is similar to Cohan's: 'I'm quite a self-conscious person, particularly in social situations. When I'm with the dancers, I completely forget about myself. I'm absolutely un-self-conscious. I just become the dancers, I know they can do something extraordinary, and I do everything to make them do it.' Crickmay's images on posters, in brochures, calendars, and books, which captured and enhanced the work so well – he has sometimes been accused of making a dancer or work seem 'better' than in reality – are so in tune with the essence of Cohan's vision that they are comparable with Barbara Morgan's groundbreaking series of photographs of Martha Graham. For many, Graham's work is defined by Morgan's images; so too is Cohan's work by Crickmay's photos. And, like many of Graham's works captured by Morgan, many of Cohan's works now only exist as photographic records. Crickmay recalls the atmosphere in the studio with Cohan as 'electric' and 'very intense and concentrated', and he was fascinated 'to see Bob taking a group of disparate people and turning them into great dancers. And by that I mean individuals.' For Crickmay, Cohan 'has always been there. He sustains friendships and will never let you down.' This is not always easy as he is 'an intellectual, well-read, intelligent and articulate' and he 'won't accept crap'; for Crickmay, who does not see himself as an intellectual, this has sometimes been difficult. On one occasion, they were having a heated discussion, taking wildly opposing points of view; the next day, returning to the discussion, Cohan started arguing Crickmay's side. When Crickmay pointed this out, Cohan said, 'I know, I just wanted to see what the other side felt like.' Artistically, however, the two trusted each other instinctively – Cohan never told Crickmay what or how to photograph, never suggested angles or movements, but there was such a bond between them that there was no need.

Just prior to the premiere of *Consolations*, the BBC showed a dance film choreographed by Cohan, called *Lifelines*. It was an eighteen-minute work created for the arts magazine programme *Review*. Returning to the subject matter of *Cell*, with music from the same composer, Ronald Lloyd, the piece was a solo for Noemi Lapzeson. Produced by Tony Staveacre and directed by Christopher Martin, the dance concerned a woman whose lover had died. Cohan particularly enjoyed working with the editor, James Mossman, who helped him realise his choreographic vision. The dance used the then cutting-edge technology of colour separation and was rather surreal in its composition – fragments of events colliding with each other with little sense of a cohesive narrative. It began with Lapzeson looking at a table which became a coffin. She then finds herself running down an endless corridor of doors; she runs through one and finds herself on the underground, and another opens onto an ocean and she runs away. Although shown only once, the film did much to raise the public's awareness of The Place and its work.

Around this time, Cohan's somewhat lonely existence was enlivened by the arrival of a long-term companion. This was Ace, a beautiful Afghan hound, who Cohan found at an animal rescue centre and who would be a constant presence for the following ten years. The dog would often accompany him on tours, and Cohan would take dog blankets, food, and toys, transporting everything in his far too small Mini Cooper, much as he had the iguana and pug in America. Contracts for Sadler's Wells, in the small print of the terms and conditions, would eventually include a clause that, 'all animals are excluded from the premises except Mr Cohan's dog'. If he was left at home, there were always people to look after him, though on one occasion a 'sitter' arrived at Cohan's mews to find Ace the worst for wear, having munched his way through most of a sizeable bag of marijuana which had inadvertently been left on the coffee table. Ace would later be joined by Alice, another beautiful afghan, and Cohan at one time had the idea of breeding them. This did not happen, which was probably a sensible idea, as the two together were more than a handful.

At about the same time as the arrival of Ace, LCDT was joined by Moshe Romano as rehearsal director. Romano, as he was always known, was Israeli and had been involved with dance in that country since the early 1960s dancing with a number of groups and eventually joining Batsheva. He had – as many would – become disenchanted with the politics of the organisation and leapt at the chance to work with Cohan in London. He remained with LCDT until it closed, apart from a short period back in Israel as artistic director of Batsheva in 1981. His flamboyant personality and ability to see and give corrections in a positive way endeared him to the dancers; and he was devoted to Cohan and his vision of dance.

Cohan's nurturing efforts were paying off, and almost everyone in the company and in the school wanted to choreograph, so there were always new works available for performance. In the company, if a work was successful it was kept for two or three seasons and then rested; many did not last, but by the presentation of their work each choreographer grew and developed. Barry Moreland began his international career with Cohan and is grateful to him for simply giving him the opportunity to make work and have it presented on a professional stage. Moreland can recall very little 'interference' from Cohan in his choreographic work, rather, Cohan instilled in them an informed independence, to 'know' themselves and develop their own artistic vision. Cohan told Tobi Tobias:

I try not to interfere because, after all, they're the ones who are going to be the choreographers of the future for the company, or for some other company in Britain. I want them to grow themselves. So we try to help them produce the works. I help them light it, talk about it, the costumes, all that, and I criticise the works only on the basis of whether or not they are working, not on what their content is. I don't care what the content is as long as they provide an interesting dance experience. I also try to keep very much in mind the fact that they're growing, so that even if I believe it is not fully justifiable to put the work on the stage, if it's a step forward for them in their own development, I think it's worth performing it a few times.[159]

This method of working – apprenticeships – would very quickly develop the next generation of British choreographers. In the school, there were nearly sixty-three students, either following the full-time course or the one-year special programme. Out of a need for performance opportunities for the students and to continue raising public awareness, the X Group was formed with third-year students. Under the direction of Flora Cushman, it toured schools and colleges with a varied repertory of student and professional work. The X did not stand for experimental, but stuck after Cohan continually wrote an X on paperwork when he was asked for a name for it and could not decide.

The Place under Cohan's guidance had been very successful – the Arts Council, in its Bulletin for Spring 1971, noted that the company were 'now established as a most valuable addition to the pattern of British Ballet'. It was still British Ballet, they could not bring themselves to acknowledge it as something else, but at least the importance was noted. In April of that year, Cohan unveiled his most successful and spectacular work to date, one that hammered home the undoubted popularity and importance of the company. The work was *Stages*, the first evening-length contemporary dance work created in Britain, although to call it a dance work is to undersell it as it was a huge multimedia extravaganza. Taking Graham's theatre of myth, metaphor, and magic to a new level, it used every possible theatrical device that The Place Theatre could muster and was years ahead of itself, pushing the dancers to new technical levels and requiring them to learn gymnastics and aerial ballet.

Stages developed from a day when Cohan found himself alone in The Place Theatre thinking about future projects. In the auditorium, he noticed that for some reason, there was a chair on the stage, so he went and sat on it and looked out at the audience. The Royal Shakespeare Company, who had previously rented the space, had moved the seating to the side of the auditorium and Cohan began to wonder how he could rearrange the space so it could be more interesting. Eventually, he devised a scheme where the audience would be seated on the stage, while the four-tiered levels of seating would be divided into one large and two smaller stages and used for the dancers and musicians, who he straight away knew had to be on stage and part of the action. The finished work would be one of the most spectacular productions yet seen in Britain, and the choreography by Cohan and designs by Peter Farmer – although in an unsuccessful Guggenheim Fellowship application, Cohan had indicated that Anthony Caro and David Hockney were interested in working on the project – would grab the audience at the start and hold them enthralled until the coup de théâtre finale had them stamping and cheering.

At the time, Cohan had been reading a lot of science fiction works and found himself drawn to Ray Bradbury's psychological work rather than pure science fiction. Bradbury has observed of his own work:

> First of all, I don't write science fiction. I've only done one science fiction book and that's *Fahrenheit 451*, based on reality. Science fiction is a depiction of the real. Fantasy is a depiction of the unreal. So *Martian Chronicles* is not science fiction, it's fantasy. It couldn't happen, you see? That's the reason it's going to be around a long time – because it's a Greek myth, and myths have staying power.[160]

Likewise, Cohan's work was a fantasy. He knew personally and had read all Joseph Campbell's works, and he was fascinated by Campbell's theory of the hero's journey or monomyth. This is the idea that a basic narrative of great significance has been and continues to be told by the whole of humanity from east to west across the centuries. One of Campbell's ideas, which he expands on in his book *The Hero with a Thousand Faces*, is that over time this story has been broken down and is reinvented in local forms. From this, Cohan developed the idea that great myths such as Hercules had become in our time animated cartoons, so that Campbell's idea of the hero's journey had been turned into comic books. He therefore set up the piece with the hero coming into the world and experiencing, literally, the journey of the hero, while the second act was the same thing seen through a comic book.

Cohan knew he had to have different music for both parts, and for part one commissioned a musique concrète score from Arne Nordheim, which he loved. For part two, he turned to Bob Downes, a jazz musician who was a virtuoso on flute, shakuhachi, and just about any other wind instrument. Cohan had met Downes after he had written music for Norman Morrice at Ballet Rambert; he was captivated by his easy-going invention and enthusiasm, and the two would collaborate on a number of other works in the 1970s.

With all the parts in place, Cohan set out to be as extravagant as he could in imagining the descent of the hero into the netherworld which really seems to have appeared out of some hallucinogenic nightmare. In 'Stage 1: Reality (impression of the world as it seems to be)-Descent-Meetings of the Goddess-Death-Reflection-Interrogation', the Hero, superbly played by William Louther, descends into the auditorium on a wire, his image distorted by strobe lighting and smoke. There, in the world of abstract, unreal creatures, he has three different life experiences. Looking back, Cohan admits to being 'embarrassed how obvious it was'; the Hero is nailed to the wheel of life, turned by the monsters, scarified; he meets the goddess spider woman, the goddess of death, the women of illusion, he gets wrapped up in his illusion of life. Then he is trapped by all the demons, executed, and when he is dead, he thinks he sees his soul, the dream of his life personified, and it turns out to be false and merely an image.

In 'Stage 2: Dream (the cartoons of what once was)-A journey-Meeting with a Monster-The sirens and another Monster-Still another Monster-Destruction of the Temple', which was set in a modern world of lurid colours and pop imagery, the Hero travels and meets the Hydra, the Minotaur, and the Sirens. In the end, he gets into a discotheque in which everyone is dancing as if their lives depended on it, when he realises who he is. While all of this chaos is going on, he climbs up the disco walls, pushes two silver pillars apart, and the whole world collapses as he walks out of the theatre underneath a flashing exit sign.

The work was an enormous success, aided by the extraordinary design and touches of popular culture, such as when Bob Downes jumped down the different levels to pass to Robert North what looked like, and many assumed to be a real, foot-long joint. It was performed almost nonstop for about 150 performances. Noel Goodwin found it 'an exciting achievement, a *Pilgrim's Progress* for our time', and that the production 'was a justification of what LCDT has sought to achieve, and a promise of significant character for the future'.[161] The work also sparked the only serious argument that Cohan had with Howard in the course of their long association. For Cohan, Howard did not realise the value or potential of the work. Howard was always looking for what was next and helping young people choreograph, which of course Cohan wanted as well, as that was the purpose of the organisation. But Cohan felt that while they had a success like *Stages* on their hands, they should tap into its commercial value and put it in the West End, where Cohan could see it selling out every night for a long run. Howard thought they shouldn't do it anywhere else, as he felt it belonged to The Place itself and he emphatically refused. Cohan got very angry and stormed out only to return and blurt out, 'If you do not want to produce *Stages*, then I don't want to be here and I'm going back to New York!' Howard was shocked by Cohan's outburst and said, 'I didn't realise you felt so strongly about it.' In the end, he gave in and the work toured the UK and Europe; they even talked about a separate company for *Stages*, but there was not enough money at the time to see this through. It was unusual for Cohan to get angry as it was usually the voluble and aristocratic Howard who would often explode into fits of rage, frequently taken his frustrations out on Mop Eager, although he would always apologise to her after, saying, 'Oh you know, it is only because I cannot say some things to him.' But he was clearly shaken by the argument and wrote Cohan a letter, which was never sent in which he talked of 'taking time off to dream together and then to try to bring our dreams back to reality – or if you prefer to redefine our objectives'. He went on to talk positively of the future, of a 'children's show' and plans to 'saturate London with our dance next year', and to admit that 'at my most pompous I even see our form of dance making a little part in changing the world'.

Not everyone, however, was taken with the work, and Cohan received a letter from a disgruntled audience member which criticised *Stages* in the strongest possible terms, accusing him of chauvinism and worse:

I cannot accept the intellectual imbalance of *Stages*, the intellectually unreal portrayal of the female. Women are not evil, treacherous, seductresses all the time we are not spider women, goddesses, narcissistic creatures and nothing else. There wasn't one balanced real portrayal of a female in *Stages*.

I found *Stages* excessively reactionary and not in touch with what is happening socially in 1972. It applauds and reinforces male chauvinism, is intellectually dishonest and is un relative to a large section of the population's experience.[162]

In the summer, the company toured Europe and it was there, on a brief visit to Switzerland, that Cohan gave his last performance. His toe was still damaged and he suffered from continual back pain but kept on dancing in *El Penitente*. During one performance, he suddenly realised that he no longer needed to dance, he could, but he did not need to. He told the dancers this when he came offstage and they were shocked; for twenty-five years, he had been one of the leading male performers of his generation, but now he could stop and concentrate his energies on choreographing and directing the company and school.

In the school, he would be aided by Jane Dudley who, after an unhappy time directing the Batsheva Company in Israel, arrived in London to head up Graham Studies. Cohan had been running the school with Pat Hutchison Mackenzie who, as well as being Principal, taught ballet, but it was too much for him – he frequently taught the 8 a.m. beginners class and would still be in the building twelve or fourteen hours later. Plans had been afoot to alleviate the situation as a letter from Robin Howard dated only 1971 shows: 'As we agreed last year you will be concentrating on the work of the company and only such matters in the school as you feel particularly strongly about'. Cohan needed someone strong who knew the Graham Technique inside out, he also needed someone that he trusted and liked. Dudley, like many after her, had had a difficult time with the unruly Batsheva dancers who wanted her to leave. Cohan wanted her as she knew all of the early Graham work and he wanted the students and, more importantly, the dancers he took into the company, to understand that work, so that when they joined him he could move on with his developments of the training.

Once installed, Dudley took some of the burden away from Cohan. She was the one who chose the teachers for the school and, between them, they arranged a syllabus. It was not an easy time as Dudley was a very strong-minded woman who alienated as many people as she inspired, and Howard's concept of 'love' seems to have entirely passed her by, but she stayed with the school for the rest of her active life and ensure that Cohan had the bodies he needed to work on. In 1972, she was joined by another former Graham dancer, Nina Fonaroff, who for the next twenty years led the choreographic studies. The two had known each other a very long time, and it was Dudley who had suggested that Fonaroff, who had been one of Louis Horst's closest assistants, be invited to teach his method. When she arrived, she taught nothing of the sort, having rejected his method many years before[163] and saying to this writer, 'I told Robin I had no idea what I would teach and I didn't; I spent two years just working things out.' This infuriated Dudley and the two would bicker throughout their time in The Place. Richard Alston remembers: 'I never really believed in the value of Jane and Nina being at each other's throats all the time. Some people thought this was a good dynamic; I didn't.'

Their arrival marked the move to a very formalised traditional dance education. This had started at the beginning of 1971 once the school was recognised by the Inner London Education Authority for accepting grant-aided students, and was more open to public scrutiny. The creative anarchy reminiscent of an art-school approach that had made the very early years of the school so exciting and unique disappeared, and it attracted a different type of students. The need to produce a professional dancing body took precedent over the need to develop a creative artist.

Cohan remembers that when the Graham Company toured abroad they became an important cultural unit that was representing not just the art form but their country – they were stars. So it was that on the foreign tours that LCDT became not just a group of dancers but representatives of the UK and of its newly developing contemporary dance culture, and when they returned, they performed better as a group. On the European tour of 1971 the group gained excellent reviews, with many commenting that the dancers gave fully to their art.

This was something Christopher Bannerman, who became a long-standing member of the company, noticed when he turned up one day to meet his friend, fellow Canadian Ross McKim, who was already a member:

> I walked into Studio 4 to meet Ross and the first thing that was interesting was that he said that the rehearsal would finish at 6.30. In my previous experience rehearsals scheduled to finish at 6.30, did finish at 6.30 because people left the room. So at six I went into this room and sat down, I didn't know exactly what was going on, people were sort of trying things out on their own and talking to each other and 6.30 came and went and nobody went anywhere, which was surprising. I slowly realised that there was somebody in charge, and the person who was in charge of this rehearsal was a man with knee high silver boots and a silver jacket and his hair down to past his shoulders and wearing dark glasses, in spite of the fact that it was very dim in that studio.[164]

The complete devotion that Cohan inspired in the venture was extraordinary. The dancers, unlike Graham's, were paid regular salaries, though not much, approximately £12 per week, but he created such a hothouse atmosphere of creative invention and dedication that, as Bannerman noted, the dancers, even those with families, could not think of anywhere they would rather be. Richard Alston has strong memories that Cohan was 'very comfortable with the idea of being a leader. Bob always expects people to do what he says, it is his nature to analyse and tell people how to do it…' In this he is similar to another American intellectual of the same vintage, the composer Ned Rorem, of whom his pupil Daron Hagen wrote: 'Like most intellectuals, he stated his opinions as fact.'[165]

If the dedication to the art was appreciated abroad, it was not always so at home as John Percival, writing in the best British critical style in the November issue of *Dance and Dancers*, commented:

> People keep telling me how exciting LCDT is nowadays and how well they are dancing. With the best will in the world I cannot see this. I want the company to succeed, but to pretend that they have done so already will do more harm than good. A lot of effort is needed (and a good deal of luck too) before they achieve their admirable aim of building a truly British modern dance tradition.[166]

The negative reaction of certain British critics made no impression on the audiences though, and 1972 began with a sold-out season at The Place. This started with two weeks of *Stages* followed by two weeks of new and repertory works. Robert Powell was to have made his debut as the hero in *Stages* but was too 'out of it' to perform, and at hours' notice William Louther returned to save the day, Powell eventually picking up the part to less than glowing reviews. Cohan's choice for visiting artist had been Anna Sokolow, another early Graham dancer who had gone on to develop her own very stylised dramatic form of dance, almost always dealing with the dark side of the human condition. Her work, *Scenes from the Music of Charles Ives*, was no exception and included her trademark 'Sokolow Stare', when the dancers would stare with menacing intensity at the audience, hoping that art would appear. Cohan may have wanted them to learn from her, but some of the group thought it was a punishment both physical and mental, as she had no qualms at screaming at the dancers, physically manhandling them, or pulling their hair to get them into the shapes she demanded. She caused problems for Mop Eager as well, as, for some reason, she refused to sleep in her hotel room alone, and for the duration of her stay, someone had to be found to share her room each night.

They had a much more enjoyable time later in the year when Cohan brought in the Puck-like Remy Charlip to work with them. Charlip had been an early member of the Cunningham Company, and brought with him the American postmodern school of choreography, based on instruction and improvisation.

Cohan had always liked Charlip as a person and he thought that it would be good for the company to experience the kind of loose choreography he did – not so much choreography as ideas about dance. It was a brave choice for Cohan, and a little unsettling, because it was the exact opposite of the technical, formal work he did. And although he was a very friendly person – at one stage the dancers arrived for rehearsal to find the room laid out for a picnic – he unsettled some by insisting they reveal their innermost secrets in rehearsals, which would then be used in the piece. His work, entitled *Dance*, consisted of almost every form of physical action but no dancing, and the dancers laughed, mimed taking a bath, and painted. They also had to respond to audience suggestions, and one evening, a viewer suggested that they should actually dance. The lengthy season which began on 16 May was to have had a new work each week, with Cohan presenting a new piece, *People*, but he became very ill and his work was cancelled.

Throughout the year, he had become more and more tired and everything he did felt 'wrong' to him. He made constant visits to his friend, Dr Patrick Woodcock, who gave him Vitamin B injections, but inexplicably never thought to take a blood sample. Instead, he suggested Cohan take himself away from the grey of England to find some sunshine, and so Cohan booked himself a two-week holiday in Marrakech which, to begin with, he found wonderful. But even in indolence, the tiredness continued; he would get up, have breakfast, swim, sunbathe, then fall asleep. Later, he would wake up and have dinner and then fall asleep again. One day, he looked in the mirror and the face staring back had a dark tan, but disturbingly dark yellow eyes. He checked straight out of the hotel and returned home. He had no idea how he caught hepatitis A and there was no cure, so he found himself confined to bed in Thurloe Place for two months, and very slowly he recovered. The illness forced him to turn down two prospective commissions, one from the Slovak National Ballet, and one from the Australia Dance Theatre. The latter was a lucrative offer for a work for the 1974 Adelaide Festival, comprising a £1,000 fee, plus £7 per performance, full transport, accommodation, and daily living expenses. This was money Cohan would have found very useful, as he always struggled on his salary, but the illness made it impossible. If it had not been the illness, it would have been his schedule with LCDT – over the years, he received a number of commissions but almost always had to turn them down because of scheduling. His work in Israel was his only real 'extracurricular activity' which usually fitted in with LCDT's holidays and which provided a much needed supplement to his London wages.

Before the hepatitis, he had been to Ibiza with Noemi Lapzeson and Robert North and may have contracted it there. Ibiza, however, stuck in his memory for a more pleasant reason, as strangely for someone so well versed in drugs, it was the first time he took LSD. The resulting trip, experienced while he floated alone in the sparkling Mediterranean, was, he recalls, 'extraordinary, amazing, me and the universe. A real trip as they say.'

The London season's programmes were rearranged and afterwards the company went to Newcastle upon Tyne to present *Stages* for the first time outside of London. At the same time, the X Group gave its first season in London at the Holland Park Open Air Theatre, following on after the Royal Ballet School's summer show. A feather in the cap for the school, by showing just how far they had come in a very short time. Although the name X Group had not originally stood for experimental, it quickly developed into an arena in which work that would not have fitted into the larger company, or would not have had another outlet, could be shown.

The company returned to London to perform at the Roundhouse and The Place in the International Carnival of Experimental Sound (ICES), a celebration of avant-garde music. The first dance in the festival was the most radical, as it was performed by Richard Alston's new company Strider, the first group to break away from the LCDT fold. Although Alston was given a number of commissions by Cohan, he had long been dissatisfied with The Place, as he told an audience there in 1979 that there were people

> … individual enough to have searched out this rather smelly cat-ridden alley [Berners Place], and they all had a very clear idea of what they wanted. Because there was no company in existence… everyone began to use their imaginations, and they all thought that something was going to be there which in the end wasn't. It was something else, it was what Bob made, and the more concrete that became the more problems there were.[167]

'Problems' was perhaps the wrong word, certainly what may have been mooted at the start was not what was developed but this was not of Cohan's creation, but rather of the demands made on him as artistic director by the Arts Council and regional theatres. They demanded value for money and 'bums on seats', and to do this Cohan had to programme a wide range of mainly accessible work. Alston now admits that 'for the first couple of years I was absolutely devoted, and then when Bob started doing more showbizzy types of work, starting with *Shanta Quintet* where they all had these blue glittery veils, which became even more showbizzy later in *Consolations of the Rising Moon*, that's when I became all serious and young and disapproving.' The needs and demands of building an audience were of little interest to the young Alston, and when

> … Bob and Robin sat me down and gave me a lecture about what sort of audience they needed and it was middle class, middle of the road, and they were saying this to a 21-year-old who was thinking, 'I don't want to do that', and that is why I started to move off… because when you're 21 you don't want to hear about how to cultivate an audience.

Cohan knew there would be a rebellion, probably by Siobhan Davies and Richard Alston, and he and Howard frequently talked about it and when it would happen.

That it happened very quickly was for them very positive. Neither Cohan nor Howard wanted LCDT to become an edifice of the establishment as had the Royal Ballet, but if it became a scratching post, against which experimentalists could rail against, then it was all for the best.

Although Alston was never technically strong enough to be considered for the company and never wanted to be a member, he had proved himself a capable choreographer. Cohan remembers vividly the day Alston broke the news that he was forming his own group:

> Robin and I were going up the stairs and Richard was coming down and he said immediately, 'Robin and Bob, I have to talk to you. I'm leaving. I'm starting my own company and it's going to be called Strider, and well, that's it.' He was very nervous, was scared to death, and he walked down the stairs and left. Robin and I started laughing and I said, 'See Robin it's already happening', and he said, 'Of course it's a great loss', but I said, 'Yes, it is the right thing', and he replied, 'I'm going to help him all I can', and I said, 'And I'm going to make it very difficult for him because he needs to be strong and you help him.' I did this by resisting, not approving, and not encouraging him. He had to stand on his own and go away and I wouldn't let him have people, dancers he wanted, etc. Robin and I often did 'good cop, bad cop' and it worked, it takes two people, we were both in charge and it was a good system.

The system worked extremely well, and the festival included experimental work from Flora Cushman, Ross McKim, Stephen Barker, Xenia Hribar, Anthony van Laast and Micha Bergese, Christopher Banner, Noemi Lapzeson, and Siobhan Davies, as well as Alston's *Tiger Balm*, which Strider performed. An example of the type of work performed can be understood from this review of Stephen Barker's *Fugue*:

> … [Robert North] wearing a ludicrously ill-fitting tailcoat with great aplomb, he unwrapped a tray full of objects: bells, gong, whistle, triangle, transistors… Each was played at least (maybe only) once, laid out on the table; then they were all wrapped up again, and as the ballet ended he was ready to start unwrapping once more. Now and again he tried to get into the action on stage, which consisted of Davies and Gibbs, in pink tights, performing dance exercises while McKim and Namron, dressed in long overcoats and big boots, but with bare legs, marched, stamped, or crawled about like raw recruits from Fred Karno's army. Stephen Barker was the choreographer a really wild invention here almost Dada in its humour.[168]

Perhaps Dada, but more clearly the influence of the Judson Dance Theater from America was being felt ten years after it began there. That loose group of artists had challenged every notion of what could be considered a dance vocabulary and very soon in the 1970s their ideas would influence the development of the New

Dance Movement in Britain. But far from being upset by it, this was what Cohan and Howard always wanted, and envisaged, their Graham-based heritage was the strong seed from which everything else grew.

After the International Carnival of Experimental Sound, LCDT moved back to The Place for a week-long season beginning on 29 August that at last saw the premiere of Cohan's postponed work. Cohan's original idea for *People*, was that the dancers should each create a scenario based on the theme of loneliness, which he would then shape into an evening-length work. Remy Charlip was very good at this, and in *Dance* he had insisted everyone create all their own material. During Cohan's illness, this idea changed partly due to time and partly due to Cohan's preference for demonstrating and creating material. The resulting work had a commissioned score from Bob Downes and choreography entirely by Cohan. Although the new work was not a full evening, there was still the intention that it should have a companion piece not yet realised.

The work had no story as such but centred on eight obsessive characters who, conditioned to their loneliness, work out their troubles alone. Their musings are interrupted by a quartet whose interventions are either serious or mocking, and whose appearances bind the work together. The costumes, by Jane Hyland, had the quartet in silver tracksuits – in later revivals these were replaced by skeleton suits, which emphasised their malevolent roles. It is interesting to note that the subtitle for Patrick Steede's early work for the Contemporary Dance Group, *Piece for Metronome and Three Dancers*, had been P*eople Alone Together and People Together Alone*, and this theme of loneliness and isolation is something very close to Cohan's experience of being in the UK. Various documentaries made at the time show how very foreign Cohan was in the context of British culture. All the main players in LCDT – Howard, Hutchison, Eager – had to a greater or lesser extent cut-glass accents which place them firmly in the upper-middle to upper-class strata of society. Cohan, by his accent and general mode of expression, is the outsider in this and this work could be seen as Cohan working out his place in the society he found himself in.

Of the characters, Robert North's was a creature – everything he touched went away or was closed to him. Irene Dilkes was a bag lady who had to gather everything up and once she had, she would lose it and had to search again. Micha Bergese was like a moth rushing towards pools of light as they appear. Noemi Lapzeson appeared in a wheelchair as she was injured at the time but insisted on being in the work. Her solo became about someone who wheels an imaginary self in a wheelchair. Linda Gibbs and Paula Lansley were like two prostitutes and Cohan created for them a duet that was not a duet – separated by a wall, they performed two dances simultaneously that had no relation to one another. Clare Duncan, in a floral dress, played the eternal spinster; ignored by two men, she is left sobbing in a corner. Namron's solo was at the end, and he appeared as a big macho man who was pushing everything around, but who ultimately was left pawing at the ground, puzzled by his own ineffectiveness.

The fragmentary nature of the work was commented on by a number of reviewers at the time, but it was mainly seen as a very powerful statement and a great success, with Peter Williams in *Dance and Dancers* finding it 'one of Cohan's best creations to date, as there is a greater depth of feeling in each of these very disparate movement sketches'.[169] The season marked the departure of some dancers, notably Clare Duncan, who had joined the company in 1967, after leaving London Festival Ballet. She was some years older than the rest of the dancers, and had begun to feel somewhat isolated particularly on tour. Cohan urged her to stay as she was an experienced performer, but his suggestion that, if she felt lonely on tour then she should socialise with him, was met with disbelief as: 'Bob wasn't a person to socialise with, not if you wanted to relax.'

If some left, then others arrived and *People Alone* marked another successful collaboration with Norberto Chiesa, whose set of multipurpose screens, each with a fragment of a pattern on them, which when laid flat acted as rostra to be climbed on, also gained praise. Chiesa, who hated New York, was by this time living in London where Cohan had suggested the two purchase a property together and renovate it. Although Cohan kept his Thurloe Place mews house, they followed through on the plan of buying a house in Elspeth Road, in the then not terribly fashionable suburb of Clapham. This set up the pattern which continued over the years, until they bought an old farmhouse in France and Chiesa moved there to supervise its renovation.

For the end-of-year season at The Place, Cohan invited May O'Donnell to visit and teach the company her own athletic development of Graham Technique and to make a dance. Cohan had loved O'Donnell since she had been his first partner in *Deaths and Entrances*, and believed that her clarity, simplicity, and American approach would be good for the dancers. In the intervening years, O'Donnell had developed into an extraordinary teacher, clear, direct, life affirming, and joyous, and counted William Louther, Dudley Williams, and Ben Vereen as three of her outstanding students. She had also built up a considerable body of work, often to the music of her philandering husband Ray Green, as would be the case on this occasion. Peter Williams wrote of the finished work: 'It could be said that one of the faults of the more recent developments in contemporary dance is that dance, in an old accepted way of using steps and things, is something that doesn't happen often. O'Donnell's *Dance Energies* is dance all the way.' He went on to note its unevenness but was happy to report that the audience got 'the feeling that the dancers were revelling in a piece that allowed them to dance...',[170] which had been exactly what Cohan wanted.

Alongside the performance work, the company was doing an enormous amount of educational work and, in contrast to the O'Donnell piece, Cohan invited the Wigman pupil Lotte Goslar to create a work especially for children. The dance, *Ends and Odds*, was given at matinées over the Christmas holidays and was a great hit with the young spectators, not least because it included audience participation.

Cohan's success was summed up in an interview he gave to the *Guardian* which was introduced by James Kennedy:

> A school, a home, a theatre, a permanent company, a distinctive homegrown repertory – these in the past five years have been Cohan's necessities just as in the thirties' they were a necessity for Dame Ninette de Valois; and now, at The Place, he has acquired a school, a home, a theatre, a company, and a homegrown repertory is on the way.[171]

He went on to note that Cohan had made twelve works for the company and that he hoped that in three years, apart from some classics, *all* the work would be home grown. This certainly did not seem too ambitious, as by the end of 1972, LCDT had presented twenty-two new works, eighteen by company members. This was an extraordinary achievement and an affirmation, if one were needed, that Cohan had been exactly the right choice for the job.

In addition to all the work in England, Cohan had found time to go to York University in Toronto, where, at the invitation of Grant Strate, he made a work on a group of eighteen students. The piece, called *Mass*, was an extension or metamorphosis of some of the material of *X*, and had its first performance at the Burton Auditorium of York University, on 19 December 1972. The costumes were by Susan MacPherson, a distinguished dancer with the Toronto Dance Theatre, and the music by York faculty member David Rosenboom. In the piece, Cohan wanted the dancers to explore more than just their bodies and the score required that they make sounds as well as move. This was, in Cohan's mind, not a complete realisation of his idea, and he would extend it dramatically in a work for LCDT. But it was a success in Toronto, and Strate wrote to him on 27 December: '*Mass* was a big hit. I liked it more each time I saw it. It seemed to grow and grow.'[172]

1973 was the year when Britain joined the Common Market, and LCDT joined the Royal Ballet, London Festival Ballet, and Scottish Ballet in the Fanfare for Europe festivities. The ballet companies presented traditional galas while Cohan, embracing the young, presented a slightly revised version of *Stages* that played to sold-out houses at The Place on 11, 12, and 13 January. He then settled into work on his new piece for the Camden Festival in February.

Commissioned by the Arts Council, this was to be the companion piece to *People Alone*; entitled *People Together*, it reunited the same collaborators: Chiesa, Downes, and Read. As the companion piece to *People Alone*, one may have expected *People Together* to be about people who connect or even love each other, but this was not to be the case. In the uncharacteristically long programme note, Cohan explained:

> *People Together* is a group dance with only one moment when two dancers are

alone on stage. Since working in Toronto last year with 25 dancers, I've been fascinated by moving large groups. People do so many things together that I had to set certain limits in order to choreograph the dance, I chose three activities as a basic structure for the entire piece – love games, conflict, prayer – and this formed a workable structure for both Bob Downes and myself. The whole dance has turned out to be a collage of events – glimpses, rather than a sequential story – of people together. But I've tried to make it run smoothly as a contrast to the episodic structure of *People Alone* in that people together appear to be more alone than people alone.

This bleak comment came from Cohan's observation of masses of people together in playgrounds, protest marches, pop festivals, and even religious gatherings, which he felt only increased the inner loneliness of the individual.

Neither work gave any hope that the loneliness might be temporary although at the beginning and end of *People Together*, the group were united in a type of whirling dervish ceremony. Cohan had seen the whirling dervishes dance in London, and had an image for the dance of a structure that disintegrates and then comes together again. The sections in-between included a slow-motion orgy, bouncing of balls as in children's games, and a disturbing warlike section for which the dancers donned battle helmets and skeletal-type masks, vaguely reminiscent of the war section in Jooss' *Green Table*. The work, as many of Cohan's from this period, uses movement and ritual bordering on dance theatre rather than pure movement. But it marked a definite choreographic development in his handling of large groups. Noel Goodwin found it 'a tragic work, expressed with stark and austere dignity...',[173] while Peter Williams observed that 'Cohan has not moved so far away from Graham as he and we might think: what he does is to relate Greek mythology to the present day.'[174]

For Cohan, 'It was a product of the time; hippies, punks, dervishes turning on those big costumes and how silly people are when they start to fight people; it was about war.' Looking back, he can see 'it was messy and it all fell apart'. But it had an interesting theatricality, as in the section where 'all the dancers had to bounce a tennis ball to a partner while one was bounced to [them]'. The conjunction of the bouncing balls and Lycra-clad bodies was very effective, though to get the effect needed many hours of rehearsal as 'some of the women and men had never had a ball in their hands in their life'.

The society Cohan drew on for his dances caused problems for him and others in the company. In the early 1970s, he started to grow his hair very long and to wear the somewhat flamboyant clothes and shoes of the day, frayed bell-bottom jeans, bright shirts and waistcoats, and silver platform shoes, and this often drew the attention the police. One night, he had parked his car in Chelsea's King's Road to look at some of the designers' windows when a policeman stopped him and questioned him as to his sobriety, as he had seen him swaying as he got out of his car. Cohan replied that he was sober, but of course he was swaying as he was wearing 3-inch platform boots; the policeman was unconvinced and it took some persuading that he was not 'under the influence'. He narrowly missed arrest on that and many other occasions. Noemi Lapzeson, likewise, had run-ins with the police and, after being wrongly accused of supplying drugs, decided that she had had enough of London and left LCDT in 1973. She had been an inspirational figure to the young dancers and a support to Cohan, although looking back now, she holds few fond memories of either the work or London.

Just as Britain moved into Europe, so did Cohan. While visiting the south of France with house-hunting friends, Cohan and Chiesa spotted a large, rambling ruined property in the hamlet of Saussine, situated between Alès and Uzès in the Languedoc-Roussillon region. They instantly fell in love with the wreck of a property in what was virtually a ghost town, borrowed the money from their companions and bought it. Over the next forty years, they would lovingly restore it, most of the work being carried out or supervised by Chiesa, who soon moved permanently to the property. Cohan would visit when he could and when he was not there he was working, most of his earnings being poured into the restoration work. The restoration is still not completed, but the two have created a magnificent home in a beautiful setting.

The spring brought the possibility of an exciting development for the Trust in the shape of a new building, new theatre, and generous funding. The Lyric Theatre Hammersmith had been demolished and the developers proposed to build a modern fully fitted theatre on the site. Hammersmith Council hinted at massive funding and the Greater London Council also expressed interest. A feasibility study went ahead and an international profile was aimed for, but in the end it all came to nothing and The Place would remain the home of the company and school, although problems were soon to emerge there.

After the Camden Festival, LCDT moved to the Oxford Playhouse to give the premiere of Cohan's *Mass*, an extension of the York University work. Back in England, Cohan set it on the company and a partial version was broadcast in the television arts programme 'Full House' on 17 February, and it was again well received. The full version seen in Oxford was the culmination of the different versions of all this work and was an extraordinary collaboration between Cohan, the dancers, and the composer Vladimir Rodzianko.

The Kagel score that Cohan used for *X* ended with a lot of screaming and Cohan wanted to develop the vocal sound world, and so decided to remake the work. He had seen the vocal performer Roy Hart, who was a pioneer of what is now called extended vocal techniques, in a performance of Peter Maxwell Davies' *Eight Songs for a Mad King*, when Daviet6 company was in residence at The Place, and knew that those types of sounds were what he wanted. He was also influenced by seeing Rudi van Dantzig's 1971 ballet *Painted Birds*, which was an early attempt at Eco Art and alerted the audience to man's ability to pollute both minds and the environment. Danzig's ballet made extensive use of film projections to illustrate and amplify the action on stage, but more importantly its final coup de théâtre came when the music by Niccolò Castiglioni gave way to a recording of the final chorale from Bach's *St Matthew Passion*, which was then taken up by the singing of the cast, the choreographer, and some of the company's staff.

Robin Howard introduced Cohan to Vladimir Rodzianko, a Russian (Ukrainian) composer who had been resident in the UK for eighteen years and was well versed in vocal techniques, and the decision was made to have the dancers sing at the same time. Then began a very difficult journey for everyone involved. Rodzianko came in to rehearse three times a week and was very demanding in the vocal skills he expected from the dancers. Some, like Celeste Dandeker and Xenia Hribar, took to it well; most enjoyed the throat singing in harmonics at the opening, but the memorisation of text from the Latin Mass, together with chanting and cries which had to be in time with the pre-recorded tape Rodzianko made, caused problems and upsets. For some, like Namron who admits to being tone deaf, it was an unbearable chore. Added to this was the choreographic problem that the dancers needed to be free when singing or able to sing when dancing.

Observers[175] noted a similarity in theme with Cohan's *People* diptych and his programme note, that described the work as 'a general requiem for the victims of man', indicates a heartfelt work yet again exploring man's inhumanity to man. His later comment that 'any gathering can become a congregation' indicates similarities with *People Together*, and the contrast of group work and the isolation felt by individuals in a group was certainly explored in the work.

In its original form, *Mass* lasted only one season as it was too hard to maintain and needed constant care. If a dancer left, then it was virtually impossible to teach the dance and vocal part to their replacement. Cohan shelved the work for a while, but after meeting the composer Judith Weir on a choreographic course, he replaced the score – including the dancers singing – with one by her. In this version, Mary Clarke wrote that '[with a] new score by Judith Weir, its theme of supplication becomes turgid'.[176] Not satisfied with that, Cohan eventually turned to Geoffrey Burgon; in this guise, Peter Williams found the work had 'lost the power it originally had'.[177] After this, the work was laid to rest.

As soon as the British season ended, the company went on their longest tour to date. This would take them to South America and they would perform in Chile, Brazil, Argentina, Colombia, Venezuela, and Mexico. It was an enormous undertaking, complex in logistical organisation and in the adaptation of the extensive repertoire – which included *Cell, Eclipse, People Alone, People Together, Cold, Cantabile,* and *Dance Energies* – to the technical help available in a wide range of theatres. But Cohan was very experienced at touring and, together with Mop, held it all together. She proved her worth in Rio de Janeiro, where quick thinking on her part and the greasing of a few palms ensured that some company members who had been arrested for trying to buy drugs were released, and an international incident was averted.

The glamour of the tour was quickly left behind when they returned to the UK, gave the first London performance of *Mass*, and then went on tour again, presenting *Stages* in Scotland for the first time. There, Cohan gave an interview to *The Scotsman*, in which he was able to note with some satisfaction that contemporary dance had become a part of the artistic life of the country telling them, 'When I came [in 1967] there were enough students to make up one class. Now I am auditioning three or four hundred people for places in the school.'[178]

The tour was a prelude to LCDT's bravest move yet in its development, a one-week season at Sadler's Wells, from 30 October to 3 November. The company had toured regional theatres extensively and had enormous success abroad, but had still been wary of tackling the cradle of British ballet. They wisely showed only one work, the crowd-pleasing *Stages*, and it worked, with Clement Crisp in the *Financial Times* noting that the first night audience was 'like an Osmond overflow in enthusiasm'.[179] In the *Guardian*, James Monahan approved of the choice, not because he saw it as the best work in the company's repertoire, but because 'it makes a show which should be enjoyed by people who would be bored or frightened by the obscurities and austerities of much of modern dance'.[180]

After such a successful year, it was sad that 1973 would end in tragedy. Touring Britain in the 1970s was always a chore and especially so in winter, where lack of heating in digs and theatres caused illness to run rife through the company. So it was at Manchester Opera House in December, when most of the company were suffering from colds and taking flu medication, that during a performance of *Stages*, Celeste Dandeker momentarily blanked out while turning on her hands, fell, and cracked a vertebra in her neck. Nowadays, shocking as that would be, everyone would know what to do and a dancer so injured would be left until medical help arrived. In 1973, the world was different and she was picked up, carried offstage and sent to hospital where it was discovered that she was almost totally paralysed. At the age of 22, the career of one of LCDT's most beautiful dancers was over. It was not until the early 1990s that she would perform again, with CandoCo, a company she founded with Adam Benjamin for disabled and able-bodied dancers. It had a devastating effect on the company and it took all of Cohan's skills to keep things together.

Chapter 7

Commentary

Those first few years I was in London were very exciting times.

It was very clear that we had this enormous task ahead of us. Reading it now in this chapter, it's hard to believe that we succeeded at all. We all worked so hard to get everything in place all at once at the beginning. Creating the entire building, making the studios and the theatre, while organising the classes and at the same time teaching, choreographing, trying to keep everything together and under one roof. There was no time to sleep. We made some mistakes on the way but we kept our momentum. I think overall the big picture was successful or, at least, it was what Robin and I were trying to do.

The moment, the scene Paul describes of Robin reading the letter from the Arts Council refusing our first request for a small grant, is etched in my memory. I still cannot believe the timing of what happened and perhaps its foreboding for the future.

Everyone involved – dancers, teachers, friends, and critics – were gathered in the large Drill Hall that was to become the theatre for the signing of the lease of The Place building and the announcement of our future plans. We all had a drink to toast the signing in our hands. There was a table set up and seated at it were Robin and his lawyer, the owners and their lawyers, with all the documents laid out. Robin tapped his glass, we all turned to him, and he started to speak about this exciting new venture, when a smallish man hurried up to the table, whispered something to him and gave him a letter. The man hurried away and Robin slowly opened the letter, read it, and carefully put it down on the table. He then continued to speak about our plans for The Place. Signed the lease and we all toasted this exciting future and applauded.

Mop and I knew something was wrong and couldn't wait to get Robin's ear. The man had whispered, 'Mr Howard I think you should read this letter before you sign the lease.' It was from the Arts Council and, of course, our first request for a small grant to start The Place was turned down.

Here we were working unreasonably hard, making studios, dressing rooms, offices, and a theatre in this derelict building, all the time thinking we were doing something important for dance and its future in Britain, and the Arts Council turned us down. Robin's simple reaction to continue to sign the lease anyway was indicative of his resolve and reassured my resolve to do what I moved to London to do, and I thought would work.

I had no problem with organising The Place. The school and theatre were there in the building. It was an organic structure and all the parts and seeds were planted in the beginning. It just had to grow as was needed. I always thought of it as a future safe house for dancers and dance.

I did have a problem with organising the future or thinking about the future of the company. I had two ways to go, and it was very clear after the first year that we could go either way. We could stay small scale, just work at The Place, and be very contemporary with new work, new ideas, and a small and knowledgeable audience. It was an exciting idea but at the same time we were being offered a touring schedule.

Every town in England had empty theatres. The old theatre schedule was breaking down. West End plays used to go on tour after their West End run, with well-known actors perform for a week and then go on to a new town. Managers were eager for anything to put in their theatres or else turn them into bingo halls. It meant that we would spread ourselves very thin just after starting, but I felt it was important to take advantage of our early success and try to make the idea of a contemporary dance company a legitimate artistic entity in Britain.

Someone once told me that Merce Cunningham said that Martha Graham's great contribution to contemporary dance was to take it out of the studio and put it in legitimate theatres on Broadway, and that idea fascinated me. She did make contemporary dance legitimate and paved the way for all of the other contemporary companies to have performances in theatres instead of obscure studios and made-to-do halls. I thought that there was an opportunity to do the same thing here in Britain. I wanted the experimental work. I wanted the new work that was sure to come, the work from Richard Alston, Sue Davies and many others, but I also wanted an audience. I wanted to legitimise the profession but above all, I wanted the dancers to be employed full-time.

Being usually employed part-time in a dubious profession, dancers cannot get a loan at a bank, so therefore they cannot get an apartment, they cannot even get a washing machine or anything that required credit. I wanted to change all that. I wanted to change their status in our society, and part of that was legitimising contemporary dance as a valid art form, as something that was right and meaningful in our society. So I wanted the dancers on full-time employment, and that meant touring at that time.

Of all the decisions, I think that the most important one was the development of the school. Unless you have a good school, you will not have a supply of well-trained dancers and choreographers in the future. Your dancers' artists will always come from somewhere else and that was not the idea of The Place that Robin and I had. The company and the school were complimentary to each other. I wanted the company to excite young people and make them want to study dance, and if they had the will and the talent, I wanted the school to be there to make that possible.

It was also important to me that the company and the school were together in the same building, using the same studios, walking past each other in the halls and eating in the same canteen. Not only to maintain the standards of the art form for the school, but so the students could see in a very real and personal sense where they could go if they wanted to be choreographers or performers.

It's true I was living alone for almost this entire time, but I wasn't alone because I was always thinking about The Place and everything that went on there. This was my work. When I went home, it was just a relief to find a little break in the schedule to eat, sleep, and then come back and do it all again.

Getting my dog Ace was very important to me as I always had a dog when I was young. Even though he was an independent Afghan, it worked out perfectly. He got used to the entire routine of going to the studio every day and going on tour. I got a little guidebook that listed all the hotels that would accept dogs. He also taught me very good lessons in movement.

There is this constant argument about whether dogs have the kind of self-awareness that maybe dolphins and elephants do. One of these tests uses their understanding of a mirror. Many dogs go up to the mirror image and smell it. If it doesn't smell like a dog, they're not interested.

At the beginning of class, when I came in, he would come with me and usually go up to the dancers to say hello, and then he would go behind the piano and lie down. At the end of class, there would be applause and he would instantly get up and start dancing. He would do exactly what the dancers did when they went across the floor leaping. He would leap across the floor on a diagonal and watch himself, like dancers do, in the full-length mirrors on the front wall of the studio. He would then just sit and look at himself in the mirror.

One time, I was standing some way to the side and behind him, I said, 'OK, it's time to go Ace.' He did not turn around to look at me, he looked at me in the mirror because he knew that the mirror was a reflection of me and he knew the dog in the mirror was a reflection of him. He got up, watching himself, and we left.

I like moments like that.

Chapter 8

I always think of Bob as a corporeal architect.

(David Earle, 2010)

1974–5

The early months of 1974 saw the return of the sweet-and-sour coupling of Anna Sokolow and Remy Charlip. Sokolow once again made a gloomy, depressing work, *Steps of Silence*, to an expensive and – by general consensus – painful score by Anatol Vieru, while Charlip reworked five earlier dances into *Mad River*, with glamorous and witty designs by Bill Gibbs. March also saw LCDT perform only the second work by Graham it would ever show. As long ago as 1972, John Percival had suggested in *Dance and Dancers*[181] that the company should acquire *Diversion of Angels*, and now they did. Cohan asked Graham for permission and she agreed, though it was not free and her manager Ron Protas asked for an astronomical fee, which Howard paid for out of his own pocket. Having been involved with the work from its creation and having danced in numerous performances, Cohan knew all of the parts and taught it to the company himself. *Diversion* is one of Graham's most technically demanding works, and Cohan's decision to acquire it heralded a coming of age in the technical development of the company, some critics even thought LCDT performed it better than Graham's own company.

Cohan was linked again with Graham when, out of the blue, he received a phone call asking him if he would like to choreograph a television production of Richard Strauss' opera *Salome*, which Götz Friedrich was to direct. This was to be a major event in conjunction with the Salzburg Festival; veteran conductor Karl Böhm would conduct the Vienna Philharmonic, and the distinguished cast would include Teresa Stratas as Salome, Bernd Weikl as Jochanaan, Astrid Varnay as Herodias, and Hans Beirer as Herod. Stratas had wanted the 80-year-old Martha Graham, who had recently returned to the word of dance after years of illness, to choreograph the highlight of the opera, the famous Dance of the Seven Veils. She turned down the request but suggested Cohan instead.

Götz Friedrich's production was extraordinarily vivid – the staging, set, costume design, and the general tone were reminiscent of a low-budget 1950s Biblical epic. The grotesque naturalism of the production could be seen as an appropriate response to the lurid, over-the-top drama with music that perfectly matched it. When composer Arnold Bax attended the 1908 premiere of the opera in Dresden, he wrote that he had watched it with 'disgusted but fascinated eyes'.[182]

Teresa Stratas, a high lyric soprano who had never performed Salome on stage, identified completely with the role as opera's most depraved teenager, and looked every inch the neurotic and misguided princess, capturing the essence of the part vocally and dramatically. Friedrich set all of the action in the courtyard of Herod's palace, but exploited the claustrophobic possibilities of limited space by his careful focussing of camera angles that follow the singers and by numerous close-ups that often show details unavailable when the opera is seen live. The cumulative effect of such close-ups heightens tension and creates an atmosphere in which the viewer is brought into the action.

The Dance of the Seven Veils appears towards the end of the opera, when Salome strips so that in return Herod will give her the head of Jochanaan (John the Baptist). It is always an eagerly anticipated moment as the staging needs to be inventive, since few opera singers are willing to remove all of their clothes. Cohan's task was therefore not easy, as he had to take into account both Friedrich's wish that there should be as much flesh as possible on show and Stratas', who was worried about a few extra pounds (she was, it must be noted, one of the sveltest singers of her day) and wanted as little as possible on show. The solo is often staged on an exposed empty stage but in this production, by the time the Dance of the Seven Veils begins, the set was crowded with a bizarre assortment of characters and caricatures of fascinating weirdness. It was not so much a personal dance for Herod as a full-scale public performance.

Friedrich wanted Stratas to move through the crowded scene, and so to help her, Cohan added four attendants to guide her and to help remove the veils. Here, the designer Jan Skalicky had opted for a full burka-style outfit with a headpiece which emphasised the reptilian slithering of her movements. In Cohan's version, the dance is no longer a solo but a quintet, and he cleverly gives most of the interesting choreographic material to the attendants, while Stratas is asked to manipulate the material, stretching it suggestively over her face, or expanding it with her arms like a peacock in heat. Cohan's Graham influence is to the fore in this work, with sections reminiscent of *Clytemnestra*. He builds the tension beautifully, and when five minutes into the dance Salome exposes her eyes for the first time, it is deeply erotic. After this point, Salome begins to writhe before Herod and, following the music exactly, the movements become more deranged, with rolling on the floor, seductive looks through unleashed hair, and impressive back bends from the knees. She keeps most of her veils on for the majority of the dance, but Friedrich's clever use of close-up and Cohan's burlesque approach, revealing far less than you think you see, are hugely effective, and it is only in the last thirty seconds that the veils drop thick and fast, the camera registering the pile at Salome's dancing feet. Friedrich insisted that Cohan mount a ladder and drop the clothing himself, the final piece being a golden brassiere, and it took a great many takes to persuade it to land cone side up.

It takes repeated viewings of Cohan's choreography to realise just how successful it is. It is certainly not the most revealing – Maria Ewing's full nudity wins the prize. But it is erotic in the best sense of the word, just as Graham's work is erotic and the best of burlesque is erotic. Cohan is adept at suggesting the psychological state of mind of the character by subtle looks and gestures, rather than being a show-stopping distraction. At the end of the dance, we know more about Salome's character at this point in the opera and the plot can move on. It is a pity Cohan did not do more in the world of opera (he only worked on *Salome*, the early *Dido and Aeneas*, and *Amahl*), where his approach to subtle character development through movement would have been welcome. He would continue to explore Eros in his own dances and burlesque in one more intriguing work.

Another screen project was *Men Seen Afar*, one of two dances for television commissioned by the BBC, the other being *6354/9116* by John Chesworth of Ballet Rambert. Cohan took as his starting point lines from William Blake's poem 'To Thomas Butts':

Each herb and each tree
Mountain, hill, earth, and sea,
Cloud, meteor, and star,
Are men seen afar.[183]

It would seem that at the time, the purpose of television dance was to demonstrate the technical effects possible on television and not the choreographic talents of the creator. So in this short work, Cohan and his director go for many kaleidoscopic close-ups of hands and feet, arms, clenched fists, interlocking fingers and swaying torsos arranged technically not choreographically. In part two, 'cloud, meteor and star', the dancers floated off into a star-filled sky, faded to blue and disappeared into heaven, appearing at the end as a circular constellation before fading to nothing. It was a diverting entertainment that provided free publicity for LCDT's autumn season, but like many of the works from this period, is hampered by inadequate technology.

As artistic director of a leading theatre company, Cohan was one of the people that all the graduates from theatre design courses of every art school were told to go and see. To begin with, Cohan was welcoming but after a while with twenty-five or so people coming every year, each with a portfolio which would take an hour to go through, he gave up. One who managed to see Cohan was Ian Murray Clark, who told Cohan that he had an idea for a dance in a public swimming pool (this was many years before Daniel Larrieu's work *Waterproof* would be staged in an actual swimming pool). Cohan thought it was so cookie and a good idea, but not for him. At the time LCDT logistically could not have done it, so he thanked him and kept his number, and four months later received a commission from the Fondation en faveur de l'Art chorégraphique to make a work for the Lausanne International Festival. The commission included money for a new set, so Cohan called Clark and asked him to design a swimming pool with one side missing; Clark found the idea funny but said yes. Robin Howard was a little more practical, and wrote to Cohan on 4 October, 'Please Bob, do not agree to commission the designer nor give any orders to have his designs made until we are quite sure that we can tour the final product.'[184] Cohan called Bob Downes, whose music he knew would be eminently suitable for the project, and then had to find a dance idea. He was lucky in finding an old book called *The Waterless Method of Swimming Instruction*, in which illustrations showed little boys on benches learning to swim, without water. In addition to this he had a *Peanuts* cartoon in which Lucy is in a booth with a sign stating 'Psychiatric Help 10¢', giving advice to Charlie Brown:

> Lucy: Maybe I can put it another way. Life, Charlie Brown, is like a deck chair.
> Charlie: Like a what?
> Lucy: Have you ever been on a cruise ship? Passengers open up these canvas deck chairs so they can sit in the sun…
> Some people place their chairs facing the rear of the ship so they can see where they have been…
> Other people face their chairs forward… They want to see where they're going!
> On the cruise ship of life Charlie Brown, which way is your deck chair facing?
> Charlie: I've never been able to get one unfolded…

Premiered at the Théâtre de Beaulieu on 11 June, *The Waterless Method of Swimming Instruction* was a light-hearted romp set on the swimming pool of an ocean liner, with the cast carrying on as though inspired by the aforementioned manual. Siobhan Davies was injured and so could not be part of the athletic movement, but gave a hilarious performance as the Siren of the Deck Chair, a Joyce Grenfell-type character for whom the erecting of a deck chair or preparing for a spot of sunbathing assumed epic proportions. Cohan admits 'it was pretty crappy, but was successful. Just a joke really, we just had fun all the time.' Not just a joke for, as Peter Williams noted it, it is one of those rare modern dance works that 'puts audiences in a good humour' and 'dispels that somewhat turgid image so often associated with contemporary dance.'[185] Siobhan Davies garnered particularly good reviews, especially from Clement Crisp who christened her the 'Beatrice Lillie of the Dance'. The dancers had great fun putting the work together, manipulating the large inflatable lifesavers and generally larking about, until Cohan like an experienced script editor pulled them all together. The work was one of the pieces filmed by the BBC in the 1980s and so has lasted in the public consciousness more than some of Cohan's weightier and more deserving creations. A lot of the movement material proved very useful to Anthony van Laast, who was in the original cast, when he came to choreograph the hugely successful musical *Mama Mia* in the 2000s.

The tour to Germany was a disaster. The promoter, Julian Braunschweg, had booked them into large theatres and some gymnasia, but this turned out to be during the Football World Cup. None of the company managers seemed to have any interest in football, or they may have foreseen the problem, which was that there were no audiences. Or, if there was an audience, then the stagehands were likely to be watching a match on television, so the scenery did not get moved. Things got worse in Düsseldorf, when Braunschweg announced he had no money to pay them; the alternatives were to continue with only the hotel bills paid or cancel and go home. They chose to continue and Braunschweg went off to sell some family jewels so he could give them their per diem. After the company returned to England, the correspondence continued with Braunschweg for almost a year in an attempt to collect all the money he had promised them.

September saw the company on another regional tour which showed the continued interest Cohan had in presenting a varied repertoire. Manchester saw the premiere of Siobhan Davies' *The Calm*, a well-received work to a beautiful score by Geoffrey Burgon who would go on to write some of the best music LCDT would have. In contrast to the homegrown work, Cohan had acquired his old friend Dan Wagoner's dance *Changing your Mind*. This was a quirky and intriguing dance, performed to the accompaniment of newspaper stories read by dancer Ross McKim.

When the tour reached Liverpool, the company premiered Robert North's *Spartan Games*, its name very soon changed to the catchier *Troy Game*. The work had its origins in the South American tour during which the dancers had seen capoeira, then barely known in the UK and every night they went samba dancing. North was very excited by the rhythm of the percussive batucada music, and had bought lots of music and instruments. He told Cohan he wanted to make a dance for all the men inspired by what he had seen and heard, and outlined it to him. In preparation, Cohan added huge amounts of jumps into the daily class to build up stamina for the piece. The work was an instant hit, its vitality and humour loved by young and old, and it remained in the company repertoire until Cohan retired in 1989.

During the course of the tour, North and Davies were named associate choreographers and it was an invigorated company that arrived in London for a three-week season at Sadler's Wells. They brought with them an extensive repertory that included *Diversion of Angels*, Ailey's *Hermit Songs* (William Louther returned for a special performance of the work), together with Cohan's classic works *Hunter of Angels* and *Eclipse*, and a new dance from him called *No Man's Land*.

This work had its origins a long time before it was made, when one day the designer Peter Farmer telephoned Cohan and said, 'I want you to see a painting ladder a friend is selling and I think you could use it.' This hardly seemed an exciting offer, but Cohan agreed and found himself looking at a huge metal structure with four heels, two ladders, and a platform for painting large canvases.

Cohan agreed to buy straight away, although he had no idea what he would do with it, and it was eventually stored unhappily at The Place.

Eventually, its time came when Cohan had an idea inspired by Jean Cocteau's 1949 film *Orphée*, that it would perhaps be possible to attach lights to the tower so that it could become the door to the underworld. In a sense, the structure made the piece because Cohan had to work with it – it was too large and impressive to be ignored. His choice of composer was the virtuoso double bass player Barry Guy, who would perform his graphic score *Statements II* live on stage as an integral part of the action.

Cohan made the dance in silence, his preferred way to work, as he likes 'to know the music so well so that I trust my inner timing so that I can choreograph in silence say for one minute and then add the music'. This he did with Siobhan Davies as Lethe, Linda Gibbs as Eurydice, Robert North as Orpheus, Anthony van Laast as Cerberus, and Patrick Harding-Irmer as Charon. Cohan decided he would not tell them who they were while he choreographed, and they kept asking him about their characters and what were they doing, but he told them to just get on with it. Then, after the fifth rehearsal Davies said, 'I know who we are!' and managed to place each character exactly, so deftly had Cohan shaped the movement for each character.[186]

Guy's involvement in the work was a joy and a problem as he was, and is, a very successful musician and was always booked up. Performances of the piece had to be scheduled around his limited availability, much as performances of *Consolations of the Rising Moon* had had to be scheduled around John Williams. Guy did try to help by making a tape of a version of the work that could have been used but the Musicians' Union would not allow it. The problem even got as far as a BBC interview, when Cohan and Guy were teamed with an official from the union. In the programme, Cohan got Guy to admit that he was probably the only person in the world who could play the score, while the union man replied that Guy had no business writing music that only he could play! Off-air the official swore at Cohan and said he would never have any personal dealings with him again. Dealings with the Musicians' Union were always difficult and this would not be the last time he would have problems with them.

Cohan's initial programme note was simple and direct:

No Man's Land

For a long time, I have wanted to do a dance about Orpheus and Eurydice and when Barry Guy played his bass solo for me I saw an opportunity to do a condensed, very literal version of the legend. The only liberty I have taken is to see it through the eyes of Lethe, the goddess of 'forgetfulness and oblivion'.

But after reports that audiences found the dance too difficult to follow, a more detailed one was added:

No Man's Land

According to ancient legend, when Eurydice died, Orpheus was so overcome with grief that he refused to sing or play the lyre and thereby plunged the whole world into silence.

The Gods, moved by his grief and dismayed that this, the greatest of poets, should sing and play no more, allowed him to find the entrance to the Underworld so that he might recover his lost wife. Their one condition, however, was that Orpheus should lead the way and not look back at Eurydice until they reached the upper air.

Through his musical genius and despite the tricks played upon him by the watchdog, Cerberus, the ferryman Charon, and Lethe, the Goddess of Forgetfulness, Orpheus regained Eurydice. In the story as told by Virgil and Ovid, just as he had the end of the passage in sight he could not refrain from turning to gaze at his wife's face, and through this excess of love he lost her forever.

In *No Man's Land*, however, it is the final trick played upon them by Cerberus which banishes Eurydice to Hades once more and leaves Orpheus with nothing but a searing image of his lost love, scorched upon his mind forever.

It was an enormous success but it was not an easy evening's viewing – Guy's music was loud and violent, and the lighting effects were reminiscent of an iron foundry. But Cohan says of the work: 'I felt the audience should have an experience, and sometimes you have to hit them hard.' The hard-hitting work, even with its large set, would be revived a number of times over the coming years. It was a particular success for Patrick Harding-Irmer whose Orpheus, Clement Crisp felt, 'remains one of the greatest individual performances of LCDT's history. In its heroic outlines, as in its subtlety of means – linear control matched by expressive dignity and a potent depiction of grief – it tells of an artist touched by the divine fire.'[187]

After the First World War, the harpist Carlos Salzedo had become very friendly with dancer Vaslav Nijinsky; at the time, Salzedo was developing a whole new technique for playing the harp. Influenced by Nijinsky and the physicality of the dancers' approach to all forms of movement, the 'Salzedo technique' looked in detail at the relationship between sound production and the harpist's physical movement, before, during, and after a sound had been struck – which part of the fingertip to use, how to attack the note, what speed should the finger close into the palm after sounding. The dancer transformed the musician's whole approach to his instrument and an entirely new sound world was opened up. Barry Guy, likewise, feels he was transformed by working with Cohan. Initially, he had been intimidated by the physicality of the dancers; intimidated yet fascinated by how they controlled and channelled their energy throughout the work, how they approached and left a movement, or phrase, or how they could change the dynamic of a gesture in an instant. He was so fascinated that he joined a Pilates studio to see if he could learn to articulate, control, and channel his physicality into playing his bass in particular ways. Out of this he developed a new way of playing his instrument; with a new physicality, new sound worlds opened up, new theatrical possibilities for the presentation of his instrument as an extension of his personality opened up, and he changed the way the double bass as an instrument was perceived.

The season, which ended with more performances of the ever-popular *Stages*, was a financial and artistic success. The company, performing better than ever, had presented six London premieres and the future looked bright. The school announced it had an incredible 330 students and that the Gulbenkian Foundation had agreed to fund the choreographic studies programme – in effect, Nina Fonaroff's salary.

In addition, the new Chairman of the Trust, appointed at the suggestion of the Arts Council, was a millionaire businessman named Gabriel Harrison. He liked what the Trust was doing and, although he never quite understood exactly how The Place operated, he made lots of promises of money. On the strength of these, the Trust went ahead with building plans costing £30,000, and they moved on, at his suggestion, to secure once and for all their building and purchase the freehold of the building. Sadly, Harrison died suddenly after a minor operation, and event which caused near catastrophic problems for the Trust. Inexplicably for a respected businessman, he left no Last Will and Testament, and none of the large sums he had promised appeared. The Arts Council refused to help, causing further bitterness at The Place, as it was they who had suggested he become Chairman in the first place. The future swiftly turned from looking very bright to very bleak – closure was a real possibility. It was only yet another selfless gesture by Howard, who mortgaged his house, that stopped it becoming an immediate reality.

In spite of the crisis, work had to continue, and in February the company performed once again at the Camden Festival. For this, Cohan reworked a dance called *Myth* which he had staged the previous year for the Bat-Dor Dance Company in Israel. This new version would have music by Burt Alcantara and designs by Norberto Chiesa, and was performed on 20 February at the Shaw Theatre.

Continuing his interest in electronic music, Cohan turned to the American composer Burt Alcantara, who worked extensively with choreographer Jennifer Muller. Unlike the music he chose for many of his other dances, Cohan wanted an attractive score for this piece, and Alcantara, who made use of the synthesiser in an accessible way, was a perfect choice. However, Cohan had made the dance in silence, and then asked the composer to come and watch it. This mode of operation had been standard in the very early days of modern dance; many of Louis Horst's scores for Graham were written in this way, but by the 1970s, most composers refused to work this way, feeling it restricted them too much. Not so Alcantara, who happily watched rehearsals, timed the dance's sections, and then went into hiding with his synthesiser. After a month or so, he played the score to Cohan, who loved it, and when it was performed alongside the dance, it fitted perfectly, much to the delight of the dancers who also loved the score and were pleased to have accessible music to dance to. Peter Williams would describe it as sounding like 'a crazed organist playing Bach',[188] its frantic tempo heightening the excitement.

The original title, *Myth*, was helpful as it was heavily influenced yet again by the writings of Joseph Campbell, the dance being based around a series of fantastical stories. These included a hero who meets his own death and a butterfly who becomes a woman. Cohan changed the title to *Masque of Separation* when he felt people were taking the work too seriously, a masque after all was a 'light' performance and he saw this work as an entertainment, not an evening of deep soul searching.

Cohan's programme note for the dance was clear and to the point:

Out of Chaos came all separate things. This is a Myth of Separation. A warrior separated from his life, death separated from his victim, a couple separated from each other, a man separated from his sorrow, and the final revenge of Chaos.

The company were billed as Daemons. American Frances Alenikoff, writing for *Dance News*, would give a lucid description of the work:

Chaos is a predatory female who emerges form a billowing black cloth, from which she also spawns her motley creatures. The first of her progeny is a warrior, who hurls himself through virtuoso karate paces. He then tangles acrobatically with death who separates him from his life only to be separated in turn from His prey. A romantic interlude includes a gauze-cladded chorus of maidens and two lovers who passionately couple, only to be finally sundered. More transpires, but Chaos triumphs, enveloping the Brood she has hatched, extinguishing them.[189]

But it mostly divided the British critics, with Edward Thorpe finding it had 'some of the most beautiful, exciting and erotic images in any modern repertoire',[190] while John Percival in *The Times* felt 'the work still makes no coherent sense', and that 'Bergese's silly costume makes him look as though he is suffering from orchitis'.[191] It is true that Chiesa allowed his imagination to run riot for the costumes, which had very exaggerated painted tights, especially for the butterfly. In this role, Paula Lansley was attached to a parachute harness, the silk billowing around her in the best Loie Fuller fashion. Even arch-Cohan supporter Clement

Crisp was 'not convinced',[192] while the writer for the *Birmingham Post* probably got it right when he wrote it was 'hard to say what it is all about but there is never a dull moment'.[193]

As part of the Camden Festival and continuing the excellent outreach work that The Place, under Cohan's direction, was developing, the public, during the festival, were given the chance to discover what exactly contemporary dance was. The options included watching choreographers at work, participating in a taster class, and for teenage boys the opportunity to see a performance of *Troy Game*. In addition, there were free gifts, lecture-demonstrations, discount classes, and tours of the school. Thirty years on, all of this sounds commonplace but at the time it was groundbreaking work, no one was doing as much to bring contemporary dance to the public as Cohan and LCDT.

This was no easy task, and although Cohan feels he was easy to get on with, he remembers:

> I had to be very strong to overcome the difficulties in England. This type of dance had not been seen before, we were under-funded, we were working harder than anyone should have been made to in order to maintain our position and we had to struggle to stay there. And we had enormous financial problems to run The Place and Robin was running out of money.

In June, there was a gala fundraising performance which saw an appearance from ballerina Lynn Seymour, who danced a duet with Robert North. The highlight of the gala was the premiere of a new work by Cohan, at the time untitled; it would soon be called *Class* and would be one of his greatest achievements.

Cohan had often thought of putting the daily classroom exercises together to formalise them. Often, when the company toured, they would present a technique class as a performance for schools and he would, as Graham had done before him, talk through the material, explaining exercises as they happened. He knew Harald Lander's ballet *Etudes*, which is a choreographed version of a ballet class from barre to grand allegro, and thought that it would be good for the contemporary world to have something similar.

As director of LCDT, Cohan was the main teacher of the company teaching them every day. He was not giving them a diet of Graham as the technique would be seen at the Graham Studio, but his version of it. As long ago as 1957, when he broke from Graham and began teaching in Boston, he had, as Gus Solomons Jr noted, thrown away and then rediscovered the essence of Graham's technique for himself. This is what he brought to England, and this is what he had been developing ever since he arrived. Commentators have often said that he adapted Graham Technique to suit British dancers' bodies and temperaments, but the reality is he needed to change little. The cool, elegant, streamlined technique that he taught was not developed on British bodies – in the early days the Company was a veritable United Nations of dancers – but had already been formed by

Cohan, and it was his already re-imagined Graham Technique that sat well in Britain. Of course, it was always developing, as he told a conference at I. M. Marsh College, 'it [the technique] keeps changing… The technique evolves, slowly, but it has to serve the dancers and it has to serve the company.' Cohan had rediscovered for himself, through his own work, the essential purpose of the Graham Technique, which is to 'reconnect oneself with instincts that were surrendered after childhood. The purpose being to burn away the blockages so that the body can become once again the clear, pure and open channel that it was born to be.' The work requires a daily assessment of one's motivations, of one's ability to communicate. One can clearly see here a connection between Graham and Gurdjieff, as both require a daily re-evaluation of the self in order to move forward as more fully informed human beings. This method, which Cohan developed to a supreme level and has now sadly disappeared, sat very well with the philosophical attitudes of many artists at the time. There was, in the late 1960s and early 1970s in Britain, a great interest in alternative philosophies, prompted in no small part by the Beatles' interest in all things Indian, and in particular transcendental meditation. Many of Cohan's dancers had been or went to study in ashrams in India – Ross McKim and Christopher Bannerman among them.

Canadian Christopher Bannerman, a former ballet dancer who danced with LCDT for fifteen years, is eloquent in his memories of these classes:

> [I] encountered a kind of exchange about dance that I'd never really encountered before. There were some very special moments when I experienced a kind of crystal clarity – I received teaching that was direct and yet linked to wider contexts which stemmed from Bob's ability to communicate very specific information and to relate it to a wider view of dance, and even life itself. This was the first time that I heard how dance was both physical and metaphysical. There was an element that we could call physiology but the physiological terms weren't limiting – there was a precision about a network of crystallised physical information that was just mind-boggling really.[194]

By the mid Seventies, Cohan had abstracted what he wanted from classic Graham Technique and from his knowledge of other techniques, and refined this into what he calls 'a purely mechanical process – a functional process that had nothing to do with art per se'. In his explanation of this, he has often used the analogy of painting, noting that 'you can't become a painter unless you can draw a line, a mark of some kind with control', though he does acknowledge that this would not be the case for naïve or folk painters. Continuing his analogy, he observes that 'the painter needs control of his or her materials, of the brush, or the paint, or knife, so too the dancer needs control of his or her back, or arm or eye'. These are of course purely mechanical concerns and have little to do with artistic expression. At LCDT, he is happy to admit he 'was in an ideal situation to do this since I did not have to worry about the imaginative or artistic part because we were doing some five or six hours of artistic work every day'. He did not therefore have to mix the purely technical with the artistic but was able to develop 'a highly refined, technical, totally abstract and functional, physically developing class'. The point of the class was not fun or enjoyment, nor to give the dancers a dancing experience – they did that all day in rehearsal. It 'was to build a very strong moveable body, a functional moving body'. In order to achieve this, he had to strip away all the significance from parts of Graham's technique to find out just what it was that Graham had invented at a mechanical level. Graham Technique at the Graham School was taught so that the dancers could dance Graham's works; his company were not training to be Graham dancers. It was not easy but his company were willing guinea pigs.

The class itself, which on rehearsal days took an hour and a quarter, required intense work both physically and mentally, and for most of the time took place in one spot. Here, the dancers would be 'constantly trying to find new sensations, new areas to awake in the body, new relationships between muscles'. His basic concept, which he had been developing and refining for twenty years, was that 'if you were completely centred and focussed on and concentrate on your centre, then you could move anywhere and you could fly across the floor'. At one stage, for over a year, the class included no jumps, only preparations for jumps which they executed endlessly. This idea was partly based on old Russian methods of ballet training, the idea of preparing and preparing and never jumping until the moment would come when the preparation was so perfect that the jump would simply happen.

After standing from the floor work, they may have taken one or two steps forward, back or to the side. A classic exercise such as the circular walks became not about walking but about 'working for a hollowing of various parts of the body in order to produce the walk'; the work was intense, focussed, and very detailed. Cohan is absolutely clear that this work was to develop the technical body and had nothing to do with the development of the person as a dancer, nor with the development of a language or vocabulary. Instead, he wanted them to participate in a ritual, which went deep into the core of their physical beings, where Bannerman recalls they would 'come into contact with a certain energy and relate that energy and our experience of it to a wider context'. Ross McKim would later coin the word sarxisty to describe this experience. Derived from the Greek for flesh, he means it to be comparable to ecstasy, but ecstasy implies stepping out of the body and sarxisty involves stepping into the body.

To ensure that his vision was not diverted, he never asked any of his old Graham Company colleagues to visit and teach the company. There would be visiting teachers; jazz teacher Matt Mattox taught sometimes, and a frequent and always welcome guest was Kazuko Hirabayashi, whose particular approach to Graham-based work fitted well with Cohan's vision; few, if any, other Graham teachers were ever invited to teach. In the school, he had wanted Jane Dudley installed so that he could be sure the students had the same foundation he had, and then when they joined him, he could lead them on a journey of his making. He paid lip service to the Graham dictum that it takes ten years to make a dancer, but in many cases this was true. He would look for potential company members in the school, or even before they arrived, he would see a talented boy or girl in a workshop or residency and encourage them to come to the school. Once there, he would monitor their progress until they were ready for the company. If they joined the company, then he began the serious work of shaping their bodies and minds for the serious work of dancing: 'Once I saw the ones I wanted, I would teach them and I would change the look of their bodies. I looked at a dancer I was teaching in relation to time, three, four years and I would spend the time to teach them.' This was always subtly done; Anthony van Laast remembers he had been working on a plié exercise in a particular way for some time when Cohan came up to him and suggested a slightly different approach, which resulted in a much more effective plié. Cohan's response to this is to say, 'I had to tell him when the time was right.' Sometimes after an exercise he would say nothing, intending that the dancers should use that moment to think for themselves, to take charge of their body and their learning. The company members were 'the chosen' and Celia Hulton recalls Cohan coming up to her one day in class and saying, 'You are here because I want you here.' If dancers thought Cohan was looking for a type, he was not, as he told Jonathan Lunn who had doubts that he should be in the company: 'I wanted you for you', and not as a copy of someone else. This policy of only taking dancers into the company who had been students in the school was a double-edged sword. Many came to the school with the main hope of getting into LCDT; obviously for the vast majority this could not happen, and for a number their failure to be accepted blighted their future careers. Even if they went on to successful work in dance, their failure to join the hallowed ranks would always see them marked out as second rate. However, not all of the 'chosen' wanted it, as Julyen Hamilton recalled:

> Cohan wanted me to join and I said no and Cohan said 'please we need another guy'. So I did join and after 2 weeks I said 'I'm sorry I can't handle it'… After 2 weeks I had a back spasm, lifting another dancer, and I said 'Please will someone teach me how to lift him, because I think I might hurt myself', and they said Ah, you'll learn after a few more injuries…! But to give him his due, it was Cohan who came and massaged me during the performances to keep me going. I didn't know how to do makeup and he showed me. He was very sweet and kind to me; he was never aggressive or pressurising, and I didn't make it easy for him.[195]

As other dancers recall, he never had to demand anything, they wanted to give him whatever he needed. Though exactly what this involved sometimes had to be learnt, as Kenneth Tharp recalls: 'I remember a company class soon after I joined the company, and Bob had shown an exercise. He asked everyone if it was clear and I started to say, 'I feel', at which point Bob cut me off saying, 'I don't care how you feel, it's how I feel!" This was, Tharp recalls, 'said with love and a twist of humour', but it did make him realise that sometimes the best experience came from doing, not questioning.

Cohan's *Class* was a synthesis of his movement vocabulary developed over thirty years of dancing, and an extraordinary testament to what he had achieved in his time at The Place in a very short time. Like Lander's ballet, it covered all the daily technique exercises which Cohan shaped into an exultant, virtuosic display. From a beautifully fluid solo from Linda Gibbs, the dance moved through the floor exercises to contrasting sections for the men and the women, broken up by some solos which explored the characters of key dancers such as Kate Harrison, Anca Frankenhauser, and Patrick Harding-Irmer, and finishing with the full ensemble performing a series of breathtaking falls.

There was never in LCDT a hierarchy such as in the ballet world, with principals, soloists, and coryphées, but everyone knew that the dancer who exemplified Cohan's aesthetic was the Australian Patrick Harding-Irmer. Harding-Irmer, known affectionately as 'The Body', owing to his extraordinary physique and presence, had begun his dance training in 1969 with Keith Bain at the Bodenweiser studios, and graduated from Sydney University with a BA in 1970, majoring in philosophy and German, followed by Dip. Ed. in 1971. He had arrived in Britain in 1972 and been spotted in an evening class – wearing a brown bell-bottomed catsuit – by Flora Cushman who told Cohan he had to see him. This Cohan did, and realised straightaway that 'he was extraordinary'; at 33, he was older than Cohan would normally have wanted, but he knew he could use him. Following some sort of procedure, he placed him briefly into the school and then got him to take company class. He ruffled some feathers by sitting in the front at Cohan's right hand with a look on his face that said, 'You tell me what to do and I will do it.' Cohan knew straight away that there would never be a question of who was boss: 'If I had said fall on your face, he would have. Not that that's what you looked for, but he challenged me to teach him as well as I could. His attitude never changed, I was the boss.' He would stay with Cohan for seventeen years, until Cohan retired, and Irmer and his wife, fellow LCDT dancer Anca Frankenhauser, moved back to Australia.

In *Class*, Cohan gave Irmer a virtuosic solo, in which he burst on the stage like a force of nature. In a series of leaps, falls, rolls and the most extraordinary balances, he demonstrated all the attributes of a Cohan-trained dancer. But what made the solo all the more powerful was not the technique and bravura but his demonstration of sarxisty. The brief solo is all Cohan's technique in microcosm.

Class was to have its premiere at a gala fundraising event at The Place and, for reasons which everyone has forgotten, Cohan left it until two weeks before the gala to ask John Keliehor to compose the music. Keliehor, a Seattle-born composer, improviser, and percussionist who had been living in England on and off since the late 1960s, had been playing for classes in the school and for the company. He was, however, nonplussed by the request. It was for an important event, Keliehor was very busy with other projects, and what Cohan described sounded very complex; when he attended a rehearsal, he saw just how complex. Cohan had rehearsed the work in silence, or rather with him shouting out counts, occasionally clapping rhythms and time changes with the dancers filling in with sounds to help them remember where they were. By the time Keliehor saw it, the structure was all there and by the end of rehearsal, he had decided it would be possible. He was further swayed 'by the look of desperation on Bob's face which nearly broke my heart'.

To the next rehearsal Keliehor brought a pad of paper and metronome in order to write down all the counts and, more importantly, the tempo changes which occurred all too frequently in every section[196] of the work. By the end of the week, he had sketched out all the bar lines with metric changes, but within these bars there were no notes and no melodic line, simply sets of directions. Keliehor got together three other musicians – a percussionist, guitarist, and double bass player – and talked them through what was supposed to happen. As the premiere approached the music and dance were still not quite together, Cohan decided that the only way it would work was if he joined in with the group playing a set of claves. Unfortunately, even that did not work and halfway through, the dance and music came unstuck. Cohan had to shout, 'Stop!' and explain to the audience what had gone wrong, then start again from the point of collapse and go on. For a perfectionist such as Cohan it was deeply embarrassing; happily, it did not prejudice the work which went on to become an audience favourite.

Mary Clarke was not alone in her view that 'Class should be required viewing for all those classically oriented people who still believe that the moderns can't dance. It is a myth that LCDT is quietly shattering.'[197] Peter Williams wrote, 'Cohan has found the contemporary answer to the classical 'défilé' work' and that '[Class] will be invaluable as an introduction to the Graham Technique wherever it goes'. Earlier in the article, he acknowledged that 'Cohan has adapted this [Graham Technique] so that it reflects the way it has been developed to suit the rather different temperament of the British dancers'.[198]

As was becoming usual, John Percival was a dissenting voice. Unknown to Cohan, in 1975 Graham had also created a technique demonstration which she named Adorations, set, curiously for Graham, to baroque music arranged for guitar. On comparing it with Class, Percival would write, 'Graham's Adorations also based on a display of the daily classroom technique is something else: the sheer virtuosity of Graham's dancers goes beyond anything LCDT has yet achieved,… and the choreography has a theatricality and structure beyond what Cohan presented'.[199] This is a curious opinion since Graham's work is a fairly static arrangement of the class exercises, while Cohan's is fully choreographed, using the exercises as a base from which to move the dancers further and further into flights of technical fantasy that are, in the end, breathtaking. *Adorations* has long since disappeared from the Graham Company repertoire, being replaced in the early 1980s with a longer work called *Acts of Light*, set again to unsuitable music, this time Nielsen's Romantic *Helios Overture*. At the time of writing the Graham Company are looking into acquiring Cohan's *Class* for their repertoire.

After the first performance, Keliehor was approached by a young woman called Morgana Taylor who wanted to introduce him to her mother Anna. They had both enjoyed the score enormously and in return for some instrumental tuition for Morgana, Mrs Taylor offered Keliehor the use of her vast and rare collection of Burmese gongs. Keliehor continued to refine the score with these gong sounds in mind and the instrumentation changed. Out went the bass and guitar and in came three more percussionists playing an array of instrument. Even then, in the early tours of version two, Cohan still played with the musicians. Eventually, version three arrived, and then version four for eight percussionists. It was this version that Noel Godwin, while acknowledging certain similarities to Britten's gamelan-inspired score for the ballet *Prince of the Pagodas*, would compare its effects to a surfeit of 'Swiss clocks'.[200] In any event, Cohan was never entirely satisfied with it feeling that the instrumentation it used lacked some lyric impulse he wanted, and it was expensive. In 1980, he asked Geoffrey Burgon to write a score with a more lyrical feel, but beautiful as it was – it gave the dance a kind of film noir feel – it was not right and was swiftly dropped and soon after, he went back to Keliehor to ask for a new version which Keliehor generously provided. This was a more elaborately scored version for six players, including Mrs Taylor's gongs and some new instruments and unusual children's toys which produced wonderful rare sounds. The subtle changes, which saw the ensemble divided into a small concertino section playing gamelan-like sounds and the larger group playing the drums, added just the right feeling which Cohan wanted, and this version became definitive. The years of waiting were worth it, and Keliehor's score *Class V* is a dance classic of kaleidoscopic rhythms, and an Aladdin's cave of instrumental colouring.

Although life carried on for most of the year, the gloom of the immense financial problems hung over all of The Place's work. Eventually, a fundraising appeal for an endowment fund was begun, with the aim to raise £1.1million. This was to purchase the lease on the current building, which could be legally terminated in 1976, and purchase and convert the building next door, as more space was desperately needed. Incredibly in such a situation on 12 November LCDT began a lengthy season at Sadler's Wells, showing seventeen works seven of which were new to the capital. Both of Cohan's contributions had been premiered elsewhere and where eagerly awaited in London.

In the mid 1970s, LCDT's music director was John Perras, who was very experienced with dance having previously worked with Paul Taylor. After sometime with the company, he began questioning Cohan as to why he always used 'difficult' music. Cohan had to agree with him, he did use and was using more and more challenging music, challenging for him, for the dancers, and more especially for the audiences. Cohan had always been drawn to musique concrète or difficult atonal works, but he tried to make the complex sound worlds more listenable through the type of movement he did to them. He found the scores challenging because 'you couldn't sit back in your memory and recreate steps, you had to make up your own steps'. In choreographing, he always tried to vary the rhythm or the structure of his material, and he found this easier with electronic music. He was never interested in copying the music, or attempting any of Ruth St Denis' music visualisations.

One day, Perras gave Cohan a tape of Vivaldi's infectiously good-humoured *Gloria in D* and said, 'Here, why don't you do something to real music for a change?!' Ignoring the insult, he took the music and listened to it 'intensively'. By this, Cohan means, and here there is an unlikely similarity with Frederick Ashton, he played it every day, possibly about sixty times in two weeks. Like Ashton, this is the only way Cohan learns the sound as he doesn't read music, he has to learn by listening. But as much as he loved the piece, he finally decided it was too big and he could not use it.

Not to be beaten, Perras presented Cohan with another Vivaldi tape, this time of the *Stabat Mater*. Cohan listened to it for several months. He loved the sound, liked the mood, liked the theme, and felt it was something he should do. He was particularly taken by the opening lines of the hymn written in the thirteenth century by Jacopone da Todi:

At the Cross her station keeping,
stood the mournful Mother weeping,
close to her son to the last.[201]

So, much to Perras' surprise – it was as radical a departure for Cohan as it had been for Paul Taylor when he used baroque music in his seminal work *Aureole* – he agreed and then straightaway put it off because he could not think of how to do it. All he could see in his mind was every trite contrived image linked to the theme, none of which he wanted to put on stage.

To push himself, he agreed to an opening date for the work in six weeks' time, but he still had no idea how to start. He retreated with the tape to his house in France and sat on the back terrace with views over the mountains and every day, all day, listened to the music. Then, one day during a beautiful sunset, which would eventually be portrayed in the costumes, he suddenly knew how to make the piece:

It was all there in the music, it would be all women – which I had not decided until then. It all came in one flash, in two or three minutes, I saw there were nine sections, nine women; first solo, then duet, trio, fourth section was a repeat of the first, fifth was a repeat of the second, sixth a repeat of the third, seventh was different, a question of the whole process, the eighth a resolution, and the last the answer to the question.

Excited, he called Mop and told her to get the dancers ready for the next day.

Cohan jumped on a plane and flew back to England, eager to start work. The vision of a dance had appeared to him and, although he had no steps in mind, he was deeply moved by the concept of actively standing still and sorrowing. This idea, together with the colour of the sunset, the textures of the music, and an understanding of the dancers he would use as aspects of Mary's experience, were the foundations of the work. When he got into the studio, Perras and Romano were waiting for him and Cohan said, 'OK, we will begin with the last section because it is the most difficult.' The dance then poured out of him, he demonstrated every step with someone at the piano, while Perras and rehearsal director Moshe Romano were running around, trying to help the dancers pick up and remember what he was doing.

Cohan cannot remember changing anything in the finished dance, he knew where everyone was supposed to be and how they were supposed to move. Like Graham, he now had a body of dancers who understood his style and methods, and they could take his material and develop it. He says of the choreography for this work and in general:

> I did not preconceive steps, I always moved from the physical intention, which is always the most fascinating thing to me in teaching a work to someone. When I work as a choreographer, I try to make the movement come from a sensation or a quality, or a need to create a certain form of expression within the form I am using, and the form is a certain set of movements that I am using. You always try to give the dancer a physical sensation, not a shape. They may come close to you, [but] it doesn't matter, if the sensation is right, they will get the movement right.

Cohan has always seen the transmission of a dance from one dancer to another as problematic as

> … those movements in sequence become the dance, then it is performed and then taught to someone else and they learn the steps, not the sensation. This is always a great problem: how to create the original meaning of the movement onto the new person. Usually, the choreographer remembers the sensation of every step they have ever made; you may not remember the step but if you see it, you will remember why you did the step thirty years ago and you will know if it is right from the sensation, not the movement. That is a difficulty of transmitting work and moving it on, and why you cannot learn

from a video; sometimes it is clear, say in a big run and a leap, but not if it is complex. It may be easier in ballet with a more set language, but you will not get the sensation. You have to have direction or intention in yourself when you choreograph. That direction creates the combinations. If you relate it to a painter, every mark on a canvas becomes a map of the process of his trip, and when he finishes all of that journey, you have a painting. Every movement is a map in time; the physical movement of where the dance is going. You may not know where you are going, but you know you are going somewhere. You may find the end first and you will know how to get there. You may have an illumination. You don't always in the process on the way.

Cohan's process in *Stabat Mater* was to follow the music, quite literally, if a musical phrase was repeated he repeated a dance phrase. This may sound simple but it is not, a lesser figure would have produced a work that mickey-moused Vivaldi, but not Cohan. His training with Horst meant he could understand the architecture of the music, and knew when to go with it and when to go against it.

Writing of *Stabat Mater* in the *Dancing Times*, James Monahan drew parallels to Graham's *Primitive Mysteries*, which he describes as her greatest achievement – 'a simple noble ritual of her own making'. And he was pleased that Cohan 'has miraculously, succeeded in exactly the same way' in his *Stabat Mater*, 'a ritual for (seven) female dancers', that is 'not derivative and is wholly convincing'.[202] But, even a work as appealing and accessible as this could not guarantee universal approval and a curious anonymous review in the *Kilburn Times* in December 1976 found, 'It was the weakest part of the evening, most of the dancers were inadequate in conveying the emotional feel of such tragedy with their, at times, awkward ungraceful movements.'[203] The *Kilburn Times* notwithstanding, *Stabat Mater* would go on to be seen as one of Cohan's finest creations, an 'outstanding work of modern dance',[204] constantly in the repertory of LCDT. Kate Harrison, the original central Mary, was so identified with the role that some writers worried that no one would be able to replace her. But their fears were unfounded, as many other dancers did take on the part over the years. *Stabat Mater* would become Cohan's most popular work and would go on to be set on a number of companies around the world. When it was restaged by Ballet Theatre Munich to celebrate his eightieth birthday it was seen as a 'quietly challenging work', and 'a revelation'.[205]

When the dance was performed on LCDT's American visit in 1977, a number of critics commented on its architectural and sculptural qualities. In the *New York Times*, Anna Kisselgoff wrote, 'It is almost Greek in the classical sense of ancient Greek drama and in the choreography's sculptural values.'[206] While in the *Philadelphia Inquirer*, Daniel Webster reported that 'Cohan's ease in moving and balancing groups, his sense of architectural and sculpted shapes and his ability to sustain this level of emotion through the length of the piece made it powerful'.[207] David Earle, who has followed Cohan's work for over fifty years, describes Cohan not so much as a choreographer, but as a 'corporeal architect' who moves his immaculately sculpted creations in perfectly organised and beautifully designed spaces. Frances Alenikoff would give a perceptive appraisal of not only the work but of Cohan's approach to choreography in general, writing: 'Cohan has a craftsman's polished awareness of the dynamics of space and the uses of metre. His compositional devices are tradition oriented and formal; circles, classic groupings, canons and fugues. Movement patterns evolve and unfold from a serene poised centre, and phrases accumulate and expand architecturally until they span the stage, sweeping it with luxuriant lyricism.'[208]

Stabat Mater was followed closely by Place of Change, which was presented at Sadler's Wells in the company's December season. It was a reworking of a dance Cohan had made during his summer break for the Bat-Dor Dance Company. After her success with Myth, Jeannette Ordman had asked for a piece and Cohan chose Arnold Schoenberg's String Quartet No. 2 as the music. Though dedicated to his wife, it was written in 1908, at a time when she was having an affair with the next door neighbour, Richard Gerstl, and is a distraught, impassioned work including Schoenberg's first real use of atonality. Unusually for a string quartet, it includes in the third and fourth movements a soprano who sings two angst-ridden poems by Stefan George, including the lines:

> Deep is the sadness that gloomily comes over me,
> Again I step, Lord, in your house.
> Long was the ride, my limbs are weary,
> The shrines are empty, only anguish is full.[209]

Never one to be concerned with the baser sides of human life, as reflected in the music's creation, nor with the self-pitying tenor of the poem, Cohan's programme note stated that 'the piece tries to demonstrate the struggle to transmute earthly love into a more selfless or Divine Love'. Cohan's work is always striving to illuminate the human existence and show the possibility for spiritual growth and transformation. Cohan created what was fundamentally a hugely elaborate duet inspired by the beautiful physicality and presence of one of the female dancers in the company. One day, he had seen her walk across the stage; this captured his imagination, and that is basically what she did, becoming for him an abstract evocation of the spirit of life. Noel Goodwin, writing in Dance and Dancers, felt that the dance paralleled the musical concept and observed that 'the first two movements seem to me to be of a preparatory nature to the other two, when the voice is added'.[210] The intricate and emotionally wrought duet in the second movement seemed to indicate a turmoil which Cohan tried to resolve in the final movements. The third movement, a fast quintet for a female soloist and four men, leads to something of a transfiguration in the finale. Cohan translated the finale's title, 'Entrückung', as 'Transport', though a better world would be Rapture:

I feel as if above the last cloud
Swimming in a sea of crystal radiance–
I am only a spark of the holy fire
I am only a whisper of the holy voice.[211]

The relationship between the 'whisper of a holy voice' and Gurdjieff's 'waking sleep' could not be more apparent.

The work had a mixed reception. Clement Crisp found it 'curiously dated in appearance', but 'well intentioned and ultimately unconvincing', while 'the path of what I take to be illumination is neither very clear nor particularly persuasive'.[212] John Percival's review concentrated on the dancers' lack of technique and contained the sort of curious sentence that could have been expected in 1954, not 1975: 'It is far harder to dance really fast with a modern dancer's bare feet than in a ballet dancer's specially designed shoes.'[213] Clearly, there was still a lot of work to be done to drag some British critics into the twentieth century. He also went on to complain that LCDT was still utilising Graham Technique and had not as yet developed a movement language of its own, commenting, 'They will I suspect find their own real creative style only when they rebel… as Graham rebelled against her predecessors.' Percival should have known better, or perhaps he did not know, that Graham's work had taken ten or fifteen years to develop. It was totally unreasonable to expect LCDT to have developed something unique in half that time, but whenever he could, he would find some way for critiquing LCDT in terms that the dancers found overly negative and unhelpful. This became so marked in the coming years that Cohan asked for a collection of the reviews to be sent to him with a view to pursuing some sort of legal action, which, happily, never occurred.

As well as Cohan's pieces, the company showed a varied programme of work by Richard Alston, Siobhan Davies, Micha Bergese, together with two intriguing collaborations between Robert North and respectively Lynn Seymour and Wayne Sleep from the Royal Ballet. All of this work had been presented on a budget of £15,000, compared with the £70,000 spent by the Royal Ballet to refurbish a perfectly satisfactory production of *Romeo and Juliet* or the £150,000 spent by London Festival Ballet on a new version of *Sleeping Beauty*. Although financially the situation would get better for contemporary dance, even now, in the second decade of the twenty-first century, the gap between the funding of the British ballet companies and the now well-established contemporary scene is still so enormous as to be unacceptable.

The year did, however, end on a very bright note, when Cohan was awarded the prestigious London Evening Standard Award 'for his tremendous achievement in moulding of the London Contemporary Dance Theatre into Europe's finest modern dance company'.[214] The award was a great vote of confidence in Cohan by the critical establishment and a tremendous thumbs down to the Arts Council. David Earle asked Cohan how he had managed to achieve so much in so short a time and was told, perhaps mischievously:

> I did three things, I knew it was a ballet city so the first year I worked on extensions so that at the first London performance all the legs were by their ears. I never did a work on opening night that had not been performed and received rave reviews from the critics before. I never open with a new work and so as they never go back on their word I start with the good works. I always planted people in the audience to lead the applause because you can never trust people to know when they have enjoyed themselves!'

1975 was a key year in development of Cohan's work; up until then all of his dances could be divided into two choreographic styles. One which he identifies as including works such as *Eclipse, Hunter of Angels, Cell, X*, etc., which were in his words 'minimalistic.' He was 'torn' between that and 'my lyrical movement style', which can be seen in works such as *Tzaikerk, Masque, Place of Change, Stabat Mater* and *Nympheas*. He was always drawn to the more minimalistic work, constructed with fewer transitions and more static movement, and feels that 'if I had gone that way I may have been more interesting as a choreographer. But it didn't satisfy me physically. I could see it was interesting and I enjoyed what I did with it, but I didn't enjoy myself as much in the studio, so I went the other way.' It was not a reasoned choice, he 'just went with it'. The move to a more consistently lyrical style had to do with the realities of developing the company. He has always said he mainly made pieces not for himself, but to develop his dancers, and by the mid Seventies, he had trained a group of superb technicians who needed to 'dance'. And the type of dancing they preferred doing was not the static minimalistic work which occasionally bordered on what we now call physical theatre, but the dancing of long lyrical phrases of movement. In addition to this, he was under pressure from outside influences, such as theatres and audiences who requested to see dancers dancing in dances that danced. He had not just himself, but many other people's livelihoods to consider, and 'we went the way that was the acceptable face of contemporary dance'. He knew that his way was not the only way, and that 'there would be a rebellion of Sue [Davies] and Richard [Alston] and Robin and I frequently talked about it. It happened very quickly and that was good.'

LCDT and London Contemporary Dance School could not be everything to everyone and by the mid Seventies, many former students were responsible for a burgeoning independent dance scene which existed outside of Ballet Rambert and LCDT. Tamara McLorg, Christine Juffs, Betsy Gregory, Kate Flatt, Maedee Dupree, Christopher Banner, and Julyen Hamilton are just a few of the personalities who were developing work that was contrary to the now established large companies. In addition, there a number of small, experimental groups, including Alston's Strider formed in 1972, Limited Dance Company, Cycles and Dance Organisation, all formed in 1974. Owing to the success of the school, even if some students disliked the regimented system, it could not be denied that it produced artists who could go on and develop alternative modes of expression. And in the coming years, this ever growing group would make demands on the limited funding available to dance in Britain, with devastating consequences for LCDT.

Chapter 8

Commentary

If the very first three years were spent finding and creating The Place, the school and the company, the next years were spent trying to make our ideas bear fruit. But, as Paul writes, we constantly had serious financial problems. Robin bore the brunt of that burden. He always said to me, 'You just tell me what you think you want to do, and it is my job to make that possible.' As wonderful as that sounds to an artist, I just could not do it. I knew what it was like to live with no money and every bill coming in the mail demanding payment or else. Robin did not have that experience.

It reminded me of a conversation I once had with Baroness Batsheva de Rothschild. She was never ostentatious, and if you met her, there was no way you would know that she was the daughter of one of the world's richest men. She had just married Donald Bloomingdale and they had an apartment on New York's Upper East Side.

I was with her in their new living room, sitting on a Louis XIV chair, with a Rembrandt and Renoirs on the wall, chatting away while waiting for Martha to arrive. After a while, she said to me that I seemed depressed and what was wrong. I suddenly let go, and told her that I had no money except for what I earned teaching, $7 a class. It was not enough to live on and I was about to have my telephone shut off and every bill I received was red and I did not know how to cope with it. She listened to me with sympathy and when I finished she said, 'How interesting, I have no experience of that feeling at all.'

This same 'lack' is what I was worried about with Robin.

Critics! Before you read what I say about dance critics, I should admit that I have twice received the National Dance Critics' Circle Award for Achievement in Dance! Which I have accepted! I have danced or choreographed for about fifty years. In that time, I have had a lot of reviews. I could write a book about how I feel about them. My particular argument with John Percival's reviews was exactly about that thing that we needed so desperately, money. I really didn't care what he wrote, but it was the prestige of the newspaper that he wrote for that made it a problem.

Foreign touring is still one of the few ways British dance companies can earn a little money. *The Times* was in every British embassy and consulate all around the world every day. We were always trying to interest the British Council into helping us organise foreign tours. How could we convince some distant arts officer to want us if the only reviews he read about London Contemporary Dance Theatre in *The Times* were dire? I saw little hope with Percival, except for *The Times* not to ever review us, but there was little chance of that, because as a major critic, he had to be seen at an opening and anyway he got paid to write the review, although I would have gladly paid him out of my own pocket not to write.

I know a lot of the difficulty with critic's reviews; they affect artists personally and that is something every artist has to deal with in their own way. For me as a dancer, after the first few years, they became much less important. I never kept them. My father did.

I always found it revealing to read several different critics' reviews of the same performance. It highlights the fact that we all see the world through our individually 'conditioned' eyes, and therefore what they each think has no more importance than anyone's personal opinion. The problem is that, even though the critic is writing their own personal opinion, they carry the weight of the newspapers status and importance they are writing for behind them.

As the director of LCDT, the critics' reviews took on a different significance.

I cared that the dancers and choreographers were personally encouraged and as well, our entire enterprise. Of course one expects and needs criticism, but I know that going on stage as a dancer is a particularly naked and vulnerable act. If there is a negative criticism that needs to be reported, in my opinion, at least it should be constructive or helpful.

Peter Williams, who was the founder and editor of *Dance and Dancers*, was for me a good example of a helpful critic, as he always put my work into an artistic context that was revealing to me.

I also cared about the reviews because the company was the publicly visible part of all the work Robin, Mop Eager and I were doing at The Place to bring this change in dance to Britain and we needed some good, 'free publicity'.

It is a sad part of the system, in our culture now, that, a person, and often an 'uncreative' one, who has worked themselves into a position of power in the media, can easily use that power, both artistically and financially, over the lives of practising artists.

Many of the critics I met became friends, but some are naïve and don't really realise the power they have over dance artists' lives and their future ability to work. Or maybe they do know their power and won't admit to it. They frequently say in defence, 'But we are only reporters.'

If so, then why don't they report that the audience loved the work even though they did not or why do they rush up the aisles in the dark and out before the bows, as if the audience's reaction might spoil their precious thoughts.

As you can see, I have studied the critics as they have studied me.

If you do read dance reviews between the lines, as it were, you can clearly see that there are some critics who have their own agenda. The fact that they have the advantage of not being subject to answer for their opinions by the artists they criticise can still make me furious.

Chapter 9

But soon as early Dawn appeared,

the rosy-fingered,

then gathered the folk about the pyre of glorious Hector.

(Iliad, xxiv. 76)

1976–9

More awards followed in 1976, when Robin Howard was created CBE in the New Year Honours List, and awarded the Royal Academy of Dance's Queen Elizabeth II Coronation Award for 'outstanding service to the art of ballet', the use of the words 'contemporary dance' still being too much for the establishment to bear. Yet, Cohan and LCDT continued to become more and more part of the establishment. Cohan in particular found calls on his time from many quarters, being asked to speak on television, at conferences, to be part of committees, to deliver workshops and classes, and to choreograph. Most of the choreographic requests he regrettably had to turn down, as LCDT's punishing schedule of touring took most of his energies, but he did continue his relationship with Israel, visiting frequently in any holiday time he could find. It is to his credit that he also almost never turned down teaching requests, perhaps seeing them as an essential part of proselytising duties appearing for any number of organisations including Inner London Dance, the Laban Guild, the Royal Academy of Dancing, and many smaller bodies. Primavera Boman remembers:

> At St Martins we had a weekly sculpture forum. People like William Burroughs came to talk, and so many other artists known in Art and Culture. So I asked Sir Anthony Caro if I could arrange for Bob to come too. Bob decided to teach a class to the sculptors. It was so hilarious that both Bob and I cracked up. It didn't take much for Bob to giggle anyway. He had a hard time hiding his grin. And so did I. For example Bob said, 'Everyone, face the front so we can begin.' One student sat on the windowsill, the others faced the back of the studio, and so on. Then triplets across the floor – opposite arms to legs – well, that was the goon show. They all enjoyed the class though; another testament to the greatness of Bob's teaching.

Later in his career and at the height of his fame, Marie McCluskey recalls asking him to teach at her Thamesdown Contemporary Dance Studio, and was surprised when he arrived early, unaccompanied, having 'just walked up from the station', his lack of ego being refreshingly unique.

He was also always looking for ways to keep the company, and himself, fresh, and beginning in 1976, they undertook a series of residencies. These had been commonplace in America since the early days of modern dance, when performance opportunities were limited. So to provide opportunities for interaction with a public, companies would take up residence in colleges and universities, where they would be able to perform as well as teach, create, and generally involve the students or communities in their work. Cohan had brought this idea with him to England, and it was to be one of the many concepts that he introduced that would change the face of British dance.

The first of these large-scale residencies took place between January and March, and for these the company was split into two. Cohan with nine dancers, a musician, and two technicians took up residence in the north of England while the remaining company either took leave of absence or worked at The Place. While primarily based at Bretton Hall College, Cohan and the dancers also did extensive work at Bradford & Bingley College, York University, Hull University, Lady Mabel College, and I. M. Marsh College. In later years, when the residencies had become well established and much in demand, both halves of the company would be working on location at the same time.

Cohan, in a lengthy interview for the April edition of *Dance and Dancers*, explained how it had all fallen into place:

> I was looking for an alternative way for the company to function. You see, our normal way of functioning now is to do between twenty and twenty-five weeks of straight performing a year. It's hard and it is, in a sense, uncreative in that the dancers never get to meet the audience or know what the audience is thinking about what they are doing. We have always tried to do lecture-demonstrations along the way, one afternoon then we would also teach some master classes. It seemed to me that this could be expanded. At the same time several members of the company who have been with us a long time wanted some time off to do some work.

Cohan also wanted to stretch not only himself, but the company as well, and in the nine weeks of the project, he certainly did that. Everyone worked extremely hard, going into an area for three days at a time, delivering lecture-demonstrations and open rehearsals, then performing for three days and then holding post-performance talks. The dancers taught a great deal, since in addition to work at the colleges, they went into schools in the locality, which in some places meant a dozen or more schools. In this, the dancers were always paired and there could be up to four classes going on in an area at any one time. All of the work paid off and the audience numbers for public rehearsals grew throughout the project: 200 in Bradford, 750 in York, and 900 in Sheffield.

The residency at Bretton Hall was mainly due to the efforts of the indefatigable Margaret Dunne, a seminal figure in dance in the north of England and a tireless

advocate for dance everywhere, and who had from the beginning been one of
the staunchest supporters of Howard and of the Trust's work. In London, she
visited Cohan with a terrifying proposal; would he be willing to choreograph
in public? She explained that her college was comfortably equipped with useful
theatre space, and that if he would choreograph on the stage, she would bring in
students to watch. At first, this appalled Cohan, although his concern was not
for himself but for the dancers. They were used to open rehearsals, but the act
of choreographing is a very sensitive, exposing situation, 'if it is going well and
everyone is getting what they want then it's fine; if it is not going well, how or
why would that be shown publicly?' It would either be a disaster or a success, but
finally after some careful thought and discussions with the company, he agreed.
The situation was helped at Bretton Hall, mainly because everything under Miss
Dunne's watchful eye was very well organised. The group had a beautiful studio
complete with stage, but on exploring the space, Cohan decided it would be
better to put the audience on the stage and the dancers in the auditorium. This
is what happened and, from 2.30 to 4 p.m., about 200 young people watched
Cohan and the dancers at work creating an, as yet, unnamed dance. But what he
had not realised, or rather what the canny Miss Dunne had not explained, was
that another 200 people would arrive at 4.30 p.m. and stay to watch the company
work until 7 p.m.

To begin with, Cohan found the work difficult as he was put on the spot; twice
a day, he had an audience who wanted to see work being created. The problem
was that each set of spectators wanted to see a finished product at the end of each
session, but choreography does not often work like that: sometimes there may
be a performable sequence, but at other times just disparate phrases and motifs.
The fact that Cohan and the dancers were under the scrutiny of not one but two
audiences daily put everyone under a great deal of pressure. Group one wanted
and expected to see the hour and half's work tied up into 'their' sequence at the
end. Then the next group would want to see something entirely new, and not a
rerun of what the first group had seen. But Cohan worked the whole event out
carefully, and while he was working with one dancer, he would ask the others
to go into the audience and sit and explain what he was doing. The dancers
also, to begin with, found the situation difficult and artificial, complaining that
they could not do everyday things such as have a cigarette or food break when
not being used, or swear when something did not go to plan. Cohan told them
that they should do all of those things, minus the swearing, as the students were
coming in to see a company at real work. In the end, it all came together and
Cohan remembers there being 'a nice friendly feeling'; sometimes the dancers
would be surprised when the audience would break into spontaneous applause
over some small experiment that had worked. He finished the dance just in time
on the final Friday night; later, the dancers would joke that the piece had a climax
every minute and a half.

When he worked in Israel, Cohan had experienced days when 'there would be a very hot wind, the air would be very difficult to breathe and the people would say [dramatic voice] 'Oh, I can't work today; Khamsin, Khamsin.' There used to be an Israeli law stating that if you killed someone during Khamsin, it was taken into account at your trial, as it can drive you crazy.' *Khamsin* would be the name of the dance. This seemed a strange topic for a dance made in a snowbound college in Yorkshire, but Cohan had it in the back of his mind, which left him free to 'just do crazy things!'

Cohan choreographed it without being quite sure whether it had any underlying meaning, rather he saw it as an entertainment; one section, however, had a more locally inspired and gruesome background. In York, he had seen a building with niches in the walls and had been told that they used to hold the heads of executed enemies and thieves as a warning. The idea of disembodied heads stuck in Cohan's imagination, and he worked out that the only way he would be able to create this on stage was to have a huge piece of stretched Lycra standing in for a wall. Slits would be cut in the material and the dancers' heads would appear. Unfortunately, once realised, the effect was not as successful as he had hoped because, effective as it was, it distracted from the dance which became about something else. Instead of a set of crazy images to a diverting score, it became about 'a woman in a cloth and a man in front of it trying to touch her, as if he were touching a woman from another world'. This overpowering image was too much for at least one reviewer, who imagined that it had almost necrophiliac connotations, 'as though Namron were trying to make love to a woman (Anca Frankenhauser) wrapped in a winding sheet'.[215]

The multicultural references continued when Chiesa dressed the dance in costumes reminiscent of a carnival in Venice, which Cohan felt perfectly reflected his idea of crazy fun; the only darker section being the York-inspired man and the veiled women. Cohan found part of the set when he was in New York in a shop on Canal Street which specialised in industrial plastic. The emporium was popular with a wide range of creative personalities who would go there to search for materials because, although its products were primarily for industrial use, they found they could make art from them. Browsing one day Cohan found some Mylar, a perfectly reflective mirror plastic, then not available in England at the time. Bringing it back to England, he had it taped to the linoleum floor, where it reflected a shimmering light onto the cyclorama and the costumes.

For the music, he turned once again to Bob Downes, who agreed to decamp to Yorkshire and improvise while Cohan choreographed. Cohan enjoyed working with Downes, as his ever fertile imagination was always ready with new ideas and also because he never tried to impose these on Cohan or the dance. He was happy to follow, but in following he gave Cohan a gallimaufry of rhythms and musical sounds to work with. Cohan often found Downes' music 'a bit from the left field and slightly jazzy, which was not quite me, but it was an easy way to work'. Downes likewise enjoyed working with Cohan, whom he found to be a quiet, 'Humphrey Bogart-type figure', and he enjoyed improvising for him but, unlike many improvisers, had no problem notating his improvisations for future reference. Once the structure of the dance was fixed, Cohan recorded it and gave it to Downes who completed the score once the residency was over.

Perhaps by the nature of its construction, *Khamsin* appeared fragmentary, giving it 'a look of skilful improvisation, smooth but not very deep'.[216] But it was welcomed as a diverting dance full of intriguing, emotional twists and surprising technical effects pulled together by Downes' music, which one critic characterised as 'Egyptian Rock'.[217] Not surprisingly, it was one of the pieces that ended up in the repertoire of the Batsheva Dance Company much to the annoyance of Jeannette Ordman who had wanted it for Bat-Dor.

In the middle of all this, Cohan returned to London to receive an Evening Standard Award at a reception held at the Savoy Hotel. Ballerina Lynn Seymour, who presented it to him, noted in her speech that Cohan was the most persuasive person she knew and that she believed he would be able to convince even critic Bernard Levin, who had a few days previously written a disparaging article on ballet in *The Times*, to don tights. In his acceptance speech, Cohan made it clear that he saw the award as being for the whole organisation, and especially Robin Howard, who 'has given all of his money to us, but it has made him happy'. He then scanned the room and with a mischievous smile said, 'If any of you would like to be very happy...'

Howard continued to sell his property and goods to pay for The Place, and on 1 March at Sotheby's he sold, for £184,000, his museum-quality collection of rare Elizabethan and Jacobean books, including the Shakespeare folios he had inherited from his father. The sale of Howard's goods went on for all his life, and Cohan believes that the funding LCDT received from the Arts Council was in inverse proportion to Howard's gifts. As Howard became poorer, the Council gave more money and took more control until eventually he was removed from the board of the trust he had created. The Council were immorally using Howard to subsidise what was now an integral part of the British cultural scene. Howard's giving frightened Cohan, because he knew Howard had never had 'nothing'; he came from a background where there was always money somewhere to pay the bills, and he worried what would happen to him when all of that was gone.

With the residencies over, Cohan and his dancers returned to London to take part once again in the annual Camden Festival. Here, the performances at The Place continued the educational themes of the residencies by including sessions in which works were analysed and discussed. In one such session, Cohan talked through *Cell* which the dancers, in practise clothes, performed in silence. Clement Crisp noted in the *Financial Times* that Cohan's analysis of the work was helpful and illuminating. The company then returned to Leeds, where on 22 March they gave the first performance of *Khamsin*. They would return to

Yorkshire in June for the premiere of another work by Cohan, which would turn out to be one of his most admired.

Cohan first had the idea for *Nympheas* in 1946, when he saw Monet's celebrated paintings of water lilies at an exhibition in New York. Even though he hadn't created any dance at the time, he knew he wanted to make something based on them. Cohan has always been drawn to abstract and impressionist painting which, far more than sculptures, more than music, dance or literature, excites him, and he is happy to admit, 'When I see painting, I get unbelievably excited, sometimes I think I should have been a painter.' When the commission came along from an arts festival in York, he bought a book on Monet and thought, 'Why not do it?' He then began discussing the project in depth with Chiesa, whose input was essential to its realisation. Straightaway, they both agreed that they wanted to find a way to project the Monet images onto the stage. Ever inventive, Chiesa made several designs and they finally settled on one with a white double wall, so that not only could the images be projected, but the dancers could walk on this raised platform which was invisible to the audience, and seemingly float in the air.

Cohan had at an early stage thought of commissioning a score, but eventually realised that what he wanted was piano music by Debussy. He therefore listened extensively to all of the composer's piano works, eventually selecting seven pieces – all but three from the *Préludes*:

Arabesque No. 1
'Feuilles Mortes' (*Préludes*, Book 2)
'Les Collines d'Anacapri' (*Préludes*, Book 1)
'Bruyères' (*Préludes* Book 2)
'Clair de Lune' (*Suite Bergamasque*)
'Ce Qu'a Vu le Vent d'Ouest' (*Préludes*, Book 1)
'Pagodes' (*Estampes*)

He thought long and hard about working with 'Clair de Lune', eventually deciding to include it in the hope that his visualisation would provide a fresh take on the somewhat hackneyed classic. After the premiere of the work, he had the idea to add an eighth dance to 'La Terrasse des Audiences au Clair de Lune' from the *Préludes*' Book 2, but time got in in the way and it tantalisingly never materialised.

Working with the music was more difficult than he had anticipated, since much of it did not feel metered, and finding a pulse to hold on to proved sometimes illusive. A further complication was that he rehearsed with recordings by several different pianists, but always intended that in performance the music would be played live. Whoever played live had to listen to the recordings Cohan had used and play in exactly the same way, with the same rubato and phrasing, which for any pianist was not an enviable task.

As the dance was a simple, honest reaction to the music, there was no need for complex explanation and he provided a simple programme note stating:

Nympheas

From the year 1899 -1909 Claude Monet worked on very large paintings, capturing the challenging light and mood of the lily pond at his home in Giverny. He called the series *Nympheas*.

Over the years the work was almost universally applauded: David Gillard in the *Daily Mail* thought it 'a magnificent new work... that weaves a gentle, wistful, notional spell'.[218] Edward Thorpe in the *Evening Standard* that:

The work is an exquisitely realised exercise in impressionism. The movements that Cohan has devised are rippling, pliable, live and fluid: the scintillation of sunlight and water, the evanescence of passing shadows. It is an astonishing departure from the 'hard-line' choreography so associated with modern dance, a kinetic adventure with new realms of lyricism.[219]

Adding more praise, Alexander Bland in *The Observer* wrote: 'He reflects the feeling of iridescence and ephemerality without imitating its appearance and produced a ballet which is seductive but not sentimental, elusive but firm.'[220] As another of the few Cohan works recorded for posterity by the BBC, it has remained in the public imagination, and though in no way representative of Cohan's oeuvre, does show the lyricism possible with his refined Graham Technique.

In the summer, as part of the United States Bicentennial celebrations, Martha Graham's company was invited to perform at the Royal Opera House in Covent Garden, their first visit to England since 1967. Since Cohan had left Graham in 1969, she had suffered from alcoholism and major illnesses that had left her incapacitated for years. Her school and company had been kept going in a small way by some of her dancers, in particular Bertram Ross and Mary Hinkson. Then, in 1973, helped by a former photographer, Ron Protas, she had returned to take control, sacking most of those who had kept her work alive. Protas, although he was disliked by almost all of her dancers, was a remarkable publicist and through various means had enabled Graham to once again enter the limelight, presenting her as the founder of modern dance and a living legend. She began to choreograph again and made works that included Nureyev, Fonteyn, Baryshnikov, and other ballet luminaries. The new dances were heavily criticised in the press for not being up to the standard of her early work, though all acknowledged that it was incredible that a woman in her late eighties and crippled with arthritis was still able to create. At home, her work was seen as very old-fashioned and outdated, while abroad she was a star, the best of America. In preparation for the visit, John Drummond convinced the BBC to show some of her work and he visited her in

New York to interview her.

As it was her first visit in many years, it was imagined that Graham would visit The Place, the only school in the world outside of her own that 'officially' taught Graham Technique. But, as John Drummond wrote in his autobiography, this was not to be as 'the infamous Ron Protas insisted that she not visit London Contemporary Dance', which 'he dismissed… as parasites deserving of neither acclaim nor notice'.[221] To Drummond, 'this seemed… wicked, and I begged Graham to go to the LCDT's studios at The Place. At once she became a troubled old lady and said sadly, 'I don't know who to believe. I don't know what to do.' It was quite tragic.'[222] Cohan was not as offended by this as was Drummond, as Graham did not like anything else but her own work and even worse, 'if you were more successful than her, she couldn't tolerate it'. In the end, she did not visit The Place, but Cohan took his dancers backstage to meet her after a performance and she loved it, saying, 'Bob, they are so beautiful.' The company were ecstatic and everyone left happy.

But the happiness was cut short by a piece of petty spitefulness and bad grace on the part of the Graham Company management, headed of course by Protas. Robin Howard had once again guaranteed the loss at the Royal Opera House, should there be one, which in the event there wasn't, and he also invited the Graham Company to a party in their honour at The Place. A great deal of effort and money had been put into decorating the building, which was laid out for an after-show reception. The clock ticked on and no one arrived. Eventually, two of the company showed up, very embarrassed, and explained to Cohan and Howard that they had been instructed not to attend on pain of losing their jobs.

In addition, Cohan was told that Ron Protas had been telling the critics that the licence to perform *Diversion of Angels* had been withdrawn because LCDT danced it badly. This could not have been further from the truth, since most reviews said that LCDT performed it better than the Graham Company. The truth was that the fee Protas had demanded for the rights to perform the work was so exorbitant that the company could not afford to keep paying it. Other rumours reached Cohan about Protas' attitude to LCDT, and Cohan decided he had to raise the matter with Graham herself, visiting her in her suite at the Savoy. For a while, they chatted as friends about gossip and nothing and how successful the season was; then, Cohan told her that he 'wanted her to shut Protas up', that it was not right that Protas was spreading lies about LCDT, and that it was disrespectful to Howard, especially after he had guaranteed the season. Graham became very angry, 'and just at that moment Ron poked his head around the door and she shouted at him, "Ron, I didn't ask you to come in, get out", and she pointed at the door.' She apologised to Cohan for him, she was angry because Protas was embarrassing her. Cohan left feeling slightly calmer, though angry and sad that he had had to bring the matter up with Graham. The changing corporate structure of what soon became almost Martha Graham PLC meant that LCDT never again performed any work of Graham's, and the name Graham Technique, which Protas had registered as a trade mark, disappeared from the school, to be replaced by the non-copyrighted Graham-based technique.

In late July, LCDT visited the Santander Festival and then returned under the auspices of the British Council, performing in Austria, Belgium, Spain, and Portugal. At the same time, the insecurities back home were solved when the Trust bought the freehold to The Place. To do this, Howard sold the rest of his book collection and all of his shares and persuaded his brother to sell a farm they owned jointly. They received £100,000 from the Arts Council, £50,000 from the Linbury Trust, and a few other small amounts, but Howard had to put in £600,000 of his own money. Cohan's fears for Howard were beginning to come true.

Cohan was diverted by an interesting trifle when he was asked, via Robert North who was always looking to extend his portfolio, to create a short piece for a nude review entitled 'Carte Blanche'. This was in some ways a long awaited sequel to *Oh Calcutta!* and was led by Kenneth Tynan and Clifford Williams. What they had wanted to do was put actual sexual intercourse on stage but, as that was illegal, they had to look for other theatrical stagings.[223] In the end, it consisted of scenes exploring a whole gamut of sexual experience from solos through to threesomes and group sex. Along the way, it took in geriatric sex as well as sadomasochism (spanking was a major interest of Tynan's) and incest. In an interview with Robert Semple in the *New York Times*, the show was described by Tynan as, 'like its predecessor, a choreography of nudes – bodies in tableaux. Its passions are heterosexual, but not entirely. It has nothing to do with courtship or marriage. It is, simply, tribute in song and dance to a three-letter word beginning with s and ending with x.'[224]

With contributions by North and ballet choreographer Peter Darrell amongst others, the show had dramatic elements taken from an eclectic mix of writers including the Earl of Rochester, Paul Verlaine, Keith Waterhouse, Molly Parkin, and Tynan himself. One of the most successful and curiously poignant sections was the Eugène Ionesco scene, which concerned an old lady who is repeatedly called to by a young man in a window, imploring her to come to him; this she does after dressing in clothing that brought back her youth. Later, before going to bed to sleep she changes back to her former self.

It was a little more than shocking, as Bob Downes who had written the music for Robert North's contribution recalls:

> The show certainly did not come under the category of 'family entertainment'! It should have been put on at the 'Windmill'. I went along to a rehearsal with my then girlfriend, Robert North and Lynn Seymour. The programme opened up with nude males and females marching on to the stage, singing, 'Fuck me – suck me – wank me, lick me', which as you can imagine astonished us. One girl

was replaced in a scene as she was criticised for not demonstrating an orgasm well enough whilst lying on a table being masturbated by a man.

All trace of the dance has disappeared, although some of the images that appeared in the April 1977 issue of *Playboy* may be of Cohan's section. Cohan recalls his 'number' involved two men, two women, and two motorbikes. They were placed on a turntable with a film of a moving street scene whizzing by and, as the turntable turned, the performers stripped while seated on the bikes. It ended with a climax in which the bikes crashed. The show played to a capacity audience at London's Phoenix Theatre when it opened on 30 September, although the reviews were generally less than complimentary. Cohan's section was described by Ivan Wardle in *The Times* as 'a ton up death orgasm that would be at home in the Raymond Revue Bar'.[225]

After the 'glamour' of 'Carte Blanche', the year continued with a tour of the regions, where LCDT frequently played to 98 per cent capacity houses. In November, they were back at Sadler's Wells for a three-week season, where they presented fourteen works by six choreographers, including *Khamsin* and *Nympheas*. During the year, LCDT had produced nine new dances, and performed over thirty-two weeks, twenty-six of which had been touring, some abroad. This was an extraordinary achievement, and something that was asked of no other company. It also placed a tremendous stress on all concerned. Touring may seem exciting but as any businessman will attest to, the constant passage on planes, trains, and automobiles swiftly becomes wearing. For the dancers, add to that attempts to find cheap 'digs' in often drab northern towns, as well as the impossibility of finding a decent meal after a show, which were often mutually exclusive activities. Patrick Harding-Irmer remembers that Cohan told him that he 'had an idea to write a book locating the best restaurants in the provinces, mostly Indian or Chinese, which stayed open late enough to eat after the show. It would have been a best seller!' Plus the wear and tear of dancing on curiously raked stages, in poorly heated theatres, and the time spent on the road becomes enervating. Injuries frequently occurred, and substitutes were more than often placed in main roles, even in new works, and at times entire dances had to be cancelled; more than once *Troy Game* had to be dropped because too few of the men were fit enough to dance it. The Seventies were a time of great financial hardship in Britain, and this sometimes led to poor audiences, particularly in northern towns. Patrick Harding-Irmer recalls that 'one year out on tour, when it was seeming quite difficult to get an audience, Bob had a great idea of doing a piece called *Bingo Here Tonight*, so that that could be put on the billboards outside the theatres!' It sadly never materialised.

The old theatre maxim 'The show must go on' was adhered to – it had to be, or they would have folded, and 1977 began with the company back for more residencies in Yorkshire and Lancashire. This time, the company gained national coverage as the Bretton Hall work was filmed by Derek Bailey for the 'Aquarius' arts programme on ITV. It was also documented by Clement Crisp, who wrote a diary about the company for the *Financial Times*. In it, he painted a picture of the extraordinary personality that Cohan was: 'Watching Cohan at work I am vividly reminded of his extraordinary qualities as a dancer with Graham – he is still effortlessly, a unique exponent of the Graham style at its most powerful. He is also a teacher and speaker, a charismatic figure...'[226] In spite of his nerves at speaking in public, Cohan had become the face of contemporary dance in Britain, appearing in documentaries and television programmes, explaining the work of The Place or the importance of contemporary dance to the health of the country. And certainly for his own company it paid off: between 1973 and 1977, attendance at performances by LCDT in Oxford and Cambridge doubled, with similar figures elsewhere in later periods.

In his article, Crisp noted that Cohan was working, once again in public, with Micha Bergese on a dance called *Successions*. This was the working title of what was to be a celebratory piece commissioned for the Queen's Silver Jubilee, to be performed at Sadler's Wells in April. The dance was to be made by four of the company – Cohan, Bergese, Davies, and North – with music by Bob Downes and set by Norberto Chiesa. By the time the work was performed, it had shrunk to three sections and the title had been changed to the rather un-celebratory *Night Watch*, and Cohan would remember it as 'one of the worst dances we did'.

Each of the choreographers made three very different sections, and Cohan was at a loss to see how they would fit together, and so he tried by making linking interludes, but it was not an easy experience. At too late a stage, it became clear to Cohan that it was impossible to contain these blossoming artists, all of whom had developed different styles and who wanted to go into different directions. He now acknowledges it was unrealistic to think they would submit to an overarching idea, as 'they were too young to be flexible and I was too unrealistic', and after all, 'we had nothing to celebrate'.

Cohan adopted the overall form of the processional for the piece, and this idea would recur throughout all the sections, as well as linking them together. In the first section, 'Evening Star', the whole company, in elaborate contrapuntal lines, crossed the stage with a series of falls and static poses. The stage cleared, leaving behind Robert North and Siobhan Davies who performed a statuesque duet and were joined part way through by Tom Jobe and Charlotte Kirkpatrick. The material gained speed as Bob Downes' score became more rhythmically charged and the cast reappeared in another processional. This one saw Linda Gibbs emerge as the others left and she introduced part two, 'Midnight Sun', which consisted of her solo and a number of separate duets happening simultaneously. The final section, 'Palais at 4 a.m.', again played on the processional theme, the dancers entering but then frequently moving into huddled clusters reminiscent of social dancing. The dance finished with another duet for Davies and North that saw Davies left alone on stage, undulating against some orange circles representing the sunrise.

Chiesa's set designs were ingenious yet frustrating – the set consisted of a two-metre high painting that moved across the stage like the passage of the night. It stopped in different place and waited for each section, and was a nightmare for the crew to hold in place, but the company couldn't afford the machinery to do the job. The set got better reviews than did the dance, for although the structure was praised for being 'seamless', which was 'doubtless the achievement of Robert Cohan, who is the best modern choreographic craftsman we have', it was generally agreed that 'choreography, like any other art, is best not done by committee'. The complete work was seen as 'efficient but characterless'.[227] The 'too many cooks making too light of their work' led, apart from a couple of moments, to a 'dull procession of Graham-inspired clichés' accompanied by another of 'Bob Downes' serviceable but same sounding scores'. The dance was quickly dropped from the repertoire, which was a pity because within it there were sections, particularly duets, of great beauty that could have had a life of their own. But it had not been a happy experience and everyone wanted to move on.

Another frustrating and high-profile work was a television version of *Job*, made for the arts programme 'Aquarius', and shown just before Easter on Thames. *Job*, is one of Vaughan Williams' finest scores and Ninette de Valois' ballet of 1931 a seminal point in the development of British ballet. But the pastoral score was not a natural choice of music for Cohan to work with, and he 'found the music corny in places'. He visited de Valois who, as was always her tactic to begin on the attack, said to him, 'I can't recognise you Robert, you always change your hair!' He told her what he had been asked to do it but that he didn't really want to, and that he felt they should do her version. She disagreed and told him that young people should do their own things, and he should do it; but she did warn him that she had found it a difficult score to work with.

The whole project turned into a very trying experience on every level – choreographic, technical, and practical. A fundamental problem was that Cohan disagreed on everything with the producer, who was unfortunately also the director, and in television it is the director who has the final say. The director wanted a literal telling of the biblical story of Job as depicted in the score but once he began work, Cohan found himself wanting to abstract the piece because he got stuck, literally, in the characters and story. This was not helped by the designer; Cohan could not get him to understand his concept, and he insisted on placing Siobhan Davies as Job's wife in a bad wig, and Robert North as Job himself in an even worse wig, plus an obviously fake beard and moustache. The whole look was wrong, and was neither natural nor artificial, but produced the effect of bad wax works. Other technical aspects went wrong and in one scene of blue screen trickery, as the angels fly through the cosmos a triangular piece of set can be seen hanging in the stars.

Cohan also felt that the director had no idea how to direct dance and, as on film all the audience sees is what the camera sees and what the camera sees is up to the director, there were arguments. The angle was wrong, the space was wrong, the lighting was wrong, there was for Cohan one missed opportunity after another. Then, they arrived at Elihu's solo; it was late, everyone was tired and they were running out of time. The whole point of this section for Cohan was that Elihu came forward and went back, but the camera stayed on him and never moved. The director refused to listen and the shot simply did not work and, as tempers flared, he left the studio. Cohan then jumped in and talked the cameramen through the dance; there was sudden silence and then everyone applauded. One cameraman came to him afterwards and told him that was the most exciting thing he had done. Cohan had such a bad experience that he did no more television work until he worked with his old friend Bob Lockyer from the BBC on the filming of some of his classic works.

One unfortunate aspect of the production must be laid at Cohan's feet, and that was the casting of Namron, the only black member of the cast, as Satan. He looks back on it now with embarrassment: 'I made a terrible mistake, it says Satan is the most beautiful man of all and I gave it to the most beautiful person in the company and he was black! It is specific in the scenario, some of my men were nice looking but Namron for me was beauty and I made his eyes glow red! Terrible!' In addition to the glowing eyes, Namron was given exceedingly long Fu Manchu-style fingernails, which caused enormous 'comfort problems' in the course of a long day's filming.

To work on this unfortunate production, Cohan had turned down a very interesting and lucrative offer from film director Ken Russell to provide the choreography for his film based on the life of Rudolph Valentino starring Rudolph Nureyev. His name had been suggested by his former lover, and had he agreed, it would have given him a very high-profile boost in publicity and a sizeable fee. But, as always with Cohan, the work with LCDT came first and he turned it down, and sadly no more films came his way.

Cohan's next work for the company almost never happened. While working on *Khamsin*, the pressure of the situation had found him make far more material than was needed for that work. He explained to the audiences that it would be a full company piece and that he would put it together with the dancers in London. Then he made *Nympheas*, which progressed so easily that he found that he had time to make another new work, at which point the dancers reminded him of the leftover material from Yorkshire, which they remembered but he had forgotten. Out of these leftovers came one of his most technically demanding works, *Forest*.

Cohan shaped the material around his memories of his childhood visits to Camp Raleigh; what he had always remembered was the sensation of being on his own in the forest: 'There a twig breaking would startle and you would look quickly to see what was there; the wind, the sound of the leaves falling from the trees, tinkling all around, and an awareness of being.' For him, 'that is what *Forest*

24 Cohan in pensive mood, 1970s.
25 Cohan teaching, from publicity material for The Place, early 1970s.

26 Cohan and Ace.
27 Robert Powell in *Stages*, 1971.

28 Kate Harrison in *Class*, 1975.
29 *Waterless Method of Swimming Instruction*, 1974.

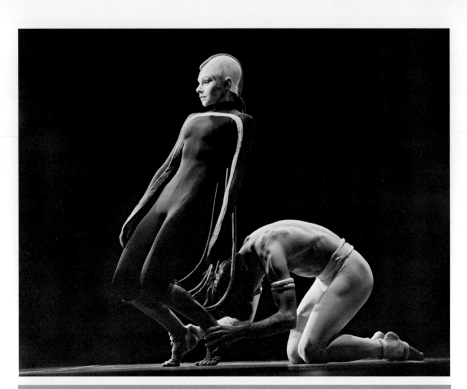

32 Robin Howard in the mid 1980s.

33 Patrick Harding-Irmer in *Skyward*, 1984.
34 *Slow Dance on a Burial Ground*, 1986.

35 Celia Boorman as Hippolyta, Alan Innes as Theseus in *A Midsummer Night's Dream*, Scottish Ballet 1993.

36 Rupert Jowett as Puck, Karl Burnett as Bottom, Galina Mezentseva as Titania in *A Midsummer Night's Dream*, Scottish Ballet 1993 Rupert Jowett as Puck, Karl Burnett as Bottom, Galina Mezentseva as Titania.

37   Cohan and Janet 'Mop' Eager at Winchester Cathedral, October 2006, on the occasion of Cohan receiving an honorary doctorate from the University of Winchester.

is about, and the dancers have to be in that state of awareness that I was in as a kid alone in the forest; that's all there is to it, if you can do that and keep it all together, then it works.'

Forest is an extremely difficult piece to perform, because there is nothing for the dancers to rely on except the painted costumes and some wind sounds. It is filled with difficult balances, particularly for the women but not only them, as the men have long sustained phrases and balances, and there are many strenuous lifts. The movement itself Cohan calls 'sensuous', the dancer has to feel the physical movement itself and its relationship to its environment. Just as he as a child was aware of everything in the living forest, so the dancer has to be aware of that entire environment – sensation, mood, smell, temperature – recreated on stage. In this work more than any of his others, the dancers have to be so skilled at performing that they can forget the audience, forget everything except the sensation of the movement. If they can do that and can enjoy and maintain their own sensation of movement, 'then the audience will become mesmerised... They won't know why but they will watch...'

In *Forest* the music, an electronic score by Brian Hodgson, follows the dancers. Cohan wanted them to take as long as they needed to fill the movement: 'They need to feel each other if they are together on the stage if they are alone and to take time and be aware.' The music therefore is open ended and could in theory last between twenty-two or forty minutes, though in practice the work usually lasted twenty-five minutes. There is no pulse or rhythm to the music and the dancers have to learn to recognise certain sounds, birds or whatever in the music and in relation to it shape the performance.

Over the years, *Forest* has come to be regarded as one of Cohan's greatest creations, and when it was restaged to celebrate his eightieth birthday, this 'feral, eerily beautiful and technically challenging work'[228] was warmly welcomed. In 1993, Cohan went to New York and with Kazuko Hirabayashi staged it on her students at Purchase College a part of the New York State University, where it drew a glowing review from Jennifer Dunning in the *New York Times*:

> Bodies move through dim light in soft-colored leotards. The eager attack is Graham. The look of limpid suspension is Merce Cunningham. The nine dancers bring a simplicity to the choreography that reveals but does not stress the dance's many small surprises.

> Overall, *Forest* is a series of cross-stage progressions, with dancers peeling off or leaving, then returning for brief duets and solos that are a fluid part of the whole. Mr Cohan's inventiveness is boundless and delicate, wearing thin only in the dance's last moments. One dancer neatly stops, another turns. A woman travels across the stage in prim little chaîné turns and notices two fallen male bodies. She pauses to stare, her hand flies up to her cheek as if in wonderment,

and she travels off again.

There are voluptuous oozes for a reappearing siren. Strange, sensuous lifts curl like plant tendrils into the air or down around the lifter's body. The dancers pass through one odd but beautiful shape or action after another. A storm comes, the dance quickens and hardens and bird and animal sounds are heard over wind, followed by rain. Every element of the dance contributes to its mood and grace, from Brian Hodgson's score to Norberto Chiesa's costumes and Mr Cohan's lighting.[229]

Yet, at its first performances, its silent rituals puzzled a number of critics, such as Noel Goodwin in the *Daily Express* who found it 'limited in contrast of pace and dynamics',[230] or James Kennedy who in the *Guardian* thought it 'a piece which is no more than an exercise for the majority of his talented group, and which lacks shape and conviction'.[231] For those, as Charles Ives might have said, with eyes to see and ears to listen, such as Clement Crisp, it was 'fluent, highly imaginative and gratifying', with a 'richness of movement imagination [which] suffices to hold our attention completely'.[232] Cohan's hopes that the dancers would be able to draw the audience into the performance were clearly successful, as Anne Morley-Priestman reported in *The Stage*: 'It held the audience's attention with the utmost seriousness indeed';[233] Richard Davies in *Classical Music Weekly* told his readers: 'The work is so self-contained and really splendid. It ratifies Cohan's position in the pantheon of modern dance choreographers.' He also said that it was 'a remarkable composition, not merely because it rendered the audience blissfully cough less, but because of its totally restful atmosphere'.[234]

Peter Knight, writing in the *Morning Star*, used his review to criticise not only *Forest* – 'we are reminded of the loneliness, claustrophobia and dankness to be found in forests – quite unintentionally I fear', but the season as a whole: 'A lacklustre production in what has proved to be a lacklustre season.' He went on to criticise what he saw as a lack of strong choreography: 'LCDT, while remaining one of the strongest companies in the country, have reached a plateau due mainly to the limited themes with which they have been presented. Such a strong, skilful and talented company could well open itself to the influence of more dynamic choreographers.'[235] This theme, criticising poor or limited choreography not up to the standard of the always superb dancers, was one that over the next few years a number of critics would raise.

On 30 June 1977, Cohan and the company took a huge step and made their first appearance in America at the American Dance Festival. On the first night, the company presented Davies' *Diary 2*, Cohan's *Cell* and *Class*, followed on the next night by *Masque of Separation*, *Stabat Mater* and *Troy Game*. These works showed the range of LCDT's style, and it was only right that four of the six should be by Cohan. He was very nervous about the whole venture. The new British style had been seeded from America, and this was the first time that the notoriously difficult New York critics would have a chance to see the work of his company which was barely ten years old. At the first performance, he stationed himself at the back of the theatre so he could watch not only the dancers, but the audience as well. When at the end of *Class*, there was a silence and then the audience stood up; he thought they were walking out, but then he heard the roar of applause and cheers and he realised it had worked. The local press ran the headline 'London Contemporary Dance Make Smashing US Debut', while Anna Kisselgoff, who was just beginning her tenure as Chief Dance Critic for the *New York Times*, wrote that they were a 'well-trained company', who 'unquestionably deserved success'.[236]

On his return to England, Cohan spent two weeks on the campus of Surrey University in Guildford to lead the International Dance Course for Professional Choreographers and Composers. This would be his first of eight visits to the course, which had begun in 1975 under the auspices of the Calouste Gulbenkian Foundation and which was 'a crash course in creative collaboration between the essential elements of dance, music and movement'. The purpose of the course was emphatically not to teach, as 'no one can teach any form of creative art where talent does not exist'. But what the course did set out to do was to 'provide a professional training for those with an already proven talent, with masters to guide them and to pass on their experience.' In 1977, the course brought together eight choreographers and eight composers who had to create works together using the twenty-five dancers and three musicians selected. Cohan was aided in this by the composer John Herbert McDowell, who had a long association with dance, going back to his days as a member of the Judson Church group. The two had not worked together before, although Cohan knew of his work with Paul Taylor. They were an unlikely 'couple' as unlike the fastidious Cohan, McDowell was a great big bear of man who, although already plagued with the emphysema that would kill him in 1987, refused to stop smoking, always wore carpet slippers and carried his life around in plastic bags. He was also very creative, very friendly, and always had positive things to say about the participants' work.

The 'master guides' in the first two courses had been Glen Tetley and Norman Morrice respectively, and a format had been set up which Cohan was happy to follow. In the mornings, there would be classes in ballet and contemporary for the dancers and 'creative work' for the musicians followed in the afternoon by the masterclass. In addition for him were to be three inviolable rules:

1. There was to be no final show
2. There was to be no invited audience
3. There was to be no sense of competition

For Cohan, what was of paramount importance was the work itself.

In addition to this, Cohan brought in Siobhan Davies (who also taught some of the contemporary classes) and Robert North who performed *Eclipse*, which he analysed in terms of form and structure. John B. Read was also called in and gave a class in lighting for dance. McDowell created a special work to show what could be achieved in fifteen minutes. For this, he commandeered all of the participants, students, staff, administrators, and technicians into a 'happening'. Here he organised folk dance for the dancers, music for the musicians, and movement for himself and the choreographers. At one point, his beard was set alight and then shaved off to the accompaniment of balloon squeaks.

This postmodern approach was in a sense at odds with Cohan's approach which was largely based on his experience of working with Graham and his studies with Horst, and by the mid 1970s could have been considered old-fashioned. Throughout the 1960s and 1970s, philosophical notions of deconstruction had come to the fore, mostly based on the works of French philosopher Jacques Derrida, and these had seeped into choreography. Cohan was not in sympathy with this as 'you can deconstruct everything but at some point you have to construct the deconstruction, you cannot simply destroy until nothing is left, well you can and then go home, and that is the way one feels sometimes in seeing choreography that is so deconstructed that all you want to do is close the door and go home.' To counteract this, Cohan always returned to Horst, who was very strict about form, as

> ... Louis made me understand that the form of the dance, whatever it is – classical, contemporary form, or moment against vibration – it is what contains the dance. I always felt, when you choreograph a movement sequence, if it all existed in space at one moment out of time, it should be a beautiful sculpture, beautiful not meaning pretty, but beautiful. It should have its inherent beauty and no matter how simplistic, angular, raucous, or whatever the movement is, it should have its own integrity and that's how you build a dance out of its own integrity, and that's what I tried to teach.

In this course on two successive days, Cohan split the choreographers into two groups; four were asked to make solos on themselves, while four could work with the dancers and explore the idea of 'an unusual space'. Other themes for the projects were left deliberately vague, Cohan only hinting at a possible theme or structure. In the second week, the projects were extended to a few days and included one much to Cohan's heart, where the dance was made in silence and the music added later. The reverse was also required with the composers asked to write five or six minutes of music for a known choreographer who would then add the movement. In the final two days of the course, Cohan brought in illustrated books on dreams, magic and fantasy as inspiration.

Lest this should sound that Cohan was doctrinaire in his approach, he was not. He was able to talk from long experience but was open to other ideas, particularly on what could be an idea for a dance. One of the students on this course was Janet Smith, who would go on to develop a successful career as a choreographer. One day, she was describing to the group what gave her ideas for choreography; one of these was a description that 'one day, she was washing dishes, the phone rang, she ran to it, shook her hands and then had an idea for a piece'. Cohan had never had that experience: 'I had never washed my hands, shaken them, and had an idea for a dance. Certainly I had washed dishes and, in that aimlessness that takes over when you do menial tasks, I have thought of movement. But never the act of shaking my hands which was what Janet had described.' But he was happy to follow on a discussion that it could be possible to be inspired in such a way. Had he been doctrinaire, it is unlikely he could have held the interest of the choreographic participants, which included a diverse range of practitioners, many of whom went on to some success – as well as Janet Smith, Reinhild Hoffmann and Ian Spink were present.

Much against his wishes, certain critics were allowed to attend the final evening's showing and after the event, one well-known critic put his arm around Cohan and said: 'You know Bob, we are all just parasites, but you just have to learn to live with us.' Cohan was incensed by the comment and put into action a plan to have made a large insect spray filled with – fake – DDT. He would then confront the critic at the next LCDT Sadler's Wells season and publicly spray him. He was sadly talked out of this by Robin Howard who, although he agreed with Cohan's sentiment, felt the ensuing publicity would not be a good idea.

In the autumn, Cohan and LCDT continued on their regional tours and it was while in Manchester that he received the devastating news of Robert Powell's death at the age of 36. Powell's mental and physical health had over the years been devastated by excessive alcohol and drug abuse, and his career had gone into a steady decline since his return to the USA in 1973. He had come from a difficult childhood in Hawaii where his mother, who worked as a prostitute, would often bring her clients home. This understandably had greatly affected his life, and led to the distressing manner of his death. On 24 October 1977, at his invitation his mother had arrived at a New York hotel; as she walked into the room, he jumped out of the window, crashing to his death. It was shocking news to Cohan and to the many company members who remembered him as a supremely gifted dancer.

In spite of this, work had to continue, as the Trust was once again in a very poor financial situation. In addition to the £400,000 spent on the freehold of The Place and its neighbouring building, another £350,000 was needed to complete the renovations and refurbishment, and an appeal was launched. At a fundraising gala in the Wells autumn season, Cohan's *Khamsin* and *Class* framed an interesting selection of works that showed the versatility of Cohan's approach. In addition to Lynn Seymour guesting in Robert North's *Scriabin Dances*, and Siobhan Davies in Jane Dudley's masterpiece *Harmonica Breakdown*, the women of the company danced in some reconstructions of works by Isadora Duncan, which were received very well. The men, however, danced in a revival of Ted Shawn's *Polonaise*, a work which showed just how far modern dance had moved on since it was made in the 1933. Clement Crisp in the *Financial Times*, described it as 'loin-clothed beefcake, self-consciously virile and irresistibly funny'.[237]

Over the years, Cohan had had an unsettled relationship with the British dance critics, the initial support for the venture wore off quite quickly, and what could be described as low-level xenophobia took over in some quarters. Richard Alston's mother surprised him one day by saying to him, 'It must be difficult for Robert Cohan, I keep reading these reviews saying what a marvellous young British choreographer you are, then they seem to pour scorn or at least are rather low key about Robert Cohan. It must be difficult, he is after all your director.' David Earle feels that 'it would be better for critics to write about things they did enjoy rather than what they did not', and that 'the only credible role for a critic in the contemporary arts is to act as a liaison between the artist and their public. I would say in my fifty years in the theatre, the biggest egos I have encountered belonged to the critics'.[238] In Cohan's case, the major problem was John Percival who wrote for a variety of publications, including *Dance and Dancers* and *The Times*. As long ago as 1972, Cohan had written to Percival: 'I apologise if I exploded at you without sufficient cause, I can only explain by saying it is the way I honestly felt.' By 1977, the negative tenor of many of his reviews had, for Cohan and the company, got out of hand – he was referred to at The Place as 'Poisonous Percival' – and the final straw was a review in *The Times* of 21 November 1977, when Percival wrote: 'As the American critic Walter Terry suggested in a recent review, LCDT is probably the best of its kind outside the United States. But compared with the leading American companies it seems to me rather small beer.' This outraged Cohan who sent the review to Terry, who in turn wrote to John Higgins at *The Times*, complaining that Percival had misrepresented him. Terry's review which Percival claimed to refer to had appeared in the *Saturday Review* of 3 September 1977, and read: 'It [LCDT] is, as far as I know, the best modern dance company abroad; and on this basis of one rousing performance I saw here, I would say it easily ranks on par with the major modern dance companies in America. I found their technical skill, performing dynamism and choreographic strength overwhelming.' This was a considerable difference to what Percival had claimed, and Terry was incensed, writing: 'I have no objection if Mr Percival shares with his readers his abysmal ignorance of American modern dance and his own curious prejudices but I resent, understandably, his unpardonable sin of omission in referring to my review thus giving the readers a blatant falsification of my considered appraisal of a major, and brilliant, dance troupe.'[239] Anthony Crickmay remembers: 'It was really terrible and got quite out of hand. A lot of people wrote [to *The Times*] and well he was not sacked but moved sideways.'

Robin Howard was always looking for ways to further 'legitimise' contemporary dance and, early on in the development of the Trust, had made overtures to the

Royal Academy of Dance, an established body well versed in 'qualifying' dance teachers. In the early 1970s, some 'highly qualified' assessors had arrived at The Place to watch Cohan teach – the same happened to Jane Dudley; he passed the inspection and he was duly approved as an RAD teacher in contemporary dance.

So it was that Cohan missed the end of the season as he flew to South Africa on 7 December. He had been asked to go by the Royal Academy of Dance to teach a week-long course in contemporary dance. Although reasonably well paid, it was rather intense, with Cohan required to teach three classes per day to thirty dancers aged 15 to 16. The visit had caused Mrs Whittaker, the RAD administrator, some stress as initially, she told Cohan he would have to use tapes as there was no live musician available. He then told them he would be happy to play for himself if they found him some bongos, but the acquisition of these instruments proved strangely impossible. Then, as luck would have it, a South African pianist, Norman Higginson, happened to be visiting London and dropped in at The Place. Cohan was happy with his playing and suggested he should play for his classes.

He had been torn by the request to go, as his union Equity was at the time boycotting South Africa over its apartheid policy, but finally decided that he wanted to see for himself what was happening there. South Africa had a well-established ballet scene, but he arrived to find that neither the teachers nor the pupils had any real idea of what he was going to teach, 'maybe a jazz class'. But they were very receptive, even though what he was doing was a long way from their world of white RAD ballet. The classes he taught were, as expected, made up of entirely white students a situation that in situ was far worse than he had imagined. Outside of the studio, he did explore for himself the painful situation of apartheid, asking to be shown around Johannesburg, where he saw how awful and hopeless it was for any of the black population; the situation reminded him of the Graham Company visits to the misery of the Deep South in the 1940s, and he vowed not to return. He made his return journey to England via Kenya, where he had a truly extraordinary time on a safari in the wildlife parks. His childhood delight in the natural world had not disappeared, and the experience of seeing so many millions of birds, together with the giant pachyderms and ungulates in their natural environment, remains with him as the high point of all his extraordinary travel experiences.

Back in the cold, wintry British Isles, the New Year began, with more residencies and performances in the north of England. During a rehearsal at Bradford's Edwardian Alhambra Theatre, Cohan took himself to the back of the theatre to check on technical matters. There he bumped into a down-to-earth elderly usherette, such as can – or could – often be found in northern theatres. He introduced himself and told her he would probably be there during the run and not to worry. She told him that she wasn't looking forward to the performances, as she didn't like 'all that modern stuff'. In his friendliest manner, he tried to turn her opinion around, and she agreed to give it a chance. He bumped into her later in the run and asked her what she thought. She told him that it wasn't as bad as she had thought it was going to be, but didn't like it as much as the ballet as 'you can't close your eyes and just listen to the music'.

In addition to his wish to 'legitimise' contemporary dance, Robin Howard's love of the form and of serving the public good knew no bounds and to this end he had, in 1975, set up an organisation called the Anglo-American Contemporary Dance Foundation, not only to foster links between the UK and USA, but to spread the word of contemporary dance around the world. It had no offices, no salaried staff, and almost no running expenses. It was maintained by private enthusiasts who gave their time, skills, and money, in fact the majority of the time and money came from Howard's own pocket. It was under the auspices of this organisation that, for a handsome fee, Cohan spent two weeks in March working with the Bermuda Dance Theatre. The Governor of Bermuda, Sir Peter Ramsbotham, was an old friend of Howard's, and it was his wife, Lady Frances, who had been a key supporter of Howard's plans for the organisation, who had asked Howard to send someone to teach and inspire the nascent company. Howard asked Cohan and 'me being obliged to say yes to everything, said yes'. In spite of the difficult times on the island – at the end of 1977 Sir Peter, who had previously been British Ambassador to America, had called in British troops to quell rioters, angered at the hanging of two men who had killed the previous Governor and his aides-de-camp – Cohan enjoyed his time there, finding the dancers young, friendly and gifted, the only overt signs of tension being the security around the Governor's mansion. Lady Ramsbotham would later write him a glowing letter of appreciation, in which she expressed the hope that he would return, something that he regrets did not happen; in any event the Ramsbothams left the island in 1980, and dance was not high on the agenda of subsequent Governors or their wives. In a letter to Howard after the visit, he wrote presciently: 'The trouble is they are company driven by their board which is a disaster for any artistic venture.'[240] In a few years' time, he would wish he had followed his own advice.

The summer saw a new venture for Cohan when his friend Grant Strate, a distinguished figure in Canadian dance, a founder member of the Canadian National Ballet and of the dance department at York University, invited him to teach on the first National Choreographic Seminar. Strate modelled the course on the Gulbenkian one and got his university to sponsor it. Joining Cohan was Adam Gatehouse, who had worked with Norman Morrice on the 1976 Gulbenkian course, and who was now music director of the Dutch National Ballet and composer Carlos Miranda, who had worked with Ballet Rambert and Lindsay Kemp. The course attracted six choreographers and six composers, along with twenty-four dancers and eight musicians. Unlike the Gulbenkian course for which there was no fee, the Canadians had in the main to fund themselves in order to take part.

There were some changes made to the Canadian format in that it lasted for four weeks instead of the two of the British one. In addition, at the end of the seminar the 'best' of what had been achieved over the period was shown to an invited audience. This was a significant change to the British model, where the emphasis had been more on the process, and certainly not a finished product. This did not seem to affect the Canadians, and Mauryne Allan made a significant breakthrough in her work only in the final week where her 'last assignment was a far cry from anything I'd ever done. I'd run out of 'isms' and had to grab something new.'[241]

Cohan left Canada and went straight to Surrey to teach on the British course, where he was joined again by John Herbert McDowell. The course followed the same format as the previous year, and many of the same themes were revisited. Projects included: a dance affecting space in a strange way, a dance to alter an audience's sense of time, and a circle dance. One difference was that a workshop was devoted to techniques of dance for television, and for this Cohan called in BBC producer Bob Lockyer, one of the pioneers of this genre. The participants were divided into four groups, provided with the equipment, and encouraged to improvise and film and dance for themselves.

One of the fruits of the Gulbenkian course was Cohan's *Falling Man* solo, made for Robert North, to music by Barrington Pheloung. Pheloung, a young Australian and student of John Lambert at the Royal Academy of Music, had been pushed by his teacher to take part in the course as a composer. But like Barry Guy before him, he was spellbound by Cohan's approach and joined in the dance classes. Cohan had been impressed with his openness and ideas, and he approached him for a score for the solo. This was the first of many works he wrote for LCDT, and he was made music director of the company in 1980. He remained with them for many years before going on to find fame and fortune writing music for television, including the hugely popular *Inspector Morse* series. Cohan's idea for the solo came out of *People Alone*, and was about someone who fell constantly, and who was unable to reach those things he needed. The character could be seen as an amalgamation of classical figures such as Tantalus or Phineas, or closer to home, Robert Powell. It was a tremendously difficult solo, requiring from North all he could give in terms of technique and stage craft. The music Pheloung wrote for himself, a graphically notated work for solo guitar, was likewise as challenging as any Barry Guy had provided. It was, as Cohan observes, 'a work of the moment. It worked when we did it but it was not meant to last. It was hard!' North had been a mainstay of the company since the very beginning and had developed into a choreographer whose blending of Graham and ballet with an innate musicality proved popular with audiences. He was, however, beginning to be restless within the LCDT family and was looking for more from life, and the solo could be seen as a way of offering him a higher profile, a promise of more to come, should he stay.

The inspiration for his next work *Eos*, was a disturbingly nightmarish electronic work of the same name by Barry Guy. Intriguingly, Guy's score had been partly inspired by time he spent on a cooperative in the Brazilian jungle. The political situation was not stable, and the sounds of the jungle were often disturbed by the sounds of gunfire and conflict. Cohan's dance was not about war or political unrest, but was concerned with the late hours of the night leading to dawn. Although Eos, the dawn goddess, sister of the sun and the moon, whose 'rosy fingers' opened the gates of heaven, was herself a beautiful and benign creature throughout history, the pre-dawn hours have been seen as dangerous and it was this that Cohan explored. The Greeks in particular developed a rich mythology around the subject; Eos is better known in her Roman version as Aurora, while Nyx, the primordial night goddess was for the Greeks the mother of Hypnos (sleep) and Thanatos (death). For Europeans, the pre-dawn hours are the reserve of ghosts, vampires and werewolves, and the Saxons called night 'the death mist.' It was not going to be a light-hearted work, for audiences or dancers.

The five couples seemed to represent each of the hours before dawn and consisted mainly of slow-moving duets, which critics noted explored 'a vocabulary of movement very different from the more conventional Graham-based technique of some of his earlier works'.[242] Some were contorted, some lyrical, and some violent but all were extremely physical, hard, and stark. These torments were all brushed away by Anca Frankenhauser as Eos, who slowly swept across the stage with white silken wings billowing behind to eventually fill the stage with light. The costumes were by the young designer Barney Wan, who would later go on to great success at *Vogue* magazine and who had been introduced to Cohan by Anthony Crickmay. Cohan had seen his work and found his creations very exciting, and on a whim decided to ask him to design for him. The simple leotards extended over the heads with skullcap hoods, leaving only strangely painted faces visible. The five couples were in various shades of grey while the night couple were in black, with silver decorations on their heads. The costumes were flecked here and there with sequins which caught the light and added to the unusual effect and were the perfect foil to Cohan's vision.

The dance, although it did not appear to be popular with audiences, was seen by James Monahan as 'the most interesting of the season',[243] while Peter Williams found it 'a most powerful expression of those disturbing images which pass through the mind in the small hours of a restless night'.[244] For Cohan, *Eos* was a very successful dance because it was the only time he received any positive criticism from Robin Howard's mother, Lady Lorna. This distinguished Edwardian lady was always sweet and friendly to Cohan but he always felt that she could never really understand what exactly it was her son was giving his life and money to. But, after a performance of *Eos*, she said to him: 'Bob, obviously you have many sleepless nights like me and I know just what you mean by that.'

Cohan's next work, *Ice*, concerned a yet more dark subject matter and had a somewhat convoluted ancestry coming about as a result of his friendship with the ice skater John Curry. Curry had gained great success in the world of ice skating, winning every major competition including the British, European, and Olympic titles in 1976, the year he was also voted BBC Sports Personality of the Year. He used his fame to create the Theatre of Ice Skating which aimed to raise the form to new artistic levels. As well as works by himself, he commissioned pieces from many choreographers, including Peter Martins, Twyla Tharp, and Cohan. Cohan and Curry had met at Peter Farmer's Sunday afternoon tea parties, a parergon to Peter Williams' dinners, and the two got along very well, with Cohan finding him charming and likeable – in the professional world, he had a reputation for being demanding and difficult, attributes which would lead to the collapse of his company in the 1980s. In one of their conversations, Curry had told Cohan of a poem in which a skater convinces himself that the cracking sounds made by the ice is Death knocking below. The subject of darkness and mystery appealed to Cohan, and he became intrigued by the possibilities of Curry's venture and was very interested in making a work for him. The work that appeared, however, was made not on Curry's group but Cohan's.

Ice, made for nine company members focussed on the figure of Tom Jobe as the central character 'trying to finally destroy the relationship between Patrick Harding-Irmer and Linda Gibbs, which has already cooled before the dance begins'. Cohan wanted the work to be the embodiment of 'that feeling we all have when we can't cope with something, when our emotions freeze, our actions freeze, we become petrified with fear'. He took that quality and personified it in the shape of Jobe to make the statement that Ice-Death comes into a relationship and separates us all. As a tour de force for Jobe, it was a success with many critics commenting on his extraordinarily flexible body which Cohan put to full use.

Cohan had been struck by the sound image of the cracking of ice that Curry had told him about, and for the music he turned to the American pioneer of electronic music Morton Subotnick. Subotnick had become famous in the 1960s with his seminal work *Silver Apples of the Moon*, the first electronic work to be commissioned by a record label (Nonesuch), and Cohan felt he would be the perfect person to write the score for a dance inspired by the sounds of ice. The dance was made in silence and a video sent to the composer, who quickly sent Cohan a tape of the work and a letter saying: 'I am very happy about the music and the dance together. I tried to make the music as though the dance was a line of the music.'[245] When Cohan heard it, he cried. For Cohan and the dancers, the faint electronic twitters and squeaks added little to the dance, doing nothing to create the sombre mood Cohan had hoped for.

Cohan had no choice but to use the score, and no one passed on any of their misgivings to an excited Subotnick when he visited England for the work's premiere and told Cohan it was 'as good as *Swan Lake*!' Although Peter Williams found it 'a well-made and enthralling piece', with Tom Jobe 'used to marvellous effect',[246] as a complete ensemble work Cohan felt it did not quite hang together and when various dancers and technicians suffered mishaps during performances, it gained a reputation as dance equivalent of the 'Scottish play' and was quietly dropped from the repertoire.

When it became clear the *Ice* would not be suitable for John Curry, Cohan offered him *Masque of Separation*, a work Curry already knew, its more theatrical aspects being very appealing to Curry's producers, added to which the scintillating music by Alcantara was just what they wanted. Cohan spent three weeks in October 1978, staying with his brother in New York and setting the work on Curry's dancers. He had skated since childhood and he had been looking forward to showing his prowess on the ice, but was somewhat disappointed when he found out that Curry always asked his choreographers to set the works on 'dry land', any adaptations being made by him once the work was on ice. The revised dance worked well but the producers decided that the whole piece was too long to be included in the show and they cut all of it except for the butterfly section, the billowing wings of which translated brilliantly to the ice.

At the premiere of Curry's show Cohan was surprised when one of the composers, 'a big Canadian lumberjack of a man', who he had worked with on the Canadian choreography course, came over to him, 'shook my hand and said, "Thank you, the course has changed my life." "How so?" asked Cohan, thinking that he had found some exciting job, the answer, "Yes, it was on that course that I found out I loved men", ' surprised him a little. But only a little as Peter Williams, who was involved the both the Gulbenkian and the Canadian courses, used to introduce the course as 'the one that will change your life'.

On returning from New York, Cohan began work on a solo for the Canadian dancer Susan MacPherson. MacPherson had studied with Cohan at the Graham school in the 1960s and along with fellow Canadian David Earle had participated in the early work of the Trust, including the very first performance in East Grinstead. Like Earle, she had returned to Canada and became a founder member of the Toronto Dance Theatre. Cohan and his work had always impressed her, and in 1978 she had participated as a dancer in the Canadian Dance Seminar. It was there she asked him to make a work for her to fit into an evening of solos she was planning to tour. Cohan readily agreed but this response, 'I always wondered what sort of solo I would make for you if you asked', took her by surprise.

The solo he made for her lasted almost fifteen minutes and was an extraordinarily difficult dance, both technically and emotionally, and stands as a testament to his high opinion of her abilities. He had in fact given her two options for a dance: one would have been a comedy number, slightly shorter but easier, but she opted for the challenge of the darker, dramatic work. Cohan chose as music Geoffrey Burgon's *Canciones del Alma* for two counter tenors and orchestra – this would also become the title of the dance. This work is a setting of two poems and part of a longer poem by the sixteenth-century mystic St John of the Cross. The three songs are 'Oh llama de amor viva' (Oh Loving Flame of Love), 'Tras de un amoroso lance' (After a Love Affair) and, finally, the last five verses of 'Canciones entre el Alma y el Esposo.'

Cohan had long been interested in the works of the Spanish mystic priest and poet, who in many of his fantastical works tried to reveal something of the mysteries of the universe. Like Cohan, the priest felt that his work was sacramental, but while noting that it was impossible for man to express in literal terms these mysteries, in his writings he observed that 'by means of figures, comparisons and similitudes, they allow something of that which they feel to overflow and utter secret mysteries from the abundance of the Spirit, rather than explain these things rationally.'[247] For St John, these 'figures, comparisons and similitudes' were his writings, for Cohan his dances.

The shape of Burgon's songs closely follow that of the poems, and the colours and textures of the music are suggested by the successive images found in the verse. Alongside this, Cohan draws a rather more homogenous line, the differences between the three poems drawn closer together with a vocabulary far more Grahamesque than he had used with his own company for many years. The gentle eroticism of the poetry is largely missing from the choreography, and Cohan paints a picture of an obsessive, possibly neurotic woman, earthbound in her movements and continually searching for something.

The first song, which begins:

O Love's living flame,
Tenderly you wound
My soul's deepest centre!
Since you no longer evade me,
Will you, please, at last conclude:
Rend the veil of this sweet encounter![248]

is formed around a cross-like floor pattern on which the dancer carves strong contracted shapes with cruciform arms and cupped hands.

The dancer returns to her starting position for the beginning of the second song:

Full of hope I climbed the day
while hunting the game of love,
and soared so high, high above
that I at last caught my prey.[249]

This shows the dancer in various bird-like poses, scurrying across the stage, but none of that suggest she may be indulging in the 'game of love'.

The words for the final song come from a long conversation between a bride and her husband with the final verses spoken by the bride:

Let us rejoice, O my Beloved!
Let us go forth to see ourselves in Your beauty,
To the mountain and the hill,
Where the pure water flows:
Let us enter into the heart of the thicket.[250]

Again the sensuality of the verse is absent and the picture of 'serene night' painted in the verse not shown. In Graham's *Errand into the Maze*, the female dancer goes on a journey leading to a harmonious ending. The three poems chosen by Burgon paint a journey to serene acceptance, but Cohan's dance seems intent on exploring the same idea without resolution and the effect is unsettling, more a response to a setting of Lorca than St John. Cohan told MacPherson that the only other dancer he would be happy performing the dance would be Siobhan Davies, but this never happened and the dance was only seen once in England at a performance at The Place, although MacPherson, after the premiere in Canada on 1 January 1979, performed it many times elsewhere and has set it on a number of her students.

From a motley group of dancers, Cohan had in a very short time created a company that was second to none in the world in terms of technique. But more than a company, he had created a tight-knit family, as Richard Alston observed: 'People came from all over to work with Bob and many stayed for a very long time.' If certain critics began to question the repertoire of LCDT, and they did, its status as an ambassador for British dance could not be questioned and in recognition of this, Cohan was awarded the Society of West End Theatre Managers annual award for 'outstanding achievement of the year in ballet'.

1979 was the company's tenth anniversary year, and Cohan could be proud of his achievement. After visits to Rome in January and Toulouse in February, the company again took part in the Camden Festival, where they presented four works by company members. Although Cohan's shaky financial position meant he needed to make money from extra work, he was seldom able to take up offers as he was dedicated to LCDT, and if there was even a question of conflict of interest, LCDT always won. So it was that in 1979 he had to turn down an offer to teach in Banff, Canada, and an interesting offer from the West Australian Ballet to choreograph a version of Stravinsky's classic score *Les Noces*, a lucrative project that would have been coupled with an offer to teach at a Music Symposium at the University of Western Australia. An Australian connection further manifested itself with the arrival of the dynamic young antipodean composer Carl Vine, who worked with LCDT for most of 1979. Ultimately, he wrote the music for two dances, Cathy Lewis' *Kisses Remembered*, and Micha Bergese's *Scene Shift*. An intriguing proposed collaboration with

Cohan on a dance on the life of Renaissance composer Gesualdo, a particular favourite of Vine's, tantalisingly did not materialise. Although a Cohan/Vine work never appeared, Vine found his time with Cohan useful and he remembers that

> … Bob did provide me with one of my favourite lines of advice for budding composers. I went to great pains, working for what I considered the greatest modern dance company in the world, to make my improvising for dance classes as inventive, quirky, and 'contemporary' as I could. This apparently wore thin at some stage, and Bob took me aside. Quietly and thoughtfully, he said, 'Don't be modern for ME.'

Vine's comment that he was working with the 'greatest modern dance company in the world' is telling of their truly international reputation and he follows up on his observation saying:

> Most of my dancer friends at Sydney Dance Company in the mid 1970s were adherents of Graham Technique, and considered Ballet Rambert too classical. Martha's own company seemed to be winding down a bit at the time, but LCDT was reaching its peak and seemed like the most exciting, adventurous company on either side of the Atlantic. (Merce Cunningham was so singular that he didn't invite comparison with anyone!) Nederlands Dans was, of course, highly regarded, but because we then had Jaap Flier running Sydney Dance, it felt a bit 'common'. I don't recall Pina Bausch being on the radar yet, and Béjart was considered simply quirky. So when I started whatever it was going to be with LCDT, I felt it was, for the time at least, the leading edge of modern dance.

It is interesting that Ballet Rambert was in the 1970s still 'considered too classical'. Since reinventing themselves in 1966, they had of course jettisoned all of their balletic works and some of their dancers, strangely including Linda Gibbs, who was told she was too classical for their new image and who then went on to be a mainstay of LCDT. But they had never wholly embraced a modern training, and classes would often begin with a ballet barre before the dancers moved on to the Graham floor exercises. The dancers therefore, if not specifically 'classical', looked very different to the clearly modern weighted style of LCDT. The relationship between the two companies was one of friendly rivalry, although they each had their own fan base. The fans could on occasion get carried away and Robert North remembers one party where the discussions of the relative merits of each company got more than heated and a fight broke out.

Cohan almost did not see out the 1970s when, on 2 May 1979, he was involved in a fire at his home at 3 Thurloe Place. Rather he was almost not involved, as he was somewhat distracted by some very good marijuana and did not notice the fire which had started in the wood-lined airing cupboard. It was only when a neighbour knocked loudly on the front door and told him she had called the fire brigade as there was smoke coming from his building that he was alerted to the danger. The fire was quickly controlled, though it did cause some damage resulting in considerable un-budgeted expense.

He was clearly not traumatised by the event, as on 6 May he taught a one-day composition seminar for the Royal Ballet School. Then, between 15 May and 9 June, LCDT presented an anniversary season at Sadler's Wells, showing nine works by Cohan, two by Micha Bergese, three by Siobhan Davies, and four by Robert North. The second week showed a wide range of shorter works by company members and demonstrated for all Cohan's remarkable achievement in developing a truly remarkable creative atmosphere at The Place. No dance company in British history had produced so many works in such a short space of time. Many of the dances created over the last ten years had had short lives, but most were at least well crafted and demonstrated a tremendous investment by Cohan in the artistic development of his dancers. And they were varied, ranging from the Cunninghamesque musings of Alston to the theatrical dreams of Bergese and the ice-cold formations of Davies. Cohan gave his dancers a space to create, both physically and mentally, and it paid off. Peter Williams noted this when he compared Cohan's achievements to those of Ninette de Valois and Marie Rambert and writing that 'no praise can be too high for the way Cohan has built up a team of creators who have been developed through the school and company workshops and through residencies... It has been a tremendous achievement and has been almost entirely responsible for the present dance explosion in Britain.'[251] This 'explosion' brought about by Cohan would become a severe threat to LCDT in the coming decade; like something out of Greek mythology, the children would devour their father.

The summer saw Cohan and the company travel to Holland and then to Israel to participate in an International Seminar on the Bible in Dance. The seminar took place at the Museum of Israel and the Jerusalem Theatre over five days and included lectures, films, and live dance. On 7 August, the company presented Cohan's *Stabat Mater*, *Hunter of Angels*, and two new pieces made for the seminar, Robert North's *The Annunciation*, and Cohan's *Song, Lamentations and Praises* (usually referred to by the company as SLAPS).

As the seminar was in Israel, the Bible that was to be discussed was the Jewish Bible, and Cohan has remarked that it was 'ballsy for me to take *Stabat Mater*'. When he received the commission for a new work, he had no idea what to do and so kept reading through the Bible, but the only thing he found that would work for him choreographically was the Song of Solomon, nothing else particularly interested him. This was a curious situation for a former Graham dancer to find himself in, as Graham often mined the Bible for any number of dances, as did his peers, Pearl Lang, Bertram Ross, Ethel Winter, and Donald McKayle. He struggled with the subject matter and it was only through close discussions with his chosen composer, Geoffrey Burgon, that he eventually decided he would use the Song of Solomon, the fall of Jerusalem and a final section of praises.

Some critics felt that the dance, because of its religious connotations, was similar to *Mass*, although movement-wise it was very different. Each section was introduced by extraordinary solos for Tom Jobe, credited as the Painter of the Soul, in which Cohan made use of his long flexible body – he was able to bend it into the most improbable shapes. Section one was constructed around a series of erotically charged duets which paralleled the quote from the Song of Solomon printed in the programme: 'Take me with you and we will run together; bring me into your chamber, O King.'[252] Burgon's music set for countertenor, percussion and electronics lifted the dance to an other-worldly level. In part two, the score included variations of impenetrable hummings or keening sounds, against which the group moved in various expressions of sorrow. The final section, 'Praises', an athletic display of joy, had been created in silence as Burgon was a little late with the score. To facilitate its completion, Cohan had set the movement to counts of three, to which Burgon's finished music provided counterpoint by hemiola constructions. Included in the music was a contribution from Moshe Romano, the company's rehearsal director, who was recorded chanting in Hebrew, the sounds of which Burgon manipulated to magnificent effect. In some ways, the finale resembled the brilliant athleticism of *Class*, and even after a final benediction solo from Tom Jobe, it always brought the house down. It was generally seen as a fine work: 'Cohan's ballet seems to have me to have found an effective choreographic imagery to distil the qualities of each in turn for the work's three contrasted sections.'[253] It was a handsome addition to the company's repertoire, in which it would remain for a number of seasons. John Percival, however, still seemed determined to cast himself as a lone Jeremiah finding, 'I did get the impression that you could take bits out of the work and replace them elsewhere without much difference. In other words, what I saw was a lot of choreographic doodling…'[25]

Cohan remained in Israel after the conference and restaged *Masque of Separation* for Bat-Dor. They had asked for *Waterless Method of Swimming Instruction*, but the problems inherent in creating the elaborate set meant the request had to be turned down. Another request to stage *Khamsin* also had to be refused, as Batsheva had the work. It is quite remarkable that Cohan was employed lucratively and often by both companies, who in Israel were deadly rivals with no love lost between either camps. But he did so for many years until a salaried position with Batsheva precluded any work for Ordman's company.

After the summer break, Cohan returned to the UK and travelled to the Theatr y Werin in Aberystwyth where, between 14 and 17 September, he took part in a Dance Appreciation Conference organised by the Welsh Dance Association and the Dance Section of the National Association of Dance Teachers in Higher Education. He contributed two sessions, one called 'The Craft of Choreography', and the second 'The Uses of Space'. The latter was foremost in his mind as he was about to begin work on a new dance for the unusual space of the Roundhouse, in Camden Town. The building, a converted railway turning shed, was of course round, and Cohan had always wanted to try to make a work for this spatial arrangement which has no front.

Dance in the round was not new to Britain: as long ago as 1960, Norman Dixon and his small company Ballet Venture had presented some dances in the round at the Pembroke Theatre, Croydon. The production prompted some discussion,[255] with the general opinion being that classical ballet was not suited to such a staging, while Peter Williams felt that Martha Graham's pieces could work. Graham, however, never made a work in the round, and it took twenty years before Williams was able to see if, in her protégé, he was right.

Cohan shared the programme with Robert North and Siobhan Davies, and each of them tried to solve the problem of the space in their own way. In Mel Brooks' comedy musical *The Producers*, Max Bialystock is said to have invented the 'Theatre in the Square', where 'nobody gets a good seat'. The same is more than often true of works in the round, the danger being that at some time three-quarters of the audience will get a side on or back view of the dancers.

Cohan says:

> I had always wanted to do it and then I found out how difficult it is and I never did it again because there is no front. I knew that, and that was the challenge, but it is too difficult. Every movement has to be in a circular phase, you have to be conscious of that as you make the material. After all, you make the material to have meaning, it has meaning if you see it one way, and another if you see it another way. So how you resolve those factors was an interesting challenge.

He wrote of the problem in the programme note: 'It has meant extending the dancers' sensations of space, or reshaping the choreographer's visual images and reconsidering our concepts of movement.'

Cohan was helped in his work by a collaboration with John Herbert McDowell who he had asked in the summer if he would like to compose the music. This was written in parallel with the dance and its style, somewhere between Stravinsky and Charles Ives, perfectly suited the textures and rhythms of the movement. It was scored for piano and small ensemble, the piano being placed at one side of the arena while the others were suspended above it. Some wondered if it would not have been better to have the musicians arranged spatially around the auditorium, making the parallel with the dance more apparent.[256]

Parallels between music and dance were not instantly apparent. Cohan, harking back to his Horstian roots, shaped the dance in a classic rondo, hence the title *Rondo*, while McDowell did not. The rondo form, found in much classical music, consists of a recurring theme separated by episodes and forms in itself a circle. In Cohan's case, there were six repetitions of the theme separated by different groupings of the eight dancers. The rondo theme had the dancers marking out the edges of the space in jogging or running patterns, something Peter Williams found 'far too obvious a way of trying to solve the spatial problem'.[257] In-between these, the episodes were shaped cumulatively for one, two, three, and four dancers. These included a characteristically dynamic solo for Harding-Irmer, and what all reviewers agreed was an enervating duet for Namron and Charlotte Kirkpatrick. The general opinion was of an interesting experiment – helped by Barney Wan's costumes beautifully knitted from different threads and wools, that were at once transparent and translucent – that, with some editing, could have been a useful addition to the repertoire, though where it would have been performed was not clear. One critic observed that perhaps the only choreographer to truly solve the problem of dance in the round was Busby Berkeley.

The Sadler's Wells season with which the year concluded saw LCDT conduct some groundbreaking market research to see exactly who their audience was and why they came to see them. They did this by handing out 2,000 questionnaires which were analysed by Natasha Newell from Queen's University, Belfast, with mainly positive results. 58 per cent of their audience regularly attended theatre, most were between 19 and 34, and many were dance or theatre students. Of those who saw the company for the first time, 75 per cent said they would be interested in returning. In the 1980s, statistical data would be used more and more to determine the all-important levels of funding the company should receive. And the company would have to work very hard to make sure the 75 per cent who were 'interested in returning' did just that and were not sucked away in the dance explosion that was about to take place in Britain in the coming decade.

Chapter 9

Commentary

In these years, our touring schedule in England was punishing.

Most of the theatres were Victorian. The front may have been modernised in some of them but backstage was really disagreeable. Sanitation was like going back in time, some corridors even had gaslights still on the walls, there were hardly any showers and the stage floor was a mess of splinters and trapdoors, or else redone with wood on steel, so it was like dancing on concrete. In addition, the theatres heating came under the Factory Act so the temperature only needed to be 56 °F (14 °C). The audience used to sit in their overcoats and the dancers were on stage in leotards. It was a recipe for dance-related injuries.

A lot of time, thought, and money were spent on overcoming these physical problems. We carried several linoleum floors, and even foam to lay under the linoleum if the floor was too hard. We used to carpet the wings and backstage space that the dancers used while waiting to perform so that their bare feet would not get splintered or greasy from years of theatre use and finally we carried heaters of various kinds to blow hot air onto the stage.

We performed two different programmes every week and at least one matinée, usually on Wednesday. We used to open on Monday, but then realised that the Sunday work for the crew was paid at twice a normal day and that extra cost could not be made back with the Monday ticket sales, so we changed to open on a Tuesday. That meant that our workweek was, in addition to technique class every day and the inevitable rehearsals to replace a sick or injured dancer:

Dress rehearsal, Tuesday afternoon
Performance, Tuesday night
Matinée, Wednesday afternoon
Performance, Wednesday night
Crew changeover to programme2
Dress rehearsal of new programme, Thursday afternoon
Performance of new programme, Thursday night
Performance, Friday night
Sometimes a Saturday matinée
Performance, Saturday night
Sunday, day off
Monday, go to next town, etc., etc.

In those years, to fulfil our grant terms with the Arts Council, we had to perform twenty-six weeks in England alone each year. When, I wonder, did we find time to do all of those new works, and no wonder I got so tired reading about it now.

But The Place, the school and the company were running well and we all had to run to keep up with the momentum.

Again, it was that simple decision I made a long time ago to say yes to every request; Robin was also saying yes, that made it all work so fast. Someone once told me that if you need something done for you, give it to the busiest person you know, not the one who has time.

As the head of the company, I had the usual problem that all directors have of keeping all of your dancers happy, and that means dancing every night. The implications are obvious, I think.

A choreographer for the company always chose the dancers they wanted to work with for a certain piece. I would of course advise if the choreographer did not know the company well, but most did know them well.

Choreographers do not always choose who may be considered the best dancers in a company for a new work. They choose for a variety of reasons. It may be their ideas are so clear that they want dancers that have a particular look, or it may be that they choose friends that will make the difficult moments in the studio easier. Most dancers have their own special performing 'color' on stage, and that may be what a choreographer needs for their work.

All of these considerations might mean that some very good dancers do not have much to do in a certain performance. Another small seeming but large problem for me was that most choreographers don't want their new work to open a program.

Still another difficulty of repertory was that most theatre managers did not want dances repeated on our next visit. Even though works may be revised or made to be seen more than once. Put that all together and you can see that a lot of the dances I choreographed during this period were in effect 'made to order'. Not necessarily the work that was burning inside, trying to come out.

I am not complaining because curiously enough, the most interesting thing about these 'problems' that I had to solve, is that some of these dances I choreographed 'to order' in this period were among the best I ever did.

Chapter 10

Love work, and despise official positions, and do not become too acquainted with the governing power.

(Pirkei Avot, 1:10)

1980–3

The 1980s saw enormous changes in the British dance scene. In spite of the financial hardships that the arts felt under the Thatcher government, the range of dance companies and opportunities for dance training grew exponentially. As a result, all aspects of The Place's operations were challenged, in terms of educational and artistic policy and financially. After the 'retirement' in 1975 of Rudolf Laban's assistant Lisa Ullman, which for many had been a long time coming, the Laban Centre for Movement and Dance began its inexorable rise to prominence. Under the leadership of Marion North and former Graham dancer Bonnie Bird, it moved on from its purely Laban roots and began offering a range of programmes of dance study, from professional to academic, which in dance technique terms included a wide range of styles from ballet and Jooss, to Graham and Cunningham. The study of dance developed at many universities and polytechnics across the country, the courses were often hidden within creative arts programmes but there nonetheless. Dartington College in Devon, which had seen some of the earliest arrivals in American modern dance, became, following Mary Fulkerson's arrival in 1973, a bastion for what became British New Dance. Influenced by Steve Paxton's Contact Improvisation, Joan Skinner's Release Technique, and the work of Anna Halprin, Fulkerson, who was interested to see what dance looked like on 'ordinary bodies', began teaching improvised and non-technique based movement. Her influence was crucial, and those in her sphere, including Rosemary Butcher, Richard Alston, Sue MacLennan and later Yolande Snaith, became the leaders in the New Dance Movement. The success of these types of artists was recognised when the X6 Collective, a group of New Dance Artists including Fergus Early and Jacky Lansley, previously based at Butler's Wharf, found new premises in the East End of London. Chisenhale Dance Space, as it became, was and is the London centre for independent and experimental dance artists.

Dance Umbrella, which Val Bourne had begun in 1978, brought avant-garde work from the United States and beyond. The first festival had presented pieces by Remy Charlip, Douglas Dunn, Brooke Myers, and Sara Rudner. At the time, they were hardly new artists, but their work was little known in the UK and what

Dance Umbrella did was to give the opportunity for exposure on a professional stage for more than a few cognoscenti. As Dance Umbrella grew, and it was very successful, it brought new European artists such as Daniel Larrieu and Anne Teresa de Keersmaeker. This style of dance was the antithesis of that developed by Cohan with LCDT, although the work of Siobhan Davies was clearly touched by it. What Val Bourne managed to do in some ways was to capture the sense of cutting-edge excitement that had been so much part of The Place in its early days, and which had been lost in the move to legitimacy.

In addition, a range of dance companies that would have seemed unthinkable in 1970 had sprung up: Second Stride, Ludus, Janet Smith and Dancers, Extemporary Dance Company, MAAS Movers, EMMA, East Anglia Dance Theatre. Many of these artists had been students at The Place, and the explosion in dance was something Cohan and Howard had hoped for, though it exceeded their wildest dreams. It also exceeded the funds of the various funding bodies and, throughout the decade, more and more artists asked for ever-shrinking money to support them, which would have dire consequences for LCDT.

At the tenth anniversary season of LCDT, Cohan suggested to Howard that they close the venture down, and he was not joking. They had, he argued, achieved what they set out to do; there were companies, schools, independent artists, and performance spaces, none of which had been there when they began. Not all of it was due to them, but they could take credit for kick-starting the revolution in contemporary dance in Britain. Howard gave the suggestion serious consideration but then told him it was not possible as so many people depended on the organisation for their livelihood and they could not possibly let them down.

Cohan therefore entered the 1980s with serious doubts about his willingness to stay at The Place, as he has said on a number of occasions, 'I was burnt out.' For ten years, he had been teacher, choreographer, manager, designer, mentor, panellist, the visible face of dance, and all this had taken its toll:

> I almost always had to do the pieces required to make the programmes work; the opening piece or a piece using everyone that wasn't in the other pieces. Or I had to make sure everyone had something to do every night, to keep the company functioning as a whole and to try to keep lots of very good dancers wanting to stay with us. I had no rules or style, consciously; I sometimes think I should have gone the way of a piece like *Cell* or *Eclipse* and develop a specific movement language, but I was always mindful of the idea to represent different ways to dance and I was running a rep company.

> I had a definite style of staging and lighting, which gave a uniformity to the look of the company, but I was also mindful that we were a touring company and we had to please audiences all over the country so they would tell their

friends to come and they would want to come back next year to see us again. It was hard to keep that balance between making entertaining contemporary dance and doing work that was too avant-garde and that we could only do successfully in London.

In addition, he had very little money as he admits: 'I never paid a bill until the final red demand came. I couldn't.' This contrasts with ballet choreographer Kenneth MacMillan whose negotiations for a part-time associate choreographer contract with American Ballet Theatre began at $100,000.[258] Cohan was also nearing retirement age and what would that bring? There would be a small pension from The Place but would it be enough? The possibility of a professorship at York University in Canada was a real and appealing possibility, providing a job with less stress and greater security, but ultimately, he made other choices.

For Cohan and the Trust, the decade began as it would go on, with serious financial problems. The building work at The Place cost £557,974, far more than the estimate of £332,000, and educational grants that should have been paid to the school were late. At one stage, it seemed a real possibility that the school would have to close. The sale of yet more of Howard's personal assets helped matters a little, but there was a curtailment of some of the Trust's activities. The 'unrest' felt in Cohan and Howard was also felt in the dancers who, in May 1980, suggested to the Board some new methods of working, which in addition to the full company seasons would enable the dancers 'to work in a new way, with a more flexible yet structured situation with workshops presented at The Place and in different venues throughout Britain. Other dancers may want to take off or want to perform or teach elsewhere.'[259] This was an exciting and radical proposal well ahead of its time, and in some ways a more structured approach to the project manner of working that took hold in contemporary dance in the 1980s, in which dancers were hired for specific projects rather than on permanent contracts. With smaller groupings allowing for greater flexibility, it was a method which could well have helped avoid the problems LCDT faced at the end of the decade, had there been money to implement it. Unfortunately as was often the case with good ideas at The Place, there was no money and the proposal was shelved.

As it was, in the spring, the company split into two, with one half directed by Micha Bergese and the other by Robert North, each visiting different areas in the south of England. Cohan's only choreography for the group was the thirty-minute *Field*, with music by Brian Hodgson and costumes by Penny King. The set, consisting of a dark green backcloth with a slit of blue at the top which Cohan designed himself, was seen as 'ravishing'.[260] He saw the dance as a more summery version of *Forest*, although some clues to a deeper meaning can be gleaned from a quote Cohan kept from John Berger's book *About Looking*: 'The field that you are standing before appears to have the same proportions as your own life.'[261] Much as in *Forest*, Cohan had reflected on his childhood, *Field* was also in some ways an assessment of his life at a crossroads, although he never made this explicit. The programmes carried a very brief note stating that 'Cohan's *Field* deals with impressions and thoughts on crossing, sitting in and watching others in a field.' In the work, which on paper reads like a ballet scenario rather than a contemporary dance one, a girl dances dreamily, she is joined by others, dances a love duet with a man; a dance with fans leads to a group finale which leaves the girl alone on the stage, dreaming across her field. The piece, although reasonably well received – Mary Clarke finding it a 'pastoral ballet' with 'a sense of light, sun and fresh air',[262] while Noel Goodwin found 'the entries, the searching, the touching and going, are the choreographic distillation of an acutely observant eye'[263] – did not satisfy Cohan. Apart from the convincing love duet for Kate Harrison and Patrick Harding-Irmer, he felt that 'the whole dance did not work. It was too low key.'

Soon after the premiere of *Field*, Cohan was getting ready to leave his Muswell Hill home when he heard the doorbell. He ignored it as it was very early, but the sound persisted and on opening the door he found a small hunchbacked man he knew vaguely. The man was William (Bill) Strum, the general manager of the Batsheva Dance Company, and he told Cohan he wanted to make him an offer.

Since 1964, when Bethsabée de Rothschild had founded the Batsheva Dance Company, it had become the flagship of the Israeli dance establishment, even though its early years had been fraught with difficulty. After the company refused to appoint de Rothschild's lover Jeannette Ordman as artistic director, she had severely cut back on her financial involvement with the group, and even founded another company, Bat-Dor, for Ordman to run. In spite of this setback and with state support, the company had grown and included in its repertoire works by well-known choreographers, including Cohan himself, Glen Tetley, Norman Morrice, Jerome Robbins, and José Limón. It could also boast some excellent dancers in Rina Schenfeld, Rena Gluck, Nurit Stern, Ehud Ben-David, Moshe Efrati, and Rahamim Ron. In spite of its many successful performances abroad and its great following in Israel, in the 1970s the group went through a difficult period with a continuous turnover of artistic directors: Jane Dudley, Norman Walker, Linda Hodes, William Louther, and Brian McDonald. Most of them came for short periods, found they could not cope with the difficult temperaments of the Israeli dancers, and left. Norman Morrice had very much wanted to take the job when it was offered to him, but Marie Rambert advised him he would be better suited to running the Royal Ballet; he accepted that role with disastrous results. Instead of Morrice, in 1977, Paul Sanasardo had taken over as artistic director and he was about to leave again in not entirely happy circumstances.

The situation could not continue as the company was tearing itself apart and the Board decided it needed someone with an international profile, respected in Israel and also Jewish, to step in. Strum, a pugnacious New Yorker had come to England to demand – Strum never asked – that Cohan go to Israel to take the helm of the company. Strum was a Zionist and felt that Cohan, as a Jew, should be willing to come to Israel for the good of the country. Cohan had other ideas. While he was happy to visit, set work and to take on choreographic assignments, he knew only too well the difficulties that awaited anyone working on a daily basis with the Batsheva Dance Company. Reviewing one of their New York performances, Don McDonagh had said there was 'something of the Wild West'[264] in their style of dancing, unruly and a little more than dangerous. Had he seen them in the studio, he would have known how right he was. There, everyone had their own ideas about what should happen, and fights could and did break out as tempers flared.

Cohan said no, but Strum was not a person used to hearing that word, he was used to banging people's heads together until he got what he wanted. Over the next few days, Strum went to see Robin Howard to convince him that it would be good for everyone, that Cohan should accept, or if he could not come full-time to Israel, then Howard should agree to free Cohan to work with Batsheva on an advisory basis. Cohan was angry that Strum had gone behind his back and talked to Howard, but Howard thought it a workable idea and, between them, they convinced Cohan he should try it. In addition, it would mean extra – much needed – money for him and, as his salary at The Place was not large and the costs of renovating the house in France were a constant drain on his resources, it seemed a reasonable request. For the next ten years, Cohan would visit Israel three or four times a year, set choreography, occasionally make a new work, and advise on all artistic matters. But, he would not be the artistic director (even though *Dance Magazine* announced him as such[265]), not be the person who was there every day, dealing with the administration of the company and the personalities. He would, however, advise on who that should be, and this was to be his first major hurdle to overcome and almost ended the arrangement.

In March 1980, Cohan went to Israel, taking with him Moshe Romano to set three of Cohan's works on the dancers – *Khamsin*, *Cell*, and *Nympheas*. The group could not afford the set for the latter piece and it was performed with curtains for the projections, an effect that was in Cohan's mind less than satisfactory. The two took costumes to lend to the Israelis and Jenny Henry, LCDT's long-time wardrobe mistress, kept detailed notes of everything they borrowed, just in case they should forget to return with them (Remy Charlip had borrowed the costumes for *Mad River* and never returned them, so she had every right to be wary). Cohan taught class, got to know the dancers, many of whom he had taught already, and all the other personalities involved. The dancers respected Cohan enormously and welcomed his personal style. Mira Edels, who was just beginning her time at the company as Strum's assistant – she would later go on to become general manager – noticed the calming effect he had on those around him. Israelis can be somewhat brusque with one another, and even in giving corrections may have said, 'That was lousy!' Cohan's way was to say, 'If I was doing that, I would…' As Edels recalls, 'he does not know what negative words are, and he would never hurt anyone'. Unfortunately in the position he was in, causing some hurt was unavoidable.

In such a small country as Israel, there were very few opportunities for dancers to follow a career as well as live in their hard-won land. In Batsheva, there were some dancers who had been with the company since its inception, fiercely dedicated to it and to the state of Israel. Two of them, Rahamim Ron and Rena Gluck, were the most senior dancers; both were extremely strong personalities and had a huge following as dancers in Israel. The year prior to Cohan's arrival, Gluck had taken a sabbatical from the company and had been visiting her homeland of America, teaching and coaching at a number of institutions, including her old school Juilliard, and at the Graham Studio and CalArts. While teaching in Canada, she had been offered a full-time position in Toronto, but the job she really wanted was artistic director of Batsheva, and it was she who had suggested Cohan's name to the Batsheva Board, expecting that he would be artistic adviser and she artistic director, the two working rather like a president and prime minister. Before turning the Canadian job down she had written to Strum and said, 'if there is anything you need to tell me, tell me now and I will not come back'.

She returned to Israel expecting to be made artistic director, but instead was summoned into a meeting with Strum and Cohan and told that there was no job for her or Ron. It was a sad start to Cohan's tenure and a sad end to her career with the company, which had been partly created by the Baroness with her in mind. It is unlikely that it will ever be clear who actually made the decision. Paul Sanasardo wrote a letter to Gluck stating that he had advised Cohan to appoint her and he had ignored it, Strum had told Cohan it was the Board's decision they should go with and he should implement it. But Gluck remembers it differently: 'They did it illegally because the Board were not told, Bill did it with Bob. Bill came to my house and he had been my friend, I told him, "I hold you beneath contempt", and he said, "It was Bob's decision." There was a great deal of discussion about the matter in the Israeli press, and the sackings caused a great deal of bad feeling, but the decision held. Ron moved to Sweden and began a second career there, and Gluck became director of the dance department at the Rubin Academy in Jerusalem. She never again attended a performance of the Batsheva Dance Company.

The decision to lose Gluck and Ron was ostensibly made to move the company forward with new blood, but then Cohan did the opposite of what was expected by installing his friend and rehearsal director of LCDT, Moshe Romano, as the artistic director. Romano had been with Batsheva at the very beginning and was an excellent rehearsal director, but he was not an artistic director, nor a choreographer, nor was he the new blood the company needed. His role as rehearsal director of LCDT was taken by former dancer Lenny Westerdijk, the wife of Gale Law.

Clearly, Cohan was not going to be an arm's length adviser because he told Dora Sowden of the *Jerusalem Post* (14 August) that 'This was not an obvious choice, because I didn't want to lose Romano in London, but it was an obvious choice because he is someone who has worked with me and the London company in a very creative way and we plan changes in the structure and the working of the Batsheva Company.'[266] Cohan was going to be very much around – the article stated three times a year – even though Romano was quoted as saying he would 'do all the work, training, rehearsing and directing'. In case anyone should worry, the article clearly stated that 'It is not Cohan's or Romano's intention to duplicate the London company here', but they would in the early stages 'rehearse works from London that would suit the company'. Although Romano carried out his job with the good humour for which he was well known, the dancers did not respect him and it was felt that he was simply following Cohan's instructions. He helped greatly in developing the educational and workshop areas of the company but, after just over a year, he returned to London.

In addition to Israel and the longest European tour that LCDT had undertaken, the summer saw Cohan again in Canada to lead another choreographic seminar. The beautiful town of Banff, where the seminar was held, provided Cohan with a welcome break from the stresses of Israel and the long tour, which had also stopped him from being there for the first week of the seminar which had been led by ballet master Tod Bolender. When he arrived, he was reunited with John Herbert McDowell, with whom he had developed an excellent working relationship, Grant Strate, the organiser, and Strate's boyfriend Earl Kraul, who was teaching the ballet classes on the course.

The participants included a range of the best of young Canadian choreographers from a variety of styles, including Christopher House, who would go onto direct the Toronto Dance Theatre, and James Kudelka, who would go on to become the director of the Canadian National Ballet. Kudelka was at first sceptical about the whole venture, as for him 'choreographing was very private and something I didn't much want to share with anyone else'.[267] But he found the atmosphere so congenial that once he got there he 'opened up considerably and found it a very safe environment. I completely misjudged the hothouse and thrived in the heat of it.' He is happy to admit that he

> … lived off and used the tools from the experience at the Banff seminar for a very long time: working quickly and concisely, surrendering to the assignment you get, or give yourself, every time you make a dance; trusting the process and not steering too much; trusting the performers to engage with you; the importance of not necessarily being able to execute every move yourself.

He directly attributes these to Cohan's exercises, which included:

> 1. Create a dance with no walking, running, or repeated movement.

2. Create a dance for a dancer while sitting in a chair, without demonstrating any movement.

3. Create a strange space.

4. Make a solo for yourself which expresses what dance means to you.

Choreographers often found the final assignment extremely challenging, with many of them creating huge swathes of dense movement in an attempt to hide themselves. In this Banff seminar, however, Brian Webb from Edmonton went to the opposite extreme and produced a dance in which, dressed only in his underpants, he sat on a cushion for what, to the audience, seemed an eternity.

Cohan's approach to choreography was described by Iro Trembeck, who as a dancer and writer in residence wrote a report of the seminar for *Dance in Canada*, as 'decomposition, the analytical approach of breaking down into component parts – time, space, energy – in finding new ways of approaching these elements'.[268]

While Cohan was out of the country, the BBC had broadcast two programmes directed by Bob Lockyer; one was of Cohan teaching a masterclass and the other consisted of a double bill of *Forest* and *Waterless Method of Swimming Instruction*. These were the first works Cohan made with Lockyer, whom he had known for many years and with whom he enjoyed a harmonious working relationship. Lockyer would be the only television director Cohan would work with from now on, and their collaboration would – although they did not realise it at the time – provide for posterity the only professional documentation of Cohan's choreography. For the dances, Cohan was paid the princely fee of £18 per minute for the right to transmit once only, repeat fees were 50 per cent of final fee with further, unspecified percentages for abroad. To put this into perspective, as Charter he was paid £450 by the Royal Opera House, Covent Garden, to light a production of *Troy Game*.

The developments in Israel and Cohan's need for a break from LCDT accounted for the significant changes in the running of the company that LCDT announced in the autumn. Mop Eager, the administrator, and Robert North, the associate choreographer, were named as associate directors, and North would be directing the company in the first half of 1981 to cover for Cohan who was to be on sabbatical. The sabbatical for Cohan was to provide him with a much needed break from the directing of the company. The time away from The Place enabled him to spend more time at his home in France which was finally taking shape under Chiesa's expert eye and fluent French. But he still had calls on his time, and he paid a number of visits to his ageing parents, still living in Sheepshead Bay, and more time than he had envisaged was spent in Israel, where, in addition to the work with Batsheva, *Tzaikerk* was acquired by Bat-Dor.

In the spring of 1981, Howard and Eager visited Cohan in France to discuss exactly what he wanted and did not want to do in relation to the work at The

Place. After much discussion, they came up with some quite detailed thoughts:
Cohan

    1. Would not like to be involved in the administrative direction

    2. Would like to choreograph/teach and oversee teaching

    3. Would like to work on technique (i.e. on students)

    4. Would like to work with small groups of selected dancers (from company if doing a special work with them) and students from school. Initially to work with group (12) from company i.e. junior members plus Barry Pheloung (Norberto [Chiesa] also working with them)

    5. Would not like to be involved in demonstrations/lectures/teaching in colleges and schools

    6. Happy to work things out on film and video to be used for above

    7. Happy to work out matinée material with Richard Mansfield (the director of educational projects) and to plan some kind of programme for this in July (possible relating ed. Work)[269]

These Howard agreed to, even though they were quite considerable changes to Cohan's work, with the overriding aim to free him up to concentrate more on choreography. He had never enjoyed and never wanted to be a bureaucrat, and yet as the company and school grew and grew he found an increasing amount of his time taken up with meetings – fundraising, staffing, managerial, etc. – and he wanted to be free of them. The discussions also included the possibility of building a studio in France so Cohan would be able to work with small groups of dancers without leaving home, but the finances were not available and the scheme was dropped.

In addition, the meeting covered strategic planning for the company's future. It was envisaged a much more businesslike approach which would leave little room for the concept of 'love' which Howard had wanted from the company's inception:

    1. For the future the company is going to have to be less 'family' more 'organisational' in its approach, i.e. consider the 'Group' rather than the individual rather more than in the past

    2. Necessary to bring in outside choreographers, less emphasis on choreographers from inside – this we plan from 82

    3. Not to continue with associate choreographers – for the immediate future to have associate directors and acting artistic directors

    4. For the autumn, Chris Bannerman to cover tour with Mop and Lenny

    5. Robert should be asked to dance and company in New York in May 83

    6. Agreed not to speak to him until after summer tour but if goes well Patrick to be acting artistic director for Dec/Jan/Feb Main Middle scale Group.[270]

Point two was a major policy shift, since for many years, the vast majority of the company's work came from company members. This is what, for many critics, had led to a stale look to LCDT's repertory. The choreographers all knew each other, and tended to make works from a very limited pallet. The bringing in of works from international figures would, it was hoped, reinvigorate the group, although all of this was dependent on having the finances to pay the fees that international choreographers expected.

Cohan was away from the company until 13 July when he returned to begin intensive work on a full-length work to be premiered at the Moray House Gymnasium on 31 August as part of the Edinburgh Festival. John Drummond, the director of the festival and a long-time intimate of Cohan's, had worked hard to secure £20,000 of funding from Tennent Caledonian to commission the work – the first commission the previous year had gone to Peter Maxwell Davies for his opera *The Lighthouse*. Entitled *Dances of Love and Death*, it would in terms of technical and staging demands rival Cohan's *Stages* from ten years earlier. Large-scale works had made something of a comeback on the contemporary dance scene and Ballet Rambert had recently had great success with the evening-length works *Cruel Garden* by Christopher Bruce and *The Tempest* by Glen Tetley. Cohan hoped his new work would similarly captivate a new audience.

The piece was based around great love stories from history, and the idea came from the death of Marilyn Monroe. Cohan had always been fascinated by her, as for him she represented the essence of the American beauty star. Cohan had seen her close up in New York, although he was not introduced. He saw her as the beginning of celebrity worship, a concept that intrigued him. When she died he had passed a news stand and the headline had read:

THE GODDESS IS DEAD

The idea that she had become the goddess Aphrodite stuck with him, and that became the start for the dance.

His collaborators on the work were once again designer Norberto Chiesa, who with a larger budget was able to let his ideas run wild and created some extraordinarily evocative costumes and sets; the lighting designer John B. Read, whose designs had to cover everything from the Greek underworld to Hollywood; and the composer Carl Davis. This would be Cohan's first collaboration with Davis, although Davis had written music for two previous LCDT works *David and Goliath* and *Gladly, Sadly, Madly, Badly*.

Cohan enjoyed working with Davis a great deal, finding his sparky American style energising, and although Cohan devised the script himself, he found it a great help to be able to bounce ideas off him. Cohan always regretted not having someone to talk over his work with; to some extent, he did use Peter Williams and occasionally John Drummond, but what he felt he needed was 'a literary person, perhaps a playwright', but he didn't have one. What usually happened was that he 'had complete freedom [but] I wanted to be able to talk it through with someone but everyone was so afraid of me, people just said what a great idea'.

In the work, Cohan wanted the structure to resemble a party in which different guests tell stories; at the end of each story, the guests are free to walk around, chat, drink, eat, but in a way unaffected or unrelated to the stories they have heard. In addition, Cohan was concerned with what people remember of famous – or infamous – love stories. How much do we remember in detail, are the details remembered the most important? In line with the fact that the work was an entertainment, Cohan knew that he would not be able to plumb any strong emotional depth, but he did not want to distort the essence of the story. This is where he chose to follow a narrative similar to the banner headline he had seen announcing Monroe's death, and indeed many times after. Included into the design concept was a type of surtitle bar which came to life with witty banner headlines and key points in the dance. In the programme notes, he wrote, 'If there is a message in this dance piece it is that the audience should sit back and enjoy the stories and be amused by the interludes.'

For the interludes, Cohan wanted to use some of Conlon Nancarrow's *Studies for Player Piano*, these frantic, hyperactive pieces created for mechanical piano as they were impossible for the human hand and mind to play, swept in in a totally illogical fashion, their rhythmic impossibilities sounding like the excited chatter of the guests at the party. They contrasted totally with Davis' score which was balletic in scope and imaginatively scored for just ten instruments (composer David Matthews brought his expert ear to the orchestrations) and which, in order to aid in the understanding of the stories, signposted each by borrowing elements of styles from the periods or countries in which the dances were set. So in the Persephone story he used Balkan folk; in Tristan a medieval pavane; the Sleeping Beauty referenced baroque music; while Cathy and Heathcliff was an extended romantic waltz. Each story was introduced by sections for the characters of Love and Death which used early eighteenth-century styles.

The finished work covered five stories ranging from ancient Greece to the twentieth century, and all concern the conflict between love and death. With a slight similarity to de Valois' ballet *Checkmate*, the characters of Love – embodied as the goddess Aphrodite – and Death manipulated the characters and shaped the action, and they begin the work. The action then moves to a scene on a beach

The stories themselves moved chronologically through the centuries, and began with Persephone and Pluto. Persephone, the daughter of Demeter the goddess of the corn, is gathering flowers with her mother and some handmaidens. Pluto, king of the underworld, finds her alone and rapes her, dragging her off to Hades where she will live forever. Demeter, looking for her daughter, finds the dress, realises what has happened, and curses the earth, making it barren. When Pluto appears, she argues violently with him. Zeus orders Persephone to be returned to her mother, but because she ate one pomegranate seed in Hades, she cannot go free. She must spend three months of each year in Hades, and during these winter months the curse and Persephone's fate are remembered. This section particularly caught the attention of John Percival who, in a review for *Dance Magazine*, told his readers that 'the enormous buttocks of Namron, playing Pluto and the more modest ones of his attendants are copiously displayed'.[271]

An interlude entitled 'After the Dance' leads to Tristan and Iseult, gazing longingly at one another. Tristan, escorting Iseult to Cornwall where she is to marry King Mark, has by accident drunk a love potion intended for Iseult and Mark. Mark, however, forgives them and Tristan leaves for Brittany where he is mortally wounded. Iseult, who has a reputation as a healer, is called to help him. Tristan's wife deceives him into thinking that Iseult has refused to come by telling him that a ship with black sails is arriving, black sails meaning she has not come. Tristan dies just as a ship with white sails bearing Iseult arrives, and she dies of a broken heart.

An interlude, 'Black Fedoras', leads to the Sleeping Beauty in which Love introduces the Prince and Death creates a thicket which will keep him away from the Princess. The Prince awakens, gets through the barrier, and awakens her with a kiss, but then she insists he goes through certain trials before she will marry him.

After the interval, the second part began with 'The Party', in which Tom Jobe as a transvestite Death tried to kill Philippe Giraudeau in as many ways as possible. Cathy and Heathcliff's tale was told complexly, using a Grahamesque structure of flashbacks and ghost sequences. On his deathbed, Heathcliff hears Cathy's voice, he imagines dancing a waltz with her, and they are soon joined by the shades of Cathy's husband Edgar and Heathcliff's wife Isabella. Heathcliff and Cathy are reunited on the moors and dance an ecstatic pas de deux, but she dies and he finds himself back on his deathbed. Not even Death can separate the two and their love continues beyond the grave.

In the final story, Cohan returned to his inspiration and Celia Hulton, whose curvaceous body and extraordinary acting skills made her the embodiment of Marilyn Monroe. Cohan showed her in her public persona and in her search for love, finally blurring her two aspects. The work was meant to be an entertainment and Cohan ended it with a final divertissement in which, in spite of the inevitability of love and death, life goes on.

The premiere was almost a disaster as, at the time, the company were trying out a new computerised lighting board, and unfortunately it failed on the day of the technical rehearsal. So Cohan had to cancel the rehearsal while another board was put into a taxi and sent up from London to Edinburgh. Everyone agreed that they would all go to the venue at 10 p.m. to finish the technical rehearsal. However, when they arrived, the theatre was closed, barred, locked and they could not rouse anyone to open it; this was a catastrophe, bearing in mind how heavy the technical demands were on the piece. They left despondently, and the next day the dress rehearsal became the technical rehearsal, and the first night became dress rehearsal. There were, as a result, mishaps in the running of the show, and John Drummond hated everything about it, in particular the music. He refused to see it again and would die with the firm belief that he had commissioned a failure. The Tennents, however, who had sponsored it, saw the show a number of times, bringing guests and telling Cohan they thoroughly enjoyed it.

The first performances were sold out and, despite the technical problems, the show was enthusiastically received by the public. The critics were mainly honest about the work, appreciating the scale and the theatricality while pointing out that it lacked coherence, that this type of work was not what Cohan was best at, and that the dancing itself could have had more life in it. Cohan admits he could have used a dramaturg to draw the work more coherently together, but their appearance on the British dance scene was some years off. The lack of drama was mostly put down to Davis' score which was criticised for being too bland.

Noel Goodwin, writing for *Dance and Dancers*, felt 'There are too many elements at play, and the result is too diffuse'.[272] Davis himself remembers that the players struggled for most of the run with the intricacies of his score which was certainly not heard to its best advantage.

Once on tour, not all the public loved the work, and after a performance in Leeds which the *Yorkshire Post* had found 'a stunning collaboration… deserving to become a classic',[273] Cohan received a letter from the group Women Against Violence Against Women who were far from enthusiastic:

> This evening we were present at a performance of *Dances of Love and Death* at the Grand Theatre in Leeds. We were shocked by the content of this dance and found it extremely offensive. Is it necessary to portray the sexual initiation of a young girl in sadomasochistic terms? The music is poignant, the choreography starkly violent. We find the representation of sexual love as automatically including dominance and violence on the part of the men and submission from the woman, totally unacceptable. Furthermore the acceptance of this by the other dancers representing society, is abhorrent.[274]

The autumn saw the company back at Sadler's Wells, where the repertory included one programme of works by Robert North, who had been unhappy with LCDT for some time and had left the company to become artistic director of Ballet Rambert. North had been with the company from the very beginning, and his dancing and his choreography had been central to LCDT's development. Cohan, Howard and Eager had played a dangerous game with North and Siobhan Davies, playing the two, very different but very long-serving members of the company, off one another. To North, they said that his work was popular with audiences and they needed it to counteract the dry, emotionless work of Davies. To Davies, they said that they needed her intellectually rigorous work, popular with critics, to counteract the cheap popular works of North. It was not a harmonious situation, being more reminiscent of the old Graham Company than the company based on 'love' that Howard wanted. North's decision, however, came as a surprise, and was a blow to Howard and Cohan who had long thought that he would be the next director of LCDT. As events played out, North would not have had to wait long, since Cohan would very soon make it clear he no longer wanted to be the sole director.

Away from the company, another side of Cohan's artistic nature was shown when, from 15 November to 8 December, the Photographers' Gallery in London showed an exhibition of his dance photography. Over the years, Cohan had taken many photographs of his dancers and the exhibition was a culmination of this. The photographs were not literal images of dancers frozen in time, but captured their movements with extended exposure times, so that what was seen were sweeps of movement, the movement paths made visible. The exhibition was a success, with Jan Murray writing in *Time Out* that 'the camera work [shows] a depth of kinetic understanding denied to people with less experience of the art form'.[275] They would later be seen at Sadler's Wells and on the covers of a number of LCDT publications, although since then they have not been seen but do deserve to be preserved, perhaps in a book or DVD format, as they are an impressive series of studies of dance and dancers.

The beginning of 1982 saw number of the long-serving members of the company, Cohan included, on leave. This left Patrick Harding-Irmer to follow through the plans that had been discussed in France to take on the role of acting artistic director and to lead an attenuated group in regional touring. The tour included Richard Kuch's Brecht-inspired *Mother Courage*; Jane Dudley had been in the original 1968 cast of the work and had suggested it to Cohan as a good acquisition, but the dancers never really took to the gloomy work and it was swiftly dropped. When the company regrouped, they began a six-week tour of *Dances of Love and Death*, which also saw the retirement of another LCDT stalwart, Namron. Namron had been involved with the school and the company from the very beginning, and was a firm favourite with dancers and audience alike, and his presence was much missed. He had decided to 'retire' at 40 while he 'could still move', and move he did in this final work. After gently complaining to Cohan that he had not had a really good solo in some time, Cohan choreographed for him, in his final appearance, a very challenging role that needed all his stamina and stage craft to bring off. Add to this some ferocious partnering and the role was a fitting end to his career with the company.

Cohan told Anthony van Laast that 'I want to build a wall so high that to get out of this place, that to leave, you have to know really why you want to go'. Cohan invested so much time in his dancers and the company that most of them stayed with him for many years, and LCDT became known as much for its dancers as for its choreography. Clare Duncan or Noemi Lapzeson, Micheline McKnight, Paula Lansley embody the first company, while the second company period, beginning in the mid 1970s, was embodied by a number of dancers, who, by the late 1970s and early 1980s, had naturally grown older and wanted to move on to pursue other paths, either professionally or to start families. Anthony van Laast, Paula Lansley, and Ross McKim left in 1979, while Micha Bergese left in 1980 and Cathy Lewis in 1981. Namron, Robert North, and Kate Harrison stayed until 1983. Leaving, as Cohan hoped, was not easy and van Laast recalls, 'I had to take a Valium and cried like a child when I told Bob I was leaving.' These were major recognisable figures in the company who had created well-known roles in what was the classic LCDT repertory, or in a number of cases had choreographed the repertory themselves and, as they left, the look of the company changed not only in physical appearance, but artistic outlook. This exodus of dancers provided openings in the company for a new generation who would come to be recognisable figures throughout the 1980s. Those including Michael Small, Paul Douglas, Lauren Potter, Darshan Singh Bhuller, Jonathan Lunn, Anne Went, Julian Moss, Kenneth Tharp, Brenda Edwards, Tamsin Hickling, and Peter Dunleavy would stay with LCDT until Cohan's retirement, and some even beyond that. The changes in personnel, coupled with the changes in artistic direction caused by Cohan's more frequent absences, however subtle they may have been, saw a very different LCDT enter the funding arena of the 1980s.

In January 1982, Cohan travelled to Canada to make a new work for Dancemakers in Toronto, entitled *When Evening Spreads Itself Across the Sky*, set to J. S. Bach's *Suite No. 5* for solo cello. The title is a paraphrase of a line from T. S. Eliot's 'The Love Song of J. Alfred Prufrock':

> Let us go then, you and I,
> When the evening is spread out against the sky
> Like a patient etherized upon a table;[276]

Put in context, these lines make the work considerably less romantic than it would first appear to be. This dark, turbulent dance looking at evening was almost a companion piece to *Eos*, which looked at the coming of dawn, and was almost as disturbing. Although they were a talented group, Cohan found working with the unfamiliar dancers difficult. He was so used to working intensively with LCDT, who were so in tune with his way of creating that they could anticipate his next thought, but in Canada he found he could not work in the same way. His memory of the work was that 'The palette was different. I was unhappy with what was coming out and that inhibited me. They found what I was doing technically very difficult and I wasn't used to that as a problem. It was a big problem, and somehow I couldn't make it easy.' Although the work, for Cohan, contained a beautiful duet and impressive costumes from Chiesa, he was not happy with the finished piece.

Cohan rejoined LCDT at the beginning of April when he began work on a new piece, *Chamber Dances*, forty minutes of pure dance set to a pre-existing score of Geoffrey Burgon to which the composer added two extra movements. The work for six couples seemed to indicate lovers who were meeting and parting, with a gradual darkening of the mood. Midway through, a woman (usually either Anca Frankenhauser or Charlotte Kirkpatrick) arrived swathed in a gigantic blue cloak, in which the men of the company became ensnared. This image was based on an Indian painting Cohan had seen, in which the figure of Night wore a blue cloak which all of the animals of the night tumbled in after her. He was not entirely happy with the effect produced and would return to it a few years later. The dance ended on a brighter note with the dancers returning to a lighter mood and mode of dancing.

The work received mixed reviews from the critics which highlighted the changing face of dance criticism which, throughout the 1980s, would see the amateur – in the best sense of the word – old school characterised by Peter Williams and Richard Buckle being replaced by the new school of academically trained critics such as Alastair Macaulay and Sarah Rubidge. This was a change that occurred throughout the dance world, and of the Americans, the distinguished writer and critic Marcia Siegel has noted that 'the new critics often seemed to write about theories of dancing rather than reporting on the dances they had seen'.[277] These changes were noted even in other fields, and the distinguished literary critic Sir Frank Kermode complained of literary critics 'who seem largely to have lost interest in literature as such'.[278]

For the young critics, Sarah Rubidge, a new addition to the *Dance and Dancers* team, in a review of *Chamber Dances*, told her readers she experienced a 'sense of déjà vu. I waited in vain for some original quirk, some unexpected development to the only too familiar material. But I was disappointed.'[279] Macaulay was equally cutting in the *Dancing Times*, where he was sharpening the claws for which he has become well known, finding that '*Chamber Dances* is long and meanders a good deal', adding 'cutting would improve every piece by Cohan that I've seen', and concluding '*Chamber Dances* is just a succession of scenes: they never cohere.'[280] Some of Cohan's previous supporters, including Noel Goodwin, tried to be more positive but the tenor of the reviews would presage much of the 1980s in relation to Cohan, as Rubidge noted: 'I was left with a sense that this was not a work of the 1980s, but was more of an example of British contemporary dance circa mid Seventies.'

Rubidge and other young critics often writing for the Laban-published *Dance Theatre Journal*, edited by Chris de Marigny, wanted to embrace 'the more experimental work that was taking place at the time', and thought that his publication should be the mouthpiece for the new generation of work that was coming through and challenging the status quo. In it, he nurtured budding writers who took a different view to the standard critics. These different views would become more and more prevalent as the years went on, and the relevance of the 'Contemporary' in London Contemporary Dance Theatre would be questioned mercilessly.

In the summer, Cohan undertook a new venture when he went with Geoffrey Burgon to teach on the first New Zealand Choreographic Seminar. News of the success of the Gulbenkian course had spread around the world, and a version of the course was arranged in Auckland, attracting a number of choreographers from the southern hemisphere. This southern course followed much the same format as the established Gulbenkian one, with Cohan and Burgon dividing the daily tasks between them. Burgon found Cohan 'a pleasure to work with', his easy open mind accommodating and willing to try out and incorporate any musical ideas the composer would put forward.

Much as he would have liked to, Cohan was not able to stay and enjoy the antipodean environment, as he had to return to Surrey University to teach on the third Gulbenkian course where he was reunited with John Herbert McDowell. The two had by now worked out a format they were happy with, and they changed the structure very little. There were seven one-day projects, and three spread over two days, which allowed between six and eight and a half hours of creative preparation. This time, however, Cohan wanted to see the works in as complete a form as possible.

The tasks were set before lunch and enabled the composers and choreographers more time for discussion and were not style specific, in fact they were deliberately opaque to allow the participants maximum creative input. These included: a dance made to music composed that morning; a dance exactly 4' 11" long which had to include a small construction, a depression, a large construction, and one surprise. They did not have to be made in that order, but the work had to have a title. He also included one of his favourite tasks to make a solo, preferably danced by the choreographer, which was a personal statement about dance. This time no one danced in their underwear.

Cohan was ever concerned with artists having a wide knowledge and a clear understanding of their place in the continuum of the artistic world, believing 'you need to know where you have come from in order to know where you are going'. So, in addition to the live choreography, Cohan showed an eclectic selection of dance films which were discussed by the whole group, including the classic *Four Pioneers* (concerning Graham, Humphrey, Holm, and Weidman), Cunningham's *Events for Television*, Bronislava Nijinska's ballet *Les Noces*, and a documentary about the course itself made in 1977 by Bob Lockyer.

In the autumn, Cohan went with LCDT on a three-week coast-to-coast tour of Canada. It was exhilarating as the company had never been there before and the audiences were hugely enthusiastic. The critical reception was, however, a mixture of brickbats and bouquets. Not having seen the work before and having for comparison only some American dance companies, the critics brought an objective viewpoint that was often missing from English critics. Of the positive ones, this, from Jacob Siskind writing in the *Ottawa Citizen*, was typical of many:

> There is a quality to all of the work of the London Contemporary Dance Theatre that sets it apart from and above most such companies currently touring. The dancers are all superbly trained and move with such incomparable ease that the tensions they produce are a result of the thought behind the movement, never the effort required to make the gesture.[281]

Other writers noted that the company had now moved so far beyond the Graham Technique that they clearly had a style entirely their own. But within these, a large number of reviews commented on the coldness of the dancers: John Ayre, in *Maclean's* magazine, while admiring their extraordinary technique, found the repertoire 'arid [and] emotionally unyielding',[282] the dancers keeping the audience at arm's length.

In an interview with Max Wyman, dance critic of the *Vancouver Sun*, Cohan acknowledged that 'There's a natural athleticism in American dance – and I'd say the same about Canadian, and Australian – and the English as a culture do tend to be more reserved. They don't run up to you in sneakers and embrace you and say a have a nice day.'[283] Some British may indeed not do this but then neither does Cohan, and what the Canadian critics had picked up on was exactly what Walter Terry had noted exactly thirty-two years previously, and worth repeating here, that 'there is a cool remoteness about Mr Cohan's work. If passion is present, it is as if it were remembered and not of the instant.'[284] It would seem reasonable to accept that the aesthetic of LCDT was a reflection of its director Cohan, just as the Graham Company was a reflection of her, or Cunningham of him. Indeed, the style of LCDT would change quite dramatically once Cohan gave up the full-time artistic direction of the company.

While visiting Canada, Cohan dropped over the border to see the Batsheva Company perform at Carnegie Hall for one night only on 26 October. The performance was to honour Jerome Robbins, who was receiving the King Solomon Award from the America-Israel Cultural Foundation. Critics lamented that the company was not as yet able to mount a full season but were full of praise for the programme carefully chosen by Cohan and Moshe Romano which showed off to their best advantage the quality of the dancers.[285] The mixed bill included a duet from *Nympheas*, as well as works by John Cranko and rising star Ohad Naharin.

It was during the Canadian tour that Cohan announced his decision to step down as artistic director of the company. A somewhat emotional sounding Cohan told Tom Sutcliffe of the *Guardian*,

> I'm tired. I've worked at this nonstop, nose to the floor, literally, 12 to 14 hours a day, for 10 or 15 years. I just can't find the energy to push harder, as hard as I

feel it should be pushed, or as hard as I've pushed in the past. I'm overworked. And for the company to go on past this vision I've given it, it needs a new push. Maybe some genius will apply for the job, and I won't have to come back. I might have some pangs of jealousy, that I couldn't do it. I'm very human.[286]

He went on to lay out some of his plans, which included writing a book on choreography and to exploring his own creative processes. As he explained very frankly,

I can make all the pieces resemble each other, and visually beautiful. They have a certain kind of class. But there's no rule through the work – I've just enjoyed doing what I wanted to do and mostly its turned out fine. If you're lucky as a creative artist, people like what you do. The others, the unlucky ones, you don't hear about.

Now I feel it's time for something different. I still have lots of ideas for dances, but now I can no longer get them to the point where I can actually do them. I've simply got to find a new artistic way of functioning. There has to be a new artistic director of LCDT because I feel, with me questioning myself so much at this point, I might make wrong decisions for the company.[287]

But his 'retirement' was some way off, and first Cohan had to get the company ready for performances at the Brooklyn Academy of Music as part of the Britain Salutes New York festival. The visit almost did not happen for the usual financial reasons, and it was only by a supreme effort from Howard and Mop that additional funds were found. For a festival called Britain Salutes New York, Cohan selected an odd programme, as three of the four choreographers, Cohan himself, Robert North, and Tom Jobe were American, while the only native British choreographer was Siobhan Davies. Nevertheless, the performances were, as they were in Canada, an enormous success as Clive Barnes, whose support had been key to the early success of LCDT, told his *New York Post* readers: 'As I left the theatre, it seemed as though the whole house was cheering. It is the kind of success that can be compared to the initial impact of the Royal Ballet in 1949.'[288] What surprised many critics was the dancers' high technical standard, rivalling as it did that of many long-established American companies. Barnes perspicaciously noted that 'Cohan's choreography and technique is no spin off of Graham, or if it is, it spins off and bounces at the speed of light'.[289] In amongst the success, however, there was dissent, which came mainly, as it did in England, from the younger generation of critics. Burt Supree writing for the *Village Voice* found 'all of the works too long' and noted that, in *Class*, 'Harder, faster, bigger are the only goals, and humanity the only flaw', while *Cell* 'demonstrates a cold self-lacerating wilfulness' which 'displayed no humanity of its own'.[290] However, Cohan's old Graham friends were impressed, telling him that it looked like the old companies used to, where everyone participated and knew why they were there. Graham herself, approaching 90 and still very active, was invited but was unable to attend owing to illness.

The illness of another person approaching 90 almost saw the visit end tragically for the Cohan family. On the closing day, they had a matinée and an evening performance. Cohan remembers being at his brother Elliot's apartment on Charles Street when his mother called and said, 'Your father just went to work and it's a Sunday.' His father, who was 85 years old and had been suffering from dementia for some years, had got up at 5 a.m. and dressed himself. This was not the first time this had occurred and Cohan's mother, thinking he would settle down and have breakfast, had not taken too much notice, but he had left the house and she later found out he had got on a bus to somewhere. She called the police, who found a man who had loaned her husband some money as he had said he had to go into Manhattan. Cohan told his mother to stay calm, and he and Elliot went looking everywhere for him. He was not at his former workplace, nor at his childhood haunt of 125th Street. Cohan ran through Harlem with photographs, asking passers-by, 'Have you seen this man?' No one had, and the family became more and more worried for his safety. He was found by the police the next day and returned home. His father's health would cause great concern for Cohan, who felt keenly that he was not able to help as much as he would have wanted, or would have done had he lived in New York. His reduced commitment to LCDT would mean he was able to visit more often, but not as often as he would have liked.

The company returned to Britain to prepare for its Sadler's Wells season, which included a gala attended by Princess Alexandra and marked Cohan's retirement as sole artistic director. In a sensitive and heartfelt tribute to Cohan, Peter Williams wrote:

> It is one thing to introduce new and developing art forms, especially in a country so classical ballet orientated as was Britain up until the early 1950's, but it takes someone with a unique personality to make it all work in a way that can eventually change a whole nation's attitude to dance… In its way, his contribution to the whole dance scene in Britain parallels that of those two other legendary pioneers – Dame Ninette de Valois and Marie Rambert.[291]

Noel Goodwin for *Ballet News* was equally appreciative of Cohan's achievements, writing:

> Robert Cohan's leadership has changed the face of dance in Britain. His work has brought about a new indigenous style of dance as an art and an entertainment, with a crossover of interest and techniques between this and the traditions of classical ballet, to the mutual advantage of both. It quickly became popular because it deals directly and vividly with experiences that are

common to all of us, searching out with equal intensity those images of beauty and life which can, in turn, enrich our capacity for human understanding.[292]

The gala programme included three Cohan classics, *Stabat Mater*, *Forest*, and *Class*, while the season as a whole ended with *Dances of Love and Death*.

Cohan's 'retirement' was short-lived – even at the leaving party, a colleague said, 'What does this mean Bob? You coming back to work tomorrow as usual?' Cohan recalls: 'I was not going to make any decisions and Robin would take my place, but every time I came to London, I would call Mop and I would end up making all kinds of decisions which Robin had not.' Cohan had said at the time that he would like his successor 'to be someone from here (LCDT) or at least from Britain, who takes over eventually',[293] while Robin Howard, ever the pragmatist, said, 'We shall be looking for the right person to undertake the next phase of our development…. But if we cannot find one such person, then we feel the company is strong enough to go forward under some form of joint leadership until such a successor can be appointed.'[294] The Trust did indeed search for a replacement but could find no one suitable, and so reluctantly Cohan agreed to come back for seven months of the year as artistic adviser. In August 1983, a triumvirate was set up with Cohan taking artistic responsibility, Siobhan Davies as resident choreographer, and Mop Eager continuing as administrator.

With Cohan taking something of a backstage role, the LCDT repertory began to change. The genius of Cohan had been to develop from nothing not one but two generations of British choreographers and in the mid 1980s, the work of Siobhan Davies, Jonathan Lunn, Darshan Singh Bhuller, Jayne Lee, and North American members of LCDT Tom Jobe and Christopher Bannerman, began to feature regularly in the company's seasons. Their extensions, developments, permutations and even rejections of Cohan's style pushed the company in new directions. Tom Jobe's high energy athletic dances, often owing much to gay disco culture, were hugely popular with audiences, while Siobhan Davies, in her beautifully crafted dances which seemed to take Cohan's air of detachment to the nth degree, found favour with critics.

In spite of his attempt to leave and his hope for a lower profile, Cohan was still the face of LCDT, and on 9 December the BBC broadcast another double bill featuring two of his dances which demonstrated the variety of his style, *Cell* and *Nympheas*. With an estimated audience of 900,000 viewers, it was one of the most successful dance broadcasts ever achieved.

Chapter 10

Commentary

The 1980s were, as is obvious, reading what Paul has written, a very difficult time for me personally. I kept saying I was burnt out, tired, and other such things, but I think what I really I felt inside was something else.

Robin had asked me to develop a high level of contemporary dance by establishing a professional school and dance company in London. I thought I had done the job and I was finished. That is what I meant when I went to Robin and said we should close the company after our Sadler's Wells season. I thought the company would look wonderful in that season, and we would have several choreographers represented and we could finish on a high note.

I often thought that the biggest mistake Robin and I made was that we did not prepare for success. We thought, I certainly did, that the job of bringing contemporary dance into the mainstream in England was going to be so difficult, and take so long, that there was no need yet for a plan for the future.

We started a search for someone to take over my job, which was Artistic Director of the Trust, not just of the company. As a part of that search and to give me some time off, several company members were given the chance to be directors for short tours. Robin and I also interviewed several possible artists privately, but we thought, to no avail.

I always had a problem with our name.

When we started, I wanted to call the company London Dance Theatre.

That name was already in use by a small company directed by Norman McDowell. Robin had actually helped that company financially before we started. I came to London as a modern dancer, as that was what we were called in the States at that time. But in England that name, modern dance was confused with ballroom dance. I did not consider myself as a contemporary but a classic modern dancer, if there was such a thing.

I thought the name London Dance Theatre would have given me a freer hand to produce any kind of dance or style in performance. When Norman stopped his company performing, I asked Robin to buy the name from him, which he said he did, but by then our advice was that we were too well known to change our name, although I still think we should have.

Another problem I had with the position of being artistic director of The Place was the need, as we grew larger, of meetings to deal with the constant emergence of problems that needed solving. These meetings were almost always in the morning. At one point, it dawned on me that for all the people at the meeting, it was one of the high or important parts of the day.

For me, the high point of my day was going to be in the studio, not in the meeting. I understood the need for them, but I used to leave the meetings mentally tired and then had to pull my brain and body up to face the rehearsals.

My experience in dance was always physical, and since the body has an infinite ability and depth to experience sensation and movement, the work never ended. This was and is as addictive as any drug, and I think that is one of the reasons why dancers work so intensely. I know about the brain releasing endorphins, but the passion goes even further.

In the film *A Dancer's World*, Martha Graham says: 'Dance is realistic. Either your foot is pointed or it is not and no amount of dreaming will point it for you.' Dancers know this and are passionate about gaining the control and strength to get every move they make right.

Chapter 11

When an elephant is in trouble, even a frog will kick him.

(Hindu proverb)

1984–9

Cohan's first new work for the company for over a year was presented after an intensive rehearsal period at the Grand Theatre in Leeds on 16 February 1984. The idea for *Agora* had first manifested during the 1960s. In those days, planes from Israel regularly made a stopover in Athens; one of these was going to be longer than usual, and Cohan decided to stay in the city. He was fascinated by and made a number of visits to the Parthenon, which was then open to visitors at any time of day or night. Very late one night, Cohan found himself in the ruins when he had 'the impression that there were ghosts coming up from subterranean passages and living their lives again. The feeling stayed and gave me the idea.'

Agora, the Greek for place of assembly or meeting place, was translated in Cohan's vision as a meeting place of ghosts. He devised the idea that there were four people who were there that night, just as he had been, as the ghosts appeared. Norberto Chiesa once again made a very effectively simple set, where the ruins were laid on stage but covered by a black cloth making little hills on the stage; when the cloth was removed, the ruins were revealed as a sort of Parthenon.

He prefaced the first section, 'Intimations', with a quote from Heraclitus: 'The Lord whose oracle is at Delphi neither speaks nor conceals. He gives signs.'[295] Set to J. S. Bach's great chaconne in D minor from the *Partita No. 2* for solo violin, Cohan created a quartet for the human characters. They entered one by one, each solo yielding to the next and, as the group assemble and as a community, they watch each other, occasionally adding a small broken phrase like a friendly comment on the newcomer's movements. Once the whole group is together, the solos, which had seemed to highlight the differences of each member, come together and the two men and two women, dressed in pale grey trousers and grey shirts with rolled up sleeves, dance together, exploring human relationships in an attempt to achieve self-consciousness. It was an unusual dance for Cohan, in that there was little contact between the dancers, rather each phrase was picked up and passed between each member until at the end they were all moving as a single harmoniously connected group. Into his classic vocabulary, Cohan added touches of everyday movement – slight leanings of a supported head, casual sitting down, or a hand casually placed on the hip. He was not entirely successful in merging the two styles, but by the end a sense of quiet intensity of purpose was achieved.

The second section, 'Chasm', was prefaced by more Heraclitus:

The Sibyl with razing mouth
Utters things laughless, unperfumed, unadorned.
Her voice will reach through a thousand years…[296]

To a sound score by Barrington Pheloung, part two was related to part one in that it was its direct opposite. It was concerned with the unconscious, repetitive violence that leads nowhere, and which Cohan feels we, as a species, carry deep within ourselves. The vocabulary here was much more classic post-Graham expressionism, oppressive, martial, and steeped in misery and grief. During the dance, the eight (new) dancers dragged onstage and constructed a structure that could be seen as a physical merism, appearing as both a war machine and a tree of life. The latter seems more likely, as the women suspended themselves in it towards the end.

The third and final section, entitled 'Hymn', was prefaced by words from the twentieth-century writer and Nobel laureate George Seferis: 'Sing little Antigone, sing, O sing… your hair with sun's thorns.'[297] The music returned to the baroque and was danced to Bach's joyous *Brandenburg Concerto No. 6*, and here Cohan tried to present a dancer's solution to the problems posed in the preceding movements. In the end, the dancers seem to achieve catharsis through dance, through the reflective gesture, and redirection through the energy of movement. In the three movements of the concerto, the opening allegro was for eight dancers (four from 'Intimations'), the adagio was for another eight (seven from 'Chasm'), and the final allegro for all the dancers. The athleticism of this last movement was an undoubted crowd-pleaser; if some in the audience were puzzled by the quotes in the programme, and by the imagery in the first two sections, these doubts were swept away by the flying and leaping of the company in the substantial finale. In his review for *Dance and Dancers*, the ever-helpful John Percival suggested the dance would be improved if 'Cohan threw away the first two sections and the setting, keeping just the concerto and leaving space for his exhilarating dances'.[298]

Separately, the individual sections worked, but as a whole, the dance did not hang together as a unity. Perhaps highlighting Cohan's slightly unformed vision for the piece, he was rethinking aspects of the movements during the first performances. Initially, the work was to have been called *Common Ground*, and the individual sections 'Separations', 'Transition', and 'Confirmation', the final version being arrived at after a few early performances. The quotes in the programme were not, with hindsight, particularly helpful, and seemed to belong to an earlier period of dance. Few, if any, works from the 1980s quoted from the Greek, and Cohan's use of them does seem to indicate a sense of insecurity in the work as whole. Looking back, Cohan sees the dance as 'A bit of a mess; but it was a good idea'. John Percival felt he had to tell his readers that 'I had not the faintest idea what Cohan is driving at', and to ask, 'How can so well-read and intelligent a man make his work so unintelligible?'[299] But at the time, it proved popular, and even Alastair Macaulay, writing in his best exasperated style in the *Dancing Times*, after bizarrely disparaging the work by comparing it to Balanchine's *Agon*, had to acknowledge it 'proved to be a huge success with the audience'.[300]

This was only the third time he had used baroque music, and he found the *Brandenburg Concerto* particularly difficult to work with, its rhythmical intricacies and heavily contrapuntal lines proving difficult to align with the movement. The chaconne, however, captivated him, and he would return to it again in a work for the Batsheva Company the following year.

In Israel, Cohan was instrumental in setting up Shades of Dance, a series of workshops which would run every two years for the purpose of encouraging Israeli choreography. In this, he was happy to be reunited with his old student Elida Gera (she would also make the costumes for his chaconne piece), who took charge of the day-to-day matters, with Cohan in the background offering his support and advice. It was an enormously successful venture which discovered and nurtured a whole new generation of choreographers, including Yossi Tamim, Siki Kol, Alice Dor-Cohen, Tamar Ben-Ami, Liat Dror, and Nir Ben-Gal. The latter two choreographers so impressed Cohan that he would, few years later, invite them to make a very successful work (*Rikud*) for LCDT.

After Leeds, most of the spring and summer were taken up with international touring. A visit to Barcelona was almost cancelled as Montserrat Caballé, a daughter of Catalunya, wanted the theatre for her birthday. Only after the company agreed to build their visit around Señora Caballé's celebrations did it go ahead. Returning to London, the summer season at Sadler's Wells had disappointing audiences, as there had been a surfeit of dance in the capital which had emptied wallets and satiated appetites. The Cuban National Ballet had just completed a visit, and both the Royal Ballet and the Moscow Classical Ballet were performing at the same time.

From London, the company went to Scandinavia and then on to America for two very high-profile engagements. One was a return to the American Dance Festival, which was celebrating its fiftieth anniversary, and where they were once again well received, and the other was to the Olympic Games held that year in Los Angeles. As representatives of British dance, the company wanted the Olympic performances to be of the highest standard, but disaster struck during a performance of *Class*, when one of the American technicians pressed the wrong button on the tape machine (even an event as high profile as this did not warrant, at least for a contemporary company, live music) nearly ten minutes before the end, and the curtain had to be brought down on a bemused audience and upset and angry dancers. While rehearsing in Los Angeles, Cohan was surprised by a visit by Dora Saunders, who he had not seen in thirty-five years, and who was now living in Claremont fifty miles east of the city. The years had not diminished the affection between the two, and Cohan surprised everyone by leaving the rehearsal to have dinner with his old friend who had given him his first breaks as a choreographer.

Back home, Cohan created a new work called *Skyward*, to a piano quintet entitled *Clouds* by the company pianist Eleanor Alberga, who was slowly developing a reputation as a composer, having successfully written the music for Jayne Lee's 1983 work *Spinnaker*. The dance was a joyous piece of pure movement based on the flight of the common skylark (at its first performance it was known as *Skylark*), a bird that has inspired many poets, artists, and composers over the centuries. The work was not overly well received by the critics and even Noel Goodwin, often a staunch supporter of Cohan and his company, found the dance 'concerned with nearly anonymous movement' that saw the company engaged in 'a contrivance of dancing which only intermittently gave the dancers a chance to shine'.[301] Unusually Chiesa's costume designs were criticised as 'more an encumbrance than an asset' and his set, a suspended metal rectangle which at one point was tilted so that it obscured the dancers' faces for six or seven minutes, infuriated many.

1985 saw LCDT and the Trust in general once again in severe financial difficulties, and for the *Financial Times* Robin Howard wrote a frighteningly honest appraisal of the company and its work, in which he questioned the company's existence. The problem, as he laid out, was twofold, on one side they did not have enough money to really invest in creativity, and on the other the Arts Council insisted they do so much touring – over thirty-six weeks – that they did not have time to breathe, take stock, and develop new work. Of Cohan, he wrote:

> We cannot give Bob Cohan, whose immense abilities made the company and the school, the breathing space his gifts merit. Choreographers in other companies can have months in which to prepare new work; Bob has half a day for six weeks, if he is lucky, during which time he is also teaching, attending committee meetings, advising all and sundry who make demands upon his time. We cannot give him the life that is essential if he is to remain the choreographer he has proved he truly is under easier circumstances.[302]

It is clear from Howard's comments that most of the changes to his working life that Cohan had hoped for when he reduced his commitment to LCDT had not occurred, and the many considerations that had nothing to do with art still bedevilled him. He continued to make decisions about who danced, who should choreograph, who needed encouragement, whether music rights were affordable, etc. The problems of selecting repertoire that satisfied the needs of the dancers, the theatres, and the funders were almost insurmountable. The Arts Council constantly berated them for not doing enough challenging work, yet if they did do challenging work, then the theatres complained that no one wanted to see it. Yet, the theatres also complained if they brought back popular repertoire. Generally, if works were successful or semi-successful, Cohan would keep them for a year, and then drop them and bring them back; but even then, theatres would complain. This is of course in complete contrast to ballet, whose bread and butter is the standard popular repertoire; no one would ever suggest that a major ballet company should drop *Swan Lake* for a few years.

But there is here, strangely, a ballet link. In an interview Cohan gave to Chris de Marigny, the editor of *Dance Theatre Journal*, in 1985, his frustrations are almost exactly the same as those expressed by Dame Ninette de Valois in her responses to criticisms of Sadler's Wells Ballet published in the *Dancing Times* in 1955. There, she responded in her typically forthright manner to complaints about: touring – too much; creation of new works – not enough time, lack of rehearsal time, see touring. To de Marigny, Cohan said:

> We are in a very interesting, difficult and unusual situation. We are a contemporary dance company – it says London Contemporary Dance Theatre – and we are asked to fill Birmingham Hippodrome, Bristol Hippodrome, Leeds… We are asked to fill big places on tour with contemporary dance and music. We are also asked to go to other smaller venues, like Mold and Warwick for example.
>
> We have been coping with this as best we can, but I don't see the logic of it. Speaking in terms of a contemporary company, it would be like saying Stockhausen's opera, *Donnerstag* [*aus Licht*], after it has done its five performances at Covent Garden should go and perform five nights in Manchester, five nights in Liverpool, five nights in Glasgow et cetera. They don't do that. It's too experimental a piece. People don't come. If they did come they would leave.[303]

Cohan was frustrated by the Arts Council policy of 'one size fits all'. He firmly believes in experimentation, but that work should take place in a studio and be shown to interested parties who give feedback on it. Then there is small-scale dance, again challenging in outlook but for the cognoscenti, but which is never going to have a large audience. Then middle scale then large scale, each should be in an appropriately sized theatre, for an appropriate audience. The problem with the Arts Council was that they wanted LCDT to present challenging works in large-scale theatres, which would be half full, and then they and the theatre managers would complain that the company had no audience.

He continued to de Marigny: 'The Arts Council's middle name now is 'accessible'. That's all it says to us all the time, that we have to be accessible. But we are not London Accessible Dance Theatre.' This conundrum is a circle that the Arts Council has never squared. They want work to be challenging to move forward the art form and yet at the same time want large audiences so that they can justify spending public money. In 1986, Robert North was dismissed from Ballet Rambert because, under his direction, the work was not seen as challenging enough, even though it brought in the public. He was replaced by Richard Alston, who was dismissed in 1991 because, under his direction, the challenging works did not bring in the public. In the 2010s, the question of challenging or accessible is still a problem for the Arts Council and its clients.

Developing new work going into challenging new directions does not just happen, it takes time, and in his interview, Cohan highlighted a further problem for himself and his company, that of research and development:

> We have reached the point where we can't afford to experiment. It's one of the burning issues as far as I am concerned. Any business our size would put something between 10 and 20 per cent of their budget on research and development. Never have we been allowed by the financial constraints to put even 1 per cent on research and development.

And so the conundrum continued. Cohan had trained extraordinary dancers whose abilities far outstripped the choreographers they worked with. This was a situation he had himself envisaged, and yet there was no time to develop the choreographers. In the early days of LCDT, most of the dancers tried their hand at choreography; the works would be tried once or twice, and then if not successful dropped. By the 1980s, LCDT was a flagship company and trying out work in the full glare of publicity was not an option. The dancers trained every day in Cohan technique, and yet as choreographers they had only occasionally a few brief weeks to experiment choreographically. There is a great difference between making work for a small workshop showing to interested parties, to making work to be danced by a major company, in the company of work by major choreographers, in major theatres. The emphasis at the time was very firmly on audience development and not artist development.

Indeed in 1985, the middle years of the Thatcher government, it seemed highly likely that money to fund the arts would be cut further. In that year, the Arts Council published a slim (twelve pages) glossy brochure entitled curiously *A Great British Success Story: An Invitation to the Nation to Invest in the Arts*. It discussed how the arts are the cornerstone of a civilised country, 'the lifeblood of a nation', and then went on to justify public funding by noting how much money was recouped in taxes, employment, and through tourism. But fundamentally, it was a begging letter: 'We are asking the nation to invest in this well-proved 'product'; to provide the cash to ensure that past glories do not become insubstantial memories, and that present achievements can be built upon for even greater returns in the future'.[304] Social historian Arthur Marwick has noted that before Thatcher, ' "public investment" meant government investment', but under Thatcher 'the phrase has a new meaning: "investment by the public" (rich ones) usually'.[305] Again, the investment in the arts by private individuals has been something Britain has struggled with. In the USA, which has minimal government funding of the arts, private individuals give generously, but this is because the donations can be heavily offset against tax demands. In the UK under Thatcher, this document suggested private individuals should give money as well as pay tax. It did not happen and would not happen, but the document shows how desperate, under Government instructions, were the Arts Council to draw in more money to support its operations. The document further muddied the waters by talking about the 'arts industry' which it defined as 'embracing high and low culture and all structures and activities relating thereto'.[306]

It was a frustrating scenario all around, and Howard in his article warned that the company was in danger of dying, that not just LCDT but 'companies like ourselves are fighting for… survival'. They would not give up without a fight and, on 11 July, LCDT held a fundraising gala at the Royal Opera House. Held in the presence of Prince Andrew, a last-minute replacement for Prince Michael of Kent, it was a glamorous affair, introduced in her engagingly eccentric English by Natalia Makarova, who presented the Alvin Ailey American Dance Theater, in Billy Wilson's Concerto in F, with Eleanor Alberga as soloist in the Gershwin's Concerto in F for piano accompanied by the Royal Opera Orchestra. The New York City Breakers introduced the latest moves from the Big Apple. New solos by Kenneth MacMillan were danced by Linda Gibbs, Ross McKim, and Christopher Bannerman, the dancers having worked with him on his choreography for Wagner's *Tannhäuser* (Howard's suggestion that he make a work for the company came to nothing). And Zizi Jeanmaire danced with Luigi Bonino in a flamboyant cabaret number by her husband Roland Petit. The whole evening rounded off with a brilliant performance of *Class*, which as ever had the audience cheering before it ended.

Cohan spent much of the year before and after the gala on choreographic matters. Between 27 May and 22 June, he had been at Simon Fraser University in Vancouver, teaching on another of the Canadian Choreographic Seminars. Then, immediately after the gala, Cohan oversaw the company's choreographic workshops. Although not open to the public, they produced eleven works by company members, and proved the company had no intention of dying. He then moved on to lead his fourth Gulbenkian course which still had the possibility to change the participants' lives. LCDT dancer Jonathan Lunn as a student had been encouraged in choreographing by Nina Fonaroff, and had had some success in workshop performances by the company. He participated in the 1985 course and, in the exercise in which the choreographers had to make a solo on themselves which expressed 'what dance means to you', he found himself paired with a jazz based composer with whom he had little affinity. The piece they made ended up being two solos; Lunn entered the stage and stood with his back to the audience, the composer played his music and when he had finished, Lunn began dancing. For some reason, it worked, and at the end not only the audience but Lunn were in tears. He had created something deeply emotional, personal, and human which touched everyone. This was a breakthrough work for him, and Cohan encouraged him, telling him this was the type of work he should be making. And he did. The following year, the beautifully observed *Hang Up* with text by Anthony Minghella, would be taken into the LCDT repertory and Lunn continued to develop the deeply personal style 'discovered' on the course.

When he had announced his retirement, Cohan had indicated that he would like to write a book on choreography, a project that has still not been realised. But in 1985, he agreed to act as editor of a new journal called *Choreography and Dance: An International Journal*, to be published by Harwood Academic Publishers. The journal would be 'analytical, critical and educational, and it will provide a forum where choreographic ideas can be exchanged and discussed'.[307] His co-editor, initially, was to be Alastair Macaulay, an interesting pairing as Macaulay had never shown any particular interest in Cohan's own work. Over the years, the publication produced invaluable issues on a wide range of topics from classical modern dance to more experimental work.

At the same time as the journal began, Cohan was working in every spare moment on *The Dance Workshop*. This had been commissioned by Gaia Books, a company specialising in literature concerning mind, body, and spirit, and was concerned not with choreography but technique. In layout, the book was similar to *Modern Dance Techniques and Training* written in 1949 by Gertrude Schurr and Rachel Yocum, which documented a version of Graham's technique and philosophy. So in his book, Cohan documented his developments in technique and dancing in general. Filled with beautiful illustrative photographs of LCDT dancers by Fausto Dorelli and line drawings by Peter Mennim, and with an introduction written by Wayne Sleep, it presented a beginner's guide to contemporary dance and, for popularity's sake, a section on jazz.

The line drawings broke down each exercise into its component parts, and with brief, careful explanations, the reader was led through the movement sequences. In a way, it can be seen as a forerunner of the current spate of books and DVDs produced by the New York City Ballet and Ailey Company amongst others, in which technical classroom exercises are presented as a way – as the dust jacket said – to 'Achieve suppleness and agility', or to 'Develop a fit and beautiful body', or to just 'Experience the joy of movement'. The current books of course have the benefit of recorded material against which the reader can judge themselves, not so in Cohan's book, where the student must interpret the diagrams and the photographs of beautiful professionals in staged poses. It was a curious outlet for Cohan's writing talents, introducing as it does many of the basic Cohan/Graham technical exercises and Cohan's philosophy on dance. Had another publisher taken it on and produced it in another format, it could have become a respected textbook. As it is, it exists as a fascinating curiosity, a beautifully written document of a style of dance that was already on the wane by the time it appeared.

In the latter half of 1985, Cohan was working with LCDT on a major new work for television. *Mass for Man* was the BBC's first dance commission in ten years and was first shown on BBC2 on 30 November. Directed by Bob Lockyer, it had a new score by Geoffrey Burgon; a special sculpture designed by Barbara Gosnold had been made by Philip King, while Glenn Carwithen created the series of graphic images based on archival film and photographic material.

The idea for the dance came to Cohan from 'Looking at the news every night with films of starving children, earthquakes, and the possibility of nuclear war; the problems of the world seemed beyond our control'. As a result, he felt that a ritualistic work was needed: 'we all need a Mass, because there is a great deal that is happening in the world that is out of control and out of our control.'

In 1980s Britain, there were few, if any, choreographers who concerned themselves with ritual as a means of bringing a community together, but to Cohan, who had grown up immersed in the work of Joseph Campbell, it seemed a natural route to follow. For Campbell, the purpose of a ritual is 'to focus your mind on the implications of what you are doing.... And so we should realise that this event here and now: our coming together to help each other in the realisation is a beautiful, beautiful ritual.'[308]

Cohan explained his decision to return to the form of the Christian mass, at the introduction to the broadcast of the dance: 'I think I have done religious works because I am basically a religious person. Now, I never say I am a religious person, but I have to face the fact that if I do one religious work after another, then it must be interesting to me in some way.' He then went on to give the clearest indication of the influence of Gurdjieff on his thinking, and how much Gurdjieff's work had meant to a man who had served in a world war:

> I do believe in working on one's self in the religious sense to be a better man. The very simple fact, that if every single man in the world was a better man today, then we would have no problems like war. If each person was better, had cleaned war out of themselves, had cleaned aggression, had overcome aggression in themselves, then we would have no war. So in a sense, I do believe that we should work on ourselves all the time. I do dances about that because that subject fascinates me, I try not to say I am a teacher or a preacher, but that is what fascinates me and that is why I do it.

Like all rituals, Cohan's *Mass* is beautifully and formally organised, nothing is out of place. In this, he was helped enormously by the work of his collaborators. For him, the set was perfect as it 'looked like the bones of a beached whale, the bones of a cathedral on a beach. It had a very strong sense of place. This was a place where a ritual could take place.' Looking at once both contemporary and ancient, its angles and lines proved the perfect landscape in which Cohan could place his dancers. Likewise, Burgon's score managed to conjure a world of mythic rites and modern menace. Scored for male voices, percussion, including the inside of a piano, bass drum, many smaller drums and four trombones, the score is a model of economy and colourful orchestration. Having worked with Cohan before, Burgon found his work 'very immediate, very emotional' and the collaboration 'not so difficult', and that a lot of it happened unconsciously.

The architecture of the design and the form of the music helped shape the dance, but even more important was his collaboration with Bob Lockyer. The two had known each other for many years, and it was largely through Lockyer that the commission had come about. They worked together closely on the production, and between them 'every angle for the dance was worked out'. As Cohan explained to viewers,

> I wanted to make something that would only work on television; that I couldn't do on the stage. People sometimes worry when they see legs and arms cut off in the televising of a staged ballet, as they long to see what the rest of the body is doing. I have to make the viewer realise that I want to be selective. I have choreographed every move expressively for the television camera, and if I only show a face or hands, then that is what I want the viewer to see. What I tried to do was to show you only feet, but to tell you at the same time that nothing was happening but only feet, so you would be content to look at just feet, or look at just a face, or look at just arms.

In addition to this, he used the technological advances that had appeared since the ill-fated production of *Job* to have 'magic entrances and exits, people appearing and disappearing. You cannot have that on stage.'

Some of the most effective technical work appeared in the antiphons, the purely instrumental sections that appeared between each choral section of the rite. Here, he used archival photographic images of war and natural disasters, including famine and earthquakes, 'to point those up as reasons why we need catharsis at this time'. Particularly effective is one where the camera breaks through outstretched arms and hands to settle on Celia Hulton's open palm, on which appears the mushroom cloud of a nuclear explosion.

Early on, Cohan had had to 'find a reason for the whole *Mass* itself, for the whole production when I had to find a point of catharsis. A point where we could identify, all of us, everybody, not just me and not just the dancers, but everyone watching it identify.'[309] This problem was taken out of his hands when Siobhan Davies, who was nearing the end of her dancing career with LCDT, but who he wanted very much to be in the piece, became pregnant. By the time it came to shoot the work, she had given birth to the baby, and 'I said, well, this is the answer and it's very logical and God answered me, I didn't have to answer it myself. She produced a beautiful child who will now be in the *Mass*.' He was at pains to point out that 'I wasn't trying to be sacrilegious in the sense of showing Jesus. I was trying to show the belief we all have that life itself is precious, and that each new life is precious, and life goes on through that.'

The work is a hugely successful piece of dance for the camera. Like Merce Cunningham's collaborations with Charles Atlas, every technical nuance is beautifully observed. The choreography is some of the best of his later years, exquisitely shaped group work, keenly observed solos, and sensitive partnering. As he would tell *Classical Music Magazine*, 'You can't be avant-garde all your life. That would be a false state not honest to yourself.... you are avant-garde only until your art takes root. You have certain values and principles you apply to your work.'[310] The vocabulary here, therefore, is his own beautifully honed development of Graham, danced to perfection by dancers he had trained and who he knew intimately. But for all of its technical perfection, it does suffer from a certain coldness, perhaps coming from, as Walter Terry had noted over twenty-five years previously, the form used. Then, as in this work, Cohan allowed the formalisation of the ritual to outweigh the humanity he wanted to express. The humanity almost comes through when Davies and her baby appear at the end of the work, but to quote Terry, 'He comes close to it but not enough.'[311]

After a year's break from new stage work for the company, Cohan produced three in 1986. All were ambitious in scope and all explored, perhaps in line with the current social climate and the state of Cohan's mind, the darker side of the human psyche. The first of the three which were first shown in Eastbourne on 14 February was called *Slow Dance on a Burial Ground*, which the programme note said 'is set on an ancient hallowed ground where the image of death reigns'. Its creation was influenced by three factors: Stephen Montague's music, Cohan's memory of ancient burial grounds, and a piece of fabric. When he first heard the music, Cohan's memory was drawn back to the company tour of South America in 1975. There, in Peru, he had seen ancient burial grounds with skeletal arms and legs protruding from the earth; these powerful images had stuck with him throughout the years. He heard the music without knowing its title, and was surprised that he had put the music and image together in his head.

The third factor in the dance was a vast piece of fabric which the female figure of death wears and which covered the whole stage. The cloth had holes in it through which could be seen the arms and legs of her prey, a clear reference to the Peruvian burial grounds. This was similar to the use of the cloth in *Chamber Dances*, which he felt he had underdeveloped.

Cohan has said that if he could, he would have had his dancers dance naked because they had worked so hard on developing their extraordinary bodies; 'Why would I cover them up?' This dance was, it would appear, the only time when it was actively mooted, if not put into practice. Kenneth Tharp recalls some interesting rehearsals, when it looked as though Cohan was going to ask for some nudity, but however dedicated his dancers were to him, this was not something they were keen on doing, and they appeared clothed.

With hindsight, Cohan can look back and ask, 'How could anyone want to see a dance called *Slow Dance on a Burial Ground*!' At the time the question was asked by a councillor in Hull, who was quoted in a local paper as saying 'No wonder no one goes to theatre when they have titles like *Slow Dance on a Burial Ground*.'

A curiously long set of 'notes' were released with the work, and showed how distant was Cohan's aesthetic from current trends in British dance. The following is only an extract:

> In the dance Cohan uses a device that he has worked on before in another dance. Most artists through the ages have felt justified in experimenting with a recurring image or set of ideas in a whole set of works. In dance, however, there has been a tendency to attempt something totally new with each new work. Nevertheless, originality, so sought after in art, does not lie in specific devices but in the context of the images. In other words, it is what happens before and after the event that makes it significant or not, original or banal.

Although it had some striking images and long programme notes, it was swiftly dropped from the repertory.

In May, Cohan led his company in a week of choreographic sessions and lecture-demonstrations at the Birmingham Hippodrome. Over the years, LCDT had developed an unrivalled educational programme, and here company members and musicians worked with local community groups on creative projects, which were presented to the public at the end of the week. In addition, the final day included an open forum in which staff from all areas of the company's work answered questions on any aspect of their work.

These educational sessions had been either extremely cheap or free to participants, and in June the company continued its efforts to reach new audiences at affordable prices by performing in a former circus tent in Norfolk Park, Sheffield. The Big Top, as it was known, had in previous years been used by Rambert and the Royal Ballet with great success, providing as it did a large stage and the possibility of charging markedly lower prices than a conventional theatre, thereby opening up the world of contemporary dance to those who might otherwise not have ventured into a conventional venue.

The summer saw the company in the Tivoli Gardens in Copenhagen, where a bit of fun on Cohan's part helped avert a possible disaster for the coming tour, as Jane Ward, then company administrator, remembers:

> Tivoli has a funfair and Bob said he wanted to go on the big ride (a sort of big dipper) and I went with him. We laughed tears down our faces as we were jolted from side to side and up and down, while also trying to avoid being seen by the Tivoli chief executive (a rather distinguished and charming man who

always wore a very smart suit). The dancers were quite impressed that we'd been on a ride but then it turned out I'd put my spine out with the jolting and they were all banned from going on it themselves.

Spinal problems would have spelt disaster for the company, who in August went to Italy where they premiered Cohan's second piece of the year, *Video Life*. This was a forty-minute work commissioned by the Meeting for Friendship among Peoples Association in Rimini, and aimed to show how the horror seen on television can lead to violence in real life. In a 1982 interview with Canadian critic Max Wyman, Cohan explained that he would like to make a dance like the dance of the Navajos that brings health to all, further explaining that 'Dance can excite you to war. It should be able to excite you to peace. It would be nice to do. I can't find quite the images.' He seems to have found the images in this work, and in the programme note, he questioned if 'It is even possible that we could ourselves be changed by what we see and slowly change into victims of violence ourselves.' And he wanted the dance to act as a warning that we should recognise the danger while still affirming the positive in life.

It was a complex work including an elaborate set of white poles by Chiesa and another challenging score by Barry Guy for live double bass and pre-recorded tape. Guy based the music on a ground bass from Monteverdi's *Vespers of 1610*, the formal structure of this masterpiece of Western art seeming to ground the work in some higher level of humanity. In addition, Darshan Singh Bhuller wielded a video camera in imitation of the invasive nature of television cameramen to catch the expressions and movements of the dancers, which were mixed into the television screens showing images of famine, war, and violence. Critics, while acknowledging that Cohan had created some 'fiercely striking dance', generally found the work either 'too long or confused',[312] and that, despite its 'convincing atmosphere of frenzied angst',[313] it remained 'largely unconvincing'.[314] For the performers, it was a challenging and moving experience, and all found themselves emotionally and physically drained at the end of performances.

Cohan's final work of the year, first shown as part of the Edinburgh Festival almost, brought his career full circle, as the original stimulus for *Interrogations* was Hamlet's famous soliloquy beginning 'To be or not to be...', which had inspired his first piece thirty-five years previously. Here, though the work did not represent a purely dance translation of the speech, the words provided the basis of the action, which was in the form of a journey which took place as it might in a dream. In the dream world, there were chance encounters, with a recurring influence being the striving for some unobtainable goal. Similarly, the characters within the dream were not directly drawn from Shakespeare, but could possibly be seen as archetypes.

The dance boasted a spectacularly dramatic set by António Lagarto, in which huge sheets of industrial metal gave the impression of some gigantic battleship; to one side were a cypress tree, a tower of scaffolding, and a crane which projected into a darkly menacing sky. The suggestively fascist costumes for the Keepers, who seemed to oppress the Traveller, the Guardian, and the Dream Lovers, rounded off what was a bleak landscape. Adding to this oppressive atmosphere was a chair hoisted to the sky at the beginning of the dance by the Keepers and suspended by a chain and a sort of cloth tie that looked for all the world like the death's head from *El Penitente*. The score, by Barrington Pheloung, offered a compelling dialogue between a computer track and live musicians and served to underline the shifting tensions of the dance.

Through this bleak landscape journeyed Darshan Singh Bhuller, who gave a very powerful performance as the Traveller who meets both good and evil characters and is forced into a series of choices, but is sustained by brief glimpses of a faceless elusive dream, of two lovers. Apart from the malevolent militaristic Keepers, other key figures in his harassed journey and eventual freedom were an androgynous Guardian played by Patrick Harding-Irmer in crocheted frock and flying coattails and a mantis-like woman played by another company veteran, Anca Frankenhauser, whose snood and long skirt looked like a period riding apparel seen through a Hollywood lens.

Much of the movement had a sinister, driven feel to it; for all of her elegant clothing, the woman had a clawing, seething angularity, while Bhuller's character put up a generally frenetic resistance to the grey stumbling lumps that were his Keepers. But there were moments of contrast, such as the *Nympheas*-like lyricism of the lovers, whose pink-hewed costumes likewise provided the only contrast to the metal grey and black of the rest of the work. The work would be seen as one of Cohan's most powerful later pieces, with Dick Godfrey in the *Newcastle Journal* finding it 'a potent allegorical vision of a man's journey through a mystical land of sky scraping cranes and mirrored walls', while Alan Hulme in the *Manchester Evening News* thought it 'dramatic and powerful with startling images'.[315]

However, of the more prominent critics, Clement Crips wrote:

> Cohan's strong sense of theatre drives the action along and, I imagine, carries the audience with it, until the finale amid strobe lighting when Mr Bhuller hangs and swings from a vast white cloth. Various characters, hideously garbed, impinge upon Mr Bhuller's nightmare, chief and most impressive among them Patrick Harding-Irmer as a Guardian, who may be Hamlet's father. I wish I felt though, that as with the better nightmares, there was some relevant matter to be gleaned from its inconsequentialities.[316]

Alastair Macaulay loathed the dance, finding it a work 'overpowered by everything except dancing', and asked his readers: 'can one describe a work like this as anything other than pretentious and pseudo-intellectual?' He went even further, stating, 'I am one of the many who don't think that he has made any work of real significance in the Eighties.'[317] Of course, he did not go on to elaborate on what he thought which works from the 1980s were significant, although he did regret the loss of Siobhan Davies who was leaving LCDT to take up a Fulbright Scholarship.

In spite of the growing criticisms, 1987 saw the Contemporary Dance Trust celebrating its twenty-first anniversary, and Cohan was in demand for the celebrations. The year was marked by a wide-ranging series of performances and celebratory events. Mary Clarke, Clement Crisp, and Anthony Crickmay produced a magnificent book, called, optimistically with hindsight, *London Contemporary Dance Theatre: The First Twenty-One Years*. The title, notwithstanding the book, focussed not only on LCDT but on the whole working of the Trust, covering the school, the choreographers, the teachers, the personalities, and dancers involved. In the light of events that followed in a few short years, it was an invaluable document of the work of the Trust and provided in a changing world a timely reminder of just exactly how much the dance world owed to Cohan and Howard. As Clarke and Crisp wrote, 'It is no exaggeration to say that the Contemporary Dance Trust, as umbrella for a school, a teaching system, a performing troupe, a manner of creativity, had altered the way a nation thought about dance and had extended its influence to Europe.'[318]

On 26 March 1987, Cohan was at the Southbank Centre in London, giving a talk on 'Ideas for Dance' as part of Articulations. This was a series of lectures by leading figures in the arts, including director Elijah Moshinsky on opera, and ballet dancer Peter Schaufuss on *The Nutcracker*. To a large audience, and with the aid of slides, Cohan covered a range of topics including creativity, choreography, and performance.

Back home in France, although he did not know it at the time, Cohan had his last meeting with Martha Graham. He had always been on friendly terms with her, but her circumstances in her later years meant that for him, as for most of her old friends, he saw very little of her. Although shrunken in old age and crippled with arthritis, Graham in her nineties was still choreographing and touring with her company, and when Cohan saw the company was to perform in Avignon, near his home, he decided to visit. Going backstage after the performance, he forced his way past Ron Protas, who tried to block his way to Graham. When he got close, she peered up at him and said, 'Bob! You've gotten older', to which he replied, 'We all have Martha, we all have.'

Graham died in 1991, active to the last, having lived to see her final complete ballet, *Maple Leaf Rag*, gain ecstatic reviews from the New York press. No one in dance had had a career as long as hers, spanning as it did almost the whole of the twentieth century. She was at first a radical outsider, then the height of fashion, then a cliché, but by the end, she had transcended all labels to become an icon of modern art. Late in her life, she was heard to compare herself to Hans Christian Andersen's Ugly Duckling, who stays so long in the water his feet are frozen in the winter ice and he is unable to escape. There are some who questioned if Cohan had not stayed too long at LCDT.

The arrangement by which he was away for a considerable part of the year was not a happy one. Although Howard had initially encouraged Cohan to take on the role with the Batsheva Company, he had quickly realised it was a mistake and had even offered Cohan money to give it up. This was something Cohan was unable or unwilling to do. The result was similar to what had occurred in the very early days of the company and had made Cohan move to the UK. When he was in residence, the company were energised, but when he was away a sort of inertia set in. The teaching of company class had, after some false starts with dancers from the current Graham Company, largely been handed over to the Swedish teacher Christel Wallin. Her precise approach to the work was as welcome as it was unusual for products of the Graham School in the 1980s, but she was not Cohan.

The ambitious plan to enrich the company's repertory by bringing in outside choreographers was snagged on the horns of limited finance. Paul Taylor's work was always welcome when they could afford it, but a number of choices did seem downright odd. Neither Rosalind Newman's nor Daniel Larrieu's work sat easily on the dancers. After years of refusing, Jerome Robbins allowed LCDT a licence to dance his ballet *Moves*. Already nearly 30 years old and danced in silence it proved a challenge to audience and dancers alike. Howard was particularly exasperated by Cohan's decision, in 1987, to bring in the young American Daniel Ezralow, who made the vampire-inspired dance *Irma Vep*. Howard found the work without artistic merit, and even questioned Mop Eager as to whether or not Cohan had brought him in because he was in love with him. The backbone of the company repertory was still Cohan's old work, with most new choreography coming from Siobhan Davies, Christopher Bannerman, and occasionally Jonathan Lunn, all three of whom had consciously rejected the house style in favour of a cool sense of detachment. Bannerman in particular fared poorly at the hands of the critics, with Alastair Macaulay finding him amongst 'the most anonymous of all'[319] current dance makers. Article headers such as Nadine Meisner's 'In Search of a Choreographer' in *Dance and Dancers* became more and more frequent.

To celebrate LCDT's anniversary, and at the suggestion of Jack Phipps from the Arts Council, who had perceived a need for full-evening works and not triple or double bills, Cohan directed an evening-length work entitled *Phantasmagoria*. As he explains,

> A Phantasmagoria was on some of the very old posters I used to see framed in many of the theatres we went to. It must have been a catch-all name given to a series of magic or eccentric acts put together in the late 1800s or early 1900s. I thought to do the same thing with choreography by different company members and myself.

The work was choreographed by Cohan, Tom Jobe, and Darshan Singh

Bhuller who, much to Howard's relief, replaced Danny Ezralow. Cohan made part one which concerned itself mainly with Greek mythology, while Singh Bhuller made the 'Smouldering Suit' section. For a work aimed at attracting a younger audience it was full of classical references, at least in part one, at a time when classical studies had long since been dropped from the school curriculum. But spectacle, not education, was the main purpose of the dance, and it certainly did not disappoint. Like its models, Cohan's staged extravaganza did not tell a story, rather it proceeded in a series of fantastic episodes, with a tenuous link in the theme of 'heroes'.

In part one, Pandora released a four-legged man on the world. This was followed by 'Slaying the Monster', in which Perseus, an appropriately athletic Michael Small, stole the seeing eye from the Graeae and killed Medusa, a scene which always received whoops from the younger audience members. In 'Web', Patrick Harding-Irmer was ingeniously and frighteningly caught in a gigantic spider's snare. In 'Camouflage', the dancers, dressed in zebra-like stripes, danced in front of a similar background, appearing and disappearing, and giving the effect of a Bridget Riley painting. These were followed by 'Earth Mother', 'Lyric Ode', 'Nymph and Shepherd', 'Smouldering Suit', and 'Spinning Man'. 'Smouldering Suit', by Singh Bhuller, was particularly effective, as Kenneth Tharp wrestled with a suit which Clement Crisp memorably described as 'having incendiary tendencies'.[320] Part one ended with Harding-Irmer inside a spinning astrolabe-like device, but not before the dancers had, inexplicably, participated in an American football game with their bare buttocks exposed for all to see. If Michael Clark could do it, why not LCDT?

Part two was by Tom Jobe, who had long since left the company to dance in commercial theatre. Cohan remembers that 'Tom wanted to choreograph and I said, 'Have a go.' His ideas were very showbiz, but they were too surreal for showbiz at that time. I thought there would be a market. I liked him and I liked the way he thought I didn't always like his camp pop attitude but when he was serious about it, it worked.' Jobe's contribution to *Phantasmagoria* did, however, veer to the camp, being a series of dances based on dead divas and gay icons:

> Part 2: Valley of the shades: Gala in the Elysian Fields, Spring to the memory of Michael Staniforth, Shade of Patsy Cline, To the memory of her, Kick Line One Eighty Seven, To the memory of Michael Bennett, Shade of Edith Piaf, To her memory, Concita Consuela de la Canria Canesta Canabe, Lio Palmeri, Shade of Maria Callas, Finale.

Like many artistic endeavours in the 1980s, it suffered by being over the top and somewhat tasteless. But as Mary Clarke observed, while it was not a masterpiece, 'the company disport themselves with relish, as if enjoying their birthday party production and all the choreographers have given them rewarding, dramatic material'.[321] And it was popular with the public, with John Percival noting, 'To judge by the enthusiastic whistling and shouting from the back of the Hippodrome Theatre at its first performance, Robert Cohan has hit the right note at least for young audiences.'[322] While Clement Crisp had to admit, 'It is, I suspect, an evening for a young audience, eager to be dazzled by such shenanigans, as well as by LCDT's magnificent dancers. They will not be disappointed[323].'

The audiences may have liked the work, but Robin Howard was not taken with it and at the premiere, Mop Eager recalls having to restrain him from using his fists to beat out a frustrated tattoo on his metal legs, saying, 'Why does he have to do these big pieces!' The expense of touring the sets by Nadine Baylis, together with the elaborate special effects, saw the work disappear very quickly.

The dance was a perfect symbol of the problems the Arts Council faced in the late 1980s: it was indeed popular with audiences and did put 'bums on seats', but it did not, as critics noted, advance the frontiers of contemporary dance, which was why the company had originally been set up. Some writers compared it to *Stages*, which was an evening-length work and had many special effects, but when that work was presented in 1971, it was contemporary, it was cutting edge. The world of theatre in England and in particular dance had moved on considerably since then, and 'serious' was just that 'serious'. It was not about glitzy special effects and spectacle, and certainly not camp homages. As David Dougill wrote, 'The *Phantasmagoria*, in what is for the company a very different vein, should augur well for the present tour, even if the production leaves longer-term problems unsolved.'[324] The problem was, as Dougill noted in his article, where should LCDT go from here? A question that would be asked more and more once the smoke from the birthday candles had disappeared.

Clement Crisp would later write of this period that he felt in Robin Howard 'a sense of resignation in the face of an uncertain future';[325] there was certainly tension. By the late 1980s, Robin Howard had become increasingly at odds with the Board of the Trust he had created. In the early days, it was peopled with artists and creative people, including Sir Henry Moore and Sir John Gielgud, but by the late 1980s, there were more businessmen and women involved. These people had a more corporate view of business, which was well in line with these high days of Thatcherite Britain. This was not Howard. His lengthy heart-on-the-sleeve article for the *Financial Times* in 1985, exposing for all to see the problems besetting the Trust, was not the sort of thing that leaders of business did. Dirty washing was not laundered in public but behind the sealed doors of the boardroom. Even the members of the Trust found him difficult to deal with; he had based the foundation of his work on 'love', and he did love what he did, but when he cried, as he did sometimes in meetings, the businessmen simply became embarrassed. He confided to Eager that 'he found himself trapped'.

Mop Eager remembers[326] that a British Council employee had noticed something unique about the company, and had put it down to the fact that it was led by two father figures Howard and Cohan, and that it had 'a feeling of family'.

This was something that was clearly out of step with the world that the Arts Council wanted to see, and one phrase that she read in one of their appraisals which the Arts Council 'used in gradually trying to wear us down' was, 'it is time it was not run as if it were a family'. In addition, Howard was not a yes man to the Arts Council, and he was therefore 'not always popular. He would fight for things; he was awkward.' Eager believes there was a 'great deal of jealousy in the outside world towards the company'. Cohan supported this view in an interview in *The Stage*, when he told Katie Philips: 'There was also a feeling that LCDT had gotten out of control – it [the Arts Council] thought that Robin [Howard] was empire building and it wanted to be more in control. We were too successful and took too many jobs away from too many people – it built up a lot of resentment.'[327]

As early as January 1988, Howard had felt an undercurrent of the Board turning against him in his role as Chairman, and by the summer had decided to take matters into his own hands. He placed on the agenda for the September Board 'The Matter of Chairman of the Board'. At the meeting, which took place on 14 September, Howard was asked to leave the room as discussion of his role took place. The outcome of the meeting was predetermined as, before the meeting, Cohan had been shown a list of the names of the Board – a majority – who would vote to remove Howard as Chairman. The employees of the Trust, including Cohan and Eager, were not allowed a vote. Considerable cogitation then took place as to what role, if any, Howard should be offered, and after much soul searching, it was decided that the title of Life President should be offered to him, along with the offer to remain a member of the Board. Howard was then invited back into the room and told he had been sacked (he would always refer to it as such).

He was courteous in his response, declining to accept immediately the offer until he had time to consider it. Eager would later tell Ross McKim 'that Robin was outrageously pushed out', and that the event destroyed him. She was told that he had been ousted because he had no more money to give and had no more use. He was not bankrupt, but all of his artistic treasures and most of his property holdings had gone, his house was mortgaged, and for the first time in his life, he had lately had to draw a salary to live off. Graham's and Cohan's fears for him from years earlier had come true. Cohan was furious at the decision, and the next day called Laurence Isaacson, who had been elected as chair, when his secretary asked, 'Does Mr Isaacson know you?' He hung up, went straight to the estate agent, and put his Muswell Hill house on the market. More importantly, he decided finally, once and for all, that he would retire from LCDT.

Away from the stresses of Britain, Cohan found some diversion in Israel, where again his experience at The Place was put to great use. Since its inception, the Batsheva Company had not had a home to call its own, and for performing used large theatres in Haifa and Tel Aviv, mainly the grand Habima, the 'National Theatre'. This was not a satisfactory situation, and in 1988, Mira Edels found a very old disused building complex, the ruins of the Alliance and Yechieli Schools, in the rundown neighbourhood of south Tel Aviv. Most of it was derelict, although a small hall was in use for Sabbath services.

At first, company manager Bill Strum refused to go into it because it was in such poor condition, but with Cohan and Edels coaxing he did, and they convinced him of the possibilities for the property. Cohan, having developed all technical aspects of The Place, of course had extensive knowledge of what was needed and what could be achieved. These premises required considerably more renovation than had The Place, but Edels knew an engineer, and he and Cohan developed the designs and specifications to transform the buildings. Financial backing was found from the London-based family of Suzanne Dellal, a young woman who had died of a drugs overdose. At first, Strum said no, not wanting the association with a tragic death, but Cohan said yes, and so with the support of the Mayor of Tel Aviv and the Israeli Arts Council, the complex was developed.

It has proven to be a hugely successful venture, home to Batsheva, a complex of offices and the finest dance stage in the Middle East. Yet, there is no mention of Cohan in either its publicity or history. As with so many projects, his enormous amount of work is hidden behind the more publicity-seeking personalities of others.

If Cohan was in need of a pick-me-up, he received it on 8 November, when he was awarded a CBE from Arts Minister Richard Luce. The awarding of honours in the twenty-first century has become more transparent, with application forms available online. In the 1980s, it was a more arcane process, and in this case had been started by Robin Howard, who led a concerted campaign of letter writing to the Government Office, recommending Cohan for some sort of award. There were many supporters from the great and the good of the British arts world – including his old sparring partner Ninette de Valois – who were in agreement with Howard who wrote, 'For over 15 years Robert Cohan has worked untiringly for very little remuneration to establish Contemporary Dance in Britain and to be one of the main leaders of this Country's dance and Ballet 'explosion'. It is hard to think of anyone this century who has contributed more to the artistic life of Britain.'[328]

Cohan's final works for his company were not his happiest creations. LCDT had an agreement with the London Sinfonietta to collaborate on a series of performances at the Queen Elizabeth Hall, London. This should have been a wonderful opportunity for the company to work with a large group of world-class musicians and create dances to music by some leading contemporary composers. The original proposal that the evening should be to specially commissioned music had been very exciting. However, for various reasons, this was not possible, and the orchestra offered instead four pieces already in their repertoire. As the leading performers of contemporary music in the UK, the Sinfonietta's repertoire, to their credit, covered a broad spectrum of music by living composers. Unfortunately, the music that the orchestra chose to offer Cohan – broad as its range was – proved of little interest to any of the choreographers he approached. Initially, Cohan and Siobhan Davies were to have shared the choreography, but after prevaricating for some time, she decided she did not want to work with any of it. Cohan then offered the music to a group of young French choreographers, including Daniel Larrieu and Angelin Preljocaj, and all of them emphatically turned the selected works down. It therefore fell to Cohan to create, in a very limited time, four dances to music which he found at best only vaguely interesting.

In *Metamorphosis*, a solo for Darshan Singh Bhuller, to Britten's *Six Metamorphoses after Ovid*, Cohan chose to look at six different aspects of one man, using the device of removing layers of clothing as if removing layers of emotional protection, and in so doing exposing more and more of the man's personality. In this, he was returning to the world of *Cell*, of twenty years earlier, although the concerns of this dance were very different. Singh Bhuller found the creation of the work 'very natural… it was like a conversation. Bob would show a movement, I would do it, and then he would give me the space to develop the phrase. He certainly knew what he wanted and was very quick on shaping the material.'

Singh Bhuller started fully clothed and, in each metamorphosis, removed an item of clothing until in the final one he was stripped to his jockstrap, revealing his body and his soul. Cohan wished to explore the idea that we present different aspects of ourselves depending on what we wear – suit, shirt and trousers, vest and underwear. As he noted in the programme, 'The different images are presented not only to the world but to ourselves, and none of them are any more truthful than the others, just different, another self.' Some younger audience members who had not read the programme found the striptease on stage a giggle-worthy affair. In addition to Bhuller on stage, Anthony Crickmay had taken a series of beautiful photographs of him, and these were projected on a screen. Crickmay's photographs captured the movement and character of each metamorphosis, and added commentary on the physical action. If the metaphysical part of the dance was not entirely successful, the dance, as dance, was, and the performances by Bhuller and Gareth Hulse on oboe, who seemed to feed off one another in an extraordinarily symbiotic way, transforming each in the process, were the highlight of the season, with David Dougill finding it 'ingenious, witty and brilliantly danced'.[329]

However, by common consent, the most wholly successful work was created to Hans Werner Henze's *Quattro Fantasie* of 1958, a setting of poems by Edna St Vincent Millay for tenor, guitar, clarinet, horn, bassoon, and string quartet, including the lines:

I cannot say what loves have come and gone,

I only know that summer sang in me
A little while, that in me sings no more.[330]

Although the Millay lines seem entirely appropriate to Cohan's mood at the time, he chose as his inspiration not the music or poetry, but his memories of a poem he had read many years before. It concerned three angels who come to earth, and each falls in love with a woman and then loses his wings – one is punished by losing his love, and the two others roam the earth forever searching for one another. The second cannot have his love until he says a magic word that makes him an angel; when he whispers it, she screams it and becomes a star, and his feathers fall off. The final one can only have his love in his angel form, but when they consummate their love, she burns to ashes. Cohan had often wanted to make a dance on the subject, and in this work, called *In Memory*, his memory of the poem proved a stronger inspiration than the music or Millay. He did not follow the story literally, but used it as a base for a tale of four men who tell of their love for each other or a woman, tying it tenuously to the Millay poem by creating a meditation on love and relationships. Using the most experienced men in the company, Christopher Bannerman, Darshan Singh Bhuller, Jonathan Lunn, and Patrick Harding-Irmer, who were able to command the stage effortlessly, Cohan's choreography interacted with the melancholy themes of the music, its ebb and flow reflecting the changing relationships on stage. The challenging, dense sound world of Henze's music was the closest to the type of music Cohan could relate to, and the theme of loss resonated with Cohan's psyche to produce one of his most striking works. In the audience for the first night, Robin Howard told Mop Eager that he thought Cohan had returned to form and that it was one of his finest pieces.

Stone Garden, by Nigel Osborne, tried to recreate in sound something of the atmosphere of timeless contemplation found in Zen gardens. The sound world Osborne devised was extraordinary and, using Western instruments, he imagined the playing of the shamisen, the stringed instrument central to so much Japanese classical music. To this music, Cohan created more of a primitive ritual, reminiscent of the world of the stone statues of Easter Island rather than a meditative Japanese stone garden. The massed groupings of men and women were not supported by the music, even in the faster sections, and the general feeling was of a work at odds with itself. Only the dramatics of Anca Frankenhauser as a sort of Priestess/Chosen One held the work together.

Cohan's least favourite piece was David Bedford's *Symphony for 12 Musicians*, which was the base for his dance *Crescendo*. Since his days as one of the British avant-garde in the 1960s, Bedford had, in the 1980s, embraced minimalism, informed in part by medieval musical techniques and rock music, and the symphony embodied this. Although it had a rather complex musical structure, it was extremely accessible, and built to an exciting climax over a long crescendo, hence Cohan's title. Cohan made some attempt to use some of Bedford's musical structures, beginning with a simple theme and elaborating on it, stopping, beginning again, and each time getting more elaborate and building to a climax. But his heart was not in it, and he relied heavily on the input of the dancers; Noel Goodwin quite rightly noted: '… the exhilarating pace accelerated to a brilliantly lit coda of acrobatics where what looked like each dancer doing an own thing'.[331] The resulting work resembled a series of classroom exercises aimed at showing off the dancers, with one reviewer noting that it 'resembled *Class*, but was diminished by comparison'.[332] But even a diminished *Class* was worth watching, and Angela Kane could find it 'vigorous and virtuosic' and that 'its formal free-from angst choreography invigorates the dancing'.[333] Bedford, who worked with the company on educational music and dance workshops, had fonder memories of the collaboration, in particular he was amazed by the size of the audience for the performances. When his music had had its premiere at the Spitalfields Festival there had been only about twenty people assembled to hear it.

Cohan was angry with the critics for the drubbing of the performances as he had explained to them the circumstances surrounding the pieces and had asked them to stay away from opening night. They did not and the idea that '[t]hese were minor works by a major master'[334] were echoed in most of the papers and journals. If the critics only saw the performed works and found them wanting, the musicians themselves had found it was a rewarding project as they relished interacting with the dancers. Most of the works were not completed by the time the dancers and musicians came together, and they were fascinated by the way the dancers worked together with Cohan to create the works, a method so totally different to the way they themselves worked, simply having to play a finished score. In addition, they were placed on stage with the dancers during performance and found that their approach to the physicality of performance a transformational experience.

The quartet of works shown at the Queen Elizabeth Hall would also be the final new works Robin Howard saw by his old friend. Following his removal as Chair of the Trust, Howard had, eventually, accepted the title of Life President, though like many presidential titles it held little executive power. He was, however, still very involved and concerned with the international world of dance, having been elected President of the International Dance Committee of the International Theatre Institute. In addition, he had spent a good deal of his time interviewing major choreographers, including Cunningham, Nikolais, Tharp, Ailey, Taylor, with a view to developing a new form of dance training. Before he could begin the interviews in the UK, while on a visit to Helsinki he suffered a massive stroke; he returned to England, where more strokes followed, and he died on 12 June 1989, aged 65.

In the very early days of LCDT, Howard would try ideas out on the young Richard Alston and in one conversation, Alston said, 'Don't you think you are pushing things too much?', to which Howard replied, 'I know my life is not going to be as long as some people's lives and I want to make sure that I have got something going.' His life was certainly longer than he expected, and he had lived long enough to see that 'something going', but he also lived long enough to see himself ejected from that which he had created, an event that Eager and Cohan are convinced destroyed him. If he was not wanted by his Board, he was wanted by the dance world, and there was huge outpouring of grief amongst the dancers and in the dance community which he had done so much to create. His obituaries were fulsome, and none so poignant as that by Clement Crisp in the *Financial Times* who wrote:

> It is impossible to overestimate the significance of Robin Howard's work in securing and fostering the growth and development of contemporary dance in Britain... Robin Howard was single-minded in his dedication, and he worked without sparing himself. His simplicity and generosity of manner, his idealism and enthusiasm, touched everyone who knew or worked with him. His best memorial is surely the grand flowering of dance in this country that he inspired and guided.[335]

Chapter 11

Commentary

In spite of all the difficulties we had with the Arts Council during this period, The Place was functioning very well. The school was turning out good dancers, many of whom came into the company. The theatre was showing a cross section of new European as well as British choreography that was almost always interesting. Robin and I were satisfied about that part of the Trust's work.

The company was touring successfully, with perhaps some smaller audiences in the regions. We were touring towns in the Midlands where many shops were boarded up and there was a definite depressed feeling, but audiences in London and abroad were good. Most importantly, members of the company had choreographed many works that were very good and in the repertory.

We were worried about the future, as Robin was running out of funds.

He saw very clearly that, unless the Arts Council was appropriating more money to dance, the future for all of us looked complicated.

We and the other dance schools were now producing many good dancers and promising choreographers every year; that had not happened in England before. There was now a need for the Arts Council to review its provision for dance and face the challenge to include those talented artists who needed financial support to further their careers.

Robin and I knew there was a dwindling supply of money in real terms for dance and he was arguing, not for more money for us, but more money for all dance. He always told the Arts Council that we were all prepared to help them take on the Government. He didn't want a bigger slice of the cake but a bigger cake. Unfortunately, I think they thought he was a little mad.

Especially in those times and even to a degree now, contemporary dance was considered the poor, minor art form that people do, who can't act, or write, or even paint. Ballet and opera, music and the national theatre are the real art forms and are worthy of sufficient support in London and a few other major cities in Britain.

I know that statement sounds more than a little defensive and feeling sorry for myself, but I would guarantee you that the people responsible for the decisions made to support the arts have all been to the Royal Opera House or the National Theatre, and very few have seen or know about the enormous amount of creative dance that was being taught and performed around the country.

It is an activity that can and does change people lives. I remember one year at this time when statistically more people attended dance performances than went to football matches.

Robin Howard came from an upper-class family and was brought up with a strong sense of responsibility to help people in our society who were not as fortunate as he was. Before he was involved with contemporary dance, he had helped many other people in the arts, such as painters and actors, with their housing and daily needs. He saw in contemporary dance a way to focus his energy and his desire to be of service.

He often said to me, 'We used to be known as a dancing nation and maybe we can help to do that again.' The point being that involving yourself in dance as audience or practitioner can help you contact parts of yourself that are otherwise not used, thereby enhancing your life. Something I agree with and know to be true.

I mention this about Robin to partly explain the utter disgust I feel with all those people who were involved with his dismissal as Chairman of the Board of the Contemporary Dance Trust, his own organisation. He had already given over the daily running of The Place to a new executive director, and the Chairmanship of the Trust was the only formal contact he had left with the organisation he gave all his money and passion to for his last twenty years.

As far as I am concerned, his untimely death a year later was directly related to that loss.

The Place and the ideas that it stands for in terms of dance artists' education and increasing the public's contact with the art of dance had become the purpose of his life.

With that contact gone there was little else left, and so he died.

Chapter 12

Be cautious regarding the ruling power. Because they only befriend a person when it serves themselves. They appear as friends when it suits them, but they do not stand by a man in his time of need.

(Pirkei Avot, 2:3)

1990–2005

Free of LCDT (although he remained on the Board), in 1990 Cohan divested himself of Batsheva as well. The ten years he had been artistic adviser had been stormy ones, but he had been a wise choice. The company was stronger technically, had a wider international presence, a wider repertory, including more works by Israeli choreographers who had been developed and encouraged under Cohan's guidance. And he believed he had seen the perfect person to take the company forward. Ohad Naharin was Israeli, had danced with the company briefly in 1974, before he went to America where he studied at the Juilliard School, and danced in the Graham Company. In the intervening years, he had developed an international reputation for his choreography which demonstrated an unshakeable belief in his own abilities. Some on the Board questioned the decision, knowing that Naharin was not really interested in running a repertory company, but Cohan was persuasive and he was appointed. It was a bold move on Cohan's part, and if only such an appointment had been possible in the UK, the impending disasters could have been averted. True, Naharin was not interested in the company's past, and very soon he dropped any sense of a varied repertory and programmed only his own works. But he reinvigorated the company and it now has an international reputation, based largely on his varied and innovative productions for the troupe. Cohan's legacy to Israeli dance, in particular the development of the Suzanne Dellal Centre, the development of a new generation of Israeli choreographers, and the emergence of a stronger, better Batsheva Company have largely gone unrecognised. But his neglect there pales beside the neglect that would soon be his reward for creating The Place.

Cohan had left LCDT at a time of enormous change in the British dance scene. When he had arrived in Britain in the mid 1960s, there were few alternatives to ballet; when he left in the late 1980s there were, if not a plethora, then a wide range of dance styles all begging for a slice of the dance budget. Some had grown up in emulation of Cohan's work, including Spiral Dance Company and Janet Smith and Dancers. Some, such as the wide range of British New Dance, including the X6 Collective, had grown up in reaction against his aesthetic. Dance Umbrella, the yearly festival which, since 1978, has brought new and challenging work from around the world to London, had gone from strength to strength and its influence was immense. In addition to the contemporary world, there were calls on funding bodies to support dances from other cultures which had long been established in the UK. The dance world was in crisis, and the Arts Council had commissioned its first report concerned entirely with dance in Britain. Published in 1989, the year Cohan retired, the Devlin report, *Stepping Forward*, heralded a major change in Arts Council policies.

In his wide-ranging report, Graham Devlin found that many of the small regional dance companies that had developed since the 1970s, including Dance Tales, Ekome, Cycles, and English Dance Theatre, had folded by 1988. Devlin argued that experimental work was as important as mainstream work, and that audiences had to be developed countrywide for experimental, as well as for the more accessible, companies. The report cited underfunding and a lack of coherent nationwide strategy and infrastructure, and found the dance profession 'deeply demoralised and nervous'.[336] This report and the Council's response to it would have far-reaching consequences for LCDT.

Amongst its key recommendations were:

The establishment of a network of national dance agencies

That the Dance Panel of the Arts Council of England adopt a more strategic role

That stronger emphasis be placed on an audience rather than an artist-centred approach to resource allocation

That additional resources be secured to fund companies more appropriately; and in the absence of this, that one or two companies be axed to fund the remaining companies more generously

That substantial funding be provided to a Black dance company (i.e. Dance of the African Diaspora)

That non-Western dance be nurtured through the proposed national dance agencies

That dialogue with the Department of Education should be advanced to clarify the parameters of educational policy from both sides.

The report never mentions axing LCDT, rather that there should be a very close reassessment of its activities and also of Rambert. If anything, alarm bells were sounded for the safety of Northern Ballet Theatre, so much so that the MP for Salford East, Mr Stanley Orme, raised the matter in a House of Commons adjournment debate on 8 March 1989. Richard Luce, the Minister for Arts, replied in wonderfully elusive political manner which allayed no one's fears.[337]

But LCDT was certainly found wanting in relation to Rambert, as the report highlights that it was a company 'in a state of transition'.[338] Rambert, however, was seen to have a clear artistic vision and Richard Alston as 'one of the few artistic directors in the country who knows exactly what he wants to do'.[339] So in the report there were no explicit threats to LCDT, although it is clear Devlin did not feel it could continue exactly as it had done.

In addition, this all took place at a time when the UK was looking more towards Europe than America for its inspirations. Initially suspicious of the Common Market, Britain had developed as a powerful member of the European Union, and the artistic potentates of the country were interested in European models of funding and artistic development. In France, in the early 1980s, the Ministry of Culture had decided that dance should be more equally spread around the country, rather than being so heavily focused in Paris. To achieve this, the government selected a range of the country's leading young choreographers, and relocated them to regional centres. This was accompanied by very generous funding, which had enabled them to establish companies, and to build both artistic and audience followings over time. This plan had the ancillary effect of attracting local and regional funding to supplement that from the centre. Named *politique d'implantation*, the policy, almost reminiscent of communist Russia, was considered by many to have been successful in growing the audience and the industry infrastructure for dance. Partly in response to Devlin's report, the Arts Council decided to follow the French model and set up six national dance agencies around the country, with a remit to serve both the local community and the dance artists. The initial project, which lasted until 1992, cost in the region of £300,000, but when it was decided to continue with the agencies, ten times that amount needed to be found to fund them. The vast amounts of money available in France were not available in the UK.

It was in this world of changing policies and financial fortunes, a time when strong leadership was needed, that LCDT found themselves at sea. When the advert for Cohan's post had appeared in the press, a flurry of excitement had gone through the British dance world, with everyone wondering who would apply and who would get the post. There was considerable surprise therefore when Dan Wagoner, another American, was chosen over any British or British-based applicants. But once the harrumphing was ignored, the reason was quite simple: at the time, the well-qualified prime candidates were otherwise happily engaged elsewhere. Robert North was working internationally, Richard Alston was directing Rambert, and Siobhan Davies was not interested in the job, preferring to work with her own small company. Dan Wagoner seemed a good choice; he was well qualified for the artistic side of the post, having been a dancer on the international scene in the companies of Graham and Taylor, he had made a substantial body of work for his own company, and he was extremely personable and a diplomatic leader. So, with long-time company member and developing choreographer Jonathan Lunn as assistant director, he got the job.

Sadly, he lasted just over a year as artistic director of LCDT. In that time, he made a good impression on the dancers, being humorous, affable, and a good teacher, even if he made it clear that the streamlined beauty of the LCDT dancers was not quite his thing. And true, he did not seem to be particularly interested in the works of other choreographers leaving that up to Lunn. But everyone seemed pleased that there was a person in charge that they were prepared to trust, although Angela Kane did flag up some warning lights in an article for the *Dancing Times* entitled 'Leader or Locum', in which she noted that 'as the LCDT season concluded, Dan Wagoner's impact remained in the realms of the unknown.'[340]

Unfortunately, Wagoner's partner of many years, the poet George Montgomery, had Huntington's disease, which causes both cognitive and psychiatric problems, and which meant that Wagoner was constantly distracted by having to look after him. Even with Jonathan Lunn's help, the stress of his personal life took its toll on Wagoner and the company, and he resigned, leaving in December 1990. Richard Alston believes that Wagoner did not intend to stay, as he was told by members of Wagoner's company in New York that they expected him to be back with them within a year. It has not been possible to confirm the exact sequence of events with Wagoner, but his early departure severely weakened the confidence of the company and the confidence of the Arts Council in the company. Things could only get worse.

The choice for his successor seems with hindsight inexplicable, flying as it did in the face of all of the signals that were coming out of the Arts Council for single choreographer-led companies. Wagoner's successor was Nancy Duncan, yet another American who was not a choreographer, but a successful administrator. In the USA, she had founded CoDanceCo, a production and performance company whose aim was 'to nurture the artistic development of contemporary dance artists'. This was a radical change of direction for LCDT and the Trust, which had always been headed by a choreographer. Her aim, 'to establish a repertoire company of international stature using international choreographers', did seem somewhat curious as many in the dance world thought that was what LCDT had been for many years. Jonathan Lunn, who had been passed over for the job, resigned and, within a year (she joined in August 1991), she had lost the confidence of the Board and had herself resigned. *Dance Theatre Journal* observed:

> There was a lot of comment at the time of the last two appointments that no British candidate was thought suitable after all these years of training people

at the London Contemporary School. It seems that at least one would have
been acceptable to the board but was not willing to take on the job on the
conditions required. Will there be any change only a year or so on?[341]

The Trust was now in a very difficult situation: in the space of just over two years,
it had lost three artistic directors, and had gone from a company with a clear
artistic policy to one with no clear policy or strategy. In looking to America,
the Trust had completely misread the signals from the Arts Council, which was
focussed on Europe for models, not only aesthetically but financially. In addition,
the school had changed dramatically with the retirement of Jane Dudley and
Nina Fonaroff, and the whole pedagogical direction of that area of the Trust's
activities was in flux as well. In consultation with the Arts Council, the Board
decided that, rather than rush straight into another round of interviews with the
possibility of making another unsuccessful appointment, it would ask Cohan to
return on a part-time basis and act as a co-ordinating artistic adviser. This was
not a post he had ever sought, and he returned somewhat reluctantly, as he told
Darshan Singh Bhuller:

> I took the company on tour and tried to keep it together but, as was clear to
> everybody, my heart was not in it. The dancers had begun to change, they were
> not the people I had trained and I was no longer teaching them. But I felt very
> strongly there was a place and room for a repertory company performing in
> the big theatres, besides Rambert. We had an audience that had been built up
> over the years very carefully and I felt it was wrong to let them down as well.[342]

Even if his heart was not in it, he still brought much needed years of experience
to the post. When Amanda Miller, who had two weeks to choreograph a new
work on the company whom she hardly knew, ran into difficulties, it was
Cohan who smoothed things over. The company were having great difficulty
understanding Miller's explanations as to what she wanted, and as one company
member remembers, 'we all started asking questions, which to her may have
looked aggressive, and she ran out of the studio crying'. It was Cohan who calmly
said to them, 'Well, if you don't understand her, copy her movements.' Whatever
the situation was, he knew how to listen to and fine-tune the company's feelings
so that the job could get done. The stress on Cohan did show, however, and it
was an uncharacteristically brusque figure who offered Fred Gehrig a place in
the company by calling him into his office and saying, 'Your job is to replace Paul
Liburd. But no one can replace Paul. OK?'

Part of the Arts Council suggesting that they should not rush into appointing a
new artistic director was that LCDT was about to be appraised by them, its major
source of funding, an event which in normal circumstances would be stressful,
but at this time pushed the Trust to breaking point. In the summer of 1992,
the Trust began a series of intensive consultations with artists, venue managers,

funders, and dance critics to gain as wide a base of opinion as possible for future developments. The Board even considered the radical possibilities of merging with Rambert Dance Company, or even closing the company down completely.

The Trust eventually opted for a model which would have seen Cohan as the director leading a team of two associate directors and four artistic associates. The day-to-day management of the company would be down to the associate directors, while the artistic associates would make work for the company and also become involved with teaching and residencies. A wide range of possible artistic associates was suggested, including Christopher Bruce, Angelin Preljocaj, and Amanda Miller. Indeed the Devlin report had recommended that the company should 'bring in a range of first-rate choreographers to develop different styles'.[343] But cracks appeared in the plan when, in late 1993, it was announced that Christopher Bruce would become artistic director of Rambert Dance Company, which had been without an artistic director since Richard Alston had been sacked in 1991 – his clear vision, that had been praised in Devlin's report, no longer being what the company wanted or needed.

LCDT was appraised by a team consisting of: Anthony Blackstock, from the Royal National Theatre; Peter Brinson, a long-time dance insider and a member of the Arts Council Advisory Panel on Dance; Kathy Gosschalk, artistic director of the Rotterdam Dance Company; Ruth Mackenzie, artistic director of the Nottingham Playhouse; Prudence Skene, chair of the Arts Council Advisory Panel for Dance; plus Julia Al-Adwani, Julia Carruthers, Sue Hoyle, Andrew Kyle, and Maddy Morton, all from various arms of the Arts Council. The appraisal took most of the year and was unusual in that it involved looking at all areas of the Trust's work, since they seemed to the Arts Council so interdependent and Devlin had recommended that all aspects of the Trust be looked at.[344] It was a dispiriting time for the Trust's employees and Karen Burgin, who headed the Evening School and Part-Time Courses, remembers it being 'a very depressing period'.

There were claims afterwards of bias against the Trust, none proven, but sufficient in the eyes of the Board that the Chair of the Trust, Peter Sarah, would raise them with Prudence Skene, writing, 'we do not believe that the company or the Trust commenced the appraisal with a level playing field'. Cohan agrees with this, as one member of the panel had previously applied for his job and been unsuccessful and Prudence Skene was seen as too close to Rambert, having worked for them from 1975 to 1986. Peter Brinson's role in the affair is somewhat murky for, although he eventually told Cohan and Eager that he did not support the Council's report and that it was released without him seeing it, he had in October 1992, well before even a draft appraisal was sent to the Trust, told the *Daily Telegraph* that 'LCDT had lost direction', and posited the question: 'So are our lead companies too large for audiences? Is their communication with the public too traditional? The answer is yes. Scratch the surface, though, and you've got a healthy core. And I would like to see dance funding restructured to enable this sort of growth.'[345] These final comments, which would later be taken up in public pronouncements by Hoyle and Carruthers, do not indicate that the panel started with an open mind.

In the middle of the crisis at The Place, in 1992, Cohan had been returning to his home in France when he bumped into Galina Samsova, the Artistic Director of Scottish Ballet, at Gatwick Airport. Out of this chance encounter, Cohan received a commission to make his first work for a ballet company. He was an unusual choice for such a commission as he had never been particularly interested in ballet as a student, had never been particularly good at fast footwork which is so much a part of ballet and, whereas colleagues such as Paul Taylor and Robert North had happily assimilated ballet into their version of contemporary, Cohan had not. Nonetheless, he was excited by the challenge, not least – as he later told Stuart Sweeney – because 'it was my first opportunity to work on pointe'.

This new work, which premiered in March 1993, was not a small-scale abstract ballet but a full-evening version of Shakespeare's *A Midsummer Night's Dream*. The play has long been popular with choreographers, and Cohan's version of the play would not be a slavish adaptation to the text but, like Balanchine and Ashton before him, he selected themes that interested him and followed these through. As one writer told his public in advance, 'it will look at the bewitched, bothered, and bewildered aspects of the different love affairs in the story'.[346]

Working with the ballet dancers was an interesting challenge for Cohan. He was used to working with dancers that knew him and his style, and could often second-guess what he wanted them to do next. He would demonstrate a phrase and the dancer could give him a possibility for going on. Not so with the Scottish Ballet dancers, as many of them were very young and most were used to learning roles in existing works. Being involved in the creation of something new, and to many of them in an alien style, was difficult. Cohan remembers on one occasion improvising a lengthy phrase of movement, then turning to the dancers expecting them to repeat it, but instead they gave him a round of applause. They had not realised he was making it up and needed them to remember it; they thought this was an elderly gentleman who had just shown that he could still move. The days when he could improvise almost all of *Stabat Mater* and have the dancers pick it up as he went along were long gone. This was going to be a challenge, but he rose to it, as Vladislav Bubnov, a Bolshoi-trained member of the cast, told *Ballet Magazine*: 'Robert Cohan made me feel at ease – I am a classically trained Russian dancer so the contemporary stuff was difficult for me.'[347]

Cohan's approach to working with ballet dancers was what he called 'fusion cooking', where he tried to fuse contemporary and balletic movement together. He told the press: 'For the choreography, I'm using ballet technique, but Graham contractions as well. I'm hoping that it will have the look of a work that has always been there, but you just haven't seen it before.'[348] He was excited by the prospect, as he told Mary Brennan: 'I love it when – in one sequence – the women are doing truly classical material, and a phrase later the men come charging out and crash to the floor.' He was fully aware that it would jar with some purists –and it did – but he believes it was worthwhile, '[b]ecause dance grows, evolves from the language that it inherits from its inventors'.[349]

Initially, Cohan had 'been swept away by Shakespeare's wonderful language', thinking 'there's nothing here; a trip to the forest, a few dances, a few spells'.[350] But in the end, his dance version did not so much tell the whole story but offer illustrations from it, together with some implied commentary. He included no Indian boy, no magic flower – Puck would wave his cloak instead. Hippolyta and Theseus – omitted entirely in Ashton's version – become as important as Titania and Oberon and, surprisingly, it is they and not the fairy king and queen who have the only grand pas de deux.

The greatest problem in creating a production of A Midsummer Night's Dream is Mendelssohn's music; there is simply not enough, as he wrote not a complete ballet score, but only about forty minutes of incidental music. John Lanchbery had ingeniously stretched that by about half as much again for Ashton's one-act version; Barrington Pheloung had to extend it to more than twice its original length. This involved fairly substantial rewriting of Mendelssohn, and Pheloung ended up with a sort of free orchestral fantasy on themes by Mendelssohn. In it, familiar tunes would sometimes take a new twist, and find themselves alongside wholly new passages, which he hoped would be seen as complementary rather than parody. There was nothing radical in the score, and the whole piece was effective when played by the fifty-piece orchestra and a ten-strong women's choir.

Like the music, Norberto Chiesa's costumes were a mixture of classic and modern, and his designs effectively set the action in a world of angular screens and curtains of silk strips. These were all white but, in classic, economic Chiesa style, they took an appropriate colour for each episode from the lighting which Cohan designed himself. Chiesa further varied these with angled mirrors for a fantasy forest in which the lovers lose themselves, and in which he placed one of those bright red sofas shaped like Mae West's lips for them to wake up on.

Before the work reached the stage, rumours were abounding in the Scottish press that it had had to be censored as it included nudity and other sexual elements, unsuitable for the inhabitants of the far-flung reaches of Scotland to which the company toured. This may have just been very clever marketing on behalf of the press office, as there was no actual nudity in the show. However, it was quite racy, as some of the scenes in the forest saw the men in costumes modified with enormous phalluses. The effect was bawdy, not raunchy, but was still too much for the Scots and they were removed. The full costumes saw the light of day a few years later, when the ballet was remounted on Sweden's Gothenburg Ballet. There was in Europe no public outcry, though Cohan does remember being amused backstage where the dancers walked around in bathrobes with the enormous appendages sticking out.

For a new venture, the critics were largely complimentary; Mary Brennan found it 'ravishing', with Cohan 'Adept at weaving observations on human nature into choreography that is utterly engaging in itself and more than ready to entertain and amuse'.[351] David Dougill in the *Sunday Times* thought,

> The resulting ballet is a rewarding cross-fertilisation of techniques and influences, with especially subtle and powerful choreography for Puck and Oberon, a very sexy treatment of Titania and Bottom, and the Pyramus and Thisbē play done as a tap routine. Barrington Pheloung has extended and developed themes from Mendelssohn's music in his own idiom, and Norberto Chiesa's ravishingly effective designs combine modern fashion with allusions to antiquity and the mysteries of nature. This *Dream* seems set to be a big success for the company. A dancer confided to me, during rehearsals: 'I like it because there's humour in it. The other contemporary pieces we've done have all been so intense and serious.'[352]

The whole project had energised the 68-year-old Cohan, who excitedly told Jeremy Hodge: 'The body directs. I'm always amazed that, after forty years of this, we can still keep making up movement, when all we've got is two arms, two legs, a front and a back. All the movement in the world comes out of that.'[353]

He needed all of the positive energy that he could muster because, back in London, the end result of the appraisal was a damning report on the Trust's activities. In particular, the panel rejected the cornerstone of the Trust's plan – the 'new model' put forward by Cohan and the Board – and in an interim report given to the Trust in December 1993, wrote: 'All the Team are agreed it was unlikely that an overall Director could lead so many artistic associates and assistants. The Team doubted that a collection of creative egos would be willing to work as a team, without an agreed philosophy and objectives.' And that 'The new model appears to be a temporary working plan rather than a permanent solution that would solve current dilemmas. In the more competitive context of the Nineties, it is hard to see how the new model will lead to the company having a unique and clear position within contemporary dance provision.'[354]

In this, they showed a singular lack of appreciation of Cohan's diplomatic skills and of the enormous respect in which he is held within the dance community. The role suggested was in a way similar to that which he had held in Israel, and which had after a period of difficulty seen the Batsheva Company reappear stronger and reinvigorated. But this was not to be and Sue Hoyle, Dance Officer of the Arts Council, at a special meeting of the Board on 4 June 1993, 'confirmed that they [the Arts Council] were not convinced by the model or that it was the way forward' and that 'The Arts Council has backed the Appraisal Team in their opinions', and that the Trust 'will have to look at other options', and if they persisted in wanting a 'repertory company they would not be funded'. The Arts Council did not believe that a repertory company with multiple artistic directors was workable and thought that the Trust needed to forget a large-scale company and start again. Hoyle went on to stress the need to find an artistic leader and that if, one was found, some sort of company would be possible.

In relation to LCDT, the Arts Council looked again to Europe, and this meant not repertory but single choreographer companies, with a clear artistic brand, such as Pina Bausch in Wuppertal, Vim Vandekeybus in Belgium, and any number of French choreographers from Daniel Larrieu to Jean-Claude Gallotta. Of course, this was not what the Arts Council wanted in terms of ballet companies, which it always saw as repertory based. It is also not what it would expect from Rambert, which from 1994 would be led by Christopher Bruce, who would never programme only his works. The goalposts seemed to have been moved.

Although not in the report on LCDT, there was much talk in the press and the dance world of the need for the Arts Council to save money. Between them, LCDT and Rambert took up 53 per cent of the Arts Council's budget for contemporary dance, and in the by now established British contemporary dance world, questions were asked why this should be so. Of course, the amount of money spent on contemporary dance paled into insignificance when looked at alongside the money spent on ballet, but there seems to have been no discussion taking place as to the possibility of closing down one of the four heavily funded ballet companies that England boasted, or of even cutting their funding and spreading the dance budget more evenly. The concerns raised in the Devlin report about Northern Ballet Theatre were never followed through as Christopher Gable, their artistic director, pulled off a series of highly successful productions. Put into context, LCDT received just under £1,000,000 per year in grant, while Twyla Tharp was paid in the region of £250,000 for her Royal Ballet commission – and disaster – *Mr Worldly Wise*. True, the Royal Ballet were extremely good in tapping into sponsorship money, but this never seemed to impact on their Arts Council grant. Translating this into ticket subsidy, LCDT received £9.50 per seat; Rambert, £12.25; Festival Ballet, £11.00; while the Royal Ballet received a massive £20.25. In addition, as mentioned previously, the newly established national dance agencies needed considerable sums of money, as did the newly emerging choreographers.

The atmosphere between LCDT and the Arts Council became acrimonious, with comments by dancers reported in the press and complained about by the Arts Council, and comments from individual members of the Appraisal Team also reported and complained about by the Trust. As already noted, Peter Brinson had begun talking to the press long before the appraisal was over, but in April 1993, Judith Mackrell reported in an article for *The Independent* that,

> … Sue Hoyle, director of Dance for the Arts Council suspects that, in the
> long term, the future of dance and choreographers may lie in organisations

far more loosely structured than old-style rep companies – and as the latter evolve they will disappear. It's possible there may be insufficient cash around to support a future for both LCDT and Rambert.[355]

As long ago as October of 1992, *The Independent* had reported that Julia Carruthers, Dance Officer at the Arts Council had said that 'Audiences are down for contemporary dance, but interest in small scale and middle scale companies is burgeoning and the new wave of multidisciplinary outfits using texts, and, in the case of DV8, having a political message about say, sexual politics or equal opportunities – not having men do all the lifts and the women simpering in the background.'[356] A year later, she told Dance UK that 'Contemporary dance is actually in a very healthy state in this country', but that 'One of the problems with the press is that the two major companies, Rambert and LCDT are just emerging from the doldrums.'[357] These comments were hardly conducive to what should have been a delicate process of negotiation.

By the late autumn, it was clear that the Arts Council was not going to agree to the Board's suggestions, and they finally withdrew their funding. Without this vital lifeline, the Board then had no choice but to close down LCDT and regroup. Laurence Isaacson, the Chair of the Trust, told the *Evening Standard* in November, 'We have put forward a number of proposals in the last 18 months to the Arts Council to ensure the continuation of the company and they have been consistently rejected.'[358] Prudence Skene also wrote to the *Evening Standard*, making it clear that it was the Trust's decision to close the company and not the Arts Council's, though quite how the Trust could have kept the company going without Arts Council funding is unclear. An article that appeared in *Dance and Dancers* after events had settled down confirmed that the Trust were 'specifically told by the Council that it was not interested in continuing to fund them as a large scale repertory company. In discussions with young choreographers outside LCDT, they found none willing to come and work on a large scale with its dancers, and the preference for small scale choreographer-led projects was strongly supported within the Arts Council.'[359] Ten years later, Cohan was still angry about the closure, telling Singh Bhuller, 'No matter what proposal we brought forward, it wasn't sufficient, because once they had made up their mind to close it, that was what they were going to do. It was done, I have to say, very badly, with a lot of deception, which was the only way they could do it...'[360] Once the news broke and the crying had stopped, the dancers began collecting signatures from their audiences, opposing closure. Company members, usually Kenneth Tharp, would make passionate appeals for audience support from the stage at the end of performances, until, that is, they were told by the Arts Council that to do so was in breach of the company contract and had to stop.

The senior critics were unanimous in their condemnation of the closure, with Clement Crisp writing:

[T]he troupe is a national treasure. We do not have anything comparable. There is nothing comparable in Europe. To sacrifice it on the altar of expediency and a chimeric re-organisation is criminal. Policy can be altered. To alter the company will be to deny its history – LCDT and its School made possible the whole modern dance movement in this country – its splendid present, and its potential for the future of dance in Britain.[361]

Even John Percival, who had often been highly critical of Cohan's work with LCDT, in a lengthy article headed 'A False Step that will Impoverish British Dance – London's Contemporary Dance Theatre', wrote: 'Who but the Arts Council would implement a policy of building up contemporary dance by killing off one of our leading international contemporary dance companies?'[362] Mary Clarke had threatened to chain herself to the railings of the Arts Council in protest, but it was all too late, and the company would give its final performance in June 1994. In the one-hundredth birthday issue of the *Dancing Times* in 2010, Mary Clarke recalled the closure of LCDT as one of the ten darkest moments in dance history. Ironically, in its final year under Cohan's direction, LCDT received its third Laurence Olivier Award.

The plans that the Trust announced were impressive, and saw The Place becoming a National Centre for Dance, while a smaller company of twelve would replace the sixteen dancers of LCDT. The new company's working name was announced as The Place Company, but this changed very quickly. The shortlist for the new artistic director was small and varied, so varied in fact that one could be forgiven for wondering if the Trust knew what it was looking for. The names, all male, came from a wide range of styles, from British New Dance, to martial arts, to more traditional forms, and only one was not from the UK. In the end, the job went to Richard Alston who, since he had been sacked from his job as Artistic Director of Rambert Dance Company, had become peripatetic, taking on a number of international commissions. His appointment, although all saw it as a 'coming home', was welcomed by some but not others. Peter Sarah, The Place's Chief Executive, told Judith Mackrell that 'He's perhaps the only person who could bring all this together – he's a very important choreographer, a great teacher and very wise and generous adviser', but then of course so was Cohan. Mackrell noted that Alston

… has his critics, too. Though Rambert went through a golden age in the Eighties – garnering awards, attracting some of the biggest names in music, painting and dance – the Nineties saw its audiences in retreat. A younger public turned away from Alston's preference for abstract and sophisticated technical dance towards the gut energy of Eurocrash. The strains of running a large company also told on the quality of Alston's own work. And he was considered by some to be artistically, if not personally, pigheaded.[363]

Alston's record in bringing people together did not look good, but he told Mackrell that he could see that he had been overly autocratic at Rambert, 'interfering with other people because I cared so much about the company'. But he assured her that in his new job, he fully intended 'letting people get on with their own job', and 'getting back in touch with movement in the studio'.[364]

How exactly this would happen was not clear, as Alston was given the almost Herculean task of integrating all of the Trust's expanded activities and to direct the new company of dancers, who, unlike their predecessors, would not be on full-time contracts but only employed for nine months of the year. For six months of the year, they would make work with Alston, while for the other three months, they would work with other choreographers, taken from four associates of the company and school. What eventually appeared, however, was the Richard Alston Dance Company, producing work entirely by Alston who, at this stage in his career, although an experienced choreographer was hardly experimental or cutting edge and certainly not what he had been in the 1970s when 'he saw himself as one of God's chosen few, going out into the wilderness to devote himself to the radical and rigorous cause of New Dance'.[365] But the Arts Council got their way.

In addition, The Place Theatre, which under John Ashford had built up an impressive performing season of thirty-nine weeks per year, would increase this to fifty weeks. Plans were also mooted for a smaller more intimate performance space for choreography, tentatively called Studio 90. There would also be an increase in services provided to independent dancers and companies. Some already had offices, there but now space would be available for storage, production, rehearsals, costumes, and set making. The cost to the companies for these services would be subsidised to take into account individual resources. The Video Place and The Data Place, which were already part of the national dance agency network, would, it was hoped, be expanded to include The Music Place.

Finally in these highly ambitious plans, the school would begin to offer daily contemporary technique classes aimed at the working professionals, who would also be able to use the conditioning studio and dance injury clinic. There would also be masterclasses, choreographic workshops, together with courses in all manner of technical support work for dance in the late twentieth century, and – essential in the economic climate at the time – a dancer's re-settlement and retraining service.

Cohan does not disagree with supporting young and experimental choreographers: 'Of course, I would support that entirely! In the time I was in England, I supported all the young choreographers that I could.' But he firmly believes that 'In the end it was short-sighted as far as I'm concerned; you need examples, you need role models and the company was that for hundreds and hundreds of dancers. I think it was penny wise or very foolish to close the company...'

After the company was closed and Alston installed as artistic director, Cohan returned to France, although he stayed on as a member of the Trust, where his role seemed to be to advise the 'youngsters' on not repeating bad decisions. It was a sad time for Cohan, as he elaborated in the film *Another Place*:

> After the company closed, I had to be very careful with myself because I had put so much of my energy, so much of my artistic creative energy and effort into the company, that I had nothing to work from. I went into a severe depression and I thought about it while I was in the depression, that this just wasn't going to work, and I can't let the people who didn't understand what we were doing affect me in this way because then they were winning and I couldn't accept that. And so for three years I plunged into painting.

Cohan had not painted since the row with his father over fifty years previously, but now he threw himself into it, painting hundreds of mainly abstract works in vivid colours. At last, he did not have to worry about pleasing funders, or theatre managers, or worry about dancers and musicians being 'happy'. He could please himself, almost.

One occasion on which he very much enjoyed himself was as period of four weeks in 1994, which he spent teaching twenty-nine pre-professional dancers at John Neumeier's school at the Hamburg State Opera. This had been financed by IBM, and Cohan found it a joy. Most of the students came from a ballet background and working with him was their first intense study of contemporary dance. The project had been arranged by Basel-born Beatrice Schickendantz-Giger, who had been a student at The Place in the early days, and it saw Cohan teaching not only technique but choreography.

The choreographic work, which was a new experience for most of the students, was very well received. Studies included one in 'restriction', where the dancers were physically tied together; a complex rhythmic study in which the dancers had to vocalise the sounds, marking out the counts. A number of the studies were shaped into one piece by Cohan and presented to the accompaniment of John Cage's prepared piano work *The Perilous Night*. The course was precisely the intense training Cohan thrived on, and which he could only regret had been lost to him in England.

After his father's death, his mother had remained in the family home; fiercely independent, she looked after herself aided by regular visits from Elliot. Then, like many elderly Jewish New Yorkers, she moved from the variable climate of New York to the sunshine and warmth of Florida. There, in West Palm Beach, she lived a very active life in what was technically a retirement complex, but where most of the residents seemed to have more energy than the staff. She died on 15 April 1996, aged 98. Her death proved a cathartic event for Cohan, and he realised he missed the world of dance and in particular choreography and, after many years of declining, gave in to David Hughes' request for a solo.

Cohan had known Hughes all the way through his training at The Place and, as a fine dancer in LCDT, since leaving the company he had danced with a range of companies, developed a solo career, and had repeatedly asked Cohan for a work. This would join other solos by a varied group of choreographers such as Christopher Bruce, Siobhan Davies, and Wayne McGregor, which Hughes would tour with great success. The piece did not come to Cohan straight away and he put off making it for many months, then one day driving home, the dance appeared. Cohan finds driving in France a chore, as French drivers can, especially on the narrow roads near his country house, be somewhat aggressive. To calm himself he would often turn to a Deutsche Grammophon CD of Herbert von Karajan conducting various popular adagios, and it was one of these pieces which suddenly inspired him.

His choice was for him most unusual, the Adagietto from Mahler's *Symphony No. 5*, famous to all who had seen the film *Death in Venice*, where its high romanticism captured the melancholy mood of death and unrequited love. It was certainly not an obvious choice for Cohan's brand of modernism, but it was not accidental, as the disc contained works by Grieg, Massenet, Pachelbel, and Albinoni among others, and any of which he could have chosen, but his mother's death and a reassessing of his life called for something unique. He called Hughes up, asked him to come to France, where he hired a local dance studio and began work. The dance flowed easily, as Cohan could clearly see in his mind images he could use, one of these was a chair. Initially, he tried to ignore this, as he has seen in his life too many bad dances made with a chair as a prop, but the image would not go away, and the chair remained. In the dance, it becomes far more than an inanimate object, it becomes a friend, a love, an object of devotion. Its role is ever changing, but its presence is constant, and the soloist constantly leaves and returns to it. The movement vocabulary is in a lyrical modern style, clearly informed by Cohan's recent work with ballet. It is concisely structured with a number of key motifs appearing in its almost fifteen-minute duration. Among these is an ecstatic movement with the body in a high arch, both arms lifted in a V shape, and the face transcendent; there are some links to *Stabat Mater*, with its theme of tragic loss. There are few high jumps – for which the athletic Hughes is well known – in the dance as the studio in which the two worked had a low roof which somewhat curtailed elevation, but there are enough dynamic changes of level, rhythm, and space that they are not missed. Judith Mackrell characterised the movement as 'slow burning passion'[366] and there is an intensity in this solo work that matches the music in a way unusual in late twentieth-century contemporary dance.

Stabat Mater appeared on the vast stage of the London Coliseum where it was restaged for Rambert Dance Company as part of their spring season. The large cathedral-like space of the venue suited the work well, and the women of the company worked hard to embody the emotional qualities of the work. Mary

Clarke found that it was performed 'with grave beauty,'[367] and that after twenty years, it held its place easily with all of the works on the programme. Sadly, Rambert did not keep the work in its repertoire and although they have bought works by other choreographers, most recently Paul Taylor's neo-romantic *Roses*, no other Cohan work has been mounted by them.

In the summer of 1996, Cohan found himself once again leading the International Dance Course for Professional Choreographers and Composers, held that year at Bretton Hall College outside of Leeds in Yorkshire. There, he was joined by composer Nigel Osborne, who he had liked personally and professionally since he had choreographed *Stone Garden* to his music in 1989. The supporting ballet classes – still required of the musicians – were taught by Ivan Kramar. The course was as selective and pressured as ever, each day beginning at 8.45 a.m. with a ballet class, and then moving on to the task for the day. Here, the composers would have to compose and record a new piece of music, and the dancers create a new dance to solve the set problem; these were as diverse and challenging as 'create a self-portrait of two people' or the always intimidatingly 'vague space'. The collaborations would be analysed and discussed in the evening, the whole process helped along by video recording. As Sheron Wray, one of the dancers, told the *Dancing Times*:

> Following our sharings and open discussions with all of the dancers and musicians, the composers and choreographers had more detailed discussions with their mentors with the previous night's video recording. I say mentors because criticisms were never directed at the particular style a choreographer worked in, it was focussing on how the problems were solved. These detailed sessions were in fact something seldom achieved in the real world. Artists sharing their ideas and problems and receiving support from each other without fear of competition or who will be held in favour by the powers that preside over the world of dance.[368]

Composer David Justin put the success of the course down to Cohan and Osborne, who 'brought the perfect spices with them: years of experience, vast knowledge, inspiration, and the all-important amount of patience. They used these ingredients to enrich our individual flavours without trying to mould us into something conventional and tried and true. They created an atmosphere that encouraged constructive criticism from everyone in the pot.'[369]

At the request of Jo Butterworth, who taught at Bretton Hall, Cohan allowed a young choreographer named Wayne McGregor to observe the course; he would later select him to participate in the 1999 event.

The experience of working on Hughes' solo and course had made Cohan realise he did want to be back in the studio, and so at the age of 71, he made it known he was available for work again. His version of *A Midsummer Night's Dream* had premiered to rather good reviews, and Galina Samsova and her dancers were very positive about the final result, and they had asked him to make a second work for them. However, the closure of LCDT and Cohan's years of depression meant that any thoughts of this second work were put on hold. But now he was ready, and fortunately so were Scottish Ballet. For this piece, Cohan returned to the baroque world of Vivaldi, using his perennially popular violin concerto *The Four Seasons* as the musical base.

In the mid 1990s, ballet in Britain was in something of a crisis – it had no choreographers. True, Bintley was succeeding in Birmingham, but MacMillan was dead and no one had replaced him at the Royal Ballet, who were reduced to importing Twyla Tharp to create a new full-length work, while English National Ballet had turned to the ice skater Christopher Dean. In Scotland, Samsova imaginatively brought together Cohan, Robert North, and Mark Baldwin, as three contemporary choreographers making work for the ballet company. The programme was provocatively called 'Sweat, Baroque and Roll' and premiered on 27 August at the Theatre Royal Glasgow.

For the designs for this work, Cohan turned once again to Norberto Chiesa, who created a series of abstract backcloths, while dressing the dancers in something approaching sportswear. The men wore shorts and the women brief floaty skirts in soft, warm colours, with flatteringly cut leotards for the principals.

In a programme note, Cohan talked about the different sections representing the different stages of life though, even with the aid of the changing coloured backdrops, in performance this was not entirely obvious, and what he produced was a largely abstract ballet to the music. As he had with his previous ballet, he blended conventional ballet steps on pointe with some quirky little touches. For reasons which he cannot now recall, each section was introduced by two men, who, dancing to the taped sounds of nature – birds, beasts, rain, and wind – acted as heralds to the action of each of the seasons. Each was built around a central pas de deux backed by the corps de ballet. Spring was danced as a green-shaded pastoral, with elegant, swift, and precise movements; the main duet was built around Nicci Theis and the Bolshoi-trained Vladislav Bubnov. Summer was designed as a beach scene in shades of yellow with the men as, possibly, lifeguards. One of their numbers, Campbell McKenzie, sunned himself with the men until Anne Christie arrived to entice him into the sunshine-laden duet. He was still attached to the Grahamesque use of props as more than décor, and in the autumn section, he choreographed a duet for Lorna Scott and Rupert Jowett, utilising a long metal pole on which she leaned or climbed, while Jowett supported her. In the winter section, Robert Hampton and Catherine Evers, dressed in blue, contrasted with the company in white, and led the company into a final tableau that united all of the seasons. Mary Brennan found the work 'haunting,'[370] while Mary Clarke rightly pointed out that in spite of Cohan's unfailing sense of theatricality, 'he was not entirely at ease writing in the classical vocabulary'.[371]

Having successfully cut his balletic teeth, so to speak, on English-speaking dancers, Cohan next accepted a commission to work in Italy, he says because he 'wanted to eat good pasta', but he also loved making dances. He had been suggested for the job by Robert North, who had developed an extensive career making contemporary/ballet dances around the world and, in particular, in the subsidised opera houses of Europe. This commission was for the 182nd season at the Teatro Sociale in Rovigo, a small town in northern Italy, which boasted a beautiful nineteenth-century opera house. In 1996, the opera house, which had no ballet company of its own, had gone into partnership with the company Fabula Saltica to produce dance works for the theatre. It was for their pick up company of dancers that Cohan made his work *Pandora Librante*, to the score of the same name by avant-garde Italian composer Claudio Ambrosini, with multimedia projections by Fabrizio Plessi. The work was premiered on 30 September 1997 at the Rovigo Opera.

The music had been composed in 1996 as a two-act ballet with the sung texts based on the American Lectures by Italo Calvino and poems by the thirteenth-century poet Cecco Angiolieri, scored for soprano, mezzo-soprano, flute, clarinet, violin, cello, piano, two percussions, and orchestra. With poetic titles ranging from dust, the nightingale, to a setting of the poem 'If I were fire', the music and poetry provided a fertile bed for Cohan's imagination. But it was not easy, the score was extremely complex, and Cohan's task was made difficult by almost never having all the company together each day. So, like Balanchine with *Serenade*, he made the sections for whoever was available on each day's rehearsal; the star of the show, Alessandro Molin, did not arrive until the last week, and so his roles were made on others and taught to him when he arrived. He was assisted in the five-week work by Claudio Ronda, the director of Fabula Saltica, an experienced dancer and rehearsal director who also translated for Cohan's culinary-inflected Italian.

As well as the difficult music, Cohan had to collaborate with Fabrizio Plessi, most famous for his site-specific installations. He had created some intriguing projections to be used in the performance, but early on in rehearsal, he complained that they were being washed out by the lighting. This enabled Cohan to happily give over to him the stage for all of the vocal sections, so that the dancers and lights would not distract from the images.

Bar one, all of Cohan's later works came about thanks to Robert North. In 1999, back in Rovigo, he and North collaborated on the forty-five-minute *Pictures*, with music by Matteo d'Amico. North had the idea of creating a dance based on classical Italian pictures, including *Cain and Abel*, *Saint Jerome in the Desert*, and *The Garden of Eden*. The opera house staff created gigantic copies of the artworks as backdrops. It was an interesting project for the two, as they deliberately made no plan as to who would do what until each day came. One of them would begin choreographing a section and then pass on the phrase to the other, an idea that may sound terrifying, but which North recalls as 'being very exciting', while Cohan found the whole experience 'energising'.

Alongside *Pictures*, Cohan collaborated with North in an unusual quadruple bill entitled 'In Mezzo… La Terra'. It comprised *Entre Dos Aguas*, *The Annunciation*, and *Italian Songs* by North, together with Cohan's duet *Eclipse*. The production toured Italy, Portugal, and Finland, where it was part of the Kuopio Dance Festival from 30 June to 6 July 1999. It was seen there by Elizabeth Kendall who, confusing the two Roberts, reviewed it for *Dance Magazine*:

> The disappointment came from Robert Cohan and Robert North's work for the earnest but feeble Fabula Saltica from Rovigo, Italy. These two choreographers of the old Martha Graham School offered one lacklustre premiere, Cohan's [sic] *Italian Songs*, about the effects of lugubrious pop tenors on young men and women in a piazza, and several recycled older pieces containing agonized angels, skittering virgins, and clamping heroes direct from some Graham central casting bureau.[372]

The summer of 1999 saw Cohan once again join Nigel Osborne at Bretton Hall, for what turned out to be the final International Course for Professional Choreographers and Composers. Political intrigues and the fatal illness of Gale Law, its director, meant this unique hothouse of creativity and experiment did not last into the twenty-first century. This was Cohan's eighth time leading the course, and he excitedly told Susan Nickalls that,

> Choreographers always work alone. What is invaluable here is that they have the chance to see how other choreographers solve the same problems. It opens their eyes. They can also ask each other questions about the work. Any artist makes work by making a series of choices and in the end it is how all of these choices are put together and how informed they are. People on this course learn about making those choices.[373]

The choreographers were as usual from a range of countries, including Holland, Portugal, and Denmark, though three came from the UK, Kenneth Tharp, Ron Howell, and Wayne McGregor, at the beginning of his rise to international acclaim.

For Kenneth Tharp, his participation was a welcome opportunity to reacquaint himself with Cohan, who he had not seen since the closure of LCDT. It was also under different circumstances, Cohan had been his boss for over ten years, and now he was acting as his mentor in choreography, something Tharp had not been noted for at LCDT. In this, Tharp found him as perceptive and helpful as ever, as he 'never taught from a sense of ego; whatever he said was to enable the choreographer to understand their own intention'.

The end of the year saw Cohan beginning work on his final ballet to date. *Aladdin*, made for Scottish Ballet had had a long gestation period. It had originally been commissioned with a working title of *The Magic Lamp* by Galina Samsova, with the idea of producing it in 1997 following *The Four Seasons*. Unfortunately, the company got into financial difficulties and Samsova left. As Carl Davis remembers, 'It was very difficult for us to know what was going on as a lot of money had already been spent on the production, I felt quite crushed. It seemed to be the end.' However, Samsova was replaced by Robert North and it was he who brought back the idea for a Christmas ballet and gave Cohan nine weeks of rehearsal to create it in 1999. Lest anyone should think that North gave his old friend carte blanche, he did not, and composer Carl Davis remembers both he and Cohan having to audition the idea for North.

When the idea for the ballet first came up, Cohan had been apprehensive, pantomimes are not an American idiom, and Cohan had never made a children's show, which is what *Aladdin* fundamentally is. But as he told Stuart Sweeney, 'I realised that this wonderful story is romantic, lyrical and magical, which are all elements that have always appealed to me and I agreed to take it forward.'[374] He added to this in conversation with Mary Brennan, telling her that the story was like a 'Romeo and Juliet love story – except they live happily ever after. And I just love doing love duets. There are four of them so my wishes are coming true.'[375]

The production was to be a spectacular Christmas entertainment, meant to last in repertory for a number of years. As such, a great deal of money was spent on it, with special effects including a flying carpet. A stellar team had been assembled and, as well as composer Carl Davis, Lez Brotherston designed the sets, Colin Falconer the costumes, and Paul Kieve the special effects.

Cohan read a great many versions of the story before settling on his libretto, and for him there was no Widow Twankey and no Wishee Washee. He saw Aladdin as a 'playful kid' whose life was transformed by the power of love, with all his exploits explained away as part of an 'inner journey'. Even here, in what is ostensibly a light-hearted piece of entertainment, Cohan still underpinned his thinking on it with a sense of spiritual journey, a theme that continually recurred in his work from *Stages*, through *No Man's Land*, to *Fabrications*. Locked in the heart of the work, he wanted his audience to recognise something that they all knew but had not yet discovered.

Once the project was given the green light, it went ahead with a great deal of excitement and enjoyment, and the first night on 20 December at the Festival Theatre in Edinburgh was eagerly awaited. The first night's audience was wildly enthusiastic, and Davis remembers all the collaborators were called back repeatedly onto the stage. Then the reviews came out and, as is often the case, did not reflect the enthusiasm of the audience. Christopher Bowen in *Scotland on Sunday* said:

> ... one would have thought that a choreographer of Cohan's experience would
> have been able to produce something better than this, even if classical idiom

and narrative structure are not his forte (the veteran choreographer was, after all, a Martha Graham disciple and is widely regarded as one of the founding fathers of British modern dance). Yet Cohan's re-telling of the familiar tale of an upwardly mobile Chinese peasant not only lacks narrative drive but dance of any real distinction to propel the story.

No one would object if Scottish Ballet pulled out the stops to make *Aladdin* a spectacular, crowd-pleasing dance entertainment, yet this it has failed to do despite some very crowd-pleasing names in the production credits.[376]

Alice Bain in the *Guardian* tried to be a little more helpful and even came up with some suggestions as to why it did not work:

Could it be that the music, with its splendidly carved filmic crescendos, is a tad on the big side for the body of the dance? Could it be that the length – though full of incidental action – requires some pruning? Could it be that, despite all the special effects, the magic lamp itself just does not work?

The dance, too, lacks presence. Though a leading member of the contemporary dance revolution in this country, Cohan takes no risks and sticks to safe, familiar balletic routines.[377]

She even found some positives:

But there is one gem. After a chitter-chattering, somersaulting village scene, Aladdin drops down a clever trapdoor into the dark, starry depths of the treasure cave, and a whirl of shiny tutus and silver skin suits begins as the jewels dance. The orchestra rolls out a grand sound for the ballerinas, pitching the white, blue, red and green set pieces from romantic bells to tick-tock rhythm. With a waltzing homage to Tchaikovsky towards the end, it's the highlight of the evening.[378]

All the collaborators were shocked and appalled by how quickly the ballet was dropped from the repertory. Although it did not gain great reviews, it did prove popular with audiences, and its demise needs to be seen in the larger picture of the cataclysmic battles that were going on backstage between the Scottish Ballet and the Scottish Arts Council. These would result in the following year in a very public battle which would see Robert North being sacked as artistic director and the company almost disbanded.

As might be expected of a person in his mid seventies, Cohan slowed down considerably and his presence as one of the founders of British contemporary dance began to fade. This was not necessarily of his own choosing, as he told Mary Brennan: '[mature artists] have something to say. They've been around. They understand things. They understand emotion. Emotion has disappeared from art, but it hasn't disappeared from life. So there's a big part of life that isn't being answered by the art of today.'[379] There were many who agreed with this view and, as Cohan approached his eightieth birthday, plans were put into place to celebrate the event in a variety of ways. A prime mover in this was Darshan Singh Bhuller, who had returned to his home town of Leeds as artistic director of Phoenix Dance Company and had revitalised this moribund company by developing a varied repertory which included Cohan's *Forest*. In addition, he had produced an hour-long documentary portrait of Cohan called *Another Place*. In it, Cohan talks about his early childhood, life with Graham, and the founding of The Place. He is surprisingly vocal about the closing of LCDT and the role played in that by the Arts Council, but ends the documentary philosophically saying he 'is in another place now'. The documentary was originally available only for an astronomical sum of money, which considerably reduced its circulation, but has since been placed, in six parts, on YouTube, providing an invaluable introduction to Cohan and his work.

In April 2005, Paul Melis at the Hochschule für Musik in Cologne presented a celebration of Cohan's work and Cohan. Kenneth Tharp and Charlotte Kirkpatrick came to help with the final rehearsals of four pieces: *Tzaikerk*, *Forest*, *Stabat Mater*, and *Class*, which Melis' students had been working on for a year. The performances with live music for *Stabat Mater* and *Class* were a tremendous achievement for the young student dancers, and Paul Melis, who did an extraordinary job in co-ordinating the school's curriculum to produce the performances. It would have been appropriate for such a project to have happened at The Place, but as none of Cohan's technique or work were now taught in his old school, they settled instead on a study day.

The event held on Sunday, 8 May, was a well-attended affair, with many students there, not just from The Place, but from the many conservatoires and universities around the capital. If his work was no longer being performed by professional companies, it was still alive in the historical syllabi of educational establishments, and the presence of so many students and young people brought a breath of fresh air to the proceedings, as these type of events can too often seem like memorial services. Most of the participants had only ever seen Cohan's work on well-used videos and the day provided the opportunity for them to see firsthand some of his technique, choreography, and of course the man himself. There was a feeling of tradition being handed down to the new generations, and a remarkable reception of this tradition, as students questioned their predecessors on the future of the art form.

The day began with a short contextual introduction by Jane Pritchard, the visible face of archival dance projects who has done so much to preserve the legacies of both Rambert Dance Company and English National Ballet. She emphasised the importance of Cohan's influence in developing an audience for contemporary dance in Britain through the work of LCDT. Darshan Singh Bhuller taught a Cohan class to members of his Phoenix Dance Theatre, which was to the many observers a revelation, particularly, and sadly, for students from the London School of Contemporary Dance, which had not taught any of Cohan's work for years. The fluidity and organic nature of the material, which flowed without stopping, was spellbinding and after the class, Bhuller was asked by a number of students why this work was not taught in the school, a question he was unable to answer.

Later, there was a screening of the BBC film of *Nympheas*, introduced by the director Bob Lockyer, who explained the process behind the recording of the different Cohan works for television. Cohan explained his original ideas for the piece and his creative process. He emphasised the importance of using one's imagination in order to fill in the gaps in the choreographic process, telling the audience that 'you've got to trust your imagination. If you don't, it just won't happen.'

His thoughts and advice on the choreographic process occurred throughout the day, in his introduction to the film, and in a rehearsal of *Eclipse*. For many of the young participants, his pronouncements were revelatory in their simplicity. When one student explained she had problems in her choreographic work because of all the ideas she wanted to work with, he told her, 'don't be a victim to your ideas'. Another questioned him about his love of form, to which he responded by asking him if he could think of any event in everyday life which did not have form. For the students growing up in a postmodern world where these concepts are often derided as old-fashioned 'formalism', it was important to hear, and to have them explained by a choreographer whose vast experience they could respect.

The day also brought together in a panel discussion a number of former LCDT members, who discussed Cohan's work with the company, without ever raising the subject of its closure. The experiences of the dancers were fascinating for the students to hear, and Cohan's comments about the closure of LCDT, that young artists need role models, were clearly brought home. The values and level of commitment that the older dancers talked about seemed as if from a different world from that of the students brought up on superficial training and quick fix choreography. But when asked by students if some of the investment in art of former times could be recovered, the replies were simple, 'Yes, if you want to fight for it.'

The study day introduced a whole new audience to Cohan and his work, but it also highlighted how fragile the world of dance is. In just over ten years, nearly twenty-five years of work had been lost; a whole period of choreographic work, a whole style of training, and a whole work ethic had been allowed to disappear. The day did not, however, end on a negative note and, as the older dancers told the dancers of tomorrow, it would be up to them to recover the past and make it relevant in their artistic lives.

The celebrations concluded on 9 May with a programme at Sadler's Wells in an evening that brought together three companies in performances of works by

Cohan. Although the event had received very little publicity, there was a good-sized audience, and the atmosphere was decidedly festive. Students from The Place had been sent along wearing 'Happy Birthday Bob' T-shirts, and mingled with the audience consisting of former company members and older followers of Cohan and his work.

Phoenix Dance Theatre performed *Forest*, while two dancers from Richard Alston's company danced the early duet *Eclipse*, and finally dancers from Ballet Theatre Munich, directed by Philip Taylor, another former LCDT member, performed *Stabat Mater*. A short film of images of Cohan's life was shown and then, following tumultuous applause, he was interviewed by Richard Alston. Cohan spoke about how he had made some of the works on the programme and recalled experiences of touring with LCDT. At the end of the evening, he was presented by Dame Beryl Grey with the Critics' Circle National Dance Awards special committee prize in recognition of his lifetime's achievement in dance, and the evening ended with a standing ovation from the very vocal audience.

In the programme for the performance, Clement Crisp, dance critic of the *Financial Times*, wrote: 'Robert Cohan was the power, the knowledge, the skill, the sheer persistence and the dedication that found how contemporary dance might be made to flourish in a new land.'[380] This theme was carried forward in reviews, with Debra Craine in *The Times* writing:

> Where would contemporary dance be in this country without this expatriate American? For twenty years, at the helm of London Contemporary Dance Theatre, Cohan helped to spawn the dance boom of the 1970s and 1980s. He trained scores of dancers, developed a generation of choreographers and made dozens of dances. This gala, on the occasion of his eightieth birthday, couldn't begin to encompass his enormous achievements, but three companies with links to Cohan did their best to honour his inspired and charismatic leadership.[381]

Jann Parry in *The Observer* noted that: 'It was moving to see how a new generation of dancers strove to honour Cohan's aesthetic, serving him instead of expressing themselves. Thanks to his influence, we've learnt how wonderfully varied dance can be.'[382] Mike Dixon, reviewing the performance in *Dance Europe*, was full of praise for the event and ended his report observing: 'Many of us feel that a knighthood is overdue for this great man who has given so much to dance in Great Britain.'[383] On the other side of the coin, *Dance Now* included what should have been a tribute to Cohan entitled 'The Godfather'; unfortunately, it was written by John Percival. He had clearly tried to rein in his antipathy to Cohan but could not resist ending his article by reiterating how much he did not like Cohan as a choreographer. In particular, he did not like *Forest*, the very work that was currently being toured by Phoenix Dance Theatre and garnering excellent notices.[384]

If the performances and study day were ephemeral, an edition of *Dance Research*, the journal of the Society for Dance Research, which had appeared in October 2004, included a substantial homage to Cohan, with memories from him and tributes from former, students, colleagues, dancers, and admirers.[385]

Cohan returned to The Place on 3 December 2005, when his first choreography for five years, a solo entitled *Study*, was performed as part of the theatre's White Christmas season. Created for Darshan Singh Bhuller, it was, as might be expected from the title, the briefest dance on a mixed programme that included work by a variety of choreographers including Khamlane Halsackda, Jeremy James, Arthur Pita, Andile Sotiya, Shobana Jeyasingh, and Luca Silvestrini. The dance was an unusual choice for a Christmas season, being very intense, bizarre, and surprising. Based loosely on the anatomy drawings of Andreas Vesalius and on the subject of fear, it was certainly not a festive piece. The écorché (flayed) figures of Vesalius are indeed fear inducing and Darshan Singh Bhuller seemed to strip the skin off his face as he slowly twirled on the spot – a very alive man imitating a dead one. A back projection gradually filled the stage with blood until the dancer disappeared in a flash of green light after just four minutes of intense drama. The work was well received, with Jann Parry writing, 'Robert Cohan needed just four [minutes] to sum up mortality in *Study*, his new solo for Darshan Singh Bhuller. Cohan, at 80, is master of them all.'[386] It also featured in the *Observer*'s year's end Top Ten awards for dance 2005.

Chapter 12

Commentary

It is still very hard for me to think and write about the closure of London Contemporary Dance Theatre without a nightmarish host of thoughts coming into my mind, so I will confine myself to just a few comments.

Dealing seriously with the Arts Council at any time was like entering a Kafka story, but during this time it was a year-long world of endless labyrinths. What I should say here is that the Board did close the Company as the Arts Council has said. What the Arts Council did not say was that the Board was told that if they did not close the company, no money would be forthcoming to The Place itself in the future. This is the Kafka part, and how you wash your hands of any guilt.

What I cannot understand is how the decision of a few people, with an agenda, I believe, can throw away millions of taxpayers' pounds with so little real dialogue. For over twenty years, we were unbelievably careful how we spent every last penny. Conscientiously using our Arts Council grant to build a large repertory of contemporary dance and carefully training dancers to do that repertory. As well we built a very large and expensive technical system of computers, lights, and all of the necessary equipment to present that repertory at the highest possible standard. But mostly, we built a very good British and international reputation and a large dedicated audience of followers. All that was easily thrown away, which makes me think that, as far as dance is concerned, the Arts Council really had no long-term coherent business policy or structure in place to deliver the art of dance to the British taxpayers who fund the Council.

What I cannot forgive was the putting out of work of twenty talented, serious dancers, artists, who had worked for many years just to be in this precise company. It not only destroyed their dreams and in some cases talent, but also cut off the dreams of all of those young people who had set their future on the same goal. I thought it was an act of artistic vandalism and I was not alone, judging from the response of all of the critics and others in the dance world at the time.

In another vein completely, I want to thank Paul Jackson for making me talk about my life to him and to make me think about why I did what I did. I am not the kind of person who goes over their past by looking at photos or recordings of old dances. This experience was a little difficult at first, but became fascinating nonetheless.

No man is an island, especially a dancer. Everything you do is in public, from your first step to your last, so I want to take this opportunity to also thank all of the people who I worked with and loved, who knowingly or not helped me over the years.

All artists, when performing and/or creating, have intense moments during their work when something special and unexpected happens.

It is difficult to describe but Martha Graham used to call them small miracles.

As I said before, for me it is the intense feeling of being in the right place at the right time and doing the right thing. When it happens, it can produce in you a surge of wonder and an inner sensation of clarity and delight that is rare in life.

I spent many years performing and literally danced around the world. I have also spent at least fifty years in dance studios, almost every day, teaching, rehearsing, or creating dance.

I have had a very large share of these 'small miracles' and mostly because of them, I can look back at my life in dance with satisfaction and pleasure.

Postlude

For O, for O, the hobby-horse is forgot

(Hamlet, III. ii. 135)

2006–

Cohan was buoyed by the success of *Study* and his enthusiasm can be seen in an interview he gave to Judith Mackrell for a short feature in the *Guardian* entitled 'The Seven Ages of...' on 8 January 2006, which was part of 'a unique survey of the various stages of the careers of performers, from pop musicians to theatre-makers'. Cohan was the oldest dancer interviewed.

'The over-70s'
'Robert Cohan, 80'

When I was small I was taught adagio, acrobatic and tap by an old woman in Brooklyn; then in high school I was head cheerleader. At 19 I went to a modern dance class at Martha Graham's studio and that was it for me. I gave up my job and within two months Martha said: 'Work hard over the summer, boy, I want you in my company.' That was 1946 and I stayed with her until 1966. I had no plans to leave New York but Martha asked me to go to London, so for the next twenty-two years I ran London Contemporary Dance Theatre. I left in 1988 and retired to France. I haven't missed dance since but I do enjoy getting back to the studio, and I've been making new work. I love being in that place again without the pressure.

The pressure was, sadly, to become even less. The success of *Study* led Cohan and Singh Bhuller to think of expanding the work into a larger project involving another former LCDT dancer Kate Coyne. The work was quite well developed, and had grown into a duet of about twenty minutes in all, and everything looked positive. All of the Arts Council funding was in place, when Singh Bhuller was told by his doctors that, owing to an injury he had sustained playing football, he should not undertake any serious performing work again. Once it was known Singh Bhuller would not be available to tour the work, the funding was withdrawn and the project has remained tantalisingly unfulfilled.

Cohan's few forays into the studio have in recent years been limited. This can in part be explained away by the ailments of old age and a slowly declining body. He is not looking to teach regular classes or workshops, as he says, 'I wouldn't like to have to stage something on my own, what I could do was choreographic coaching. I wouldn't want to run a course but I could do it on a professional level. I could certainly be a mentor.' The lack of interest shown in using the skills of one of the world's most experienced choreographers in leading the occasional advanced choreographic workshop or seminar is strange. Certainly in Britain, contemporary dance world seems to be the domain of youth, with most choreographers being in their 20s or 30s. Richard Alston, Siobhan Davies, and Christopher Bruce, now in their 60s, lead from experience, though none of them show any signs of having the longevity of a Graham or Cunningham. But even there, there are problems: Alston has fallen into the old LCDT rut of too much touring, Davies has semi-retired, and Bruce's new work is mainly created abroad. Of the experienced and very successful 50-year olds, Lea Anderson and Michael Clarke had their funding cancelled in an Arts Council cull. When Cohan said to Mary Brennan, 'there's a big part of life that isn't being answered by the art of today,'[387] he was correct. There are no longer any advanced professional choreographic courses as there were in the 1980s, and young choreographers leave college to make do as best they can. In an interview, Cohan told Sue Hoyle that 'You become an artist to create art, not as a career move. You don't think, I'm going to make a lot of money, making dances.'[388] The vagaries of Arts Council funding policy in the twenty-first century make the possibility of that even more difficult.

In an article published in *The Times* when LCDT was being closed down, John Percival wrote,

> The Arts Council's line is that it does not want to support a large scale repertory company. The dogmatists who shape the council's dance policies prefer to support small, sometimes transitory, choreographer-led ventures. They think there is more energy there (a debatable belief) and are prepared to overlook the fact that the energy is not always backed up with enough talent.[389]

His opinion seems to have been borne out in the years since. The Place Theatre did indeed become a palace for young choreographers to present their work; but how many of the hundreds who presented work in the regular seasons known as Spring Loaded or Resolutions continued for more than a few years? Very few indeed. John Ashford, who was for twenty-three years director of the theatre and the person who programmed the neophytes, gave a scathing assessment of current British dance to Lyndsey Winship when he stepped down in 2009:

> 'British dance is timorous, and therefore often dull,' says John Ashford… Too often he sees young artists 'doing what they've been taught in school' rather than 'truly reflecting the world as seen by that artist'.

And he laid the problem for this squarely at the Arts Council's door,

> Then there's the funding issue; that's the Arts Council's fault. Firstly for abandoning peer review, secondly for inputting a 'madcap' funding agenda

that values community outreach over artistry, and then for leaving the fate of young artists up to the Lottery-funded Grants for the Arts.

'I don't see why a game of chance should influence why or not promising young artists should get money to begin their careers,' says Ashford.

'I seriously believe the reason [British dance] is timorous is because it has been coerced into obeying that agenda in order to achieve any professional level of funding.'[390]

Ashford sees the tick-boxing, form-filling culture and obsession with youth that the Arts Council promulgates as a major stumbling block for any hope that British contemporary dance will become a major player on the international dance scene. The excitement that, it was hoped, would follow the closing of LCDT and of the British adopting a European approach to dance, has been scuppered in the quicksand of Arts Council policy, which has of course to follow the quixotic decisions of the Ministry of Culture, Media and Sport, themselves based on expediency rather than strategic planning.

In the light of this, it is understandable that most of Cohan's work has been limited to coaching. Occasionally, this has been for the Graham Company, which has soldiered on since its founder's death, and where Janet Eilber, the current artistic director, is happy to welcome him as 'a great and valued artist'. In the UK, the coaching is to students from those schools with the foresight to think it would be a useful to learn some of his dances. The Rambert School, headed by Ross McKim, has staged *Forest* on two occasions. On both of these, the dance was set by the late Charlotte Kirkpatrick who, until her untimely death, had been invaluable to Cohan in remounting his work. Cohan would attend later rehearsals, aiming to transmit his now unfamiliar style on the young bodies.

Another institution, the Arts Educational School in Tring, a co-educational school for pupils aged 8-18, has gone even further. There, Rachel Rist, the head of dance and an enthusiast for Cohan's work, has worked closely with Anne Went, a former LCDT dancer who now lectures at Middlesex University, to stage some of Cohan's work, including *Stabat Mater* in 2006, and in 2007 a valiant attempt at *Class*. Both of those institutions have Graham-based work as an essential part of their contemporary training, Rambert even going so far as to call it Cohan technique.

The list does not include the London School of Contemporary Dance, where none of Cohan's work, neither choreographic nor technical, is offered. Nor has he been invited to lead any sort of masterclass or workshop, even though as a trustee he is in the building three or four times a year. In the course of researching this book, this point has been raised a number of times by many people and Veronica Lewis, the director of the school, was asked several times to comment, but ultimately did not. But as Cohan says, 'I simply haven't been asked.'

Whatever views may be held on the quality of Cohan's choreography, no one has anything but praise for the quality and rigour of his teaching; he is simply acknowledged as one of the greatest teachers in the world. Since the demise of LCDT and the many changes to contemporary training in the UK, the loss of Cohan's technique is something that has vexed many people. Graham-based work of varying quality is available at a number of conservatoires and many universities and colleges, but it is Cohan's development of this that is in danger of being lost. Many of Cohan's former dancers did not retire into teaching, at least on a regular basis, and of those still working, Ross McKim teaches Cohan's work at the Rambert School, Anne Went at Middlesex University, others teach infrequently. It was to stop this loss that Paula Lansley, together with Anne Went, Rachel Grist, and director-producer Anne Maguire, set up a project to document Cohan's teaching, the idea being to produce a DVD and a booklet.

To this end seed money was found, and utilising the facilities at Arts Educational, many hours were filmed with Cohan talking to camera and then teaching exercises to a select group of advanced students, with expert demonstrations from former LCDT dancers Kate Coyne and Paul Liburd. As is often the case with such projects, the financial costs spiralled and to date, the many hours of recordings lie unedited, awaiting the necessary funding to produce what should be a fascinating document. Middlesex University is now fully involved in the project but until a DVD appears, the only real document of Cohan teaching is the class filmed for the BBC in 1978, which again, tantalisingly, is not available commercially. It is, however, available in institutions who recorded it on one of its rare outings on television in the 1980s, and where those who search it out still find it useful. Fred Gehrig, who was a dancer in the last year of LCDT, recently revisited the tape, and although he does not teach Graham-based work, he found in Cohan's pedagogy many invaluable truths that he has been able to include in his teaching practice.

Indeed, the strongest witness to Cohan's skills as a teacher and trainer and of his approach to teaching is the range of careers that his students have moved into. None were limited by his teaching, and they can be found in every style of dancing available. Siobhan Davies, Lauren Potter, Paul Douglas moved easily into release technique; Barry Moreland, Brenda Edwards, Paul Liburd into ballet; the late Tom Jobe, Michael Small, and Anita Griffin into commercial dance. His technique is a real technique, one that frees those who master it and gives them the ability to move in many areas.

Of the choreographers who came out of LCDT, they too have moved into most spheres of dance: Anthony van Laast has had a very successful career in commercial shows in the West End, on Broadway, in Las Vegas, and on film; Micha Bergese has moved into theatrical spectacle, choreographing for, amongst others, Shaolin monks and the theatre work that was part of the Millennium celebrations in the Dome; Robert North has gone on to take his brand of contemporary ballet to many companies throughout Europe; likewise, Aletta Collins has choreographed operas and musicals as well as very successful contemporary dance works. Of all his students, it is Darshan Singh Bhuller whose work has moved forward Cohan's work. As a filmmaker, choreographer, and company director, his aesthetic is closest to Cohan's own, his work mixing spectacle with a sense of social responsibility, as his 1998 dance *Planted Seeds*, based on the Yugoslav/Bosnian conflict, shockingly showed.

Cohan has received occasional requests to write some of his thoughts or articles on dance. One such appeared in a Place newsletter, though he admits it was particularly aimed at 'dumb ministers who think the arts are indulgences we should do without'.

Dance education is an education for living.

Dance teaches you where you are in your body, how well you know it, and how to become more connected to it. That only makes sense because your body is where you will live all of your life.

Dance teaches you where you are in space and how to relate and be exactly aware of where you are in it. A sense that helps you function in the space of your world.

Dance is a reality check on what you think you are doing and what is really happening. Either your knee is straight or it is bent. No amount of dreaming will straighten it for you.

Dance teaches you logic. The body is a beautifully logical creation that has slowly and carefully evolved to move as efficiently as possible. Our out of control emotions and the stresses of life tend to disorganise this logic with disruptive tensions that lift shoulders, curve backs defensively and ruin spines. The study of dance helps us to find these broken physical pathways in our own bodies and helps you to learn, not only to recognise them, but to logically repair the damage.

Dance teaches you relationships. You cannot learn anything unless you establish a working relationship to it, especially your own body. A wonderful objectivity develops as you train in dance between your mental self, and your body as your instrument. It is a strange relationship as you discover that you can give your body instructions that your body follows and on the other hand it gives you information back as to how things are going and instructions on how to make it work better. Dance is often learned in a group or as part of a group. You will learn how to tune yourself to those around you and without words, begin to feel empathy with other people so that you can work as part of a team.

Dance training teaches you attention. You cannot learn to move well without paying attention to not only what you are doing but also how you are doing it. In dance, the 'how' is more important than anything else and that requires undivided attention. A simple example is that if you repeatedly do a movement the wrong way you are teaching yourself and your body to do it wrongly, just in the same way that if you do something correctly, you teach yourself a correct way of moving. Only learning how to pay constant attention to yourself can keep you improving.

Dance teaches you how to make and control effort. Dance training, by its very physical nature can be difficult. To improve and learn requires teaching yourself how to apply and even control effort on yourself and your body. You learn how much effort is needed to walk well and how much more is needed to run and then how much more to leap and jump. You not only learn how much effort is needed for different tasks but you learn to increase your ability to work and how much further you can push yourself than you thought you could. That single achievement can sometimes change your life.

Perhaps best of all, after working well, in a good dance class, there can be a feeling of real physical use and tangible accomplishment. You may have even expressed some emotions that are unsayable in words.

You are sure to have discovered new physical sensations that enrich your imagination. Hidden in the study of dance can be the experience of comfort in your own physical world, your body. It is there waiting for your own personal discovery.

The study of dance will give you tools with which to enhance your life

2009/10 was celebrated as the fortieth anniversary of The Place, and it saw a year of celebrations of everything that had gone on in the building since it was founded. It culminated with a series of performances in The Place Theatre, curated by Aletta Collins and entitled 'This is The Place'. On Saturday, 22 May 2010, the daytime was given over to a reunion of LCDT which began at 2 p.m., when Cohan was interviewed by Richard Alston and Kenneth Tharp.

The interview was in front of a packed house of former LCDT members, from the dancers through to the musicians, technical crew, and educational staff, and was an informal affair touched with great emotion. Cohan entered to a standing ovation which lasted some minutes, and once settled into a comfortable sofa answered questions from his old pupils. The full forty years of Place dancers were there, and in the course of the interview, some would join Cohan on stage, share an anecdote or memory, and return to the audience. What came out from all of those assembled was how much they owed to Cohan, for many their entire careers. But what could have become maudlin and sentimental did not because it was all done so honestly and naturally. This sense of an extended community continued in a session which followed and was held in the company studio. There, the company members were grouped on tables according to their period working with the company and, with the help of a facilitator, encouraged to dredge up memories of what had been a tremendous journey for all those assembled.

In the evening came the performance, drawn together by Collins from the forty-year performance history of the theatre. After a claustrophobic site-specific piece held in the crowded bar, perhaps made in homage to the events that had heralded the opening of the building in 1969, the performance moved to the theatre proper. After a short collage of film clips, Namron walked onto the stage in darkness and began talking in his lilting Jamaican accent about the first performance in 1969. Standing on the same spot as he had all those years ago he slowly moved into material from *Cell*, the stage presence that had marked him out in his dancing years effortlessly holding the audience. As his words and movement disappeared into the darkness to tumultuous applause, two dancers appeared stage right. It took the audience some moments to realise it was Patrick Harding-Irmer and Anca Frankenhauser, who were performing a duet from *Forest*. At least it looked like that until words replaced movement: 'That was a jump', 'That was a lift', said the two as the material that was now physically beyond them was mimed to the amusement of the audience. What was not beyond them, however, was the quality, the sheer stage presence that two seasoned artists of their calibre can bring, and a deep understanding held in their muscle memory of a work that had been central to their careers. Once they left the stage, they were replaced by two dancers from Richard Alston's company who were to perform the same duet. Their performance and embodiment of the work was of course not comparable to the older couple; they had not the physical instruments nor the years of experience to support them, but still it was strangely exciting to see movement that, because it had not been seen for so long, seemed new. As Sanjoy Roy wrote in his guide to Robert Cohan in the *Guardian*, the work is 'no longer current'.[391] But what was exciting was Cohan's movement; shown in the context of the newer works, it seemed not new and original, but timeless and original. Wholly concerned with the body as an expressive instrument, wholly concerned with the art of choreography and not, as were many of the other works shown, with the anonymous theatricality of Eurocrash. As Roy noted in his review of the evening, 'These pieces [the early Place works] made me wish modern dance kept more of its own heritage alive.'[392]

The very long evening – the show lasted over three hours – concluded with Victoria Marks' *Dancing to Music*. This had been made in 1988 for students in the school but had been restaged in 1993 when the main roles were taken by four women associated with The Place – Jane Dudley, Judyth Knight, Ruth Moss, and Louise Donald. It is a powerfully quiet, contemplative dance with minimal movement, and for this occasion it had been suggested that Cohan dance in the work and at first, he was excited by the possibility. Then the reality of the situation set in, and he realised that he would not have the stamina for a long day's work and then a late performance, and had to regretfully back out. In the end, the main roles were taken by Richard Alston, Kenneth Tharp, Eddie Dixon (director of the theatre), and Dominick Mitchell-Bennett (a student in the school), with the rest of the cast joining in for what was a quiet and deeply moving end to a thrilling evening.

In his little guide to Cohan, Roy observed that 'If you see a Robert Cohan piece – well, you're lucky. Once the mainstay of Britain's premier modern dance company, his works are now rarely seen.' After The Place celebrations, the next opportunity to see a Cohan work occurred a year later when Richard Alston's company decided to restage In Memory, Cohan's 1989 work about loss. Supported by funding from the soon-to-be-closed Robin Howard Foundation, it was an intriguing choice which highlighted the problems of British contemporary dance in the twenty-first century.

To begin with, there were problems with the music. The work had originally been choreographed to music by Hans Werner Henze; but even Richard Alston's company, one the major funded contemporary groups in England, could not afford the musicians to perform that work, and so Cohan had to search for some 'affordable' music. This took some time, and with his own unique ear, he eventually settled on Hindemith's deeply challenging – for performer and audience alike – Sonata for solo viola. Hindemith is not a popular composer these days, and this sonata is one of his least popular works. The viola is the Cinderella of the string family, sitting between the soaring violin and the deeply expressive cello; it does not have a powerful voice and what it does have is often acerbic. It was not the best replacement for the Henze.

The dancers in Alston's company learnt the material from a video of the 1989 performance with help from Darshan Singh Bhuller and Richard Alston. Once the material was learnt, Cohan arrived to coach them and to make the considerable changes needed to accommodate the change of score. The rehearsals went slowly, as the very young dancers were in awe of him. Rehearsing in the Robert Cohan Studio with Robert Cohan, they tried desperately to give him everything thing he asked of them. But in doing this, they forgot about the dancing and even at the dress rehearsal, the piece was not jelling. Eventually, Cohan told them, 'forget about me and just dance', and they did.

The work was shown in a mixed programme of very early and new work by Alston, together with a duet by his protégé Martin Lawrance. The dancers moved very well, considering they had not been trained in Cohan's technique or aesthetic and, in addition, his movement vocabulary was completely alien to them. The basic shape of the movement and the formal structure of the piece came together in spite of the Hindemith music which was performed live on stage. What was missing was any sense of the meaning of the work; as Cohan joked, 'I made the piece on dancers in their 30s. They had memories, these people don't have any yet.' But in spite of these shortcomings, it was an important occasion. In 1996, at the time of Rambert Dance Company's revival of *Stabat Mater*, John Drummond wrote that it was so important 'to have a chance of seeing some of it [Cohan's work] again, and in different circumstances'.[393] His observation was even more relevant now, as a British dance world more and more obsessed with youth forgets where it came from.

Ultimately, very few reviews of this important event appeared in the press, either at the time of the first showing or on the subsequent tour. Of those that did, most chose to ignore Cohan's work entirely, although in one he was referred to as 'a choreographic legend',[394] a review which then did not mention *In Memory* at all. Those who did comment could not agree, Sanjoy Roy thinking that 'It all feels rather dated and heavy handed',[395] while another writer found it strangely modern and wondered how much influence Cohan had on the early work of the BalletBoyz.[396]

Long-standing British dance pioneer Marie McCluskey feels that 'the contemporary dance world is cannibalistic' and 'has no respect for its past', while Janet Eilber, the current director of the Graham Company, feels 'It's time for modern dance... to come to grips with the fact that it has an important past.' When contemporary dance was beginning it of course did not have a history, but as Eilber observes, after 100 years it does have a past that it struggles to live with. Contemporary dance is no longer merely the dance of now, it is part of an extended family; we may not like all of the family members, but we ignore them at our peril. We can see here the real difference between the worlds of modern dance and modern music. I began this book mentioning Pierre Boulez, Cohan's exact contemporary, who is now still feted as a pioneer of twentieth-century music. His works are regularly performed, even though the musical world has moved on and embraced a whole myriad of styles, and the reception of his work is not always positive. His music still has something to say musically, aesthetically, and culturally to the modern world.

In the worlds of music, art, and drama, the past and the present mingle and serve each other; the presence of an old work bringing into relief a new one and vice versa. A contemporary playwright or painter is not threatened by the appearance of early works. Indeed, they embrace and comment on them – David Hockney is an expert on the work of Turner and Tom Stoppard memorably comments on Shakespeare in his play *Rosencranz and Guildenstern are Dead*. Contemporary dancers do not do that. Writing in *Dance Theatre Journal* in 1998, Alexandra Carter, in an article that looked at how dance works may be preserved and revisited, asked the question: '[A]re we to lose the whole of Robert Cohan's repertoire for London Contemporary Dance Theatre', and pointed out that 'to suggest it could not be performed as techniques, performing styles and bodies have changed is untenable'.[397] She made the point that dancers' bodies have not changed, only their attitude to older work; and until that attitude or mindset that contemporary means youth, then the 'immature work' which John Drummond worried about will become the norm and will do so to the detriment of the art form.

In a 1980 interview with Tobi Tobias, Cohan said,

The important things in my life have always been the work. It's hard to convey. I spend most of my time in the studio working, and that is where the life is. It was so with Graham, first in class and then in the rehearsal room. Doing the actual work was the exciting time that one talks about. But that took up hours, and hours, and hours of everyday. The same thing now in London Contemporary Dance Theatre, the important thing is the work that one does, and the time that one works: the hours, and hours, and hours in dance that you spend in the studio, actually doing the physical work. That is what is exciting about it and makes it still alive. And all the theories about it, and my talking about insurance and not making the same mistakes, all that is how you keep that sense of work alive for yourself and for the other people.[398]

Robert Cohan is still available to continue that work today.

Endnotes

Prelude

1. Paul Taylor Dance Company's website, http://www.ptdc.org/artists-dances/paul-taylor
2. Butterworth 2012, p. 95
3. ISKCON'S Ideology, 24 October 2012, http://www.oneiskcon.com/2012/10/iskcons-ideology-part-seven
4. Interview with the Dhananjayans, http://kathak.org/traditionsengaged/ 2010/08/interview-with-the-dhananjayans/
5. Interview with Pandit Chitresh Das, http://kathak.org/traditionsengaged/about/about-festival/
6. It can be found at http://www.partrealpartdream.com/
7. *Guardian*, 29 November 2011, http://www.guardian.co.uk/artanddesign/jonathanjones blog/2011/nov/29/mourning-ken-russell-cy-twombly

Chapter 1

The majority of the material came from Cohan and his brother and sister Dolly and Elliot Cohan.

8. Rumi, "Mathnawi", II, 450–4
9. Hodes 2012

Chapter 2

10. Much of the material in this chapter came from Cohan and the following were invaluable resources: ASTP, http://www.astpww2.org/; 89th Infantry Division of World War II, http://www.89infdivww2.org/memories/levequeastp.htm; Louis E. Keefer, The Army Specialized Training Program in World War II, http://www.pierce-evans.org/ASTP%20in%20WWII.htm, as were Delaforce 2004, Dupuy 1994, Keegan 1992, Kershaw 2004, Mitcham 2006, Parker 1991, Shaw 2000, Toland 1999, Zaloga 2004
11. Ouspensky 1949/2001, p. 176
12. Gurdjieff 1957/2000, p. 84
13. Vidal 1996, p. 95
14. Keefer, http://www.pierce-evans.org/ASTP%20in%20WWII.htm
15. Spark 1999, p. 1
16. Gow 1970, p. 186

Chapter 3

17. McDonagh 1973, p.181
18. Leatherman 1966, p. 46
19. Graham 1991, p. 184
20. Soares 1992, p. 165
21. Ibid., p. 167
22. Graham 1991, p. 161
23. Hodes 2011
24. Graham 1991, p. 199
25. *Washington Post* 25 February 1947
26. Hodes op. cit.

27. *New York Herald Tribune* 15 August 1948
28. *New York Star* 17 August 1948
29. Early programme notes for the piece
30. Programme notes, early 1950s
31. *Atlanta Journal* 1 March 1949
32. Hodes op. cit.
33. *Houston Post* 13 March 1949
34. *Chicago Daily Tribune* 25 November 1949
35. *Christian Science Monitor* 25 January 1950
36. According to Stuart Hodes, Janet Soares records this as "Angst and Hogwash". Soares 1992, p. 204.
37. *New York Times* 25 January 1950
38. Ibid.
39. *New York Herald Tribune* 25 January 1950
40. McDonagh 1973, p. 166
41. 30 March 1950, private collection
42. Redfern 1965, p.7
43. *The Manichi* 15 November 1957

Chapter 4
44. Barnes 1954
45. Ibid.
46. In Ralph ed. 2004, p. 95
47. Barnes op. cit.
48. Hunt 1954
49. *Hamlet* (III, i, 65–68)
50. Graham 1991, p. 200
51. Graham 1973, p.271
52. Todd 1953, p. 21
53. *New York Times* 6 May 1955
54. Woods 1999, p. 50
55. Ibid.
56. *The Times* 11 March 1954
57. *Empire News* 12 March 1954
58. Netter ed. 1979, p. 166
59. Richard Buckle, *The Observer* 7 March 1954
60. Alexander Bland, *The Observer* 21 March 1954
61. Clarke 1954
62. Contemporary Dance Trust Archive, V&A Museum
63. McKayle 2002, p. 78
64. *Christian Science Monitor* 11 June 1955
65. In "Martha Graham in Asia", *Dance Magazine* March 1956
66. McKayle 2002, p. 78
67. Woods 1999, p. 50
68. *Time Magazine* 25 June 1956
69. Last Night's play by F. R. J., "*Shangri-La* Elaborately Staged at Shubert", *New Haven Journal Courier* 15 June 1956
70. F. R. J. in *New Haven Courier* 13 May 1956
71. Tokunaga 2008, p. 103

Chapter 5
72. Tracy 1997, p. 260
73. Loney 1984, p. 104
74. Christine Gratto, *Rochester and Democrat Chronicle* 5 April 1959
75. "Take off Your Shoes", uncredited article in *The Rochester News* 6 April 1959
76. H. W. S. in *The Rochester News* 5 April 1959
77. Tracy op. cit., p. 212
78. *Rochester Herald* 10 November 1959
79. Walter Terry, *New York Herald Tribune* 4 August 1960
80. Marjory Adams, *Boston Globe* 20 July 1961
81. Walter Terry, *New York Times* 31 October 1960
82. *Youth Magazine* 1960
83. Elinor Hughes, *Boston Sun Herald* 16 October 1960
84. Ibid.
85. Manchester 1960
86. Ibid.
87. Hughes, op. cit.
88. Manchester op. cit.
89. Hughes, op. cit.
90. Isabel Ferguson, *Christian Science Monitor* 17 October 1960
91. Walter Terry, *New York Herald Tribune* 31 October 1960
92. Ibid.
93. Ibid.
94. Gurdjieff Studies, http://www.gurdjieff.org.uk/gs7.htm
95. Terry op. cit.
96. John Martin, *New York Times* 6 November 1960
97. Robert Taylor, *Boston Herald* 19 May 1961
98. Kevin Kelly, *Boston Globe* 19 May 1961
99. Isabel Ferguson, *Christian Science Monitor* 26 May 1962
100. Judith Mackrell, *Guardian* 12 May 2005
101. "Campus Times", *Rochester Herald* 6 May 1961
102. Cavendish 1977, p. 22
103. Video of *Hunter of Angels*, University of Surrey National Resource Centre for Dance, 1982
104. *Boston Herald* 26 May 1962
105. Ferguson op. cit.
106. *Boston Herald* op. cit.
107. Kathleen Cannell, 26 May 1962
108. *Boston Herald* 26 May 1962
109. Todd 1962

Chapter 6
110. Elinor Hughes, *Boston Herald* 8 April 1963
111. Margaret von Szeliski, *Harvard Crimson* 9 April 1963
112. Isabel Ferguson, *Christian Science Monitor* 30 April 1963
113. Ibid.
114. Ibid.
115. Hughes, op. cit.
116. Ferguson, op. cit.

117. Billington 2007, p. 123
118. Teresa Early in Mackrell 1992, p. 5
119. *Glasgow Herald* 27 August 1963
120. *Edinburgh News* 27 August 1963
121. J. W. *Evening Dispatch* 28 August 1963
122. Richard Buckle, *Sunday Times* 8 September 1963
123. Clarke and Crisp 1989, p. 16
124. Ouspensky 1950, p. 236
125. Clarke and Crisp op. cit., p. 18
126. *Dance and Dancers* October 1966
127. In the Contemporary Dance Trust Archive at V&A Museum, but also quoted in Clarke and Crisp 1989.
128. Margo Miller, *Boston Herald* 8 March 1965
129. Alta Maloney, *Boston Traveller* 5 March 1965
130. Batsheva Company programme for premieres
131. Hutchinson and Early 1965
132. Walter Terry, *New York Herald* Tribune 3 November 1965
133. Ibid.
134. Clive Barnes, *New York Times* 8 November 1965
135. Clive Barnes, *New York Times* 6 November 1965
136. Clive Barnes, *New York Times* 6 November 1965
137. Walter Terry, *New York Herald* Tribune 6 November 1965
138. Clive Barnes, *New York Times* 8 November 1965
139. Williams 1967a
140. *Dance and Dancers* September 1967
141. Williams 1967b
142. John Percival, *The Times* 12 October 1967
143. Alexander Bland, *The Observer* 14 October 1967
144. Nicholas Dromgoole, *Sunday Telegraph* 14 October 1967
145. Hering 1968
146. Ibid.
147. Allen Hughes, *New York Times* 18 October 1968
148. Lapzeson has no memory of these events.

Chapter 7
149. Cruickshank 1976
150. Contemporary Dance Trust Archive, V&A Museum
151. Richard Buckle, *Sunday Times* 14 September 1969
152. Alexander Bland, *The Observer* 14 September 1969
153. Nicholas Dromgoole, *Sunday Telegraph* 14 September 1969
154. Buckle op. cit.
155. John Percival, *The Times* 12 September 1969
156. Williams 1970c
157. Nugent 1991
158. Ibid.
159. Unpublished interview courtesy of Cohan
160. Gerken et al 1999, p. 66
161. Williams and Goodwin 1971
162. Contemporary Dance Trust Archive, V&A Museum

163. Soares 1991, p. 196
164. McKim, "Contemporary heritage: a fusion of horizons", The Place 28 November 2006
165. Hagen 2010
166. Percival 1972a
167. Jordan 1992, p. 2
168. "Experimental Summer", *Dance and Dancers* November 1972
169. Williams, Percival and Goodwin 1972a
170. Williams, Percival and Goodwin 1973b
171. Clarke and Crisp 1989, p. 71
172. Letter from Strate to Cohan
173. Williams and Goodwin 1973
174. Ibid.
175. Cowan 1973
176. Clarke 1978, p. 204
177. Williams and Goodwin 1978
178. Clarke and Crisp 1989, p. 77
179. Ibid.
180. Ibid.

Chapter 8
181. Williams, Percival and Goodwin 1972b
182. Gordon and Gordon 2005, p. 193
183. Erdman ed. 1965, p. 712
184. Contemporary Dance Trust Archive, V&A Museum
185. Wiliiams, Goodwin and Percival 1975
186. If the principals were sure who they were, a number of the supporting dancers found themselves completely at a loss as to their role.
187. Clement Crisp, *Financial Times* 12 December 1985
188. Williams and Goodwin, 1975
189. Alenikoff 1977
190. Edward Thorpe, *Evening Standard* 13 November 1975
191. John Percival, *The Times* 13 November 1975
192. Clement Crisp, *Financial Times* 13 November 1975
193. *Birmingham Post* 9 April 1976
194. Bannerman, "Contemporary heritage: a fusion of horizons", The Place 28 November 2006
195. Lansley and Early 2011, p. 64. Hamilton would go onto become one of the leading dance improvisers.
196. The very thing Judyth Knight always refused to allow Cohan.
197. Clarke 1978
198. Williams and Goodwin 1976
199. Percival 1976
200. Williams and Goodwin op. cit.
201. O'Connell and Finberg 1958, p. 426
202. Monahan 1976
203. *Kilburn Times* 17 December 1976
204. Williams, Goodwin and Percival 1979a
205. Sarah Frater, *Evening Standard* 10 May 2005
206. Anna Kisselgoff, *New York Times* 3 July 1977

207. Daniel Webster, *Philadelphia Inquirer* 9 July 1977
208. Alenikoff 1977
209. North Valhope and Morwitz trans. and eds. 1946, p. 28
210. Goodwin 1976
211. North Valhope and Morwitz op. cit.
212. Clement Crisp, *Financial Times* 10 December 1975
213. John Percival *The Times* 10 December 1975

Chapter 9
214. Clarke and Crisp 1989, p. 103
215. John Percival, *The Times* 15 December 1976
216. Ibid.
217. Ibid.
218. David Gillard, *Daily Mail* 24 June 1976
219. Edward Thorpe, *Evening Standard* 1 December 1976
220. Alexander Bland, *The Observer* 5 December 1976
221. Drummond 2001, p. 209
222. Ibid., pp. 208–10
223. Tynan 1988, p. 357
224. "California Here Comes Tynan", *New York Times* 31 October 1976
225. Ivan Wardle, "Rapture Flawed by Porn Shop Dialogue", *The Times* 1 October 1976
226. In Clarke and Crisp 1989, p. 77
227. Monahan 1977a
228. Jenny Gilbert, *The Independent* 27 March 2005
229. Jennifer Dunning, *New York Times* 1 March 1993
230. Noel Goodwin, *Daily Express* 16 April 1977
231. James Kennedy, *Guardian* 17 April 1977
232. Clement Crisp, *Financial Times* 14 April 1977
233. Anne Morley-Priestman, *The Stage*, 20 April 1977
234. Richard Davies, *Classical Music Weekly* 21 April 1977
235. Peter Knight, *Morning Star* 26 April 1977
236. Anna Kisselgoff, *New York Times* 3 July 1977
237. In Clarke and Crisp 1989, p. 122
238. Green 2006, p.84
239. Contemporary Dance Trust Archive, V&A Museum
240. Ibid.
241. Zimmer 1978
242. Williams, Percival and Goodwin 1979a
243. Monahan 1977a
244. Williams and Goodwin 1977a
245. Contemporary Dance Trust Archive, V&A Museum
246. Williams, Percival and Goodwin 1979a
247. Silverio de Santa Teresa trans. 1935/1978, p. 24
248. Barnstone trans. 1972, p. 57
249. Ibid., p. 67
250. Ibid., p. 53
251. Williams, Percival and Goodwin op. cit.
252. LCDT programme notes
253. Williams, Percival and Goodwin 1979b

254. Ibid.
255. See *Dance and Dancers* April 1960
256. The Roundhouse would see such an arrangement of musicians when the Cunningham company presented Ocean there in 2006.
257. Williams and Goodwin 1979b

Chapter 10
258. Parry 2010, p. 594
259. Contemporary Dance Trust Archive, V&A Museum
260. Clarke 1981
261. LCDT programme notes
262. Clarke op. cit.
263. Goodwin 1981
264. McDonagh 1973, p. 271
265. *Dance Magazine* February 1980, p. 5
266. Dora Sowden, "Transforming Batsheva", *Jerusalem Post* 14 August 1980
267. Pepper 2008, p. 30
268. Ibid.
269. Contemporary Dance Trust Archive, V&A Museum
270. Ibid.
271. Percival 1982
272. Goodwin 1981b
273. *Yorkshire Post* 18 February 1981
274. Contemporary Dance Trust Archive, V&A Museum
275. Jan Murray, *Time Out* 12 November 1981
276. Eliot 2004, p. 66
277. Talk at University of Winchester, 27 September 2010
278. Davies et al. eds. 2009, p. 215
279. Rubidge 1982
280. Macaulay 1983
281. Jacob Siskind, *Ottawa Citizen* 19 October 1982
282. Ayre 1982
283. Max Wyman, *Vancouver Sun* 31 October 1982
284. Walter Terry, *New York Herald Tribune* 31 October 1960
285. Clive Barnes, *New York Post* 27 October 1982
286. "The Dance Has to Stop", *Guardian* 22 November 1982
287. Ibid.
288. Clive Barnes, *New York Post* 6 May 1983
289. Ibid.
290. Burt Supree, *Village Voice* 17 May 1983
291. In Clarke and Crisp 1989, pp. 163–4
292. Goodwin 1983
293. "Handing Over", *Dance and Dancers* 1982
294. Ibid.

Chapter 11
295. LCDT programme notes
296. Ibid.
297. Ibid.

298. Percival 1984
299. Ibid.
300. Macaulay 1984
301. Goodwin 1985
302. In Clarke and Crisp 1989, p. 176
303. Cohan 1985
304. Marwick 2003, pp. 316–17
305. Ibid.
306. Arts Council of Great Britain 1985, p. 3
307. Publicity material for *Harwood Academic*
308. Osbon ed. 1991, p. 93
309. TV broadcast of Mass on BBC2
310. Davies in Mackrell, Davies and Kay 1987, pp. 12–13
311. Walter Terry, *New York Herald Tribune* 31 October 1960
312. Katherine Sorley Walker, *Daily Telegraph* 2 July 1987
313. Keith Watson, *Ham & High* 2 July 1987
314. Edward Thorpe, *Evening Standard* 2 July 1987
315. Alan Hulme, *Manchester Evening News* 26 September 1986
316. Clement Crisp, *Financial Times* 19 November 1987
317. Macaulay 1987
318. Clarke and Crisp 1989, p. 187
319. Macaulay op. cit.
320. Crisp op. cit.
321. Clarke 1987
322. John Percival, *The Times* 1 October 1987
323. *Financial Times* op. cit.
324. David Dougill, *The Times* 14 October 1987
325. Clement Crisp, *Financial Times* 13 October 2001
326. McKim 2004, p. 98
327. Interview with Katie Philips, *The Stage* 5 May 2005
328. Contemporary Dance Trust Archive, V&A Museum
329. David Dougill, *The Times* 23 April 1989
330. St Vincent Millay 1988 (sonnet XLIII)
331. Goodwin 1989a
332. Burnside 1989
333. Kane 1989
334. Burnside op. cit.
335. Clement Crisp, *Financial Times* 14 June 1989

Chapter 12
Much of the material for this chapter which concerns the closure of LCDT is in the Contemporary Dance Trust Archive held at the V&A Museum.
336. Devlin 1989, p. 19, paragraph 2
337. *Hansard* 1989
338. Devlin op. cit., p. 70, paragraph 294
339. Devlin op. cit., p. 72, paragraph 304
340. Kane 1990
341. *Dance Theatre Journal* 1992
342. In Another Place, documentary by Darshan Singh Bhuller, 2005

343. Devlin op. cit., p. 72, paragraph 302
344. Devlin op. cit., p. 71, paragraph 299
345. Daily Telegraph 19 October 1982
346. Peter Easton, *The Herald Scotland* 25 February 1993
347. Lumley 2001
348. Sweeney 2000
349. Interview with Mary Brennan, *Scottish Herald* 21 March 1993
350. Jeremy Hodges, *Sunday Times* 14 May 1993
351. Mary Brennan, *The Herald* 28 March 1993
352. David Dougill, *Sunday Times* 28 March 1993
353. Interview with Jeremy Hodge, *Sunday Times* 14 May 1993
354. Arts Council of Great Britain report, Contemporary Dance Trust Archive, V&A Museum
355. Judith Mackrell, *The Independent* 19 April 1993
356. David Lister, "Modern Dance World Split as Ticket Sales Fall: The Boom in Dance Seems to Be Over, and Accusations of Self-Indulgence are Flying", *The Independent* 19 October 1992
357. *The Independent* October 1993
358. Reported in *Dance and Dancers* November 1993
359. *Dance and Dancers* 1994
360. Another Place, documentary by Darshan Singh Bhuller, 2005
361. Clement Crisp, *Financial Times* 25 November 1993
362. John Percival, *The Times* 11 November 1993
363. Judith Mackrell, *The Independent* 27 November 1993
364. Ibid.
365. Ibid.
366. Mackrell 1996
367. Clarke 1996a
368. Wray, de Jong and Justin 1996
369. Ibid.
370. *The Herald* 28 August 1993
371. Clarke 1996
372. Kendall 1999
373. Nickalls 1999
374. Sweeney 2000
375. Interview with Mary Brennan, *Herald Scotland* 5 December 2000
376. Christopher Bowen, *Scotland on Sunday* 7 January 2001
377. Alice Bain, *Guardian* 22 December 2000
378. Ibid.
379. *Herald Scotland* op. cit.
380. Clement Crisp, *Financial Times* 12 May 2005
381. Debra Craine *The Times* 12 May 2005
382. Jann Parry, *The Observer* 15 May 2005
383. Dixon 2005
384. Percival 2005
385. Ralph ed. 2004, pp. 95–156
386. Jann Parry, *The Guardian* 11 December 2005

Postlude
387. Interview with Mary Brennan, *Herald Scotland* 12 November 2005
388. Butterworth ed. 1999, p. 22

389. John Percival, *The Times* 11 November 1993
390. Lyndsey Winship, *Time Out* 8 June 2009
391. Sanjoy Roy, "Step-by-step Guide to Dance: Robert Cohan", *Guardian*, 18 May 2010, http://www.guardian.co.uk/stage/2010/may/18/dance-robert-cohan
392. Sanjoy Roy, *Guardian* 5 May 2010
393. Drummond 1996
394. Kelly Apter, "Review: Richard Alston Dance Company – Edinburgh Festival Theatre", 24 November 2011, scotsman.com, http://www.scotsman.com/lifestyle/performing-arts/dance-reviews/review_richard_alston_dance_company_edinburgh_festival_theatre_1_1980894
395. Sanjoy Roy, *Guardian* 21 October 2011
396. Guevara 2011
397. Carter 1998
398. Unpublished interview, courtesy of Cohan

Robert Cohan's choreographies, 1952–2011

The following list is sadly not complete – the inaccessibility of the Bat-Dor and Batsheva archives has precluded the inclusion of many of the works Cohan made for those companies. There are also works Cohan made but forgot where or when, so they could not be traced. Any information regarding omissions would be gratefully received by the author and choreographer.

Fp refers to the first performance of a work.

1952
Title: *Perchance to Dream*
Music: Claude Debussy
Design: Robert Cohan
Dancer: Robert Cohan
Notes: Utilised chair from Martha Graham's *Gospel of Eve* designed by Oliver Smith
Fp: 28 July, Connecticut College, New London

1958
Title: *Streams*
Music: Alan Hovhaness
Design: Robert Cohan
Dancer: Robert Cohan

1959
Title: *Praises*
Music: Alan Hovhaness
Design: Robert Cohan
Dancers: Robert Cohan, Matt Turney
Fp: 8 November, Strong Auditorium, University of Rochester

Title: *Vestige* (solo on the death of Pan)
Music: Eugene Lester
Design: Walter Martin
Dancer: Robert Cohan
Fp: 8 November, Strong Auditorium, University of Rochester

1960
Title: *Seaborne*
Music: James Anderson
Design: Walter Martin
Dancer: Robert Cohan
Fp: 2 April, Strong Auditorium, University of Rochester

Title: *The Pass: A Rehearsal in Evil*
Music: Eugene Lester
Design: Walter Martin
Dancers: Robert Cohan, Matt Turney
Fp: 2 April, Strong Auditorium, University of Rochester

Title: *The New Boy* (musical)
Pilgrim Fellowship of the First Church in Cambridge Congregational, Boston

Title: *The Quest: An Allegory of the Soul*
Music: Eugene Lester
Design: Walter Martin
Dancers: Robert Cohan, Matt Turney
Fp: 8 October, Strong Auditorium, University of Rochester

Title: *Veiled Woman*
Music: Leonard Taffs
Design: Walter Martin
Dancer: Matt Turney
Fp: 8 October, Strong Auditorium, University of Rochester

1961
Title: *Dido and Aeneas*
Music: Henry Purcell
Fp: 18 May, Jordan Hall, Boston

Title: *Eclipse*
Music: Eugene Lester
Design: Robert Cohan
Dancers: Robert Cohan, Matt Turney
Fp: American Dance Festival, Connecticut College

1962
Title: *Hunter of Angels*
Music: Bruno Maderna
Design: Robert Cohan
Dancers: Robert Cohan, Bertram Ross
Fp: 25 May, Loeb Drama Center, Boston

Title: *Chamber of the Liar*
Music: Eugene Lester
Design: Walter Martin
Dancers: Robert Cohan, Bertram Ross, Linda Hodes, Mary Hinkson
Fp: 25 May, Loeb Drama Center, Boston

Title: *Luna Park: An excursion*

Music: Eugene Lester
Design: Walter Martin
Dancers: Robert Cohan, Bertram Ross, Linda Hodes, Mary Hinkson
Fp: 25 May, Loeb Drama Center, Boston

1963
Title: *Ceremony for Serpents*
Music: Eugene Lester
Design: Walter Martin
Dancers: Robert Cohan, Robert Powell, Matt Turney, Carol Drisin
Fp: 28 April, John Hancock Hall, Boston

Title: *Ornaments and Ashes*
Music: Eugene Lester
Design: Walter Martin
Dancers: Robert Cohan, Robert Powell, Matt Turney, Carol Drisin
Fp: 28 April, John Hancock Hall, Boston

1965
Title: *Siddartha*
Music and libretto: James T. Anderson
Dancers: Robert Cohan, Matt Turney and ensemble
Fp: 4 March, Loeb Drama Center, Boston

Title: *Celebrants*
Music: Surinach
Design: Robert Cohan
Dancers: Batsheva Dance Company

Title: *Tent of Vision*
Music: Noam Sharif
Design: Dani Karavan
Dancers: Batsheva Dance Company
Fp: 5 August, Habima Theatre, Tel Aviv

1967
Title: *Sky*
Music: Eugene Lester
Lighting: Robert Cohan
Design: Peter Farmer
Dancers: London Contemporary Dance Group (LCDT)
Fp: 10 October, Adeline Genée Theatre, East Grinstead

Title: *Tzaikerk*
Music: Alan Hovhaness
Lighting: Brian Benn

Design: Norberto Chiesa
Dancers: LCDT
Fp: 10 October, Adeline Genée Theatre, East Grinstead

1969
Title: *Side Scene*
Music: early music
Lighting: Robert Cohan
Design: Norberto Chiesa
Dancers: LCDT
Fp: 2 September, The Place, London

Title: *Shanta Quintet*
Music: John Mayer
Lighting: Robert Cohan
Design: Robert Cohan
Dancers: LCDT
Fp: 4 September, The Place, London

Title: *Cell*
Music: Ronald Lloyd
Lighting: John B. Read
Design: Norberto Chiesa
Costumes: Robert Cohan
Dancers: LCDT
Fp: 11 September, The Place, London

1971
Title: *Lifelines*, dance for television
Broadcast: 8 January, BBC2

Title: *The Consolation of the Rising Moon*
Music: John Williams
Lighting: Robert Cohan
Design: Peter Farmer
Dancers: LCDT
Fp: 13 January, The Place, London

Title: *Stages*
Music: Arne Nordheim, Bob Downes
Lighting: John B. Read
Design: Peter Farmer
Film: Anthony McCall
Dancers: LCDT
Fp: 21 April, The Place, London

1972
Title: *People Alone*
Music: Bob Downes
Lighting: John B. Read
Costumes: Jane Hyland
Design: Norberto Chiesa
Dancers: LCDT
Fp: 29 August, The Place, London

1973
Title: *People Together*
Music: Bob Downes
Lighting: Robert Cohan
Costumes: Robert Cohan
Design: Norberto Chiesa
Dancers: LCDT
Fp: 26 February, The Place, London

Title: *Mass*
Music: Vladimir Rodzianko (1973), Judith Weir (1974)
Lighting: John B. Read
Costumes: Robert Cohan
Design: Norberto Chiesa
Dancers: LCDT
Fp: 3 April, Oxford Playhouse, Oxford

1974
Title: *Waterless Method of Swimming Instruction*
Music: Bob Downes
Lighting: Robert Cohan
Design: Ian Murray Clark
Dancers: LCDT
Fp: 11 June, Théâtre de Beaulieu, Lausanne Festival

Title: *No Man's Land*
Music: Barry Guy
Lighting: Richard Casswell
Design: Peter Farmer
Dancers: LCDT
Fp: 13 November, Sadler's Wells Theatre, London

Title: *Men Seen Afar*, dance for television
Broadcast: 16 November, BBC2

Title: "Dance of the Seven Veils", dance for video production of *Salome*

1975
Title: *Masque of Separation*
Music: Burt Alcantara
Lighting: John B. Read
Design: Norberto Chiesa
Dancers: LCDT
Fp: 20 February, Shaw Theatre, London (as *Myth*)

Title: *Class*
Music: John Keliehor (1975), Geoffrey Burgon (1980), John Keliehor (1981 onwards)
Lighting: John B. Read
Design: Robert Cohan
Dancers: LCDT
Fp: 4 June, The Place, London

Title: *Stabat Mater*
Music: Antonio Vivaldi
Lighting: John B. Read
Design: Robert Cohan
Dancers: LCDT
Fp: 29 September, MacRobert Arts Centre, Stirling

Title: *Place of Change*
Music: Arnold Schoenberg
Lighting: Robert Cohan (Bat-Dor), John B. Read (LCDT, 1981)
Design: Charter
Dancers: Bat-Dor, LCDT
Fp: Bat-Dor, unknown; LCDT, 22 December, Sadler's Wells Theatre, London

1976
Title: *Khamsin*
Music: Bob Downes
Lighting: Robert Cohan
Design: Norberto Chiesa
Dancers: LCDT
Fp: 22 March, The Playhouse, Leeds

Title: *Nympheas*
Music: Claude Debussy
Lighting: John B. Read
Design: Norberto Chiesa
Dancers: LCDT
Fp: 22 June, Theatre Royal, York

Title: *Carte Blanche*, nude review directed by Clifford Williams

Lighting: Andrew Bridge
Design: Farrah and Judith Bland
Dancers: ensemble
Fp: 30 September, Phoenix Theatre, London

1977
Title: *Night Watch*
Choreography: Robert Cohan, Micha Bergese, Robert North, Siobhan Davies
Music: Bob Downes
Lighting: Robert Cohan
Design: Norberto Chiesa
Dancers: LCDT
Fp: 5 April, Sadler's Wells Theatre, London

1978
Title: *Falling Man Solo*
Music: Barrington Pheloung
Lighting: Robert Cohan
Design: Robert Cohan
Dancer: Robert North
Fp: 18 May, Coliseum, London

Title: *Eos*
Music: Barry Guy
Design: Barney Wan
Dancers: LCDT
Fp: 3 October, Pavilion Theatre, Bournemouth

Title: *Ice*
Music: Morton Subotnick
Lighting: John B. Read
Design: Norberto Chiesa
Dancers: LCDT
Fp: 5 December, Sadler's Wells Theatre, London

1979
Title: *Songs, Lamentations and Praises*
Music: Geoffrey Burgon
Lighting: John B. Read
Design: Norberto Chiesa
Dancers: LCDT
Fp: 7 August, Jerusalem

Title: *Rondo*
Music: John Herbert McDowell
Lighting: Robert Cohan

Design: Barney Wan
Dancers: LCDT
Fp: 2 October, The Roundhouse, London

1980
Title: *Canciones del Alma*
Music Geoffrey Burgon
Lighting: Robert Cohan
Design: Robert Cohan
Dancer: Susan MacPherson
Fp: 1 January, Toronto

Title: *Field*
Music: Brian Hodgson
Lighting: Robert Cohan
Design: Penny King
Dancers: LCDT
Fp: 12 February, Christ's Hospital Arts Centre, Horsham

1981
Title: *Dances of Love and Death*
Music: Carl Davis, Conlon Nancarrow
Lighting: John B. Read
Design: Norberto Chiesa
Dancers: London Contemporary Dance Theatre
Fp: 31 October, Edinburgh Festival

1982
Title: *Chamber Dances*
Music: Geoffrey Burgon
Lighting: John B. Read
Design: Norberto Chiesa
Dancers: LCDT
Fp: 16 September, Sadler's Wells Theatre, London

Title: *When Evening Spreads Itself Against the Sky*
Music: J. S. Bach
Lighting: Robert Cohan
Design: Robert Cohan
Dancers: Dancemakers, Toronto

1984
Title: *Agora*
Music: J. S. Bach, Barrington Pheloung
Lighting: Mark Henderson
Design: Norberto Chiesa

Dancers: LCDT
Fp: 16 February, Grand Theatre, Leeds (working title: *Common Land*)

1985
Title: *Mass for Man*, dance for television
Broadcast: 17 November, BBC2

1986
Title: *Ceremony/Slow Dance on a Burial Ground*
Music: Stephen Montague
Lighting: Robert Cohan
Costumes: Audrey Gie
Set: Norberto Chiesa
Dancers: LCDT
Fp: 14 February, Royal Hippodrome, Eastbourne

Title: *Video Life*
Music: Barry Guy
Lighting: Robert Cohan
Design: Norberto Chiesa
Dancers: LCDT
Fp: 27 August, Queen Elizabeth Hall, London

Title: *Interrogations*
Music: Barrington Pheloung
Lighting: Robert Cohan
Design: António Lagarto
Dancers: LCDT
Fp: 24 September, Queen Elizabeth Hall, London

1987
Title: *The Phantasmagoria*
Choreography: Robert Cohan, Tom Jobe, Darshan Singh Bhuller
Music: Barrington Pheloung
Lighting: Graham Large
Design: Nadine Baylis
Dancers: LCDT
Fp: 29 September, Birmingham Hippodrome

1989
Title: *In Memory*
Music: Hans Werner Henze
Lighting: John B. Read
Design: Peter Farmer
Dancers: LCDT
Fp: 18 April, Queen Elizabeth Hall, London

Title: *Metamorphoses*
Music: Benjamin Britten
Lighting: John B. Read
Design: Peter Farmer
Dancer: Darshan Singh Bhuller
Fp: 18 April, Queen Elizabeth Hall, London

Title: *Crescendo*
Music: David Bedford
Lighting: John B. Read
Design: Peter Farmer
Dancers: LCDT
Fp: 18 April, Queen Elizabeth Hall, London

Title: *Stone Garden*
Music: Nigel Osborne
Lighting: John B. Read
Design: Peter Farmer
Dancers: LCDT
Fp: 18 April, Queen Elizabeth Hall, London

1993
Title: *A Midsummer Night's Dream*
Music: Felix Mendelssohn, Barrington Pheloung
Lighting: Robert Cohan
Design: Norberto Chiesa
Dancers: Scottish Ballet
Fp: 20 March, Theatre Royal, Glasgow

1996
Title: *The Four Seasons*
Music: Antonio Vivaldi
Lighting: Robert Cohan
Design: Norberto Chiesa
Dancers: Scottish Ballet
Fp: 26 August, in "Sweat Rock n'Roll", Theatre Royal, Glasgow

Title: *Adagietto*
Music: Gustav Mahler
Lighting: Robert Cohan
Design: Robert Cohan
Dancer: David Hughes

1997
Title: *Pictures*
Choreography: Robert Cohan and Robert North

Lighting: Robert Cohan
Dancers: Compagnia Fabula Saltica
Fp: Teatro di Rovigo, Italy

2000
Title: *Aladdin*
Music: Carl Davis
Lighting: Robert Cohan
Design: Lez Brotherston
Dancers: Scottish Ballet
Fp: 20 December, Festival Theatre, Edinburgh

2005
Title: *Study*
Lighting: Robert Cohan
Design: Robert Cohan
Dancers: Darshan Singh Bhuller
Fp: 8 December, The Place, London

Television and film

5 October1969: *The Place*, 15-minute film in programme "Music Now", BBC2

8 January 1971: *Lifelines*, 18-minute dance piece created for the arts magazine programme "Review", BBC2

14 January 1972: *The Place*, 20-minute film about the building and its work in the arts magazine "Review", BBC2

8 October 1972: "The Body", interview with Cohan in a programme looking at the body as a medium of expression. Dancers included Siobhan Davies, Xenia Hribar, Noemi Lapzeson, Micha Bergese.

17 February 1973: *Mass*, 15-minute extract in the arts programme "Full House", BBC2

1974: Dance of the Seven Veils in *Salome* (directed by Götz Friedrich, starring Teresa Stratas)

16 November 1974: *Men Seen Afar*, commissioned by the arts magazine "2nd House", BBC2

1977: Residency at Bretton College filmed by Derek Bailey for the "Aquarius" arts programme, ITV

1977: *Job*, ITV

13 April 1979: *Stabat Mater*, BBC2

25 May 1979: Extract from *Solo Ride* (choreographed by Micha Bergese) to celebrate the tenth anniversary of LCDT

19 November 1979: *The Magic of the Dance* (BBC2 series). In part 3, "What's New?", performance of a section of *Khamsin*

19 June 1980: Cohan masterclass, BBC2

22 June 1980: *Forest* and *Waterless Method of Swimming Instruction*, Dance Month, BBC2

13 November 1981: Clip from *Dances of Love and Death* in the programme "On the Town", BBC2

29 January 1983: *Cell*, BBC2

9 December 1983: *Nympheas*, BBC2

11 November 1984: *Dancer* (BBC series). In episode 3, "New Moves", Peter Schaufuss introduces extracts from *Class*.

17 November 1985: *Mass for Man*, BBC2

Robert Cohan's dancers

Robert Cohan and Dancers (1959–66)
Matt Turney
Bertram Ross
Robert Powell
Mary Hinkson
Juliet Fisher
Linda Hodes
Carol Drisin

London Contemporary Dance Theatre (1969–94)
Dinah Goodes (1969)
Dawn Susuki (1969)
Elsa Piperno (1969–70)
Ruth Posner (1969–70)
Maria Casey (1969–71)
Franca Telesio (1969–71)
Bob Smith (1969–71)
Micheline McKnight (1969–71)
William Louther (1969–71, 1975)
Barry Moreland (1969–71)
Irene Dilks (1969–72)
Robert Powell (1969–72)
Clare Duncan (1969–72)
Derek Linton (1969–72)
Noemi Lapzeson (1969–73)
Xenia Hribar (1969–74)
Namron (1969–83)
Robert North (1969–83)
Siobhan Davies (1969–87)
Linda Gibbs (1969–88)
Jack Nightingale (1970)
Janet Aaron (1970)
Stephen Barker (1970–4)
Juliet Fisher (1970–4)
Micha Bergese (1970–80)
Rita Levtinen (1971)
Celeste Dandeker (1971–4)
Anthony van Laast (1971–9)
Paula Lansley (1971–9)
Ross McKim (1972–9)
Kate Harrison (1972–83)
Larrio Ekson (1973)
Eva Lundqvist (1973)
Anca Frankenhauser (1973–89)
Patrick Harding-Irmer (1973–91)
Charlotte Milner (1974–8)

Cathy Lewis (1974–81)
Celia Hulton (1974–90)
Nick Farrant (1975)
Jean-Louis Morin (1975)
Charlotte Kirkpatrick (1975–89)
Tom Jobe (1975/77–82)
Sallie Estep (1975–87)
Christopher Bannerman (1975–90)
Julyen Hamilton (Peter Page) (1976–7)
Philippe Giraudeau (1977–82)
Anita Griffin (1977–86)
Serena Ward (1979)
Lizzie Saunderson (1979–83)
Jayne Lee (1979–83)
Michael Small (1979–90)
Janet Smith (1980)
Philip Taylor (1980–1)
Lenny Westerdijk (1980–6)
Paul Douglas (1980–8)
Lauren Potter (1980–9)
Darshan Singh Bhuller (1980–94)
Jonathan Lunn (1981–91)
Anne Went (1981–91)
Julian Moss (1982–90)
Kenneth Tharp (1982–4)
Brenda Edwards (1984–7)
Tamsin Hickling (1984–8)
Peter Dunleavy (1984–94)
Melinda Mckenna (1987–8)
Kerry Woodward (1987–9)
Paul Liburd (1987–91)
Tracey Fitzgerald (1987–94)
Helen Beattie (1988–91)
Kate Coyne (1988–94)
Isabel Tamen (1988–94)
Andrew Robinson (1988–94)
Isabel Mortimer (1989–93)
David Hughes (1989–94)
Sheron Wray (1989–94)
Leesa Phillips (1989–94)
Bernadette Iglich (1989–94)
Aletta Collins (1989–90)
Tom Ward (1990–2)
Elizabeth Fancourt (1991–4)
Stephanie Ross-Russell (1993–4)
Chris Tudor (1993–4)
Richard Witter (1993–4)
Karen Woo (1993–4)
Fred Gehrig (1993–4)

Bibliography

Adshead, Janet and Mansfield, Richard, *London Contemporary Dance Theatre, 1967–1975*. University of Surrey: National Resource Centre for Dance, 1985.

—— and Pritchard, Jane, *Ballet Rambert, 1965–1975*. University of Surrey: National Resource Centre for Dance, 1985.

Alenikoff, Frances, "The London Contemporary Dance Company [sic] Connecticut College, New London", *Dance News*, October 1977, p. 11.

Anderson, Jack, "Some Personal Grumbles about Martha Graham", *Ballet Review*, Vol. 2, No. 1, 1967, pp. 25–30.

Armitage, Merle (ed.), *Martha Graham*. Los Angeles: Merle Armitage, 1937.

—— and Corle, Edwin (eds.), *Dance Memoranda*. New York: Duell, Sloan & Pearce, 1946, pp. 55–58.

Arts Council of Great Britain, *A Great British Success Story: An Invitation to the Nation to Invest in the Arts*, London: ACGB, 1985.

—— *The Policy for Dance of the English Funding System*, London: ACE, 1996.

Ayre, John, "Some anarchy from the UK", *Maclean's*, October 1982, p. 77.

"Graham: 'I Am a Dancer'", Ballet Review, Vol. 12, No. 3, Fall 1984, pp. 59–71. Extract from *Deep Song: The Dance Story of Martha Graham*. New York: Schirmer Books; London: Collier Macmillan Publishers, 1984.

"Graham Without Graham, 1991", *Ballet Review*, Vol. 20, No. 3, Fall 1992, pp. 29–35.

"Martha Graham (1894–1991). Reminiscences by Marian Seldes, May O'Donnell, Stuart Hodes and Francis Mason", *Ballet Review*, Vol. 19, No. 3, Summer 1996, pp. 18–31.

Barnes, C., "First Steps into the Maze", *Dance and Dancers*, April 1954, pp. 12–13.

—— "Modern Dance: Has it a Future?", *Dance and Dancers*, October 1980, pp. 31–3.

Barnstone, Willis (trans.), *The Poems of St John of The Cross*. New York: New Directions Publishing, 1972.

Bayston, Michael, "Dancers on Television", *Dancing Times*, November 1974, p. 149.

—— "Dancers on Television", *Dancing Times*, April 1983, p. 865.

—— "Dancers on Television", *Dancing Times*, August 1983, p. 975.

—— "Dancers on Television", *Dancing Times*, August 1984, p. 939.

—— "Dancers on Television", *Dancing Times*, January 1986, p. 329.

Benedict, Ruth, *The Chrysanthemum and the Sword*. Boston: Houghton Mifflin reprint, 1988.

Billington, Michael, *The State of the Nation: British Theatre since 1945*. London: Faber and Faber, 2007.

Bliss, P. M., "A Natural Collaboration", *Society of Dance History Scholars Proceedings*, Twelfth Annual Conference, Temple, AZ: Arizona State University, 17–19 February 1989, pp. 82–7.

Brinson, Peter and Dick, Fiona, *Fit to Dance?* London: Gulbenkian Foundation, 1996.

Brown, J. M. (ed.), *The Vision of Modern Dance*. Princeton, NJ: Princeton Book Company, 1979, pp. 48–53.

Burnside, Fiona, "Music and Dance: A Collaboration between LCDT and the London Sinfonietta", *Dance Theatre Journal*, Vol. 7, No. 2, 1989, p. 38.

Butterworth, Jo (ed.), *The Art and Science of Nurturing Dance Makers*, papers from The Greenhouse Effect Conference, Leeds: Centre for Dance and Theatre Studies, Bretton Hall College, 1999.

—— *The Dance Book*, Oxford: Routledge, 2012.

Campbell, Joseph, *The Flight of the Wild Gander: Explorations in the Mythological Dimension*. New York: Viking Press, 1968.

—— *The Hero with a Thousand Faces*. 1968; repr. Princeton, NJ: Princeton University Press / Novato, California: New World Library, 2008.

—— *Myths to Live By*. New York: Viking Press, 1972.

—— *The Mythic Image*. Princeton, NJ: Princeton University Press, 1974.

—— *The Inner Reaches of Outer Space: Metaphor as Myth and as Religion*. New York: Alfred van der Marck Editions, 1986.

—— *Transformations of Myth Through Time*. New York: Harper & Row, 1990.

Carter, Alexandra, "Reconstruction, the Case for Preservation", *Dance Theatre Journal*, Vol. 14, No. 2, 1998, pp. 26–9.

Cavendish, Richard, *The Black Arts*, 1967 repr. London: Picador, 1977.

Clarke, M., "Graham in London", *Dance Magazine*, May 1954, p. 32.

—— "LCDT at Sadler's Wells", *Dancing Times*, January 1978, p. 204.

—— "LCDT", *Dancing Times*, July 1978, p. 640.

—— "LCDT at Sadler's Wells", *Dancing Times*, January 1979, p. 214.

—— "LCDT at the ICA", *Dancing Times*, March 1980, p. 387.

—— "LCDT", *Dancing Times*, January 1981, p. 241.

—— "LCDT at Sadler's Wells", *Dancing Times*, January 1984, p. 306.

—— "LCDT", *Dancing Times*, January 1985, p. 315.

—— "LCDT at Sadler's Wells", *Dancing Times*, July 1985, p. 864.

—— "LCDT", *Dancing Times*, February 1986, p. 420.

—— "The Phantasmagoria", *Dancing Times*, November 1987, p. 124.

—— "Rambert at the Coliseum", *Dancing Times*, August 1996a, pp. 1060–1.

—— "Dance Scene, Scottish Ballet", *Dancing Times*, October 1996b, p. 34.

—— and Crisp, Clement, *London Contemporary Dance Theatre*. London: Dance Books, 1989.

Cohan, R., "Survival", *Dance and Dancers*, February 1972, p. 22.

—— "Getting to Know You", *Dance and Dancers*, April 1976, p. 21.

—— "Robert Cohan Talks to Gordon Gow", *Dancing Times*, April 1976, p. 361.

—— "Robert Cohan Talks to Chris de Marigny", *Dance Theatre Journal*, Vol. 3, No. 4, April 1985, pp. 2–5.

—— *The Dance Workshop*. London: George Allen and Unwin, 1986.

Cohen, Selma Jeanne, "The Achievement of Martha Graham", *Chrysalis*, Vol. 11, Nos. 5–6, 1958, pp. 3–11.

Coton, A. V., *Writings on Dance, 1938–68*. London: Dance Books, 1975.

Cousineau, Phil (ed.), *The Hero's Journey: Joseph Campbell on His Life and Work*. 3rd ed., Novato, CA: New World Library, 2003.

Cowan, John, "LCDT at Oxford Playhouse. *Mass*", *Dance and Dancers*, June 1973, p. 46.

Croce, Arlene, "Tell Me, Doctor", *Ballet Review*, Vol. 2, No. 4, 1968, pp. 12–18.

Crow, Susan, "International Dance Course for Choreographers and Composers",

Dancing Times, November 1983, p. 122.

Cruickshank, Judith, "At First Sight", *Dance and Dancers*, September 1976, p. 25.

"Graham, Martha", *Current Biography Yearbook 1944*, New York: The H. S. Wilson Company, 1944, pp. 251–3.

"Graham, Martha", *Current Biography Yearbook 1961*, New York: The H. S. Wilson Company, 1961, pp. 182–5.

"Transatlantic Influence", *Dance and Dancers*, October 1966, pp. 28-31.

Review of LCDT performances at Adeline Genée Theatre, East Grinstead, *Dance and Dancers*, December 1967, p. 20.

"Curtain up Home for Dance, LCDG Move to Euston, *Dance and Dancers*, February 1969, p. 20.

"LCDG at the Collegiate Theatre Tour Plus One", *Dance and Dancers*, August 1969, p. 43.

Article on LCDT, *Dance and Dancers*, August 1969, p. 54.

"Explorations", *Dance and Dancers*, September 1969, p. 25.

Article on John B. Read, shows lighting plan for *Cell, Dance and Dancers*, February 1971, p. 17.

"Experimental Summer, X Group", *Dance and Dancers*, November 1972, p. 46.

"Handing Over", *Dance and Dancers*, October 1982, p. 11.

Reviews of LCDT, *Dance and Dancers*, November 1982, p. 28.

"How Britain Went Modern", *Dance and Dancers*, December 1986, p. 24.

"Trick or Treat. LCDT's *The Phantasmagoria*", *Dance and Dancers*, November 1987, p. 24.

"A Dancer You Should Know: Kenneth Tharp", *Dance and Dancers*, December 1987, p. 32.

"A Year of Dance", *Dance and Dancers*, January 1988, p. 8, p. 21.

Commentary, *Dance and Dancers*, February 1989, p. 2.

"London Contemporary, End of an Era, Another Begins", *Dance and Dancers*, Vol. 5, No. 6, 1994, p. 40.

"Robert Cohan Receives his CBE from Richard Luce", *Dance and Dancers*, March 1989, p. 34.

"Martha Graham in Asia", *Dance Magazine*, March 1956, pp. 25–9.

"Graham." A four-part *Dance Magazine* Portfolio. Feature articles: Tobi Tobias, "The Graham Season: April 15–May 4, 1974" (pp. 44–5); Jean Nuchtern, "Martha Graham's Women Speak" (pp. 46–9); Doris Hering, "But Not For Clytemnestra: Comments on the Notebooks of Martha Graham" (pp. 52–5); Joel Shapiro, "Martha Graham at the Eastman School" (pp. 55–7), *Dance Magazine*, Vol. 48, No. 7, July 1974.

A special memorial issue celebrating the art of Martha Graham. Feature articles: Joseph H. Mazo, "Martha Remembered" (pp. 34–45); Marian Horosko, "Martha's Prince" (pp. 46–7); Tim Wengerd, "Martha's Men" (pp. 48–52); Walter Sorell, "Martha and Myth" (pp. 53–5); "Martha's Dances: A Catalogue of Graham's Works from 1926 to 1990" (pp. 56–7); Gary Parks, "Martha Affirmed" (p. 58), *Dance Magazine*, Vol. 65, No. 7, July 1991.

"Director Leaves", *Dance Theatre Journal*, Vol. 10, No. 1, July 1992, p. 44.

"The Graham Classes", *Dancing Times*, December 1965, pp. 62–89.

"Dance 1, 2, 4", *Dancing Times*, December 1967, p. 126.

"London Contemporary Dance Theatre", *Dancing Times*, April 1972, p. 363.

"Dance at The Place", *Dancing Times*, June 1972, p. 467.

"The Versatile Talents of Remy Charlip", *Dancing Times*, April 1974, p. 399.

"The Contemporaries at the Shaw Theatre", *Dancing Times*, April 1975, p. 362.

"Workshops at LCDS", *Dancing Times*, August 1975, p. 592.

Davies, Stephen et al. (eds.), *A Companion to Aesthetics*. Oxford: Wiley Blackwell, 2009.

Delaforce, P., *The Battle of the Bulge: Hitler's Final Gamble*. Harlow: Pearson Higher Education, 2004.

Dell, C., "Random Graham", *Dance Scope*, No. 2, Spring 1966, pp. 21–6.

de Mille, Agnes, *Dance to the Piper*. Boston: Little, Brown and Company, 1952, pp. 144–60.

—— *Martha: The Life and Work of Martha Graham*. New York: Random House, 1991.

Devlin, Graham, *Stepping Forward: Some Thoughts for the Development of Dance in England during the 1990s*. London: Arts Council of Great Britain Dance Department, 1989.

Dixon, Mike, "Robert Cohan at 80", *Dance Europe*, June 2005 p. 31.

Dodd, Clare, "All Fall Down", *Dance and Dancers*, July 1969, p. 526.

—— "Contemporary Dance in London", *Dance and Dancers*, July 1970, p. 517.

—— "Contemporary Dance", *Dance and Dancers*, December 1970, p. 147.

—— "Contemporary Dance in London", *Dance and Dancers*, May 1971, p. 304.

Drummond, John, *The Turn of Dance? A Feasibility Study Towards the Establishment of a National Dance House*. London: Arts Council of Great Britain, 1984.

—— "A Golden Stage", *Dance Theatre Journal*, Vol. 13, No. 2, 1996, pp. 10–12.

—— *Tainted by Experience: A Life in the Arts*. London: Faber and Faber, 2001.

Dudley, Jane, "Teachers and Teaching, Jane Dudley Talks about the Schools of Graham and Wigman", *Dance and Dancers*, May 1971, p. 54.

Dupuy, T. N., *Hitler's Last Gamble: The Battle of the Bulge, December 1944 – January 1945*. New York: HarperCollins, 1994.

Elgin, Karen, "For the Love of Dance", *Dance and Dancers*, May 1982, p. 38.

Eliot, T. S., *The Complete Poems and Plays of T. S. Eliot*. London: Faber and Faber, 2004.

Erdman, David V. (ed.), *The Complete Poetry and Prose of William Blake*. Berkeley and Los Angeles: University of California Press, 1965.

Foster, Susan Leigh, *Reading Dancing: Bodies and Subjects in Contemporary American Dance*. Berkeley, Los Angeles, London: University of California Press, 1986, pp. 23–32.

Fraser, John, "Martha Graham: Into the Cool Lucid Light of a Seer", *York Dance Review*, Issue No. 2, Fall 1973, pp. 23–9.

Gardner, Howard, "Martha Graham: Discovering the Dance of America", *Ballet Review*, Vol. 22, No. 1, Spring 1994, pp. 67–93. Reprinted from Howard Gardner, *Creating Minds: An Anatomy of Creativity Seen Through the Lives of Freud, Einstein, Picasso, Stravinsky, Eliot, Graham and Gandhi*, New York: Basic Books, 1993.

Garfunkel, Trudy, *Letter to the World: The Life and Dances of Martha Graham*. Boston, New York, London, Toronto: Little, Brown and Company, 1995.

Gerken, Wil et al., "Books: Grandfather Time", *Weekly Alibi*, 27 September 1999, <http://weeklywire.com/ww/09-27-99/alibi_feat1.html>, retrieved 14 February 2010.

Goodwin, Noel, "Placed Sounds. Music for London Contemporary Dance Theatre", *Dance and Dancers*, August 1970, p. 33.

—— "The Richness of Change", *Dance and Dancers*, February 1976, pp. 34–5.

—— LCDT review, *Ballet News*, February 1981a, pp. 36–7.

—— "Ballads of our Time", *Dance and Dancers*, October 1981b, p.?

—— "London Contemporary Dance Theatre", *Dance and Dancers*, February 1982, p. 25.

—— "Based on Love", *Ballet News*, Vol. 4, No. 10, April 1983, pp. 18–21.

—— "Look and Listen. London Contemporary Dance Theatre", *Dance and Dancers*, February 1984a, p. 10.

—— Reviews, London Contemporary Dance Theatre. *Dance and Dancers*, July 1984b, p. 23.

—— "Are the Dancers Too Good?", *Dance and Dancers*, January 1985, p. 20.

—— "Relationships in Mutation", *Dance and Dancers*, February 1986, p. 12.

—— "An Adventurous Farewell", *Dance and Dancers*, June 1989a, p. 12.

—— "A Marriage of the Arts", *Dance and Dancers*, November 1989b, p. 20.

—— "London Contemporary Dance Theatre", *Dance and Dancers*, January 1991, pp. 31–2.

—— and Dougill, David, "Ballads for Our Time", *Dance and Dancers*, October 1981, p. 19.

Gordon, David and Gordon, Peter, *Musical Visitors to Britain*. UK: Routledge, 2005.

Gow. Gordon. "Cohan in Interview", *Dancing Times*, October 1970, p. 112.

—— "Cohan and Contemporary Dance", *Dancing Times*, January 1972, p. 186.

—— "Anthony van Laast in Conversation", *Dancing Times*, October 1983, p. 42.

Graham, Martha, *The Notebooks of Martha Graham*. New York: Harcourt Brace Jovanovich, 1973.

—— *Blood Memory*. New York: Doubleday, 1991.

Green, M., *David Earle: A Choreographic Biography*. Toronto: Danse Collection, 2006.

Gruen, J., "Reviews, New York City", *Dance Magazine*, August 1983, pp. 97–8.

Guevara, Chantal, "Richard Alston at Home", Cloud Dance Festival, 23 October 2011, <http://www.cloud-dance-festival.org.uk/reviews/richard-alston-at-home.html>

Gulbenkian Foundation, *Dance Education and Training*, London: Gulbenkian Foundation, 1980.

Gurdjieff, G., *Meetings with Remarkable Men*. 1933, 1971; repr. London: Penguin, 1985.

—— *The Herald of Coming Good*. 1933, 1971; repr. Sequim, WA: Holmes Publishing Group, 1987.

—— *Beelzebub's Tales to his Grandson*. 1933, 1971, 1988; repr. London: Penguin, 2000.

—— *Views from the Real World: Early Talks as Recollected by his Pupils*. 1973; repr. New York: E. P. Dutton, 1975.

Hagen, Daron, "A composer's life", 22 December 2010, <http://networkedblogs.com/ea9Ax>

Hall, Fernau, *An Anatomy of Ballet*. London: Andrew Melrose, 1953. Published simultaneously in the United States as *World Dance*, New York: A. A. Wyn, pp. 14–19.

"Northern Ballet Theatre", Hansard, HC Deb, Vol. 148, cols. 1007–14 (8 March 1989),<http://hansard.millbanksystems.com/commons/1989/mar/08/northern-ballet-theatre>

Helpern, Alice, *The Technique of Martha Graham*. Dobbs Ferry, NY: Morgan & Morgan, 1994. Originally published in *Studies in Dance History*, Vol. 2, No. 2, Spring/Summer 1991.

Hering, Doris, "Snow Prayer, and Sleep", *Dance Magazine*, September 1968, p. 28–32.

Hodes, Stuart, "Three Brides in Spring", *Ballet Review*, Vol. 18, No. 4, Winter 1990/91, pp. 9–14.

—— *Part Real Part Dream, Dancing with Martha Graham* [online text], Conchord Epress, 2011, <http://www.concordepress.com/part_real_part_dream>

—— "Akin let the cat out the bag", 101% American, 22 August 2012, <http://www.101american.com/1/archives/08-2012/1.html>

Holder, Geoffrey, "Martha Graham: American Original", *Show*, Vol. 3, No. 11, November 1963, pp. 86–7, pp. 118–20.

Horosko, Marian (ed.), *Martha Graham: The Evolution of Her Dance Theory and Training 1926–1991*. Pennington, NJ: A Cappella Books, 1991.

Howard, Robin, *First Real Draft and Submission to Trusts*. London: LCDT Archive, V&A, 1967.

Hunt, David, "Music for Graham", *Dance and Dancers*, May 1954, p. 20.

Jackson, George, "The Roots of Heaven: Sexuality in the Work of Martha Graham", in Diane Theodores Taplin (ed.), *Dance Spectrum: Critical and Philosophical Enquiry*, Waterloo, ON: Otium Publications; Dublin: Parsons Press, 1983, pp. 50–60.

Hutchinson, Pat and Early, Teresa, "The Graham Class", *Dancing Times*, September 1965, pp. 628–9.

Johnston, J., "Martha Graham: An Irresponsible Study... The Head of her Father", *Ballet Review*, Vol. 2, No. 4, 1968, pp. 6–12.

Jordan, Stephanie, "LCDT Workshop Season", *Dancing Times*, July 1981, p. 690.

—— "LCDT at the Wells", *Dancing Times*, February 1982, p. 336.

—— *Striding Out: Aspects of Contemporary and New Dance in Britain*. London: Dance Books, 1992.

Kane, Angela, "LCDT at QEH: Vision and Valediction", *Dancing Times,* June 1989, p. 834.

—— "Leader or Locum – LCDT and Dan Wagoner", *Dancing Times,* January 1990, p. 353.

Keefer, Louis E., "The Army Specialized Training Program in World War II", <http://www.pierce-evans.org/ASTP%20in%20WWII.htm>

Keegan, John, *Six Armies in Normandy, From D Day to the Liberation of Paris*. London: Pimlico, 1992.

Kendall, Elizabeth, "Reviews International", *Dance Magazine,* December 1999, pp. 118–19.

Kennedy, Edward (ed.), *Thou Art That: Transforming Religious Metaphor*. Novato,

CA: New World Library, 2001.

Kerensky, Oleg, "Review of Adeline Genée performance", *Dancing Times*, February 1967, p. 70.

Kersaw, Alex, *The Longest Winter*. Cambridge, MA: Da Capo Press, 2004.

Kriegsman, Sali Ann, *Modern Dance in America: The Bennington Years*. Boston: G. K. Hall & Co, 1981.

Lansley, Jacky and Early, Fergus (eds.), *The Wise Body*. London: Intellect Ltd, 2011.

Leatherman, Leroy, *Martha Graham: Portrait of the Lady as an Artist*. New York: Knopf, 1966.

Lloyd, Margret, *The Borzoi Book of Modern Dance*. New York: Knopf, 1949.

Loney, Glen, *Unsung Genius: The Passion of Dancer Jack Cole*. New York: Watts, 1984.

Lumley, Margaret, "Interview: Vladislav Bubnov", *Ballet Magazine*, April 2001, <http://www.ballet.co.uk/magazines/yr_01/apr01/interview_vladislav_bubnov.htm>

Macaulay, Alastair, "More or Less Contemporary", *Dancing Times*, January 1983, p. 277.

—— "Two New for LCDT", *Dancing Times*, April 1984, p. 578.

—— "LCDT Dancing LCDT Choreography", *Dancing Times*, January 1987, pp. 306–8.

McDonagh, Don, "A Chat with Martha Graham", *Ballet Review*, Vol. 2, No. 4, 1968, pp. 18–28.

—— *Martha Graham: A Biography*. Henry Holt & Company, Inc., 1973.

McGehee, Helen, "Working for Martha Graham", *Dance Research*, Vol. 3, No. 2, Autumn 1985, pp. 56–64.

—— *To Be A Dancer*. Lynchburg, VA: Editions Heraclita, 1989.

McKayle, Donald, *Transcending Boundaries: My Dancing Life*. London: Routledge, 2002.

McKim, Ross, *The Essential Inheritance of LCDT*. Alton: Dance Books, 2004.

McKittrich, D., "LCDT at I. M. Marsh College", *Dancing Times*, June 1976, p. 471.

Mackrell, Judith, *Out of Line: The Story of British New Dance*. London: Dance Books, 1992.

—— "Rambert at the Coliseum", *Dancing Times*, August 1996, pp. 1060–1.

——, Davies, Richard and Kay, Graeme, "LCDT 21 Not Out", *Classical Music Magazine*, 20 June 1987, pp. 12–13.

Madden, Dorothy, *"You Call me Louis not Mr Horst"*. Amsterdam, Harwood Academic Publishers, 1997.

Magriel, Paul (ed.), *Chronicles of the American Dance*. New York: Henry Holt, 1948, pp. 238–59.

Manchester, P. W., "The Season in Review", *Dance News*, December 1960, p. 8.

Martin, John, *America Dancing: The Background and Personalities of the Modern Dance*. New York: Dodge Publishing, 1936, pp. 187–205.

Marwick, Arthur, *British Society since 1945*. London: Pelican, 2003, pp. 316–17.

Mason, Francis (ed.), "Robin Howard, 1924–1989", *Ballet Review*, Fall 1989, p. 75.

Massie, Andrew (comp.), *Dancing in Time*, London: Gulbenkian Foundation, 1983.

Mazo, Joseph. H. *Prime Movers: The Makers of Modern Dance in America*. New York: William Morrow, 1977, pp. 153–96.

Meisner, Nadine. "In Search of a Choreographer", *Dance and Dancers*, May 1987, p. 8.

Merrett, Sharon, "Dance Scene: Scottish Ballet", *Dancing Times*, November 1995, p. 125.

Mitcham, Samuel. W., *Panzers in Winter: Hitler's Army and the Battle of the Bulge.* Westport, CT: Praeger, 2006.

Monahan, James, "The Place: Robin Howard's Triumph", *Dancing Times*, October 1969, p. 14.

—— "LCDT", *Dancing Times*, July 1972a, p. 535.

—— "*People Alone*", *Dancing Times*, October 1972b, p. 19.

—— "People at The Place", *Dancing Times*, April 1973, p. 371.

—— "LCDT at the Wells", *Dancing Times*, December 1974, p. 131.

—— "LCDT Comes of Age", *Dancing Times*, January 1976, p. 184.

—— "LCDT at the Wells", *Dancing Times*, February 1977a, p. 265.

—— "Contemporary Dance in London. Camden Festivals", *Dancing Times*, May 1977b, p. 448.

Myers, Gerald E., *Who's not Afraid of Martha Graham?* Durham, NC: American Dance Festival Publication, 2008.

Netter, Lucienne (ed.), *Heinrich Heine. Pariser Berichte 1840-1848. Säkularausgabe: Werke, Briefwechsel, Lebenszeugnisse.* Vienna: Wiley VCH, 1979.

Nickalls, Susan, "International Course for Professional Choreographers and Composers", *Dancing Times*, November 1999, pp. 118–19.

Noguchi, Isamu, "Noguchi: Collaborating with Graham", in Diane Apostolos-Cappadona and Bruce Altshuler (eds.), *Isamu Noguchi: Essays and Conversations.* New York: Abrams, in association with the Isamu Noguchi Foundation, 1994, pp. 80–9.

North Valhope, Carol and Morwitz, Ernst (trans. and eds.), *Stefan George. Poems.* New York: Pantheon, 1946.

Nugent, Ann, "A Seed in the Desert, the London Contemporary Dance Experience", *Dance and Dancers*, January 1983, p. 32.

—— "Three Dancers of LCDT", *Dance and Dancers*, December 1985, p. 24.

—— "Crickpix", *Dance*, Spring 1991, p. 10–13.

O'Connell Rev, John and Finberg, Howard, *The Missal in Latin and English.* London: Burns Oates and Washbourne Ltd, 1958.

Osbon, Diane K. (ed.), *Reflections on the Art of Living: A Joseph Campbell Companion.* New York: HarperCollins, 1991.

Oswald, Geraldine, "Myth and Legend in Martha Graham's *Night Journey*", *Dance Research Annual* XIV, 1983, pp. 42–9.

Ouspensky, P., *In Search of the Miraculous: The Definitive Exploration of G. I. Gurdjieff's Mystical Thought and Universal View.* New York: Taylor and Francis, 1950, p. 236.

—— *The Fourth Way: Teachings of G. I. Gurdjieff.* 1957; repr. New York: Random House, 2000.

Palmer, Winthrop, *Theatrical Dancing in America: The Development of the Ballet from 1900.* New York: Bernard Ackerman, 1945, pp. 43–57.

Parker, Danny, *Battle of the Bulge: Hitler's Ardennes Offensive, 1944–1945.* Cambridge, Mass.: Combined Books, 1991.

Parry, Jann, "Too Often in Limbo", *Dance and Dancers*, February 1982, p. 14.

—— *Different Drummer: The Life of Kenneth MacMillan*. London: Faber, 2010.

Pepper, Kaija, "National Choreographic Seminars", *Dance Collection Danse*, Fall 2008, pp. 27–32.

Percival, John, "This Must Be…", *Dance Magazine*, May 1972, pp. 32–42.

—— "LCDT at Sadler's Wells: Finding a Voice", *Dance and Dancers*, February 1976, p. 34.

—— Reviews, *Dance Magazine*, January 1982, pp. 22–3.

—— "Two of a Kind. Siobhan Davies and Richard Alston", *Dance and Dancers*, April 1983, pp. 14–17.

—— "New and Unusual", *Dance and Dancers*, May 1984, p. 14.

—— "Movement and Character", *Dance and Dancers*, December 1985, p. 23.

—— "The Godfather", *Dance Now*, Vol. 14, No. 2, Summer 2005, pp. 55–8.

Polcari, Steven, "Martha Graham and Abstract Expressionism", *Smithsonian Studies in American Art*, Vol. 4, No. 1, 1990, pp. 32–7.

Pritchard, Jane (comp.), *Rambert. A Celebration. The First Seventy Years*. London: Rambert Dance Company, 1996.

Ralph, Richard (ed.), "Robert Cohan Eightieth Birthday Tribute", *Dance Research*, Vol. 22, No. 2, October 2004, pp. 95–156.

Redfern, Betty, *Introducing Laban Art of Movement*. London: Macdonald and Evans, 1965.

Rogosin, Elinor, *The Dance Makers: Conversations with American Choreographers*. New York: Walker & Company, 1980, pp. 25–40.

Roy, Sanjoy, "Step-by-step Guide to Dance: Robert Cohan", *Guardian*, 18 May 2010, <http://www.guardian.co.uk/stage/2010/may/18/dance-robert-cohan>

Rubidge, Sarah, "Chamber Dances", *Dance and Dancers*, December 1982, p. 18.

—— (comp.), *Choreography: The State of the Art*. Proceedings of conference held on 3, 4 May 1992, Swindon: Borough of Thamesdown, 1992.

Rumi, "Mathnawi", Suphism, <http://www.sufism.org.pk/poetries_rumi.php>

St Vincent Millay, Edna, *Edna St Vincent Millay. Collected Sonnets*. New York: Harper Perennial, 1988.

de Salzmann, Jeanne, *The Reality of Being: The Fourth Way of Gurdjieff*. Boston, MA: Shambhala Publications, 2010.

Savage-King, Chris, "LCDT: Working Out?", *Dance Theatre Journal*, Vol. 2, No. 4, 1984, p. 18.

Schoff, Wilfred and Carus, Paul, *Tammuz, Pan and Christ: Notes on a Typical Case of Myth Transference and Development*. Chicago: The Open Court Publishing Co, 1912.

Sears, D., "Graham Masterworks in Revival", *Ballet Review*, Vol. 10, No. 2, Summer 1982, pp. 25–34.

—— "Martha Graham: The Golden Thread", *Ballet Review*, Vol. 14, No. 3, Fall 1986, pp. 44–64.

Shaw, Antony, *World War II Day by Day*. Osceola, FL: MBI Pub. Co., 2000.

Silverio de Santa Teresa C. D., P. (trans.), *The Spiritual Canticle and Poems of St John of The Cross*. 1935; repr. London: Burns and Oates, 1978.

Snyder, Diana Marie, "Theatre as Verb: The Theatre Art of Martha Graham, 1923–1958", unpublished dissertation, University of Illinois at Urbana Champaign, 1980. Ann Arbor, MI.: University Microfilms International, 1981. Order NO. 810, 8668.

DAT 4111A.

Soares, Janet Mansfield, *Louis Horst: Musician in a Dancer's World*. Durham, NC & London: Duke University Press, 1992.

Sorell, Walter (ed.), *The Dance Has Many Faces*. Cleveland & New York: World Publishing, 1951, pp. 170–81.

Sorley, Walker Katherine, "LCDT – The Biblical Programme", *Dancing Times*, February 1980, p. 318.

—— "Robert Cohan's Dream in Scotland", *Dancing Times*, May 1993, pp. 773–4.

Spark, Muriel, *A Girl of Slender Means*. 1963; repr. London: Penguin, 1999.

Stodelle, Ernestine, *Deep Song: The Dance Story of Martha Graham*. New York: Schirmer Books; London: Collier MacMillan Publishers, 1984.

Strate, Grant, *Grant Strate: A Memoir*, Toronto: Danse Collection, 2002.

Sweeney, Stuart, "An Interview with Robert Cohan", *Dance Europe*, October 2000, <http://www.criticaldance.com/interviews/2001/rcohan010310.html>

Terry, Walter, *The Dance in America*, rev. ed. New York: Harper & Row, 1971; repr. New York: Da Capo Press, 1981, pp. 83–99.

—— *Frontiers of Dance: The Life of Martha Graham*. Women of America. New York: Thomas Y. Crowell Company, 1975.

Todd, Anne, "Dance and Dancers in America; Martha Graham", *Dance and Dancers*, June 1953, p. 21.

—— "Graham Limon in the Wrong", *Dance Magazine*, September 1962, p. 7.

Toland, John, *Battle: The Story of the Bulge*. Lincoln: University of Nebraska Press, 1999.

Tracy, Robert. "Noguchi: Collaborating with Graham", *Ballet Review*, Vol. 13, No. 4, Winter 1986, pp. 9–17.

—— *Goddess: Martha Graham's Dancers Remember*. New York: Limelight Editions, 1997.

Tokunaga Eiko, *Yuriko, An American Japanese Dancer: To Wash in the Rain and to Polish with the Rain*, USA: Tokunaga Dance Ko [sic], 2008.

Tynan, Kenneth, *The Life of Kenneth Tynan*. London: Methuen, 1988.

de Valois, Ninette, "What I am up against", *Dancing Times*, March 1955, p. 9.

Vaughan, David, "Two New Works at The Place. *Mass* and *Layout*", *Dancing Times*, October 1973, p. 29.

—— "*Stages* at the Wells", *Dancing Times*, December 1973, p. 148.

Veldhuis, J. J., "Robert Cohan in Hamburg", *Tanz und Gymnastik*. Zürich. Jahrg. 50, Nr. 4, 1994, p. 402. Ill.

Venables, Lucy, "The Contemporary Ballet Trust", *Dancing Times*, September 1969, p. 634.

Vidal, Gore, *Palimpsest: A Memoir*. New York, Abacus, 1996, p.95.

White, Joan, *Twentieth-Century Dance in Britain: A History of Major Dance Companies in Britain*. London: Dance Books, 1985.

Williams, Peter, "Cortege of Angels, Acrobats, and Eagles and Things that Go Bump in the Night", *Dance and Dancers*, May 1967a, pp. 9–13.

—— "Contemporary Breakout", *Dance and Dancers*, December 1967b, pp. 20–2, p. 42.

—— "Placed", *Dance and Dancers*, July 1970a, p. 30.

—— "The 21 Years that Changed British Ballet, Brunch Dancing", *Dance and Dancers*, December 1970b, p. 23, p. 50.

—— "Rainmaking and Other Rites", *Dance and Dancers*, December 1970c, pp. 40–2.

—— and Goodwin, Noel, "*Stages*", *Dance and Dancers*, May 1971, pp. 27–31.

—— "People Together", *Dance and Dancers*, April 1973, p. 34.

—— "Myths and Memories. Four Creations of LCDT at the Shaw Theatre" (includes *Myth*), *Dance and Dancers*, April 1975, p. 18.

—— "Defying the Auguries, LCDT at Sadler's Wells", *Dance and Dancers*, January 1976, p. 16.

—— "Internal Creative Force" (includes *Khamsin* and *Nympheas*), *Dance and Dancers*, February 1977a, p. 18, p. 34.

—— "Romantic Inclinations" (includes *Forest* and *Nightwatch*), *Dance and Dancers*, June 1977b, p. 28.

—— "Assembly of Sights and Sounds in a New World", *Dance and Dancers*, January 1978, p. 19.

—— "LCDT at Sadler's Wells", *Dance and Dancers*, June 1979a, p. 33.

—— "Spatial Assessment: LCDT at the Roundhouse", *Dance and Dancers*, November 1979b, p. 28.

—— and Percival, John, "Digging in at The Place. Three Reviews of LCDG's First Season", *Dance and Dancers*, November 1969, p. 23.

—— "Six Years at The Place" (includes reviews of *Sky* and *Consolations*), *Dance and Dancers*, March 1971, p. 26.

—— "Five Placed", *Dance and Dancers*, March 1972a, pp. 30–8.

—— "New Arrivals at The Place (Charlip and Alston)", "London Contemporary X Group", *Dance and Dancers*, July 1972b, p. 31, p. 46.

—— "*People Alone*", *Dance and Dancers*, October 1972c, p. 26.

—— "American Influence", *Dance and Dancers*, February 1973a, p. 31.

—— "Contemporary Variety", *Dance and Dancers*, April 1973b, p. 25, p. 30.

—— "Two Creations Placed: *Mass* and *Layout*", *Dance and Dancers*, October 1973c, p. 42.

—— "Contemporary Maturity: *Diversion of Angels, Eclipse, No Man's Land, Stages*", *Dance and Dancers*, January 1975, pp. 18–25.

—— "A Family Affair: LCDT at Sadler's Wells", *Dance and Dancers*, February 1979a, p. 20.

—— "Biblical and Secular", *Dance and Dancers*, December 1979b, p. 12.

Woods, David, *On Angels and Devils and Stages Between, Contemporary Lives in Contemporary Dance*, Amsterdam: Harwood Academic, 1999.

Wray, Sheron, de Jong, Cynthie and Justin, David, "Coming Together, Dance and Music", *Dancing Times*, October 1996, pp. 66–7.

"Teens Create New Musical", *Youth Magazine*, 6 November 1960, pp. 18–20.

Zaloga, Steven, *Battle of the Bulge 1944* (2), Oxford: Osprey Publishing Ltd, 2004.

Zimmer, Elisabeth, "The Month of the Long Days", *Dance in Canada*, autumn 1978.

Index